Yankee Don't Go Home!

THE
LUTHER
HARTWELL
HODGES
SERIES

ON
BUSINESS,
SOCIETY,
AND THE
STATE

William H. Becker, editor

JULIO MORENO

Yankee Don't Go Home!

Mexican Nationalism, American Business Culture,

and the Shaping of Modern Mexico, 1920-1950

The University of North Carolina Press — Chapel Hill and London

0807828025

Designed by Barbara Williams
Set in ITC Charter with Clarendon display
by Tseng Information Systems, Inc.

The paper in this book meets the guidelines for permanence
and durability of the Committee on Production Guidelines for
Book Longevity of the Council on Library Resources.

Library of Congress Cataloging-in-Publication Data
Moreno, Julio, 1970–
Yankee don't go home! : Mexican nationalism, American
business culture, and the shaping of modern Mexico,
1920–1950 / by Julio Moreno.
p. cm. — (The Luther Hartwell Hodges series on business,
society, and the state)
Includes bibliographical references and index.
ISBN 0-8078-2802-5 (cloth : alk. paper) —
ISBN 0-8078-5478-6 (pbk. : alk. paper)
1. Industrial policy—Mexico—History—20th century.
2. Capitalism—Mexico—History—20th century.
3. Consumption (Economics)—Mexico—History—20th
century.   4. Mexico—Foreign relations—United States.
5. United States—Foreign relations—Mexico.
6. Advertising—Mexico—History—20th century.
7. Nationalism—Mexico—History—20th century.
8. Mexico—Politics and government—1910–1946.
9. Mexico—Politics and government—1946–1970.
10. J. Walter Thompson Company.   11. Sears, Roebuck
and Company.   I. Title.   II. Series.
HD3616.M42 M67 2003
337.72073′09′041—dc21

2003007366

cloth   07   06   05   04   03   5   4   3   2   1
paper   07   06   05   04   03   5   4   3   2   1

To my family:
my son, David; wife, Mónica;
mother, Maria Santos Linares;
brothers, Alvaro Abrego and Francisco Moreno;
stepfather, Jose Abrego;
and nephew, Nick Moreno

And to my extended family:
my grandmother, Margarita Interiano,
and uncles, Virgilio Interiano, Rogelio Interiano,
Isidro Interiano, and Mauro Moreno,
for assuming parental roles after the tragic death of
my father when I was one year old and for offering love,
support, and guidance when my mother was forced
to leave our village in Camones to work as a maid in
Santa Ana, El Salvador

Contents

Illustrations

Acknowledgments

This book is the product of the selfless acts of numerous individuals who provided invaluable support through the various stages of this decade-long undertaking. I certainly did not spend my youth on track to enter the world of academia. Growing up as a peasant harvesting corn and picking coffee in civil war–torn El Salvador, I did not even consider a life outside of agriculture an option. My situation after arriving in the United States as a Salvadoran refugee did not offer many options either. As recent undocumented immigrants, my brother Francisco and I had to work full time at the Farwest Wood Factory at the ages of fourteen and fifteen in order to contribute to the family income. Although academic achievement was a priority in my family, spending late nights and early-morning hours making bed frames at Farwest, and later, cleaning offices at the Sears Regional Division Building in Los Angeles, made it seem like an impossible task. It was only with the help of caring family, friends, mentors, and teachers that, against such odds, I was able to achieve my academic goals and complete this book.

I owe heartfelt thanks to Steven Topik at the University of California in Irvine for his guidance, support, and mentorship throughout graduate school. Steve provided constructive feedback and encouragement from the first draft of the book to the finished product. I appreciate his dedication and commitment. I am also grateful to Heidi Tinsman, who, along with Steve, provided extensive feedback. Heidi supplied a much-needed academic and moral boost in the last stages of preparing the book. Jaime Rodriguez completed the puzzle by introducing me to different aspects of academia. I thank him for insisting that I link a study of American business in 1940s Mexico to specific historical processes within Mexican society dating back to the early nineteenth century. I am also indebted to Roland Marchand, Sandra Kuntz Ficker, Linda Hall, Anne Rubenstein, and Emily Rosenberg for their interest and support. Roland Marchand was particularly helpful in the early stages of my research, before he tragically passed away in 1998. I am grateful to him for introducing me to the Sears Archives and the Hartman Center for Sales, Advertising, and Marketing Research at Duke University. His encouragement, friendship, and support contributed to the completion of this work.

I would not have finished this book without the support of colleagues, the Irvine Scholar Foundation, the Faculty Development Fund, and the School of Arts and Sciences at the University of San Francisco. An encouraging environment is crucial to one's development, and these individuals and institutions provided just that. I would like to thank friends and colleagues Gerardo Marin, Kathy Nasstrom, Becky King-O'Brien, Lois Lorentzen, Sharon Li, and Eduardo Mendieta for making USF a nurturing environment. I extend special thanks to Mike Stanfield for his lively conversations during our runs through Golden Gate Park and the Presidio in San Francisco. Mike has supported my professional development, and I thank him for providing feedback and making numerous recommendations that improved this book. I am also grateful for the support of colleagues Uldis Kruze, Tony Fells, Andrew Heinze, Elliot Neaman, Marty Claussen, and Paul Murphy. Finally, the help of my assistants and friends at USF proved invaluable, especially Maggie Red, Salvador Alcantara, Ana Ruíz, Mónica Adame, Susy Chavez, and Eileen Woodbury. A special thanks to Anne Hieber for selflessly serving as copyeditor and providing valuable feedback.

I am very grateful to the personnel of different archives and research centers for their assistance, including the Asociación Nacional de Publicidad; Archivo General de la Nación; Asociación Mexicana de Agencias de Publicidad; Hemeroteca Nacional; Asociación de Radiodifusores del Valle de México; Archivos Economicos de la Biblioteca Lerdo de Tejada; Biblioteca Fundación Miguel Alemán; Archivos Históricos de Banamex; Archivo Histórico del Arzobispado de México; Biblioteca Francisco Xavier Clavigero, Acervos Históricos; U.S. National Archives; Nettie Lee Benson Library at the University of Texas; the Film Archives at the University of California at Los Angeles; Bancroft Library at UC Berkeley; Hartman Center for Sales, Advertising, and Marketing Research at Duke University; Sears Roebuck and Company Archives; Rockefeller University Archives; and Advertising Research Foundation. I am greatly indebted to the staffs at these research centers for providing professional expertise and support.

Entering the world of academia, becoming a college professor, and completing this book became options only after caring mentors encouraged me to consider different possibilities. I am indebted to my friend and former director of the Graduate and Professional Opportunity Program at UC Irvine, Peggy Garcia Bockman, for spending many hours explaining various aspects of academia and coaching me on ways to explore different options. Prior to my arrival at Irvine, Timothy Harding, Marjorie Bray, Don Bray, Gloria Romero, Carol Shrole, and Francisco Balderrama at California State University in Los Angeles offered concern, encouragement, and guidance. My warmest thanks to each of them for their support. Going back even further, Bill Rumble and Clara Gomez of Wilson High School were instrumental in advising me to seek higher education. These individuals, as well as many others, made it possible for me to undertake what seemed like an impossible task: entering and successfully navigating through the world of academia.

The early stages of this book and my experience in graduate school would not have been the same without friends and peers such as Elizabeth Gelmini, Jose and Lani Alamillo, Dennis Kourthour, Teresa Romero, Rick Weiner, Jocelyn Pacleb, Wilson Chen, Ken Wong, and Amelito Enriquez. These individuals made graduate school an unforgettable experience. The mutual support, kamikaze debates over current events that lasted into the early hours of the morning, and modest but memorable entertainments are memories that I truly cherish. I also appreciate the engaging intellectual discussions with friends and colleagues in Mexico, including Armando Rojas, Javier Riojas, and Juan José Delgado.

This book would not have been completed without the love and support that only a family and dear friends can provide. Knowing that my son David, with his funny letters and daily phone calls, was in a loving and supportive environment facilitated my work on this book. My sincerest thanks to his mother, Linda Jimenez, his aunt, Olivia Jimenez, and his grandmother, Julia Jimenez, for providing a nurturing environment for him. I extend affectionate thanks to my mother, Maria Santos Linares, my brothers, Francisco and Alvaro, my nephew, Nicky, and my stepfather, Jose, for their love, patience, and understanding during the long periods when I could not visit because I needed to complete a chapter or go to another archive. They never complained—instead, they kept in touch and provided endless encouragement. Last but not least, I thank my wife, Mónica, for making our home a comfortable place to work, for proofreading the book and making suggestions, and for sharing her love and support.

Abbreviations

AAAA	Association of American Advertising Agencies
ACW	Advertising Clubs of the World
ANA	Asociación Nacional de Almacenistas
ANP	Asociación Nacional de Publicidad
AP	Asociación de Profesionales
CCCP	Comisión Central de Censo y Publicidad
CCPE	Comisión Central de Publicidad y Estadistica
CCV	Cámara de Comercio de Veracruz
CDAV	Comité en Defensa de los Anuncios Visuales
CDC	Comité en Defensa del Comercio
CNAP	Confederación Nacional de Asociaciones Profesionales
CNC	Cámara Nacional de Comercio
CNCA	Comité Nacional en Contra del Alcohol
CNCC	Confederación Nacional de las Camaras de Comercio
CNIT	Cámara Nacional de la Industria de Transformación
CRMS	Comité Regulador del Mercado de Subsistencias
CTM	Confederación de Trabajadores Mexicanos
DGP	Dirrección General de Profesionistas
Eximbank	Export Import Bank of Washington
FBI	Federal Bureau of Investigation
GTRC	General Tire and Rubber Company
IEM	Industria Electrica de Mexico
ISI	Import Substitution Industrialization
LEV	Liga de Empleados Veracruzanos
NAFTA	North American Free Trade Agreement
NDR	Nacional Distribuidora y Reguladora
OIAA	Office of Inter-American Affairs
ONCRETP	Oficina Nacional de Control y Registro de Escuelas y Títulos Profesionales
PAAF	Pan-American Advertising Federation
PAN	Partido de Acción Nacional
PEMEX	Petróleos Mexicanos
PRI	Partido Revolucionario Institucional
SEN	Secretaría de Economía Nacional
SEP	Secretaría de Educación Pública
SICT	Secretaría de Industria, Comercio, y Trabajo
UFCM	Unión Femenina Católica Mexicana
UNAM	Universidad Nacional Autónoma de México

Introduction

An observer at the grand opening of Sears Roebuck's first store in Mexico City on February 28, 1947, described Mexican customers as generally well behaved but extremely impatient.[1] Employees panicked "as a sea of hands thrust pesos toward them, into their pockets, into their blouses, anywhere—just to complete a purchase. Shopping-crazed crowds anxiously screamed, 'Let us in! Let us in!' They waved money at [the employees]. They tried to sneak in through the back doors, and they even cut the ropes guarding the entrance."[2] Sears's vice president for Latin American operations later reported that people fainted because of the heat and the agitation of the crowds.[3] Over 100,000 customers visited the store during the first three days of operation. The almost hysterical response to the grand opening surprised American investors, who previously had considered Mexico's political and economic climate unfriendly.[4]

Popular nationalism and radical social upheaval made investment in Mexico too risky for American companies from the 1920s to 1950. American companies feared political leaders and workers who sought to defend the ideals of the revolution as outlined in the 1917 constitution. For example, President Plutarco Elías Calles ordered government institutions to boycott American companies in 1927 to "combat" American imperialism.[5] Similarly, the mayor of Juárez launched a national "buy at home" campaign in 1931 when he declared a boycott against American merchandise.[6] Store owners in Mexico City in the early 1930s also threatened to stop purchasing American products if federal authorities did not block plans by foreign distributors to charge in dollars for their merchandise. The biggest threat, still fresh in the minds of American investors in the 1940s, was the 1938 nationalization of oil companies, during which Mexican children marched holding signs that read, "Our cooperation to pay the oil debt: Tuesday, no milk; Thursday, no meat; Saturday, no fruit; Sunday, no bread."[7] Peasants walked barefoot to cities to bring chickens, pigs, vegetables, and other goods as donations for government agencies to nationalize American and British oil companies.[8]

The contrast between the 1930s and the 1940s in Mexico raises a number of questions that are central to this work. Why was Sears so successful at entering the Mexican market a few years after popular nationalism drove American companies out of Mexico? Which aspects of American investment did Mexicans reject and which did they welcome in the 1930s, and how did these preferences change in the 1940s? How did nationalist and revolutionary rhetoric shape Mexican and American government policies and business operations? How did efforts to end the bitter regional and social tensions of the Mexican Revolution lead to the changes of the 1940s? How did the Mexican state's efforts to industrialize and become competitive in the international arena contribute to the increasing acceptance of American companies and business culture by the 1940s? To what extent did the changes of the 1940s, represented by the shopping-crazed mobs trying to enter Sears, indicate a reconstruction of Mexican society and identity? What was the significance of these changes for the emerging urban middle class and other sectors of Mexican society? To what degree did they represent a shift in or reconstruction of the ideals of the Mexican Revolution? How did they reinforce or challenge late-nineteenth-century liberal ideals, such as the perception that material prosperity was needed for national progress?

Nationalist and revolutionary policies might have threatened foreign companies (primarily the export industry), but Mexicans welcomed American businesses that supported industrial and commercial growth. Mexicans rejected the imperialist attitudes of foreign investors but accepted business practices that reinforced nationalist and revolutionary ideals. U.S. government officials like Nelson Rockefeller and American companies like Sears encouraged a new way of doing business in 1940s Mexico. *Harper's Magazine* took notice of America's new diplomatic relations when it characterized Sears's introduction into the Mexican market as a peaceful but powerful revolution, a "consumer revolution."[9] It argued that Sears encouraged good relations between Mexico and the United States and the type of business that supported upward mobility into the ranks of the middle class. The *Saturday Evening Post* suggested in a similar tone that Sears had been a better diplomat than the U.S. government.[10] These articles accurately evaluated the significance of consumer culture in 1940s Mexico, but the forces behind Mexico's consumer revolution went far beyond Sears or American diplomacy. Mexican intellectuals, government officials, business executives, and advertising agents, among others, formed a "pro-industrial and commercial growth sector" that led Mexico's consumer revolution, along with the U.S. government and American companies.

Sears's explosive entrance into Mexico and Mexico's consumer revolution as described in U.S. magazines did not take place in a vacuum; they were products of the reconstruction of modern Mexico. Supporters of modern industrial capitalism led this reconstruction from the 1920s to 1950. They defined modern industrial and commercial development as the engine of economic growth, national progress, material prosperity, and upward mobility. They associated the consumption of advertised products, an urban lifestyle, and the modern industrial setting with, to borrow from U.S. historiography, a new form of democracy, a "consumer democracy."[11] Moreover, they suggested that the consumption of advertised products offered Mexicans material abundance, product variety, individual choice, happiness, self-realization, and a new and improved personal image. Proponents of industrial and commercial growth defined Mexico as a country that was heroically leaving behind a convoluted past to become a promising modern industrial society. They classified 1940s Mexico as a society in which hard work, efficiency, standardization, and cooperation with government authorities guaranteed individual prosperity and a higher standard of living. They represented the nation's economic growth, industrial development, and political progress as alternatives to previous forms of social and political upheaval. They suggested that social tensions, concerns about social inequality, and political disagreements could be negotiated and resolved through proper mechanisms headed by the state instead of through armed resistance.

The use of consumption and material prosperity as synonyms for democracy and national identity was not a new phenomenon in postrevolutionary Mexico, but only a few scholars have recognized the significance of such a process. Mexico had earned a reputation as a promising and wealthy region that had offered opportunities for upward mobility since the colonial period. According to Daniel Cosío Villegas, one of Mexico's leading intellectuals of the twentieth century, Europeans created the myth of Mexico's wealth during the colonial period when they described the region as rich and prosperous.[12] Accounts of Mexico's wealth served as a hallmark of Creole pride by the seventeenth century. Mexican Creoles during the colonial period conveniently used Mexico's wealth to develop Creole identity and distinguished New Spain (Mexico) from the Spanish Empire.[13] Travel accounts during the early nineteenth century maintained the "myth" of Mexico's wealth despite the social, political, and institutional chaos of the time.[14] The victory of late-nineteenth-century liberals made the exploitation of natural resources, the connection of Mexico to the world economy, the establishment of legitimate institutions, and the standardization of the means of production or administration symbols of Mexico's progress and capitalist development.[15] The same trends continued in postrevolutionary Mexico after the 1920s, when Mexican and American political leaders, corporate executives, and advertising agents regarded Mexico's race toward modern industrial capitalism as the key to material prosperity, upward mobility, democracy, happiness, and self-realization.[16] However, the 1910 revolution forced them to filter Mexico's search for modern industrial capitalism, as well as other corporate, institutional, and personal interests, through popular nationalist and revolutionary rhetoric.[17]

The Reconstruction of Modern Mexico and
U.S.-Mexican Relations in Context

This work is grounded on studies of state formation, nation building, and the legitimacy of the revolutionary government. Scholars of twentieth-century Mexico explain the emergence of state legitimacy after the 1920s (through the lens of Max Weber) as the result of efforts of the well-crafted political machinery headed by the Institutional Revolutionary Party (Partido Revolucionario Institucional or PRI).[18] These scholars focus their analysis on political institutions or government policies. They suggest that public spending and support for industrial growth revealed government commitment to the revolution as defined by political leaders. Other scholars look at the interaction between government institutions and people in different areas of the country. They claim that local residents, political leaders, and cultures shaped how the federal government introduced education policy, sanitary campaigns, literacy programs, and cultural missions in different regions.[19] These interpretations present the process of state formation as a product of either state institutions or the "dialogue" between local communities and state representatives (expressed through social, political, or cultural interaction). According to another group of scholars, the consolidation of the Mexican state was an "ideological process" grounded on the theoretical approach of the Frankfurt school. These scholars argue that mass culture, consumerism, and "legends of wealth" romanticized Mexico's past and strengthened state legitimacy through ideology or false representations of the truth.[20]

My work makes a distinction between the role of state institutions and the appropriation of nationalist and revolutionary rhetoric, which some scholars define as ideology.[21] It also interprets both processes (the interaction of the public with institutions and the more abstract use of values and traditions by government or business representatives) as historical agents that shaped the reconstruction of modern Mexico and the process of state formation after the 1920s. It acknowledges numerous studies that show how people, values, and traditions in local regions shaped Mexican identity and increased the legitimacy of the revolutionary government. However, my research suggests that the process by which local communities shaped Mexico's identity romanticized the lifestyle and status of people in local regions (the *patria chica*) as well as the relationship of local communities to the nation. The new image of Mexico represented the country as an all-inclusive nation where political leaders established a government that patriotically carried out revolutionary ideals and elevated local cultures to the national and international scene. In this context, nationalist and revolutionary rhetoric defined the grounds on which specific national programs, political and economic agendas, institutions, and international diplomatic relations were negotiated or settled.

This book provides a theoretical analysis of the interplay between agency and ideology by looking at the introduction of American companies in Mexico, specifically Sears and J. Walter Thompson. Sears used nationalist and revolutionary rhetoric in its publicity because it feared any other strategy would trigger adverse results. In the process, it created expectations among Mexican employees. In 1949, Mexican employees effectively used Sears's marketing approach to organize and demand that the company address their needs. The employees forced the firing of Sears's top executive in Mexico and a restructuring of the company. The company's advertising approach represented Sears's efforts to acclimate to local conditions in Mexico. It also served as a tool for Mexican employees, who by 1949 demanded that the company respect national traditions and allow Mexicans opportunities for upward mobility. Mexicans might have influenced Sears's operations and publicity, but they did not exercise "agency" or control over Sears. Nor were they fooled by Sears's publicity after their victory in 1949, as scholars who look at marketing through the lens of the Frankfurt school might conclude. Mexican employees consciously utilized Sears's marketing strategy and the nation's nationalist and revolutionary heritage as tools for accomplishing specific goals, but they did not reject American investment. They rejected the attitude of American investors and the extent to which American business executives stepped outside the boundaries of what Mexicans considered acceptable. In other words, American companies had to understand and operate within the political and cultural balance that characterized Mexico during the 1940s.[22]

The reconstruction of modern Mexico, combined with international events such as the Great Depression and World War II, redefined U.S.-Mexican relations by the 1940s, but most scholars have interpreted this period as a time when Mexicans either carried out revolutionary and nationalist agendas or sold out to foreigners. Peter Smith and James Wilkie, among others, argue that during the 1940s in Mexico, the political class that had emerged out of the revolution implemented nationalist and social democratic programs.[23] They claim that revolutionary leaders made state institutions and the government, headed by the PRI, more responsive to the needs of the masses. In contrast, other scholars such as Carlos Monsiváis, José Agustín, and Nora Hamilton see the 1940s as a period of decline when conservative political leaders and American companies and culture "wiped out" the nationalist and revolutionary aspects of the revolution.[24] Some scholars have looked at the way in which Mexico played imperial powers off one another in order to carry out policies that benefited Mexicans. According to them, political instability and international events such as the "communist" or "Nazi" threat gave Mexicans leverage to negotiate foreign policy.[25] More recently, Gilbert Joseph and Seth Fein, among others, have used Mary Louise Pratt's concept of "contact zones" to explain the cross-cultural encounter between Mexicans and Americans through audio, visual, and textual expressions in film, technology, and other cultural mediums.[26] They suggest that the Mexican people (through their participation in and response to popular culture) shaped the introduction of American culture, diplomacy, and business in Mexico.

My work draws on different historical interpretations of postrevolutionary Mexico as it looks at the cross-cultural encounter between Mexicans and Americans through government institutions, business practices, and other forms of interaction. It relies heavily on the concept of a "cultural middle ground" to explain the interaction between Mexicans and Americans from the 1930s through the 1940s. I have borrowed this concept from Richard White's study of the cultural interaction between the Great Lakes Indians and the French colonizers during the eighteenth century. I find his work helpful in explaining the boundaries between proper and improper business practices in Mexico during the 1930s and 1940s. White defined the formation of the middle ground as the forging of legitimate cultural premises by the French and the Indians as the French attempted to "understand the world and reasoning of the other and to assimilate enough of that reasoning to put it to their own purposes."[27] My work focuses on the way in which Americans and Mexicans consciously "syncretized" values and practices as they insisted that modern industrial capitalism was mutually beneficial to Mexico and the United States. I see the syncretizing of American and Mexican values as the forging of a middle ground that allowed the coexistence of apparently conflicting values at a time when Mexican society and culture were rapidly changing.[28]

The syncretism of American and Mexican values was not accidental. Mexican and American political leaders, advertising agents, and business representatives defined the boundaries of Mexico's "middle ground." They romanticized Mexico's revolution as a radical break from the period of Porfirio Díaz (1876–1910) while implicitly encouraging aspects of Porfirian liberalism. They elevated Mexican nationalism while suggesting that Mexicans had to learn values and practices from industrialized countries in order to become competitive in the international arena. Supporters of modern industrial capitalism embraced American ideals, lifestyle, and leadership as models for Mexico's development. However, they presented Mexico's industrial and economic development as a unique Mexican process that was a product of the heroic struggle of the Mexican people during the revolution.[29]

This book also looks at contradictions that emerged in Mexico's modern industrial capitalism and the way government officials, business executives, and advertising agents maintained the coexistence of those contradictions. Scholars have explained the social and cultural changes triggered by Mexico's economic development using the analogy of "the traditional versus the modern." They associate the city with progress and the countryside with a "traditional" lifestyle, backwardness, poverty, and lack of civilization. Government programs or commercial activities originating in cities during the 1920s and 1930s were often seen as progressive efforts to promote economic growth and political stability. Among other scholars, Luis González y González endorses this approach by suggesting that stories about life in the modern industrial setting radically transformed the lifestyle in provincial areas. According to him, residents in San José de Gracia wanted to identify with life in the big city, not with the local lifestyle.[30] Questioning the "passivity" of provincial residents in González y Gonzalez's work, Mary Kay Vaughan suggests that residents in provincial areas were selective about the values and practices they adopted from federal representatives and urban areas.[31] Similar to Vaughan, scholars who study music, *charrerías*, and other folk cultural expressions suggest that provincial cultural traditions became symbols of an inclusive and unified Mexico by the 1930s.[32] In other words, contradictions were inevitable. The revolutionary practice of idealizing Mexico's folk, indigenous, and peasant heritage clashed with the late-nineteenth-century modernizing vision of Mexico in which the metropolitan industrial setting represented prosperity. Mexican and American political leaders and business executives reinterpreted the inherent conflicts between city and rural life or the struggle between "modern" and "traditional" practices. They provided a romanticized version of the countryside and traditional lifestyle while simultaneously suggesting that they coexisted with Mexico's modern industrial capitalist development. In this context, appropriating rural or traditional values did not necessarily contradict the country's modern industrial development.

This book shows how different strands of U.S. foreign policy and international events during the 1930s and 1940s shaped and were shaped by the reconstruction of modern Mexico. Similar to the works of Emily Rosenberg and Thomas O'Brien, it suggests that government officials and business executives championed a "missionary approach" as they introduced aspects of American capitalism to Mexico.[33] The book looks at how international events such as World War II accelerated America's "mission" to disseminate American ideals and shape public opinion in Mexico. Yet it shows how different factions within the U.S. government and corporate sector proposed different diplomatic platforms on U.S.-Mexican relations. It delves into the various ideological strands that drove U.S. politicians and corporations to support two different diplomatic strategies toward Latin America. Some American politicians and companies like Thompson adopted a rather arrogant approach as they promoted the spread of American capitalism to Latin America by the late 1930s. Thompson executives, like U.S. financial advisers in Latin America prior to the 1930s, expected Mexicans to accept American business strategies and projected a sense of American superiority over Mexican society and culture.

Other factions within the U.S. government and corporate sector, such as Nelson Rockefeller's Office of Inter-American Affairs (OIAA) and Sears, endorsed a form of diplomacy that insisted on understanding, respecting, and even romanticizing Mexican culture in order to cement a solid and mutually beneficial relationship between the two countries. They encouraged American diplomats and business executives to become culturally literate on "Mexico," arguing that an understanding of Mexican culture and society was the basis for efficient policies and business strategies. They developed a progressive strand of American diplomacy and advocated the use of Mexican industrial capitalism to increase the standard of living among Mexicans. They considered an increase in the Mexican standard of living a diplomatic tool against Nazi or communist influence in Mexico and a viable strategy to guarantee the expansion of American capitalism, a measure that, according to them, would also guarantee a good standard of living in the United States. This book shows how concerns about Nazi or communist influence as well as American economic expansion gave supporters of a progressive form of diplomacy the upper hand in U.S.-Mexican relations throughout most of the 1940s. Most important, it illustrates how different sectors of Mexican society understood, interacted with, and often shaped American diplomacy and business. However, the ability to influence American diplomacy or business depended on international issues or the willingness of Americans to operate within the boundaries generally accepted by Mexican society. The willingness to accept these boundaries varied and was often driven by the pursuit of specific objectives by different sectors in the United States. For example, a decline in the importance of Mexico in U.S. foreign policy during the Cold War, as Sergio Aguayo Quezada suggests, reduced Mexico's autonomy and its ability to negotiate with the United States.[34] In the end, the multifaceted relationship between the two countries was based on the establishment of cultural boundaries or a "middle ground" that ended what up to 1940 had been a bitter and tense binational relationship. The sealing of this relationship between the two countries in the 1940s set the stage for U.S.-Mexican relations in the post–World War II era, the stage on which contemporary binational agreements have been negotiated.

Themes in the Reconstruction of Modern Mexico

Mexico's regional diversity has led scholars to question the existence of a unified Mexico before the 1920s. Before 1920, Mexicans preferred to identify with their local region, the *patria chica*, rather than with the nation as a whole.[35] The outburst of regional upheavals during the revolution triggered efforts to define national ideals and find a common ground with which Mexicans from different regions could identify.[36] Mexicans embraced the country's indigenous and mestizo background while at the same time regarding José Vasconcelos's fascination with Mexico's colonial heritage and the country's "cosmic race" as the key to national progress. They idealized Mexico's indigenous and folk heritage as a symbol of national identity.[37] They also adopted a rather romanticized version of Mexico's past as a heroic and revolutionary struggle that had progressively made the country a social democratic society. Yet these expressions of Mexican "identity" coexisted with the country's commitment to industrial development, commercial growth, and the reconstruction of modern Mexico. Mexicans defined national identity as an all-inclusive concept that elevated the indigenous heritage, peasant tradition, entrepreneurship, industrial spirit, and regional diversity of the country as patriotic symbols and products of the revolution. Scholars like Daniel Cosío Villegas and Salvador Novo suggest that material wealth, abundance, and an optimistic outlook on Mexico's economic and industrial growth defined Mexico as a nation that proudly celebrated its diverse heritage by the 1940s.[38] Mexican and American government officials and business executives during the 1940s drew on Mexico's diversity, nationalism, and revolutionary traditions for commercial and diplomatic purposes while implicitly suggesting that the country had to welcome foreign investment, industries, and business practices in order to become competitive in the global setting. They forged a middle ground.

The first chapter of this book provides an analysis of the hotly debated role of the state in postrevolutionary Mexico by looking at government institutions, policies, and programs specifically designed to support industrial capitalist development from the 1920s to 1950. The reconstruction of the Mexican state under the 1917 constitution mandated the creation of public programs and institutions that would foster the economic prosperity of Mexicans. To this end, government institutions established programs that supported commercial activities. They sponsored nationwide advertising fairs in Mexico City's downtown area, organized consumer boycotts, established consumer cooperatives, opened popular stores, and created a major government-owned distribution plant, the National Distributor and Regulator (Nacional Distribuidora y Reguladora or NDR). Government institutions also undertook major reforms aimed at

revamping Mexico's technical and higher education programs as officials realized that Mexico's economic and industrial development required qualified personnel who followed "professional" standards. Government officials, newspaper
columnists, and newspaper readers engaged in a twenty-year public discussion
on how to establish and regulate professional programs, a measure they considered essential to modern industrial capitalism.

Government programs, institutions, and initiatives from the 1920s to 1950
went far beyond regulating or supporting Mexico's commercial and economic
growth. They were central to the reconstruction of modern Mexico and the
legitimacy of the Mexican state. Mexico's revolutionary government increased
its authority and legitimized the Mexican state by mediating public disputes
over corporate issues, professional standards, and commercial practices. The
legitimacy of the revolutionary government depended on its interaction with
different social and corporate sectors that turned to state institutions for either
protection or mediation of disputes.[39] State representatives adopted different
forms of paternalism as small businesses, large corporations, manufacturers,
and the general public asked for government protection and assistance in times
of crisis and professional or corporate "anarchy." They portrayed the mediation
of public disputes or the protection of different sectors as a product of the social
democratic reform Mexicans had heroically achieved through the revolution.

Chapter 2 captures the panic of U.S. government officials during World War II
as they tried to turn Mexicans into loyal allies of the United States. Extensive
research findings on Mexican public opinion shocked American government
officials during World War II. Nelson Rockefeller reported that public opinion surveys conducted in 1940 and 1941 showed that Mexicans were predominantly anti-American and in many cases supported Germany. Alarmed at these
findings, Rockefeller's OIAA set out to radically innovate Mexico's communication industry; censor (with the cooperation of the Mexican government) pro-
German advertising; and devise pro-American content in audio, visual, and textual publicity. As an emergency war agency, the OIAA worked with U.S. and
Mexican government officials and business executives to combat Nazi influence in Mexico. Rockefeller convinced American companies through incentives
such as tax breaks to continue to advertise in Mexico even though no merchandise was available there. In its efforts to influence public opinion, the OIAA
linked anti-Nazi messages to commercial advertising. U.S. companies championed American leadership in science, industrial development, economic prosperity, and democratic values in their publicity. Rockefeller's OIAA urged companies to carefully craft pro-American messages and to make sure that commercial
advertising did not reinforce a negative image of the United States. Furthermore, the OIAA instructed companies to reassure Mexicans that Mexico's nation-

alist and revolutionary heritage would continue through mutual friendship, co-operation, and modern industrial capitalism.

American companies and military operations during the war were not presented as imperialist endeavors or as threats to Mexican sovereignty. They were depicted as products of the new relationship between the two countries outlined in the Good Neighbor Policy. This policy and efforts to combat Nazi influence in Mexico during the war allowed American companies to enter the Mexican market and promote the "American way" (American investment and business practices) as a solution to Mexico's underdevelopment as well as a model for Mexico's modern industrial progress. They suggested that Mexico was moving toward a prosperous postwar era in which abundance, democracy, and modern economic development would provide opportunities for upward mobility and fulfill the nationalist and social democratic promises of the revolution. In this context, American investment supported the nation's industrial and commercial growth, reinforcing rather than undermining the reconstruction of modern Mexico.

Mexican advertising agents, as chapter 3 illustrates, appealed to the social democratic ideals of the revolution while highlighting American advertising and business practices Mexicans should emulate in order to make Mexico competitive in the international arena. They presented modern industrial capitalism as the key to national prosperity after 1922 when they began to promote advertising as an effective business practice among store owners and provincial merchants who considered publicity a waste of money.[40] Their twenty-year effort to legitimize their work as a "profession" suffered a major setback in 1943 when a constitutional reform excluded advertising from classification as an official profession. Advertising agents argued that professional advertising services were central to the progress and development enjoyed by Europe and the United States and that Mexico's prosperity and competitiveness depended on the establishment of professional publicity services. They suggested that Mexican advertisers had much to learn from advertisers in the United States, where publicity had achieved the highest reputation for accelerating commercial growth. They developed associations such as the National Association of Advertising (Asociación Nacional de Publicidad or ANP), adopted international standards, and utilized American advertising as a model. However, their focus on international publicity as an example of effective advertising did not mean they readily invited American advertising agents into the country. They allowed American advertising agencies to operate in Mexico but convinced them that commercial publicity in Mexico required a "Mexican flavor" that only Mexicans could provide.

Mexican advertising agents defined their field as a profession independent from government institutions during the late 1940s by making it a symbol of

Mexico's patriotic commitment to industrial capitalism. They argued that advertising required the development of pedagogical institutions and the implementation of research methods aimed at studying consumer behavior. They presented themselves as agents of modernity and claimed that their work would help Mexico achieve the industrial and economic development of industrialized countries. They argued that Mexican advertisers should adopt the technological innovations used by American advertising agencies. Advertising agents defined themselves as "prophets of capitalism" who supported Mexico's prosperity by generating economic growth that would raise the standard of living for Mexicans. They also suggested that advertising made way for modern industrial capitalism. They restored late-nineteenth-century liberal ideals of progress, faith in the market, and trust in the commercial sector. Yet advertising agents also endorsed the nationalist and social democratic ideals of the Mexican Revolution.

Chapter 4 provides an analysis of how advertising images reconstructed Mexico's national identity.[41] Advertising images during the 1940s suggested that Mexicans could experience individual freedom, abundance, happiness, excitement, and self-realization through the consumption of products. According to advertising, the patriotic and courageous struggle of the Mexican people during the revolution had made it possible for them to enjoy the comfort, satisfaction, and "consumer democracy" that provided an alternative to previous forms of oppression based on class, race, and gender. Advertising portrayed city life, industrialization, Western science, and standardized practices as symbols of progress and modern industrial capitalism, further supporting upward mobility and a lifestyle similar to that in industrialized countries. To this end, individual and national success depended on the ability to integrate and effectively function in an urban setting exemplified by Mexico City and the already industrialized world. Advertising images used nationalist and revolutionary rhetoric as they sold American merchandise and presented the middle-class lifestyle and ideals of Americans as models for Mexicans to emulate. They encouraged women to liberate themselves from traditional gender roles and even become "seductive" by embracing the latest cosmetics and pursuing professional careers while implicitly suggesting that women should honor traditional norms involving household duties, marriage, and sexual practices. This chapter examines the coexistence of such conflicting values through the construction of a middle ground. It suggests that the middle ground provided a neutral territory that allowed for the advertising of specific products in a way that did not necessarily embrace or reject any particular audience member based on his or her moral and ethical judgment.

Chapter 5 looks at the introduction of American business practices through the lens of an advertising agency, J. Walter Thompson. It suggests that Thompson's poor planning, disregard for Mexican traditions and business practices, and international operations made the company unprofitable until 1948, five years after its arrival in Mexico. Thompson's decision to open a branch in Mexico City was a response to the needs of U.S. clients with operations in Mexico and Rockefeller's plea that companies continue advertising American merchandise during World War II. Thompson followed Rockefeller's cue in trying to acclimate to Mexican culture but did not go far enough. For example, Thompson offered a Christmas bonus to Mexican employees in 1945, not realizing that they would expect the same bonus the following year. The loss of profits and clients and the misunderstandings between the Mexican representative and the New York headquarters led to tense management relations in December 1946, when Mexican employees demanded their Christmas bonus. Unlike other companies that selectively utilized Mexican nationalism as an effective advertising strategy, Thompson blamed Mexican nationalism for the company's failure in Mexico.

Despite its failure to generate profits and its tense relationship with Mexicans before 1948, Thompson introduced innovative international advertising and research methods during the early 1940s as it learned the ground rules for doing business in Mexico. Thompson representatives had to adopt acceptable business and personal manners in order to become a successful advertising agency in Mexico. To this end, Thompson's experience from 1943 to 1948 was a learning process that eventually led the company to become a prominent advertising agency by the late 1940s. During this period, Thompson built its infrastructure by hiring qualified Mexican personnel, carrying out marketing research for specific products, and making the Mexico City branch its operating center for Mexico, Central America, and part of South America. Thompson's success after 1948 depended on the company's ability to operate within a middle ground and the increasing legitimacy Mexicans gave to American advertising.

Chapter 6 provides a counterexample to Thompson as it uncovers the secrets of Sears's success in Mexico. Sears's dramatic success as an American retailer in Mexico was the result of its marketing strategies and its approach to doing business in Latin America during the post–World War II period. The company's marketing and commercial operations complemented Mexico's commitment to modern industrial capitalism, encouraged friendly U.S.-Mexican relations, promoted revolutionary ideals, and supported development strategies. Sears marketed its store as an innovative American retail establishment that would create a space for customers to purchase American merchandise and "experience" a middle-class lifestyle through consumption. Advertising agents presented Sears as a company that would help Mexicans climb the social ladder by providing relatively high wages for young Mexican men and women who were entering the job market as sales associates, accountants, translators, and customer service representatives. They also suggested that Sears supported Mexico's modern industrial development by purchasing merchandise from Mexican industrialists and even financing small manufacturers willing to produce Sears merchandise. Sears was presented as an American company that introduced American consumer habits while honoring Mexico's nationalist and revolutionary ideals by offering a variety of employee benefits, including a profit-sharing program.

Ironically, Sears's marketing and company operations were driven by Mexican government policies, employee expectations, and the company's willingness to operate within a framework that was in line with diplomatic economic development policies. Sears's commitment to operating within Mexico's middle ground allowed the company to successfully make profits despite setbacks caused by protectionist economic policies and employee demands. Sears's representatives in Chicago perceived company operations in Mexico as "a commercial laboratory" for further expansion into Latin America. U.S. government officials, according to *Harpers' Magazine*, described Sears as having the most effective diplomatic business strategy in Latin America during the postwar era. They presented Sears as proof that previous anti-American nationalism, American imperialism, and the tense relationship between Mexico and the United States no longer served as barriers to economic development. For them, Sears became a model company that supported Mexico's middle class, the platform of Mexican government officials, American commercial expansion, a strong U.S. economy, and the comfortable standard of living Americans had come to expect.

Chapter 7 delves into the private thoughts of Mexicans as expressed in letters addressed to newspaper columnists and Mexico City's archbishop, Luis María Martínez. Newspaper readers and devoted Catholics who wrote to the archbishop for personal advice identified individual happiness, self-realization, and national prosperity with the purchase and consumption of advertised products. Stories of family disputes, broken marriages, and community tensions implicitly defined consumption and material wealth as either the cause of or the solution to individual problems. They measured the degree of individual success or failure by the degree of access to material products. They also raised concerns about the decline of spiritual aspects of life as the urban industrial setting encouraged a material lifestyle.[42]

Archbishop Martínez did not object to modern industrial capitalism. On the contrary, he used Mexico's industrial and commercial growth to revitalize the power and public presence of the church following the bitter church-state tensions prior to the 1940s. He mediated tensions between proponents of anti-American consumer boycotts in 1945 and American government and business representatives. He participated in commercial marketing campaigns headed by Sears and requested loans from American financial institutions. Martínez also addressed popular concerns about the decline of spiritual values. Like newspaper columnists, he assumed the role of a "spiritual" or "psychological" adviser as he taught Mexicans strategies for accepting life in the urban industrial setting without disregarding spiritual matters or the romanticized vision of a tranquil rural setting.[43] He encouraged Mexicans to balance the material and spiritual aspects of life. In other words, public figures such as Archbishop Martínez coached Mexicans on strategies for coping with the changes brought about in their society by the rise of modern industrial capitalism and the increasing dependence on consumption.

chapter 1

Liberalism, the State, and Modern Industrial Capitalism in Postrevolutionary Mexico

Celebrations for the fiftieth anniversary of the Mexican Revolution designated 1910 as the year that marked the beginning of a social democratic process in Mexico. Political leaders credited the revolution with raising the standard of living, reducing class differences, transforming the country into a modern industrial society, and allowing the nation to earn the respect of the international community. They argued that Mexico's prosperity required state leadership and the precise implementation of economic doctrines based on the ideals of the revolution. They recognized the state's role in accelerating industrial growth, making businesses and industries available to the masses, introducing development programs, and opening schools that provided training for different industrial and commercial activities.[1] Government officials exaggerated the social democratic aspects of the Mexican state and downplayed the roots and the impact of Mexico's industrial and commercial growth. However, they accurately described the state as an active agent in Mexico's industrial capitalism.

The Mexican government's impact on constitutional, commercial, and diplomatic issues drove Mexico's industrial capitalism after 1917. In contrast to the United States, where, according to Alfred D. Chandler, a managerial revolution in the business sector served as the engine of capitalism, Mexican government officials sponsored, directed, and regulated the nation's industrial and commercial growth. According to Chandler, railroad companies and retailers in the United States led a revolution in which the coordination of business units and networks supported industrial capitalism from the 1850s to the 1920s. Their operations served as the "visible hand of management that replaced what Adam Smith referred to as the invisible hand of market forces."[2] The Mexican state turned Chandler's managerial revolution and Adam Smith's invisible hand of market forces into carefully planned economic and industrial development programs in its efforts to overturn a century of political instability, contested economic ideologies, and radical social upheaval after 1917.

Mexican government officials made the state the engine of modern industrial capitalism from the 1920s to 1950. They regulated professions, arguing that material prosperity and progress required legitimate standards that supported efficient management. They provided training and coerced Mexicans into accepting standardized practices, technical training, and rationalized procedures. They required professionals to master skills that emphasized efficiency in business, technocratic, and service operations. Government representatives sponsored commercial activities, regulated the market, protected national industries, and promoted popular nationalism in their efforts to make Mexico a modern industrial society in a highly unstable international market. Most important, they used the role of the government in industrial capitalism to legitimize and centralize authority in the hands of what had been a highly contested federal government since the country's independence from Spain in 1821. Ironically, political leaders selectively recast processes and ideologies embedded within Mexican liberalism (the same processes and ideologies that had triggered a century of social and political unrest) as they pushed for reconstruction, industrial development, and commercial growth under the banner of the Mexican Revolution. They drew on Mexican liberalism and the ideals of the 1910 revolution to define the rules of the game for modern industrial capitalism. In other words, government representatives after 1917 recycled nineteenth-century liberalism under the banner of the revolution as they set the boundaries for business in Mexico from the 1920s to 1950.

Recasting Mexican Liberalism in the Reconstruction of Modern Mexico after 1917

Nineteenth-century liberalism and processes emanating from the Mexican Revolution shaped the role of the Mexican state in modern industrial capitalism. Similar to nineteenth-century liberals, government representatives after 1917 linked social progress and economic development to material wealth. However, whereas nineteenth-century liberals did not agree on how to achieve material wealth or on the function of the government in national industries, political leaders after the 1920s did not question the need for state intervention in achieving Mexico's prosperity and individual progress. Renowned early-nineteenth-century liberals such as Esteban de Antuñano and Melchor Ocampo promoted temporary government protection of national industries, arguing that it would support industrial and economic growth, thus allowing liberal laws to triumph. According to these liberals, prosperous national industries and wealth were needed to foster a middle class that would serve as the foundation for a democratic society.[3]

Late-nineteenth-century liberal leaders under Porfirio Díaz (1876–1910) did not make protection of national industries or the creation of a middle class as the foundation for a democratic society a top priority. Díaz, abandoning early-nineteenth-century liberalism, advocated attracting foreign capital and mobilizing national investment by the landed elite in new industries as the formula for Mexico's prosperity.[4] Like other liberals in Latin America, he hoped to acquire a comparative advantage in the extraction of natural resources, such as coffee, henequen, and oil, for exports.[5] At the heart of Díaz's development policy was the belief that economic prosperity through exports would generate material wealth, support Mexico's progress, and create the basis for a strong nation. His formula triggered foreign dominance and new methods of state building and social engineering.[6] It established institutions, standardized procedures, and rationalized measures that supported industrial capitalism. Díaz welcomed the introduction of northern European and American management strategies—strategies that had driven America's managerial revolution and served as the engine of American capitalism. He allowed elite Mexican families to control national industries and gain monopolies over economic and political resources.[7] In turn, these families capitalized on their close alliance with Díaz to establish the first large companies and industrial complexes in cities like Monterrey. Mexican elites took pride in their association with Díaz and flaunted their aristocratic lifestyle before an increasingly dissatisfied middle class and an impoverished peasant and working class. The Mexican Revolution in 1910 challenged Díaz's policies, his abandonment of democratic ideals outlined by early-nineteenth-century liberals, and his close alliance with foreign companies and the national elite. The revolution triggered policies and regulations that promoted economic sovereignty and social democracy within the framework of modern industrial capitalism.

The social and political upheaval of the military phase of the Mexican Revolution (1910–17) forced state institutions to adopt a "social democratic dialogue," changing the interaction between state institutions and different sectors of Mexican society.[8] State institutions became mediators in public disputes between federal authorities and political bosses, community representatives, and the corporate sector.[9] Recovering the social democratic dialogue led to the political centralization of the federal government. Centralizing federal authority in the hands of legitimate state institutions had not been an easy task in Mexico prior to 1917. Liberal leaders in the nineteenth century had tried to establish a "regime of legal uniformity" by replacing corporate entities such as the church with secular state institutions. They founded institutions, procedures, and programs that legitimized the state and centralized federal authority in Mexico City under the banner of the 1857 constitution—a process Mexican scholars have referred to as "constitutionalism."

The commitment to centralizing and strengthening state authority marked what Charles Hale has described as "the transformation of Mexican liberalism from an ideology in combat with an inherited set of institutions, social arrangements, and values into a unifying political myth." Liberalism as a unifying political myth, according to Hale, became the official liberal tradition after 1867.[10] Although Hale argues that political leaders after 1910 further consolidated the liberal tradition of 1867, other scholars, such as Jesús Reyes Heroles and Arnaldo Córdova, suggest that these political leaders adopted early-nineteenth-century liberal ideals as outlined in the 1857 constitution.[11] Political leaders after 1917 presented their platform as a product of the revolution and a break from Díaz, but their reconstruction of modern Mexico under the 1917 constitution drew on aspects of both early- and late-nineteenth-century liberalism. Radical social upheaval during the 1910s forced them to portray government intervention and sponsorship of social and commercial issues as expressions of state paternalism. Similar to Díaz, political leaders after 1917 focused on centralizing federal authority and establishing state and constitutional legitimacy, but they filtered government programs and initiatives through nationalist and revolutionary rhetoric.[12]

Mexican political leaders presented the 1917 constitution as a revolutionary and nationalist symbol of the social democratic state that would heroically defend national sovereignty and protect the disenfranchised. Depending on the political views of each president, government rhetoric and policies shifted to the left or the right during the 1920s to 1950, but each administration ultimately aimed at revamping Mexico's industrial capitalism. Even President Lázaro Cárdenas pushed for Mexico's modern industrial and capitalist development, despite his socialist rhetoric.[13] Unlike the Díaz administration, government representatives after 1917 believed that the state should sponsor or direct the economy and, if necessary, compete with the private sector in order to forge a class consensus.[14] They also believed the state should actively support Mexico's industrial and commercial growth in order to be competitive in the international market. Through industrial development, commercial growth, and the development of new professional fields, according to government officials after 1917, state institutions could promote upward mobility and the well-being of the disenfranchised. In order words, the state advocated material progress and modern industrial capitalism, echoing late-nineteenth-century Porfirian ideals, but added a nationalist and social component as it presented material progress and modern industrial capitalism as the solution to, not the cause of, social inequality.

Modern Professions as the Backbone of Industrial Capitalism

Students, legislators, professionals, and journalists during the 1930s requested government support in their efforts to battle what they referred to as "professional anarchy." According to them, the lack of professional standards and the large number of charlatans who claimed to be "professional" undermined state authority and industrial capitalism. They led a movement (1920s–43) to reform Article 4 of the 1917 constitution, arguing that the constitution set the ground rules for the development of modern professions but its loose enforcement had failed to establish an adequate pool of certified professionals capable of leading Mexico's industrial and commercial growth. They advocated government regulation and the creation of an academic infrastructure for training and monitoring certified professionals. Constitutional reform leaders blamed the government for failing to stop an "evil plague of charlatans" that, according to them, was holding Mexico back.[15]

Charlatans became so common in Mexico that they found their way into popular culture as fictional characters. For example, Doctor Merólico became one of the most popular fictional characters in comedy shows in small towns by the mid-nineteenth century. According to popular legend, Dr. Merólico became wealthy by selling medical products based on his false "professional expertise" in medicine.[16] His popularity escalated to the point that charlatans or people without certified training or official authority who sold their services or merchandise as professionals became known as *merólicos*. These people cut costs by skipping formal education and eliminating bureaucratic expenses. They also had the ability to sweet-talk customers into buying products and to connect with the common people. Peasants and urban working-class residents often preferred to use the services of trusted *merólicos* or cheap products from local shops rather than paying higher prices for certified professionals or brand-name merchandise. In this way, *merólicos* challenged the certified professions, government institutions, and "regime of legal uniformity" that government representatives considered crucial for making a modern Mexico.

Constitutional reform leaders argued that the state should eradicate *merólicos* as a service to its citizens. They claimed that *merólicos* operated illegitimately and discouraged Mexicans from acquiring specialized training and expertise required for Mexico's industrial capitalism. Reform leaders also classified *merólicos* as a subversive force that threatened federal institutions that had the authority to certify professionals.[17] They claimed that government regulation was needed to protect people from *merólicos*, echoing demands for the establishment of constitutional authority of late-nineteenth-century liberals. However, they filtered their petition through social democratic and revolutionary rhetoric, arguing that government regulation would "protect the disenfranchised." In other words, reform leaders put a "revolutionary" spin on the century-long struggle to establish constitutional authority after 1917.

Constitutionalism drove the war against *merólicos* from the 1920s to 1943. A liberal tradition based on the 1857 constitution, constitutionalism before 1910 called for state mechanisms that created a "regime of legal uniformity" by requiring an individual to receive a title certified by the state before practicing medicine, dentistry, law, or other fields. The 1917 constitution continued Mexico's constitutionalist tradition by requiring professionals to certify their titles with state governments under Article 4.[18] The lack of professional training and academic institutions in provincial areas often led state governments to grant professional titles to individuals who demonstrated knowledge and skills in specific areas. Authorities referred to these certificates as "red titles," and the requirements for acquiring them varied in each state.[19] Not recognized at the national level, red titles authorized individuals to operate only in certain regions, but people who held red titles often practiced in other areas, including Mexico City. Constitutional reformers reported that many government leaders in provincial areas sold red titles to people who did not have the proper training or experience to perform a particular task.[20] This loose enforcement of professional standards by the federal government in Mexico City and state governments in provincial areas triggered the constitutional reform movement. Some reformers nevertheless argued that the "backwardness" and "naive" sympathy for *merólicos* of the peasant or working class caused the professional anarchy that undermined modern industrial capitalism.

Constitutional reform leaders upheld northern European and North American models as they constructed a bourgeois definition of their status as professionals during the 1930s and early 1940s. A representative of the Legislative Branch Commission assigned to study the reform of Article 4, César Gariaurieta, reported that the commission was currently seeking suggestions from the governments of France, Denmark, and the United States before presenting a constitutional reform that would regulate professions in Mexico.[21] Like Gariaurieta, other reform leaders described *merólicos* as "enemies of the country who prevented the formation of a national soul" because they had no "culture" and lacked the scientific knowledge of professionals in developed countries.[22] They implicitly defined "culture" as a bourgeois lifestyle, the ideal for Mexican professionals. They considered the certification of professionals crucial to eliminating the plebian aspects of different fields and raising the status of various professionals to that of their counterparts in Europe and the United States. Certified professionals identified themselves as middle class prior to the 1910 revolution by drawing on bourgeois culture rather than popular culture. For them, education, hard work, good deeds, and humility characterized professional and middle-class status.[23]

Unlike Gariaurieta, other constitutional reform leaders couched their arguments in defense of professionals in social rather than cultural terms.[24] According to Francisco Carreño from the National Supreme Court, industrial capitalism had triggered a "technocratization" of society that had turned Mexican professionals into a "class" that was subject to the same exploitation as the working class.[25] Unfortunately, Carreño lamented, no government program protected professionals. On the contrary, government officials left professionals at the mercy of charlatans by not regulating the professions. Carreño, like other constitutional reform leaders, described certified professionals as an urban middle class that deserved the same protection the state granted to other social classes in Mexico.[26] This argument was successful in supporting constitutional reform. However, lumping professionals with a diverse middle class (small store owners, non–college graduates who had worked their way up the corporate ladder, and ranchers, among others) debunked the "bourgeois" status that certified professionals had historically associated with the middle class. It "democratized" the concept of the middle class by loosening the boundaries of what constituted middle-class status. Most important, it gave government institutions authority over this loose definition as government leaders boasted that the state, thanks to the revolution, was defending the interests of the middle class by the 1940s. American companies like Sears tapped into this process by promising to democratize the concept of middle-class status.

Government officials conveniently used discussions of constitutional reform to present the state as a social democratic body that embraced public opinion and the participation of different sectors of society in state programs. Discussions of reforms to Article 4 of the 1917 constitution began in the late 1920s as a result of numerous complaints by certified professionals. The National Confederation of Professional Associations (Confederación Nacional de Asociaciones Profesionales or CNAP), which represented certified professionals in the country, organized the first congress for its 80,000 members in 1934.[27] Doctors, dentists, lawyers, and graduates of the National Autonomous University of Mexico (Universidad Nacional Autónoma de México or UNAM) attended the congress and resolved that all certified professionals be consulted on how reforms should be implemented and that the CNAP continue to participate in the legislative process.[28] The CNAP's arguments in favor of regulating professions strengthened the power of the federal government in provincial areas by suggesting that the federal government rather than state governments control the granting of professional titles.[29] The CNAP sent a survey to every professional certified by a government institution as a followup to the congress. These surveys were submitted to the nation's Chamber of Deputies as proof that most members favored requiring certified professionals to perform social service.[30] A second congress in 1937 outlined specific resolutions for government officials to implement. These resolutions called for the legislature to pass a federal law designating the professions that required a certified title and outlined the technical and scientific training the state should require of certified professionals.[31] The National Council of Superior Education and Scientific Research (Consejo Nacional de la Educación Superior y la Investigación Científica) welcomed the proposal and formed a commission to study how the resolutions could be carried out nationwide.[32]

Political leaders placed federalism, the revolution, and the state at the forefront of constitutional reform. Professional associations represented at the 1934 congress proposed the creation of a federal office to regulate and supervise the granting of professional degrees throughout the country.[33] In response to the second CNAP congress in 1937, the federal government established the National Office of Registration of Schools and Professional Titles (Oficina Nacional de Control y Registro de Escuelas y Títulos Profesionales or ONCRETP). A temporary office, the ONCRETP examined the proposed reforms to Article 4 outlined by professionals in 1937. The proposed constitutional changes required Mexicans "to exercise their professions in the name of collective social interests," thus defining professional work as a service to society rather than a simple mechanism to gain material wealth.[34] The belief that professionals were servants of society was not a new phenomenon.[35] The government promised to establish professional training centers that would provide academic and practical training throughout the country. Officials authorized to grant professional titles were required to attend federal conferences or Regulating Congresses (Congresos Reguladores). Training centers were required to have proper facilities and qualified faculty, to expect students to perform social service, to register their programs with the ONCRETP, and to publish a list of annual graduates. Graduates had to become members of the national association in their field. Most important, every graduate recognized by the ONCRETP would be officially recognized nationwide. Professional leaders were required to attend Regulating Congresses and contribute to nationwide curriculum development. These congresses were to outline government policies and provide instruction in the latest developments in each profession. Professional associations were also asked to report the illegal granting of certificates to ensure that jobs be filled with qualified professionals.[36]

The reform of Article 4 in 1943 established federal authority over professional titles but allowed some room for local control. It gave the Public Education Secretariat (Secretaría de Educación Pública or SEP) (instead of the ONCRETP) full authority as a federal institution over the granting of professional titles. Institutions of higher education approved by the SEP could grant professional titles only if they met specific requirements. Institutions had to have a curriculum that encompassed vocational, scientific, theoretical, and practical training. Federal authorities reserved the right to determine whether institutions met requirements, and graduates had to provide social service in exchange for their education.[37] However, the General Office of Professionals (Dirrección General de Profesionistas or DGP) remained independent from the SEP and maintained the authority to grant temporary professional titles based on the bylaws of the CNAP. The decree further ruled that practicing professionals had to obtain a license from the state and register with the Association of Professionals (Asociación de Profesionales or AP). Local branches of the AP were asked to participate in designing the curriculum for training in their respective fields. They were required to report irregularities, and they had the authority to cancel professional titles. In other words, the SEP authorized the granting of professional titles, but individual associations of professionals could use the semiautonomous DGP status to operate independently from the SEP. Individual associations under the DGP claimed to "defend the ethical standards and reputation of their organization" and their profession. Most important, different associations or local organizations could address and even negotiate their concerns with federal authorities under the leadership of the DGP.[38]

The public discussion of the regulation of professions reached far beyond constitutional and professional circles. It served as a public forum on the exercise of social democracy. Newspaper journalists and government officials reported popular views on constitutional reform. The newspaper *Novedades* published excerpts of interviews with people from different social sectors and occupations—mechanics, artists, and transportation employees, among others—in its "Reportero preguntón" section. According to *Novedades*, its readers favored reforms to Article 4 because they believed the government should protect the public, enforce the constitution, and restore faith in the professions.[39] Felipe García, a worker, reported being "disappointed at the fact that since the time of Carranza the president had not enforced Article 4."[40] Similarly, Santiago Pérez, a public transportation employee, argued that the "constitution looked like a lie after twenty-four years because there were many important articles that had not been enforced."[41] Others argued that government representatives should consider the needs of families that might face starvation as a result of proposed reforms to Article 4. According to them, honest Mexicans who had mastered their skills independent of government institutions would be displaced as a result of reforms to Article 4. Manuel Graciano Montes and Julio Garín from Querétaro suggested that reforms should leave room for workers who had practiced their occupations for years and were more qualified than those who graduated from the UNAM.[42] Their approach echoed popular opinion among peasants and working-class residents who did not think certified professionals were necessarily more qualified than *merólicos*. Although popular opinion on constitutional reform was diverse, the public debate in congresses, interviews, and newspaper articles indicated that state regulation of professions was the product of a social democratic dialogue. The twenty-year-long discussion of reforms to Article 4 of the constitution increased the legitimacy of the state as an arbitrator of public issues. Most important, it defined certified professionals as public servants with a patriotic task: the making of modern industrial capitalism in Mexico.

Advertising as the Engine of Modern Industrial Capitalism

Government leaders in the 1930s saw advertising as the driving force of Mexico's industrial and commercial growth. They pointed to the success of American and European advertising in their efforts to convince Mexican businesses to adopt similar publicity methods. They argued that studies in the United States and Europe showed that despite the impact of the Great Depression, businesses that had either maintained or increased their advertising expenditures were performing much better than those that had reduced them.[43] Mexican government officials used U.S. businesses as a model for Mexico's development. However, their ultimate goal was one of the key ingredients of nineteenth-century liberalism: the support of social progress through economic development.[44]

Alarmed that advertising was not a high priority among Mexican businesses, government officials directed the National Secretariat of the Economy (Secretaría de Economía Nacional or SEN) to coordinate efforts to publicize the effectiveness of advertising in increasing sales. SEN representatives claimed that their task required aggressive government action. They described their work as a "civilizing mission" that included coaching Mexicans in the use of modern business practices. They argued that, with the exception of a few national and foreign corporations, most Mexican business owners believed their products would sell regardless of how much they spent on advertising.[45] Most commercial advertising did not reach provincial areas, they reported, and when it did, it focused on clothing, medicine, furniture, and automobile products. They warned that Mexico's industrial capitalism would not advance without adequate mechanisms of publicity.[46]

The SEN established its own advertising division in October 1935 in an effort to publicize government services and legitimize advertising as a vehicle of commercial growth. According to the director of the division, José M. Campistro de Cáceres, advertising would help the SEN promote national production, encourage consumption, and carry out development programs. Campistro argued that the SEN was planning to "use advertising as a vehicle to announce the diverse operations of the SEN, and most important, to convince Mexicans of the value of publicity."[47] The SEN instructed Mexicans on ways to expand their business, increase demand, and profit through publicity.[48] Although the SEN urged Mexican exporters to increase their publicity abroad, most of its work focused on increasing national consumption.[49] It launched a campaign to convince small and medium-sized businesses to adopt advertising as a mechanism to boost consumption in the midst of the Great Depression.[50] It declared April 23 the Day of Publicity in an attempt to honor the role of advertising in Mexico and celebrate Mexico's industrial, artistic, and commercial activities.[51] Government officials also hoped to encourage merchants, industrialists, and small business owners to increase their advertising through its official declaration of the Day of Publicity.[52] They presented advertising as "the soul of commerce, the engine of industry, and the spirit of individuals or associations that served the public."[53] Although the official declaration of the Day of Publicity did not establish a long-standing tradition of honoring publicity, it revealed the significance government officials gave to advertising and its role in Mexico's development. SEN representatives used the latest technology in their efforts to boost confidence in publicity. They broadcast radio announcements informing the public that advertising benefited the nation by encouraging consumption.[54] Advertising became synonymous with service to the nation.

Political leaders saw advertising as a powerful force that went far beyond the simple act of making a sale. *El Nacional* described it as the "engine of modern commerce," arguing that it had the power to stimulate demand. It suggested that commercial success in modern industrial societies required expertise in publicity.[55] Similarly, the National Chamber of Commerce claimed that advertising stimulated the consumption of a variety of products and expanded Mexico's production capacity. It asserted that the expansion of production created jobs and a competitive economy that supported national progress.[56] Lucio Mendieta y Nuñez argued in *El Universal* that scientific and technical innovations had turned advertising into a vital force for making Mexico's economy competitive. Nuñez also claimed that the application of psychological and sociological principles made advertising an effective tool for cultivating "national consciousness." He emphasized that the forging of national unity in postrevolutionary Mexico required rudimentary strategies used prior to 1910.[57]

Liberal leaders under Díaz adopted a bourgeois definition of "culture" and "civilization" (terms that were used interchangeably) as centered in cities (specifically Mexico City) and carried out by institutions to achieve national unity. According to these leaders, nationhood and constitutional legitimacy required federal institutions to impose a bourgeois notion of "culture" and "civilization" on different sectors of society. Nuñez and other leaders of the 1930s and 1940s claimed that advertising had the potential to reach deep into the soul of the masses to build popular nationhood and patriotism in support of Mexico's constitutional authority.[58] In other words, they defined advertising as a tool that complemented federal efforts to unify the nation. However, they rejected the bourgeois aspects of prerevolutionary nationhood and culture. Their analysis "democratized" nationhood by adopting a popular notion of culture. They argued that efforts to unify Mexico required that state institutions adopt or react to popular attitudes rather than imposing a bourgeois notion of civilization on the masses. Adopting a more "democratic" notion of nationhood and constitutional legitimacy did not mean that government representatives did not impose values on the masses. It simply meant that the process of state building after the 1920s required a social democratic dialogue through which government officials tried to increase state legitimacy by either incorporating or responding to popular attitudes. Government institutions had to present their operations as work in tune with popular attitudes or actions that benefited the nation. The social democratic dialogue that emerged by the 1930s allowed different sectors of Mexican society to negotiate the boundaries of accepted norms. This dialogue became central to PRI politics from 1929 to 2000. It made Mexico the most politically stable country in Latin America after 1929.

Efforts to legitimize advertising during the 1930s included collective promotional activities. The Office of the President, the Secretariat of Industry, the Chamber of Commerce, and the National Bank of Mexico, among others, sponsored weeklong commercial exhibits and contests in Mexico City. Downtown businesses presented almost 300 window displays advertising national products in March 1931. The event also included a parade of 200 floats exhibiting a variety of products manufactured by national industries. The parade ended at La Esmeralda Jewelry, where "jewels and other gifts made by humble Mexican workers were offered to the president."[59] Public interest in this event did not decline as Mexico City residents and provincial merchants poured into the city's downtown to purchase the latest products manufactured by national industries. *Excélsior* reported that two days after the opening, floods of people continued to prevent spectators from enjoying a clear view of the spectacular window displays.[60] The nationwide contest included awards for the three best displays, based on artistic merit. The first-place award of 3,000 pesos and a gold medal went to the Atoyac Company, whose display featured a replica of Chichén Itza, an ancient indigenous pyramid, and the company's mascot, the Atoyac Indian. The second-place prize was 2,000 pesos and a silver medal, and the third-place winner received 1,000 pesos and a bronze medal.[61]

This commercial exhibit brought government officials and national business representatives together to work for a common goal: increasing the consumption of national products. Merchants thanked government institutions as they reported making as much as 20,000 pesos in sales during the event.[62] Fernando García from the President's Office deemed the event a commercial and political success. He reported that many provincial merchants who had attended had requested that the Office of the President organize commercial exhibits in their home states.[63] The president responded by sending letters urging governors to organize similar events. The Secretariat of Industry and the Chamber of Commerce started a campaign to increase the consumption of national products in May 1931, two months after the Mexico City exhibition.[64] Promotional events continued, although the nature of each event varied.

By 1933, promotional events attempted to balance supply and demand within a specific sector of the economy. The SEN organized manufacturers, distributors, and merchants in the summer of 1933 for its first White Week promotional sales events.[65] Organizers urged newspaper readers and radio listeners to take advantage of the opportunity to purchase products at lower prices.[66] They instructed national manufacturers, chambers of commerce, and distributors to lower prices during the events.[67] The SEN declared White Week clothing sales in April 1933 a major success that reduced an oversupply of textile products.[68] Shoe manufacturers and retailers hoped to achieve the same success during their promotional sales week in June 1933, when they launched a nationwide publicity campaign accompanied by a reduction in prices, special offers, and free publicity sponsored by government and private institutions.[69]

Government reports highlighted the short-term success of these events. Although promotional events generated a high volume of sales, they did not provide an effective mechanism for balancing supply and demand as government officials had claimed. Conscious of the limitations of publicity as a mechanism for regulating the market, the Mexican government declared the textile industry to be "saturated" under a 1937 law that gave the president the power to regulate production, profits, wages, and prices in industries that were declared saturated.[70] Government institutions used the 1937 "law of saturation" in their efforts to control market forces in the midst of the Great Depression and World War II. Declaring textiles a "saturated industry" suggests that promotional events did not succeed as a mechanism to balance supply and demand. However, government leaders vigorously defended the principle behind promotional events on the grounds that it made the state and the business sector partners in a process that would "democratize" consumption by accelerating Mexico's commercial activities—a phenomenon they believed would ultimately reduce prices.

The rationale for lowering prices during promotional events was based on a model central to American capitalism, but Mexican government leaders presented it as a product of the revolution. SEN representatives argued that lowering prices would allow consumers to purchase more products, thus increasing sales and forcing a rapid movement of merchandise. According to Alfred D. Chandler, the success of industrial capitalism in the United States depended on the expansion of administrative networks and the coordination of the flow of merchandise from suppliers to consumers by mass retailers, which increased the turnover of stock. Chandler suggests that a managerial revolution in the corporate sector triggered this transformation of American capitalism from 1850 to the 1920s.[71] In Mexico, government institutions such as the SEN, instead of the corporate sector, served as the force behind such changes by the 1930s. The SEN argued that accelerating the commercial process through mass marketing or high-volume sales at low prices would increase the flow of capital and ultimately benefit industrialists, merchants, and consumers.[72] Most important, it presented this process as a democratizing force and a product of the Mexican Revolution.

Popular Demands for Government Regulation of Advertising

Government officials during the 1930s argued that government regulation of advertising would protect the nation and different sectors of society. In January 1932, the official government newspaper, *El Nacional*, advocated a presidential decree regulating advertising. It argued that such a decree would improve the appearance of cities and make Mexico City one of the most beautiful cities in the world.[73] An official decree based on the 1917 constitution set the ground rules for publicity in Mexico in 1929, but businesses rarely observed advertising laws by the early 1930s. The 1929 patent and brand-name law required businesses to register their publicity and display a copyright statement on their merchandise. It also mandated that they display a "Hecho en México" label if the product was manufactured in Mexico.[74] The Secretariat of Industry, Commerce, and Labor (Secretaría de Industria, Comercio, y Trabajo or SICT) reported in November 1932 that many companies refused to display the "Hecho en México" label on their merchandise because they believed their customers considered foreign products superior.[75] The SICT accused many merchants of refusing to identify their products with national industries and trying to make them appear foreign. It argued that the government should force stores to label products manufactured in the country as Mexican merchandise.

The loose regulation of advertising under the 1929 decree allowed for the continuation of public discussions of the role of the government in advertising. Government authorities by 1938 claimed that ongoing concerns about publicity had forced political leaders in Mexico City to regulate billboard advertising and any form of publicity in public and private areas. According to them, government regulation was needed to protect private and public property from the "anarchy" of street advertising.[76] Responding to such complaints, government leaders passed a 1938 decree that made the 1929 advertising law more specific. The

1938 decree restricted the areas where ads could be placed and regulated their content, prohibiting the placement of ads on wooden boards or public buildings and the use of loud speakers or other devices that disturbed the public.[77] It also gave city government leaders the resources to enforce the law. However, the 1938 decree did not stop complaints against the lack of government regulation of foreign-language advertising.[78] El Universal reported in 1938 that there were so many ads in English on downtown streets in Mexico City that it looked like an English-speaking city.[79]

Another factor that triggered popular demands for government regulation of advertising was the concern over declining morals. Residents worked with government representatives in the 1930s to establish local "anti-alcohol campaign" committees throughout the nation in their efforts to restrict publicity that encouraged alcohol drinking.[80] The Department of Public Health (Departamento de Salubridad Pública) reported that citizens from remote areas such as Chalchicomula requested government regulation of cantinas and stores that sold alcohol.[81] Other requests from the National Committee against Alcohol (Comité Nacional en Contra del Alcohol or CNCA) demanded government "restrictions of alcohol production, arguing that producers wasted a lot of money on intensive advertising campaigns."[82] The CNCA accused advertising agents, beer manufacturers, and alcohol producers of launching advertising campaigns that "falsely claimed alcoholic beverages had nutritional value and were capable of providing vigor, strength, and youth."[83] Similarly, La Prensa denounced the use of some people's misfortune for commercial publicity as immoral. It requested government regulation of the use of catastrophes, tragic accidents, and national disasters in advertising by July 1933.[84] La Prensa referred to the recent disappearance of Spanish pilots Mariano Barbrán and Joaquin Collar during a flight from Havana to Mexico as an example of the type of incident used by advertising agents and businesses in their unethical and inhumane "commercialization of pain."[85]

Popular requests for government regulation of advertising also sought to preserve rigid gender lines. Mexico City residents voiced their opposition to the advertising strategy used at a store that hired a man to act as a woman trying to seduce passersby to enter the store. The use of cross-dressing, according to El Universal, ridiculed family traditions and was offensive to the public.[86] The newspaper argued that this type of publicity violated individual rights and represented an intrusion into public space since "people who walked on the street were forced to see a rather offensive spectacle." It demanded that the government establish rules governing how businesses could use public spaces for commercial publicity. El Universal specifically objected to the "offensive nature" of publicity that used cross-dressing and its "blurring" of gender lines, classifying cross-dressing as morally and ethically wrong.[87]

Charges against illicit advertising triggered requests for government regulation in defense of small to medium-sized businesses. Mexico City businesses launched a campaign to protect metropolitan merchants in 1931. They selected Rodrigo Montes de Oca to head their campaign as the leader of the Mexico City Advising Council.[88] Montes de Oca reported that numerous businesses were victims of advertising fraud, and he demanded that the National Chamber of Commerce (Cámara Nacional de Comercio or CNC) take immediate action.[89] He accused some advertising agents of charging merchants for advertising that was never implemented. He also condemned advertising agents who reported higher magazine and newspaper distribution rates in order to increase their fees. Other institutions, such as the National Confederation of Chambers of Commerce (Confederación Nacional de las Camaras de Comercio or CNCC), also urged government authorities to regulate the alarming amount of advertising and commercial practices that did not comply with ethical business norms.[90] The CNCC cited numerous cases in which businesses failed because, according to the CNCC, they trusted their advertising to people who did not have adequate training or professional standards in publicity.[91] The CNCC promised to combat advertising that did not follow ethical commercial norms in order to protect the interests of merchants and consumers. It launched a moralization campaign to end the type of publicity that damaged commerce and the reputation of advertising.[92] The CNCC condemned advertising that either exaggerated or mystified products as unethical and classified it as unpatriotic and detrimental to Mexico's industrial capitalism.[93]

The Mexican government changed the tone of its efforts to regulate advertising by the late 1940s. Although it did not abandon state paternalism, it no longer depicted government regulation of publicity as a mechanism for state legitimacy. Instead, government institutions focused on convincing Mexican businesses that advertising and brand-name recognition were fundamental to their survival in modern industrial capitalism. They launched aggressive campaigns to convince Mexicans that using sophisticated methods of publicity was good business. The National Chamber for Industry Transformation (Cámara Nacional de la Industria de Transformación or CNIT) and the Nacional Financiera, which assumed the responsibility for assisting Mexican industrialists and businesses throughout the 1940s, took the lead in delineating the significance of publicity. The CNIT distributed booklets stating that publicity and brand-name trademarks benefited businesses because they guaranteed uniform quality for consumers. It presented government legislation regulating publicity as a positive force that benefited business. The CNIT also argued that government laws required the proper identification of merchandise so customers could easily locate a specific brand-name product and that publicity granted the product more credibility.[94] The CNIT presented government regulation of publicity as a "paternalist" protection of the business sector.

The CNIT also instructed Mexican businesses to avoid making their merchandise look foreign. Ironically, it did not condemn the foreign appearance of products in publicity as unpatriotic or a disservice to the nation as other government institutions had done in the 1930s. Instead, it argued that although the foreign appearance of products could be good in the short term, it would be disastrous in the long run. The CNIT added to its compelling argument in favor of publicity a friendly reminder that businesses were required by law to display the "Hecho en México" label in Spanish and that businesses that displayed the label in English would be punished.[95] The CNIT argued that lying or promoting values that were contrary to high moral standards was not a good long-term business approach, but again it implied that government officials would punish anyone who did not comply with acceptable ethical standards. In other words, government institutions by the late 1940s promised to reduce state intervention in advertising and suggested that businesses would learn that the use of sophisticated advertising practices was good for business. However, the CNIT reminded the private sector that the state would serve as a "referee" and monitor publicity in order to safeguard Mexican values. The state paternalism in advertising policies and debates of the 1930s continued into the late 1940s even though government institutions pretended to be less interventionist at the national level. Not surprisingly, the role of the Mexican government in marketing followed a similar pattern.

The State as a Protectorate of Consumers: Commercial Gifts and Popular Stores

The emergence of new commercial practices, such as distributing commercial gifts and trading stamps, triggered government intervention in the market during the 1930s. The Garceran Brothers had introduced trading stamps for promotional retailing in the mid-1920s. They sold booklets of 1,000 stamps to store owners at three pesos each. Store owners, in turn, gave customers a stamp for every ten cents they spent at the store. In exchange for 500 stamps, customers received a gift worth a peso and fifty cents from the Central Commercial Gift Store in Mexico City's downtown.[96] The Garceran Brothers managed and ran the gift store, but their business increased so rapidly that they transferred management and operations to the Empresa del Timbre Comercial by 1934. Most gifts were domestic and home-decorating products. Not surprisingly, commercial gifts were particularly popular among Mexico City women. Some housewives reported that they had decorated their kitchens and dining rooms with the products they received from trading stamps.[97] *El Universal* wrote positive reviews of the operations at the Commercial Gift Store, reporting that women from different social sectors arrived at the store with their stamps and were immediately welcomed by a large number of store representatives.[98]

Mexico City merchants argued that commercial gift stores violated Mexican law and ultimately harmed consumers. Salvador López Moreno led the opposition as the president of the Cámara Popular in 1931. He organized small-scale merchants and requested the intervention of government institutions to stop the exploitation of Mexican consumers.[99] Merchants formed the Committee in Defense of Commerce (Comité en Defensa del Comercio or CDC), among other institutions, to stop the use of trading stamps and commercial gifts.[100] According to the committee, the use of trading stamps was detrimental to consumers because in the end they paid more than the actual cost of each gift since the large stores that offered the stamps charged higher prices. The CDC argued that these large stores maliciously wanted to drive small store owners and merchants out of business.[101] Opposition to trading stamps and commercial gifts led to a December 1931 constitutional decree that outlawed commercial gifts, but the SICT apparently decided not to enforce the policy after meeting with prominent industrialists and merchants who offered trading stamps.[102]

Opposition to the lack of regulation of commercial gifts grew stronger and more radical by December 1934 when merchants gathered at the Monument of the Revolution and then walked to the National Palace to demand that the government enforce the law banning the use of trading stamps.[103] They argued that Article 28 of the 1917 constitution "did not allow the use of commercial advertising through gifts," thus making trading stamps and commercial gift stores illegal.[104] Protesters urged President Cárdenas to protect small merchants from commercial gift stores that lied to customers and led to unfair competition. Cárdenas listened to protesters and promised to review their request. Ironically, he did not mention that the SEN had instructed the President's Office to stop granting permits to merchants who used commercial gifts or raffles as advertising.[105] The SEN reported that it had recently "conducted a study of commercial gifts and raffles after numerous complaints from Mexico City merchants and industrialists who had been affected by this system of advertising."[106] According to the SEN, government regulation was necessary because commercial gifts led to unfair competition and encouraged monopolies by large companies.[107] Cárdenas described his decision to ban commercial gifts as a response to popular demand and a result of his meeting with small merchants. He used the banning of commercial gifts to depict the president as a paternal figure heading a social democratic state that defended small merchants and consumers from big businesses. Cárdenas's decision to portray the state as a defender of small businesses and small industries was part of the country's capitalist-development formula adopted after 1917—a formula that Cárdenas and Ávila Camacho supported.

Government representatives under Cárdenas and Ávila Camacho used market uncertainty and social unrest as an opportunity to present government programs as a "safety net" for Mexicans. The Great Depression and World War II prompted popular demands for government regulation of the price of food and other basic necessities.[108] Bad harvests and a decline in the value of Mexican currency in the mid-1930s were partly responsible for high food prices, but accusations against unscrupulous merchants who hoarded products in order to increase prices were common.[109] The government did not hesitate to declare war against price speculation. It promised to guarantee fixed prices and threatened to close down Mexican and foreign merchants who increased prices and relied on speculation for profits. The Organic Law of Article 28 in December 1931 gave government authorities the power to intervene in the marketing of staple goods.[110] The government not only printed official prices but also authorized police officers to assist shoppers who accused store owners of charging high prices.[111]

Demands for government control led President Cárdenas to form the Subsistence Market Regulating Committee (Comité Regulador del Mercado de Subsistencias or CRMS) in March 1938. The committee was directed to combat food shortages, end poor distribution of products, and prevent abnormal fluctuations in the market that were contrary to the interests of consumers, particularly the working classes. President Ávila Camacho turned Cárdenas's CRMS into a more powerful institution during the early 1940s, renaming it the National Distributor and Regulator. The NDR used government funding to distribute products at lower prices through popular stores (*tiendas populares*) and financed families willing to operate popular stores according to NDR guidelines. There were 688 popular stores in Mexico by 1945, 190 of which were in Mexico City.[112] According to Enrique Ochoa, the number of stores increased to 2,500 by 1946, including 40 "mobile truck stores that sold basic food products, such as beans, corn, rice, sugar, powdered milk, and coffee."[113] Owners of popular stores could earn 3 to 10 percent of their merchandise investment, and they could only sell products from the NDR.[114]

Government sponsorship of popular stores during the early 1940s met with bitter resistance from Mexico City merchants. The National Association of Retailers (Asociación Nacional de Almacenistas or ANA) argued that the government should allow organizations such as the NDR to regulate the market only if the private sector used unfair business practices.[115] Others were more criti-cal. They argued that "under the excuse of benefiting the masses and providing social service, the NDR was gradually forcing the sale of expensive low-quality products and creating arbitrary monopolies by privileging some companies."[116] According to NDR critics like Concha Villarreal, the NDR prevented the sale of high-quality products and did not take consumer demand for high quality into account. She argued that, at a practical level, NDR contracts excluded the sale of well-known brands in popular stores.[117] The National Association of Food Prod-uct Merchants (Unión Nacional de Comerciantes en Víveres) complained that NDR actions would have a negative impact, claiming that "'civilized' nations re-spected commerce and that the damage the NDR was doing to Mexican com-merce harmed the interests of the nation."[118] The ANA threatened to boycott pro-ducers and distributors that sold to the NDR. Its goal was to handicap the NDR and prevent it from selling to popular stores.[119]

NDR representatives responded to critics by 1945 in their efforts to restore the reputation of the NDR as an organization that benefited Mexican consumers. They argued that consumers had a choice of merchandise in popular stores and promised to discontinue selling unwanted products.[120] They claimed that the accusations against them were false and vicious. They specifically responded to Villarreal's charges in *Excélsior* that a contract between Canada Dry and the NDR prevented popular stores from selling other soft drinks like Coca-Cola, Pepsi-Cola, and Mundet.[121] NDR representatives explained that the NDR distributed Canada Dry beverages instead of Coca-Cola or Pepsi-Cola because "after totaling the requests from the popular stores, Canada Dry was the most popular drink and because Canada Dry provided the most lucrative contract to the NDR."[122] Nazario Ortíz Garza, the general director of the NDR, argued that the quality of NDR merchandise was evaluated by "laboratories [that] examined the mer-chandise and then determined whether the merchandise was appropriate for consumers based on quality and price."[123] The technical division of the NDR also periodically checked the merchandise that the purchasing division and the di-rectors of popular stores decided to purchase.

Accusations against the NDR triggered a restructuring of its objectives and operations. Ortíz Garza reported that he would not tolerate unethical practices at popular stores. He closed popular stores accused of forcing customers to buy another product in order to purchase a reduced-price item. He also promised to punish people who purchased products in popular stores in order to sell them at higher prices on the black market.[124] The NDR established Price Vigilance Committees in every state to prevent price speculation.[125] It invited members of the Price Investigating Commission from the nation's Chamber of Deputies to visit different neighborhoods to monitor popular store operations.[126] Ortíz Garza tried to restore the image of the NDR as an institution at the service of lower sectors of society by initiating a program to distribute powdered milk imported from the United States by mid-1945. Mexicans received coupons for the milk from labor unions.[127] The NDR expanded this initiative when it established milk distribution centers throughout Mexico City in order to solve milk shortages.[128] NDR representatives described the NDR as an institution that carried out a "patriotic and humane commitment on the part of the government: meeting the needs of the masses."[129] They argued that the NDR protected consumers from greedy merchants and companies that, contrary to government efforts to lower the cost of living, took advantage of any opportunity to make profits at the expense of Mexican consumers.[130]

The power of the NDR increased during the first half of the 1940s. Its budget grew from 700,000 pesos in 1941 to 300 million pesos in 1945 at the request of the Confederation of Mexican Workers (Confederación de Trabajadores Mexicanos or CTM).[131] The CTM also asked that the government increase the number of labor union stores (*tiendas sindicales*) and consumer cooperatives.[132] The power of the NDR by the mid-1940s raised concerns about what Alejandro Noye, the president of the Confederation of Chambers of Commerce, saw as an alarming degree of state intervention in the market and the private sector.[133] According to Noye, established private businesses throughout the country should carry out NDR operations. He condemned the opening of popular stores as counterproductive because they led to unfair competition.[134] Noye compared popular stores to U.S. chain stores but argued that this model would not work in Mexico because the country was not ready for such a complicated organization. According to him, merchants in the United States purchased surplus food products from the government, but they always had enough room for profits within established price caps. The U.S. chain store model, according to Noye, provided ways in which the government could direct instead of control the economy.[135]

The postwar climate, increasing criticism of the NDR, and the election of Miguel Alemán forced a restructuring of the NDR. The government announced in January 1946 that the NDR would continue to operate but popular stores would be able to sell non-NDR merchandise and would be taxed like other businesses.[136] The new NDR director appointed by Alemán, Carlos Cinta, opted for a conciliatory approach. He "met with merchants who expressed their willingness to cooperate and work with the government as long as NDR actions did not 'invade their commercial practices.'"[137] Cinta promised to work with merchants and reassured the public that the NDR would remain an organization that would "carry out the government's commitment to social services and defend the working class from being exploited."[138] Not surprisingly, the strategy for defending and representing the interests of the working class had changed by October 1947, when the NDR embraced a less-interventionist approach and promised to continue to make products available to the lower sectors of society in a free market. By 1947, NDR distribution centers could sell merchandise to any business instead of limiting their sales to popular stores. Some of the new customers included members of the ANA—the same organization that had fought bitterly against the NDR since 1941.[139]

_____ The change in the NDR was in line with Alemán's initial economic policy and planning. Alemán wanted to reduce price controls and make the state less responsible for subsidizing food products. Hoping to boost an efficient and inexpensive food distribution system in the private sector, he sought to "provide incentives for the private sector, encourage low prices," and enforce laws that nurtured such a distribution system.[140] The government stopped NDR funding, and existing popular stores became independent, family-owned operations subject to the same regulations and policies as other businesses. According to *El Nacional*, the NDR's policy of regulating prices in order to balance market conditions had been altered to meet post–World War II conditions. However, it insisted that the government's original mission of protecting consumers, producers, and the public in general had not changed.[141] Other government institutions and businesses by 1947 took up the NDR's banner and promised to facilitate rather than actively direct the market as they had done during the 1930s and early 1940s. They insisted that these changes were not a betrayal of the revolution. Instead, they argued that new market conditions required that government leaders carry out revolutionary ideals in a different manner.

The changes in the NDR in 1947 transformed the relationship of consumers to the private and public sectors, but these changes did not necessarily make the Alemán administration different from the previous administration. The new relationship made Mexicans more vulnerable to market fluctuations as President Alemán eliminated the NDR's "safety net" and market-regulating capacity. To this end, the Alemán administration distanced government institutions further from direct regulation of the national market than the administrations of Lázaro Cárdenas and Ávila Camacho. However, Cárdenas's CRMS and Ávila Camacho's NDR were not direct results of the Mexican Revolution, despite their efforts to associate these institutions with the revolution. The social and political upheaval of the 1910s gave government officials the flexibility to take bold steps, but the CRMS and the NDR were practical measures designed to deal with the laws of supply and demand. However, Alemán's decapitation of the NDR and his "friendlier" attitude toward the business sector did not make his administration less interventionist or less "revolutionary."

Revolutionary and nationalist patterns after 1910 created a collage of processes that traced their origin to different ideals and leaders of the revolution. Alemán and his predecessors did not endorse a particular outcome of the revolution other than the ideals outlined in the 1917 constitution. Yet each administration insisted on establishing an "official version" of the revolution in order to justify its political agenda.[142] All administrations filtered their agendas through nationalist and revolutionary rhetoric.[143] They also made state legitimacy, national unity, and modern industrial capitalism top priorities. In other words, Alemán changed the nature of government institutions by the late 1940s, but he did not abandon the ideals of the revolution. Instead, he built his administration on different strands of the revolution. By distancing the presidency from Cárdenas's "socialist" rhetoric, he avoided presenting the government as the sole defender of the peasant and urban working classes. He also distanced himself from Ávila Camacho's persuasive appeal for unity as a militaristic security issue. However, like his predecessors, he made industrial capitalism central to his agenda. He took the nation's commitment to industrial capitalism a step further by linking it to the revolution and specifically to Mexico's middle class. He dropped the rhetoric of social equality and presented modern industrial capitalism as the key to upward mobility into the ranks of the urban middle class. He supported economic growth, progress, and social peace as the basis for national unity. In this context, state leadership of Mexico's modern industrial capitalism, Alemán insisted, was the ultimate goal of the revolution. Alemán redefined the revolution and invented new forms of nationalism as he, like his predecessors, placed his presidential mark on Mexico's revolution. He used the nationalist banner in his version of the revolution and what it meant to Mexico in the postwar era.

Popular Nationalism and Consumer Boycotts

Mexican political leaders from the 1920s to 1950 used popular nationalism to support Mexico's industrial capitalism and establish economic nationalist rhetoric as a symbol of Mexico's revolution. They used consumer boycotts during the 1920s and 1930s as expressions of national sovereignty and public spectacles of state mediation of disputes and protection of the Mexican population. The first effort to boycott American products occurred in May 1927 when Mexican government representatives distributed a pamphlet protesting American imperialism in Latin America to Latin American embassies in Washington, D.C. Mexican authorities released the pamphlet shortly after President Plutarco Elias Calles ordered state institutions to stop purchasing furniture, machinery, and other products from foreign countries. Calles asked government institutions to purchase their supplies from Mexican manufacturers.[144] Although Calles's order was not in itself a major break from U.S.-Mexican relations, it questioned U.S. dominance in Latin America and used boycotting as a weapon against the United States. It also represented broader Pan-American protests over U.S. imperialism after the invasions of Nicaragua and other countries in the Caribbean.

Consumer resistance to American products in Mexico took on a nationalist bent as tensions escalated between political leaders and merchants in Juárez and El Paso at the Mexican-U.S. border in the early 1930s. Juárez's mayor, Arturo Flores, ordered a boycott of American merchandise in January 1931 as a result of numerous complaints by city residents against American authorities.[145] The incident that triggered the boycott encouraged Mexican men to protect the moral integrity of Mexican women. Flores ordered the boycott immediately after Angel Juarrieta reported that American authorities had insulted his wife by questioning her moral character when she attempted to cross into El Paso on a shopping trip.[146] Flores expanded the boycott to a nationalist "buy at home" campaign by March 1931. Federal representatives offered to facilitate the distribution of national products in Juárez and asked Mexican manufacturers and merchants to express their support for Flores.[147] They set special freight fares to expedite the rapid movement of products from the interior of the country to Juárez. They also promised to support businesses and industries owned by Mexicans in order to reduce imports. The boycott ended after representatives from both cities conducted a symbolic investigation that led them to conclude, as Juárez city clerk Manuel García stated, that "the two towns were so interdependent that to hurt one meant hurting both."[148] Other boycotts in the early 1930s had a slightly different anti-American tone, but none led to a major diplomatic crisis between Mexico and the United States. However, they linked a type of "commercial nationalism" to Mexican-U.S. relations.

Commercial nationalism intensified in 1932 as supporters of boycotts against Spanish and Chinese businesses demanded that the government defend Mexican workers. The Veracruz Employee League (Liga de Empleados Veracruzanos or LEV) started a three-month boycott against Spanish and Chinese businesses in Córdoba in September 1932. It argued that "Chinese and Spanish store owners did not obey Article 9 of the Worker's Law, which required that 90 percent of the personnel hired by foreign companies be of Mexican citizenship."[149] Besides not complying with Article 9, the LEV charged, these businesses formed foreign associations. The LEV sent guards to prevent customers from entering stores such as La Valenciana (a shoe store owned by Spaniards) and El Rayo (a store owned by Chinese).[150] By late September, Spanish-owned hardware stores such as La Soriana in Veracruz were forced to close by LEV guards.[151] In October 1932, the Veracruz Chamber of Commerce (Cámara de Comercio de Veracruz or CCV) asked the government to send federal troops to stop the boycott against foreign-owned businesses.[152] Municipal authorities acknowledged the need to stop the boycott, arguing that it harmed all commercial activity in Córdoba and hindered the mechanism for the distribution of products to other parts of the country.[153] However, they admitted that they could not control tensions and that the intervention of federal authorities was required.[154]

Spanish and Chinese businesses obtained protection from Córdoba's Chamber of Commerce. The Chamber of Commerce explained that its members "respected federal laws, but decided to close down their businesses in order to reject the boycott, which the LEV had illegally launched with the support of some municipal authorities."[155] It also described its decision as a cautious effort to save money and prevent violent confrontations between LEV guards and customers.[156] Córdoba's Chamber of Commerce members promised to reopen their businesses as soon as federal authorities could guarantee peaceful operations. The CNCC met with the president in Cuernavaca on December 30, 1932, to try to solve the crisis. The president ordered federal authorities, including military representatives, to intervene to protect foreign-owned businesses in Córdoba, but he stressed the need to settle tensions through proper mechanisms of the CCV, which represented merchants at the local, state, and federal level.[157] Newspapers reported no violent clashes between LEV guards and federal authorities, but the tense confrontation triggered a process of negotiation between LEV representatives and federal government officials. The boycott of Spanish and Chinese businesses placed topics such as labor, nationalism, constitutionalism, and the role of local and federal authorities at the forefront of discussions of legitimate and illegitimate business practices by foreign companies. In the end, the federal government increased its power over local regions by assuming the role of mediator in the dispute. Not surprisingly, the settling of disputes in provincial regions by federal authorities increased the legitimacy of the state. It also made Mexican government authorities appear patriotic and nationalist.

Popular nationalism during the 1930s allowed Lázaro Cárdenas to enact bold measures that threatened foreign businesses in specific industries. The government decided to nationalize industries that it considered vital to Mexico's development, such as railroads and oil. The nationalization came shortly after the 1936 Law of Expropriation of Article 27 of the 1917 constitution. Article 27 allowed for the nationalization of Mexico's subsoils, but no political leader had dared to enforce it before 1937. Backed by popular support in the midst of an alarming international crisis triggered by Nazi influence in Europe and Latin America, Cárdenas decided to nationalize British and American oil companies in 1938.[158] Nationalized companies became government-owned or "parastate" commercial institutions. Mexican oil companies became part of Petróleos Mexicanos or PEMEX. The Mexican government nationalized only a few industries from the mid-1930s to the mid-1940s, but PEMEX, like other commercial institutions owned by the state, became a symbol of Mexican nationalism and the revolution.

Bold measures such as the nationalization of foreign companies suggested that the Cárdenas administration was antibusiness, nationalist, and prosocialist.[159] Cárdenas was not opposed to business or foreign investment. He supported workers' benefits but rejected organized-labor initiatives that threatened capitalist development. Contrary to popular belief, Mexican government officials under Cárdenas accused radical syndicalist labor activists who proposed a strike against American companies in late 1938 of being unpatriotic because a strike would have threatened the nation's development.[160] Very few American companies were nationalized under Cárdenas, but international attention to commercial nationalism and socialist rhetoric during the 1930s shaped the interactions between political leaders and business executives in the United States and Mexico in the 1940s.

Mexican political leaders nationalized specific industries so state institutions could lead the country's industrial capitalism. The state assumed leadership of the country's industrialization because no adequate infrastructure or business network existed.[161] A new generation of political leaders in the 1920s redefined the role of the state in their efforts to establish modern capitalist economic structures that would "make industrial capitalism work for Mexicans."[162] Foreign control over oil, transportation, electricity, and other industries vital to Mexico's development challenged state legitimacy and posed a potential threat to Mexico's industrial and commercial growth. Essentially, the nationalization of key industries and the establishment of state-owned companies in the 1930s and 1940s were nationalist measures aimed at giving Mexicans control over industries that were fundamental to the nation's industrial capitalism. They represented a form of economic nationalism. However, state ownership of some foreign companies represented Mexico's commitment to industrial capitalism more than the nation's radical revolutionary and nationalist heritage. Yet many national and international leaders based their actions on the nationalist and revolutionary rhetoric associated with the nationalization of a few foreign companies rather than the rationale behind it.

Economic nationalism took on new forms in the 1940s, but its ultimate goal remained the same: government sponsorship and leadership of Mexico's industrial capitalism. Efforts to protect national industries from the international market triggered policies like Import Substitution Industrialization (ISI). ISI welcomed foreign products that facilitated the local manufacturing of merchandise that was previously imported. Its ultimate goal was to stimulate the growth of national industries in order to stop the import of products. The formula was successful during the early 1940s because World War II drastically reduced Mexican imports. Mexico gained a favorable balance of trade, and a number of industries that supplied products to the United States made large profits. However, the $300 million trade surplus Mexico had acquired during the war dwindled by 1946 as American companies flooded the Mexican market with manufactured goods (refrigerators, dishwashers, and automobiles, among other items). The alarming trade balance triggered aggressive government intervention in the summer of 1947, when President Alemán placed high tariffs on imports and prohibited the import of numerous items classified as either "luxury" or manufactured.[163] Alemán's policies sought to protect national industries and the country's balance of trade in the international market, and to this end, he endorsed a form of economic and industrial nationalism. However, neither ISI nor government laws prohibiting imports rejected foreign capital.

ISI linked national companies to foreign capital as government officials adopted a number of measures geared toward developing national industries. Mexican political leaders had long considered national and foreign capital crucial to the nation's development. They established the Banco de México and the Nacional Financiera in the 1920s and 1930s to facilitate Mexico's economic development. Both institutions took pride in presenting their operations as a patriotic service for the creation of "sovereign" national industries and businesses. According to Roderic Camp, the Banco de México trumpeted its services as measures that would ultimately lead to economic independence from the United States.[164] The services provided by the Banco de México and the Nacional Financiera had a nationalist spin, but the flow of foreign capital through these institutions softened their nationalist rhetoric. Ávila Camacho turned Cárdenas's 1934 Nacional Financiera into a credit institution for the promotion of industrial development on September 1, 1941.[165] By 1946, the Nacional Financiera had become a financial agent for the federal government and had received the authority to negotiate national and foreign loans. It also had the power to approve loans requested by public and private institutions at the state level.[166] It negotiated loans with international banks, including the World Bank. It received a loan from the Export Import Bank of Washington (Eximbank) for $50 million in 1947 and a second loan for $150 million in 1950. It owed close to $100 million to Eximbank and the World Bank by 1952.[167] As a financial institution, the Nacional Financiera was vital to the development of national industries, but it funded the new businesses with foreign capital, thus blurring the lines between national and foreign support of new industries.

Mexican government officials also mobilized the flow of foreign capital by authorizing national and foreign co-ownership of companies in a constitutional decree in 1944. The decree allowed Mexican companies to own no less than 51 percent and foreign interests to own up to 49 percent of a company. Celanese

Mexicana de América was one of the most successful examples of binational companies. The company started as a joint venture in 1944 with a $20 million investment for the opening of rayon factories in Guadalajara. The Nacional Financiera owned about 13 percent of the company, Mexican investors owned about 38 percent, and the Celanese Corporation of America owned about 49 percent. By 1947, Celanese Mexicana controlled the rayon industry, with a production of 9 million pounds of rayon a year.[168] Co-ownership, according to Flavia Derossi, benefited many family-owned businesses that decided to join forces with foreign investors and gain corporation status. According to Derossi, many of these corporations (92 percent of 332 companies) remained under the control of family members even though the board of directors often included professional managers not affiliated with the family.[169] Family-owned businesses represented one aspect of the diverse business sector in Mexican society. The amount of foreign ownership of a particular company varied despite the 1944 decree because government institutions reserved the right to make exceptions. For example, International Harvester did not open its ownership to Mexican investors throughout the 1940s.[170]

Various Mexican business and industrial sectors responded differently to government policies during the 1930s and 1940s. Northern industrial elites centered in Monterrey developed a tense relationship with government officials after 1910. These industrialists were descendants of the Porfirian elites. After losing their close alliance with political leaders under Díaz, they became targets of revolutionary politicians after 1910 but ultimately survived the social and political unrest of the revolution.[171] These elites took pride in their leadership of Mexican industries since Díaz, developed a strong sense of unity, and did not hesitate to present themselves as independent from the government.[172] Northern industrialist elites expressed their opposition to the government party by joining the National Action Party (Partido de Acción Nacional or PAN) in the 1940s. Not surprisingly, PAN members were primarily from sectors of Mexican society that felt threatened by revolutionary leaders and government institutions from 1910 to the 1940s, namely northern industrialist elites and the church.

Government policies in the 1930s and 1940s gave rise to a new group of industrialists that became vital to Mexico's industrial capitalism. These "new industrialists" welcomed cooperation with the government even though they were likely to favor business intervention in the government rather than government intervention in business.[173] They were generally concentrated in central Mexico and were the primary beneficiaries of government policies by the 1940s.[174] Many gained lucrative government contracts. They also benefited from the Industry Transformation Law (Ley de Industrias de Transformación) of 1941, which gave five-year tax exemptions to manufacturing firms considered necessary to the country's economy. The law extended tax exemptions to ten years in 1946.[175] A 1944 decree exempted industries in Mexico City from paying taxes for two to eight years. Tax exemptions were neither new nor coincidental given that government leaders under Calles and Cárdenas had approved tax exemption policies in 1926, 1932, and 1939.[176] They were part of the government's formula to facilitate industrial capitalism. Not surprisingly, new industrialists often endorsed the government's nationalist and revolutionary agenda. Echoing 1940s political leaders, new industrialists argued that commercial growth represented "a higher phase of the Mexican Revolution."[177] They defined Mexico's industrial capitalism as a product of the revolution and identified themselves as "revolutionary leaders" who were providing a service to the state and society.[178]

Conclusion

The social and political upheaval of the 1910s gave Mexico's efforts to develop industrial capitalism a nationalist and revolutionary spin. As a result, political leaders and other sectors of Mexican society after 1917 filtered different agendas through nationalist and revolutionary rhetoric. They presented Mexico's industrial capitalism as a product of the revolution that would elevate the standard of living among Mexicans. In the process, they disguised the facets of Mexican liberalism that characterized Mexico's pursuit of industrial capitalism. State intervention in Mexico's commercial and industrial growth was presented as a service to the public and a measure that was necessary to implement revolutionary ideals. Such intervention strengthened and legitimized institutions as it increased the authority of the state headed by federal officials in Mexico City. In other words, the issues, programs, and institutions that emerged in support of Mexico's industrial capitalism reinforced state legitimacy and nation building. Political leaders by the 1930s felt they had enough leverage to establish national industrial development programs even if they faced opposition. Their approach and development strategies received a mixed response at the national and international level.

Spreading the American Dream: Information, Technology, and World War II

The information and content division of the OIAA launched an aggressive campaign to combat Nazi influence and "win the hearts and minds" of Mexicans in the early 1940s. The campaign was a response to research conducted under the leadership of Nelson Rockefeller that indicated that Mexicans had little sympathy for the United States. Most important, the findings showed that peasants and working-class residents had a positive image of Germany (though not of Hitler) and were openly hostile to the United States.[1] These alarming results presented a crisis in American diplomacy. In addition to Rockefeller's disturbing reports, unsettled disputes over the nationalization of American oil companies in 1938 and the developing relationship between Mexico and Germany concerned U.S. officials. Mexican trade with Germany, Italy, and Japan had increased in the late 1930s in response to an international boycott conducted by Standard Oil and Dutch Shell to force President Cárdenas to retreat from nationalization.[2] By 1940, the U.S. State Department discovered several Nazi spy rings operating in Mexico and learned of anti-American propaganda supervised by the German embassy.[3] U.S. intelligence also reported that well-known German firms such as the Bayer Company (Casa Bayer) were filtering Nazi propaganda through the business sector. Anti-American sentiment and increasing German influence in Mexico at a time when Hitler was advancing rapidly through Europe panicked the U.S. government. American military officials understood that fighting the Axis powers at the U.S.-Mexican border would be devastating. Alarmed at this potential threat, the U.S. government considered gaining Mexicans' favor a top priority for American national security.

U.S. and Mexican government officials worked to resolve tensions between the two countries in the early 1940s. U.S. government officials learned that Mexican political leaders, including President Cárdenas and his successor Ávila Camacho, valued a good relationship with the United States and did not support Hitler despite their commercial dealings with Germany. They also understood that Mexico would not retreat from the nationalization of the oil companies and that efforts to undermine the Mexican government would be counterproductive.[4] Mexican and American political leaders settled their oil disputes, although Standard Oil did not accept the settlement until September 1943. They reached a Reciprocal Trade Agreement in 1942 that facilitated the flow of merchandise and cooperation between the two countries. U.S. Secretary of State Cordell Hull considered reciprocal trade agreements a vital diplomatic tool in U.S. foreign policy.[5] Not surprisingly, Mexico signed agreements that authorized U.S. aircraft to fly over Sonora and Baja California the same year it signed the Reciprocal Trade Agreement with the United States. It also authorized U.S. military officials to inspect Mexican aircraft in Tampico and other strategic areas.[6] However, the Mexican government limited its cooperation by requiring U.S. military officials in Tampico to wear civilian clothing, arguing that the presence of uniformed U.S. military personnel on Mexican soil would trigger anti-American protests. Cárdenas objected to having U.S. military troops stationed in Mexico despite his willingness to cooperate.[7] Cárdenas's support was crucial to the United States because President Ávila Camacho (1940–46) had given him military command over Mexico's northern Pacific region, an area the U.S. military wanted to protect from a possible German or Japanese invasion. Mexico did not enter the war until mid-1942, but both the Mexican government and the U.S. government were determined to stop Nazi influence in Mexico by 1941.

U.S. efforts to change public opinion in Mexico revolutionized the Mexican information industry as government officials used print, audio, and visual materials as weapons to fight the negative image of the United States and combat Nazi propaganda. Rockefeller's OIAA revitalized Mexico's communication infrastructure and introduced standardized research methods to monitor the information industry and measure public opinion. It blacklisted companies, articles, and programs that were classified as pro-Nazi and reported them to the Mexican government. Punishment for pro-Nazi leanings varied from a slap on the wrist by Mexican government authorities to full expropriation of corporate assets. The OIAA initiated an unprecedented boom in Mexico's communication, advertising, and entertainment industries by increasing the flow of cash from U.S. government agencies and businesses to Mexican magazines, newspapers, and radio stations. The U.S. government paid for publicity and print, visual, and audio materials. It indirectly paid for commercial advertising by offering tax breaks to American companies that continued publicity during the war. Rockefeller encouraged American companies to continue their publicity in Mexico even if they had no merchandise for sale, reminding them that advertising would guarantee prosperous markets in the postwar era. He also hired top researchers and advertising agents to design pro-American publicity.

The U.S. government and commercial advertising headed by Rockefeller's OIAA championed American leadership in science, industry, and art—American ideals and the American way of life, the "American dream." The OIAA presented the United States as a nation of abundance, freedom, democracy, and modern economic development. It insisted that Mexicans and Americans had common goals: the pursuit of democracy, material prosperity, and upward mobility. It suggested that Mexicans could achieve these goals through mutual cooperation and friendship with the United States under the Good Neighbor Policy. It presented the United States as a partner instead of a threat to Mexican nationalism. Most important, American publicity suggested that both Mexican and U.S. government officials were committed to the goals Mexicans had heroically defended during the revolution. Like Mexican political leaders, Rockefeller's OIAA defined Mexico's revolution as a struggle for capitalist democracy, which would support industrial capitalism and upward mobility into the middle class. To this end, American publicity blurred the lines between Mexico's revolution and American capitalism. In other words, Rockefeller presented the syncretism of American and Mexican culture as the basis for successful diplomacy in Latin America. This strategy was fundamental to the reconstruction of U.S.-Mexican relations during World War II.

From "Big Stick" Politics and Dollar Diplomacy to the Good Neighbor Policy

The dispute over the nationalization of American oil companies (1938–41) stretched the diplomatic boundaries between Mexico and the United States. The final settlement ended a century of tense and sometimes bitter relations. It marked a shift in U.S. foreign policy toward Mexico as U.S. government officials gave priority to Mexico's friendship over the economic interests of American oil companies.[8] On the surface, the 1942 settlement was a response to fears that Nazis might gain access to a strategic military zone south of the border. However, it also recycled the 1933 Good Neighbor Policy, which until then had been primarily a rhetorical gesture. It introduced a diplomatic approach that promised to cement good relations between the two countries. U.S. diplomats under President Franklin D. Roosevelt were instructed to inform Mexicans of different aspects of American capitalism and culture, and Rockefeller's OIAA was charged with teaching Americans to respect Mexican culture. Nazi influence in Mexico led the U.S. government to abandon its tradition of siding with the oil companies after it realized that Mexicans would not accept any other settlement.

Rockefeller's diplomacy under Roosevelt's leadership redefined U.S.-Mexican relations and put a progressive spin on America's Good Neighbor Policy. Aware of previous tensions triggered by American prejudice, Rockefeller insisted on syncretizing Mexican and American culture, which he saw as compatible. Rockefeller encouraged social and corporate welfare and a less confrontational attitude toward Latin America. He supported higher wages, better health care, and an improved standard of living among Latin Americans. He promoted Mexico's industrial and economic development policies, including protectionist measures under ISI. Yet neither charity nor international goodwill was the driving force behind Rockefeller's approach. The economic chaos of the Great Depression and the political crisis of World War II shaped his policies toward Latin America. Rockefeller argued that a diplomatic partnership with Mexico and Latin America was vital to U.S. national security. He insisted that social and corporate welfare was beneficial to both American and Mexican capitalism, declaring that the United States did not have the luxury of pretending to be divorced from the rest of the world.[9] According to Rockefeller, the United States had to help raise the standard of living among Latin Americans in order to create a pool of consumers that would allow American capitalist expansion.

The phrase "Good Neighbor Policy" was coined by Herbert Hoover during his 1927 visit to South America and later adopted by Roosevelt as a rejection of military force and financial coercion under America's "big stick" politics and dollar diplomacy.[10] Tumultuous protests by people holding signs that read "Yankees Go Home!" apparently prompted Hoover to suggest that military intervention was not in line with the United States' efforts to promote democracy and establish friendly relations with its neighbors. U.S. military intervention in Haiti (1915–30), military intervention in the Dominican Republic (1916–24), and the ongoing invasions of Nicaragua and other countries outraged many Latin Americans and created discomfort in some sectors of American society by the 1920s. In Mexico, images of crushing defeat by American troops and the loss of half of the country's territory during the Mexican-American War (1845–48) often surfaced during diplomatic conflicts between the two countries. Public monuments in Mexico City such as Niños Héroes honored the youth who preferred to die in defense of Mexico rather than surrender to U.S. military forces that entered Mexico City in the 1840s. After the 1880s, Mexican immigrants' complaints about discrimination at the hands of American authorities contributed to the antagonism toward the United States. Mexicans often reported being humiliated by U.S. officials who forced them to remove their clothes so they could be disinfected and then herded them into public baths before allowing them to enter the United States.[11] The deployment of American troops in Veracruz (1914) and Pershing's expedition in northern Mexico (1916) also alarmed Mexicans. Yet nothing disturbed U.S.-Mexican relations more than Mexico's efforts to nationalize the oil companies.

Social upheaval, opposition to recent American invasions of Mexico, and U.S. fear of a German-Mexican alliance during World War I gave Mexican constitutionalists, who had the upper hand over other revolutionary factions in the 1910s, the leverage to ratify the 1917 constitution.[12] U.S. officials voiced opposition to Article 27, which authorized the nationalization of American oil companies, immediately after the constitution was ratified. Mexico's leverage rapidly declined as the threat of a German-Mexican alliance diminished and Mexico's economy worsened. Aware of these conditions, J. P. Morgan denied Mexico a desperately needed loan in 1917. However, Morgan adopted a cooperative stance at the request of President Woodrow Wilson after President Venustiano Carranza agreed to comply with U.S. demands that he hire Edwin Krammer to design a gold standard currency and central bank program.[13] Tensions continued through 1919, when the oil companies demanded a military solution to the conflict and the U.S. State Department advocated withholding recognition of the Mexican government and credit until Mexico agreed to protect the rights of foreign investors.[14] Attempts by President Alvaro Obregón to raise taxes on oil exports failed in 1921 after American companies suspended oil shipments. Siding with the oil companies, the Harding administration in 1923 made recognition of Obregón's government conditional on Mexico's acceptance of the Bucareli Agreement, which protected American companies from Article 27.[15] The Bucareli Agreement offered only a temporary solution. Tensions resurfaced in 1925 when President Calles passed a law that regulated oil exploitation and restricted the rights of foreigners to own land in Mexico. A combination of prejudice, poor diplomacy on the part of Ambassador James Rockwell Sheffield, and the bullying attitude of Secretary of State Frank Kellogg elevated tensions as the State Department discussed a plot to overthrow Calles in February 1926.[16] Fortunately for the two countries, the U.S. Congress recommended a diplomatic settlement under the Robinson Resolution after thirty U.S. officials visited Mexico and rejected Kellogg's policy.[17]

Similar to Carranza and Obregón, Calles retreated from his original restriction of U.S. interests in Mexico, but the tensions between Calles and the United States (1925–27) altered the dynamics of U.S.-Mexican relations. The U.S. government became more critical of its diplomats and appointed officials who favored peaceful cooperation and were in tune with Mexican culture. Herbert Hoover and the ambassador who replaced Sheffield in 1927, Dwight Morrow, adopted a less aggressive tone and openly opposed military intervention as a diplomatic tool. Morrow (a former president of J. P. Morgan Company) represented a cadre of American businessmen and diplomats who considered Mexico a lucrative market for U.S. investments and thought U.S. military force counterproductive. American businesses such as Ford Motors, ITT, and National City Bank entered the Mexican market in the 1920s. They favored a friendly, less rigid tone in U.S. diplomacy. Yet U.S.-Mexican relations, according to Daniela

Spenser, remained rigid concerning anticommunism and the interests of the oil companies. Despite the change in U.S.-Mexican relations, tensions resurfaced at certain points. For example, Elmer Jones from the International Committee of Bankers in Mexico implied in a conversation with the president of Mexico's National Bank that a U.S. military invasion of Mexico would teach Mexicans to respect American property.[18]

The change in U.S.-Mexican relations in the late 1920s was part of a larger movement that questioned American imperialism and dollar diplomacy. According to Emily Rosenberg, anti-imperialism in the United States reached its peak when scholars, the popular press, reform organizations, and congressional insurgents demanded an end to government involvement in foreign financial arrangements during the 1925 foreign-loan hearings headed by Senator Edwin Ladd.[19] Even leading figures such as Franklin D. Roosevelt flirted with anti-imperialism in the mid-1920s. Roosevelt called for a change in foreign policy and condemned the use of military force in defense of economic interests, which he said was responsible for "the hate and dislike of America shared by every other civilized nation in the world."[20] What bothered Roosevelt and other anti-imperialists was the blatant use of force and coercive financial arrangements by the U.S. government after 1898. Similar to Roosevelt, Sumner Welles considered the U.S. occupation of Latin American countries a failure in American diplomacy. According to Welles, the United States had failed in countries like the Dominican Republic because American leaders were prejudiced and ignorant of local cultures.[21] Critics like Roosevelt and Welles contributed to the anti-imperialism that altered U.S. diplomacy toward Latin America. However, 1920s anti-imperialists mistakenly restricted American imperialism to the direct use of force or financial maneuvering, thus limiting the potential for a radical transformation of U.S.–Latin American relations. They underestimated the power of imperialism and its multiple discourses in American corporate capitalism.

American imperialism reached far beyond the use of military force or economic coercion. Influential U.S. senior advisers and policy makers such as Charles A. Conant linked America's capitalism to imperialism and global investment during the early twentieth century. According to Conant's theory of marginal utility, by the 1890s industrial capitalism in the United States had reached a point where the nation's economic development and abundant capital limited the profitability of new investments. Conant proposed increasing productivity and investing abroad under "capital investment imperialism" as a formula for sustaining rising wages in the United States without diminishing the rates of return. In other words, he argued that investing in developing countries where capital was scarce would yield higher profits than investing in the United States.[22] However, investing in underdeveloped areas required the transformation of monetary, banking, and tax systems that facilitated foreign exchange as well as the transfer and repatriation of capital. U.S. political leaders, businessmen, and financial advisers in Latin America championed Conant's capital investment imperialism under the banner of dollar diplomacy.[23]

U.S. imperialism encompassed multiple discourses in American corporate culture. A professional managerial discourse (prompted by a revolution in the corporate management of American business) promised to stabilize Latin America's capitalist structures by emphasizing rationalization of business, social control, and professional expertise. It stressed the application of scientific research to corporate structures. It also suggested that specialization of professionals and standardization of capitalist procedures supported prosperity.[24] Another discourse presented individualism, competition, and openness to change as the keys to material progress. U.S. diplomats and businessmen who assumed the role of "capitalist missionaries" often defined resistance to these values as a "barbaric opposition to civilization."[25] A consumer discourse within American corporate culture promoted the belief that capitalism offered the opportunity to live a "good life" and that a person's ability to participate as a consumer and enjoy America's wealth and abundance was an exercise in capitalist democracy. Under the banner of capitalist democracy, American consumer culture served as a powerful symbol of U.S. corporate success among Latin Americans.[26]

America's corporate culture also endorsed discourses that favored welfare capitalism (1880s–1920s) as a savvy public relations strategy and business formula. According to Roland Marchand, welfare capitalists tried to humanize their companies by projecting a nurturing image, promoting the need to achieve something higher than profits, and trumpeting their lunch programs, free or low-cost medical care, company picnics, and profit sharing.[27] Marchand and other scholars of American history argue that welfare capitalism ended in the 1930s because government programs under Roosevelt's New Deal became more reliable than corporate welfare from the private sector. However, Sanford M. Jacoby has shown that companies like Sears modernized welfare capitalism during and after the 1930s.[28] The intervention of the U.S. government in the economy and the establishment of social programs under Roosevelt's New Deal added new dimensions to America's corporate culture and the role of the state. Ironically, Roosevelt's New Deal resembled the economic development policies of the Mexican government that U.S. officials had opposed prior to the 1940s. A more radical antibanking discourse in American society presented money as the source of greed, corruption, and exploitation.[29] This discourse (promoted by America's progressive movement and endorsed by anti-imperialists and the Left during the 1920s and 1930s) triggered sympathy for the popular radicalism of Emiliano Zapata and Francisco "Pancho" Villa, the most radical leaders of the revolution.[30] In other words, the 1910 revolution triggered American interest in the politics, history, and rich indigenous background of Mexico.[31] Even one of America's wealthiest families, the Rockefellers, expressed their artistic taste for Mexico's revolutionary art when they hired renowned muralist Diego Rivera to add "a piece of Mexico" to their private collection. American interest in Mexico led to discourses that presented a mixed image of Mexicans and their relationship to Americans. They depicted Mexicans as backward and even "uncivilized" while portraying a romanticized image of Mexico's past and its revolutionary and indigenous heritage.

Josephus Daniels personified different discourses of American imperialism and corporate capitalism as U.S. ambassador to Mexico from 1933 to 1941. As secretary of the U.S. Navy during the 1914 invasion of Veracruz, Daniels had represented America's militaristic "big stick" politics of the early twentieth century. Leftist and nationalist factions in Mexico took notice of Daniels's record and stoned the U.S. embassy to protest his appointment in March 1933. Protesters carried signs that read "Affront Yankee imperialism, mobilize the masses against Daniels!"[32] Yet most Mexicans (including Cárdenas) welcomed Daniels's diplomacy. In fact, Mexican politicians were protective of Daniels. They postponed his inauguration, which was originally scheduled at the same time as a ceremony honoring soldiers who defended the country in the 1914 Veracruz incident, in order to prevent protests.[33] Nearly 100 Mexicans died in the invasion of Veracruz in 1914, but most Mexicans (with the exception of radical nationalists) preferred to see Daniels's "progressive side" in a highly charged nationalist context.

Anti-imperialism, Roosevelt's New Deal, and increasing criticism of monopoly capitalism had changed Daniels's diplomacy by the mid-1930s. He became critical of large corporations and monopolies that disregarded the laws of other nations because he believed their actions were counterproductive to American diplomacy and American capitalism. He favored a New Deal approach to foreign policy. He strongly rejected the use of American military intervention as a tool for defending business interests, arguing that U.S. investment "did not carry the right to a warship from Uncle Sam to control" governments in foreign countries.[34] Daniels understood that Latin American markets were crucial to the United States economically, politically, and (by the late 1930s) militarily. He accurately identified the Cárdenas administration as a reformist government that sought a more equitable distribution of wealth, which according to him would increase the purchasing power of Mexicans and create customers for American companies. In other words, Daniels, like Rockefeller, considered Mexican reforms beneficial to the United States. Daniels also defended Cárdenas and offered an alternative to the aggressive sanctions against Mexico proposed by the State Department, the Treasury Department, and the Federal Bureau of Investigation (FBI) after 1938. He insisted that lack of cooperation by foreign companies had compelled Mexicans to nationalize the oil companies to gain control of the economy.[35] Daniels's diplomacy gave Cárdenas room to negotiate with the United States at a different level from previous administrations as it struck the progressive chords of U.S. diplomacy. However, his approach did not represent a unified policy toward Mexico.

Displacement of German Influence in Mexico, 1938–1942

Despite various reactions to Mexico's nationalization of American oil companies in 1938, the U.S. government developed a unified policy to displace German influence in Mexico under the leadership of Nelson Rockefeller. The range of responses to the nationalization of Mexican oil was not surprising given the multiple discourses of U.S. corporate capitalism and the different ideological strands of U.S. foreign policy. U.S. government concerns about German commercial influence in Mexico emerged by 1938, but the diverse ideological and diplomatic tendencies of different agencies hindered early efforts to oust German companies from the Mexican market. Similarly, American businesses were divided over the issue. While some companies restricted their commercial relationship with Mexico, others believed that investing in Mexico not only was lucrative but also served a diplomatic function by contributing to the displacement of German companies. Hoping to develop a unified policy to end Nazi influence in Mexico, Roosevelt established the Coordinator's Office, which later became the OIAA, as a war emergency agency. Daniels and Rockefeller formulated an effective diplomatic policy within the boundaries defined by Mexicans in the midst of an international crisis. Yet their diplomatic approach was highly contested by some sectors of American society in the late 1930s.

The U.S. State Department, the Treasury Department, and American oil companies declared a boycott against Mexico and launched an aggressive anti-Mexican campaign immediately after Cárdenas nationalized American oil companies. Standard Oil hired Steve Hanngan, who had earned a reputation in advertising for his Miami tourism campaign, to head the campaign against Mexico. Hanngan characterized Cárdenas's actions in major U.S. newspapers as communist and fascist plots that promoted the stealing of American property. U.S. newspapers depicted Cárdenas as a bully and ridiculed the U.S. government for not being aggressive enough toward Mexico. According to Lorenzo Meyer, Hanngan's campaign led some companies to take action against Mexico. Twenty-four American companies boycotted Mexico following the nationalization of the oil companies. Other U.S. corporations, such as General Electric and

Westinghouse, temporarily suspended operations as a result of the political uncertainty and fear fostered by Hanngan.[36] The State Department and Treasury Department sided with Standard Oil and approved of the boycott. They also persuaded Eximbank to deny loans to Mexico, hoping that Cárdenas would retreat as a result of economic pressure.[37] Cárdenas did not reject American investment, despite the nationalization of the oil companies. On the contrary, he protected American companies from radical organized labor in late 1938.[38] He opposed efforts by American companies to control the Mexican government through military threats or economic sabotage, as the oil companies had done prior to his administration. In other words, Cárdenas's approach conformed to the progressive diplomacy championed by Daniels, Welles, and Rockefeller. Yet the anti-Mexican faction in the United States misrepresented the Cárdenas administration in order to promote a military resolution based on America's "big stick" policies and dollar diplomacy. However, its approach and actions were not in line with Cárdenas's Mexico or the international climate of the late 1930s.

The economic sabotage and aggressive actions of the United States strengthened the already well-established commercial relationship between Mexico and Germany. According to Alfred Tischendorf, Germany had become a major economic player in Mexico by 1910, second only to the United States.[39] The development of railroad networks had given the United States an advantage as a Mexican trading partner. However, Germany had displaced England and other European countries as a major economic partner with Mexico primarily because Germans had met Mexican demands for cheap and lightweight products.[40] German investment controlled "retail and wholesale distribution, foreign trade, commodity brokerage, and drug compounding and distribution."[41] As a result, many American companies used German distributors to market their merchandise in Mexico. For example, the Bayer Company manufactured its own products but also distributed medicine produced by American manufacturers. Germans temporarily reduced their trade with Latin America during World War I, but they regained their commercial influence in Mexico during the 1920s when German exporters used inflation to their advantage. According to Rockefeller, Germans in the 1920s undercut foreign competitors in Mexico by "dumping goods at exceedingly low prices."[42] Studies conducted by U.S. commercial attachés in early 1939 warned Roosevelt of German influence in Mexico's economy. The reports indicated that German drug, chemical, and dyestuff products had gained a reputation of being superior.[43] These reports, a barter trade agreement between Mexico and Germany following a boycott by some American companies, and a 40 percent increase in Mexican-German trade from mid-1938 to mid-1939 forced Roosevelt to take action. He instructed commercial attachés to coordinate efforts to replace German products with American merchandise as Daniels sought a peaceful solution to the oil crisis.[44]

U.S. commercial attachés' mission to replace German products in 1939 was not any easier than Daniels's diplomatic maneuvering for a peaceful settlement to the oil crisis. German products' reputation for quality, according to John Bankhead, assistant trade commissioner in Mexico, made replacing them very difficult.[45] One problem was that American products were difficult to market in Mexico. For example, American companies produced heavy, expensive bicycles, whereas German bicycles were small, light, and inexpensive. According to Bankhead, to compete against German bicycle manufacturers, U.S. manufacturers had to produce lightweight bicycles at prices Mexicans could afford.[46] He also urged American manufacturers to meet the expectations that German products in the automotive industry had created. According to Bankhead, the task was challenging because Germans dominated the automotive market even though American companies, such as Ford Motors, had been operating in Mexico since the 1920s. Of the engines imported before 1939, 50 percent came from Germany and only 25 percent came from the United States.[47] Bankhead reported that German automotive products were 25 percent less expensive than American products. American engines were also heavier, and to make matters worse, Mexican importers demanded that U.S. engines meet German standards.[48] Bankhead reported in 1939 what extensive OIAA research confirmed by 1942: Mexicans preferred German products because they considered them better than American merchandise.[49]

The intensity of German influence in Mexico increased from mid-1939 to mid-1940. German officials appointed Arthur Dietrich press attaché charged with a specific assignment: to influence Mexican public opinion in favor of Germany. He received over 100,000 pesos a month from German businesses in Mexico, including contributions from the Bayer Company. He paid editors of *El Timón* and *Hoy!* to promote German interests, and his influence apparently reached major newspapers such as *Excélsior, El Universal,* and *Novedades.* Dietrich also provided economic support to the Proneutrality Patriotic Committee headed by Adolfo León Osorio.[50] This committee bitterly opposed Mexico's involvement in the war. Some Mexican politicians on Dietrich's payroll formed a proneutrality bloc in Congress. Ismael Falcón, the leader of the bloc, provided secret information to Dietrich. Ironically, the U.S. government classified Mexican neutrality as pro-German by late 1940 while at the same time preaching neutrality as its official policy. Some Mexican authorities, according to María Emilia Paz, passively supported Germany by allowing the export of strategic raw materials and turning a blind eye to German intelligence and propaganda as a result of Cár-

denas's "antipathy toward the United States."[51] However, Cárdenas's friendship
with Daniels, protection of other American companies from radical sectors in
Mexico, and efforts to be on good terms with the progressive cadre of U.S. diplomats suggest, as Meyer shows, that his flirtation with Germany was a diplomatic
strategy to gain leverage in negotiations with the United States.[52] Cárdenas's
scheme was effective.

Increasing German influence in Mexico by mid-1940 led Rockefeller to turn
efforts to achieve a quick and peaceful settlement of U.S.-Mexican conflict and
good commercial relations with Latin America into a war strategy. Rockefeller
argued that the United States had to protect its position in Mexico by implement-
ing economic measures against Nazi businesses. He did not participate in the
settlement of oil disputes (the Rockefellers were among the largest oil investors
in Latin America). However, he argued that economic cooperation and mutual
prosperity were the "best weapon against Germany," thus promoting good U.S.-
Mexican relations as a war strategy.[53] Endorsing Rockefeller's diplomatic approach, President Roosevelt instructed his cabinet to give Latin American economic cooperation top priority by September 1940, arguing that not doing so
could lead to a Nazi alliance with countries in the Americas.[54] Roosevelt assigned Rockefeller the task of coordinating the efforts of U.S. government programs and agencies to develop a unified policy of friendship and cooperation.
Daniels, Rockefeller, and Roosevelt increasingly pressured Mexico, in a friendly
manner, to reject German investment and influence by mid-1940.

The election of the more conservative President Ávila Camacho, anti-Nazi actions by the Mexican government, and Roosevelt's decision to develop a unified
policy under the leadership of Rockefeller ended conflicts over the nationalization of the oil companies and led Mexico to declare war on Germany. Compared
to Cárdenas, Ávila Camacho was seen as a less nationalist and less radical leader
by the U.S. State Department and American oil companies. Roosevelt's decision
to classify the effort to improve U.S.–Latin American commercial relations as an
anti-Nazi strategy increased pressure for a peaceful settlement. Signs of Mexican rejection of Nazi influence also pleased (at least ideologically and strategi-
cally) sectors of the United States that had bitterly opposed Cárdenas after 1938.
Cárdenas, for example, decided to close down the pro-Nazi newspaper, *Diario
de la Guerra*, as a cooperative gesture in March 1940. Ávila Camacho rapidly
increased Mexico's cooperation with the United States. He allowed U.S. intelligence operations in Mexico and blacklisted suspicious German companies. He
increased government surveillance on German citizens, including Mexican citizens of German background. Ávila Camacho developed mechanisms to monitor
foreign-language or coded messages and phone calls. He also froze all Japanese
and German bank accounts by late 1941.[55] Thus, by 1941 the United States had

won the battle to gain the full cooperation of the Mexican government with the Allies.

After 1941, as part of its cooperation with the United States under the banner of Rockefeller's Good Neighbor Policy, the Mexican government confiscated those German companies the United States could not replace through capitalist competition in 1939. As Stephen Niblo and Brígida Von Mentz have indicated, Mexico's Administrative Junta for the Vigilance of Foreign Property registered close to 350 firms, of which about 250 were placed under government control as a result of the June 1942 Decree relating to Property and Business of the Enemy (Ley relativa a Propiedades de Negocios del Enemigo).[56] The decree was renewed in February 1944 and was in effect until 1945. The assets of German firms under the control of the Mexican government were transferred to the National Bank of Mexico, which by 1943 had acquired a total of 12,377,904 Mexican pesos from German firms.[57] Forty-three German firms, including the Bayer Company, were confiscated. After entering the Mexican market in 1921, Bayer had earned the reputation of being one of Mexico's most prominent pharmaceutical companies by the 1940s.[58] In 1937 the company had renewed the contract authorizing its registered trademark and patent rights for fifty years. The contract granted the right to manufacture and import dental products, photo materials, and veterinary and agricultural products. Bayer was blacklisted for making financial contributions to Nazi campaigns and allegedly importing photo materials used by German spies to design coded messages on microdots.[59]

According to Paz, Germany trained prominent businessmen in Mexico such as Arnold Karl Franz Juachim Rügue to design coded messages on microdots and send them to South America, Spain, Portugal, and Sweden for broadcasting in Germany to prevent interception by the Allies.[60] Arguing that the Bayer-Nazi connection was a threat to national security, the Mexican government took control of Bayer's advertising and operations immediately after the June 1942 decree was announced.[61] However, complete confiscation did not take place until October 1942, and the government did not claim full control of the Bayer patent and trademark until 1944.[62] Nacional Financiera seized the company's financial resources, and a presidential decree in October 1949 transferred Bayer products, technology, and patent rights to the Industria Nacional Químico Farmacéutica, a company owned partly by the Mexican government.[63] The government returned the Bayer Company to its corporate owners in 1955 with full payment for confiscated property and a percentage of the profits made since 1942. In exchange, Bayer owners declared that they approved of the actions of the Mexican government in 1942 and would not pursue international legal action against Mexico.[64]

Mexico did not declare war on the Axis powers until May 1942, after Germans attacked two Mexican ships, the *Faja de Oro* and the *Potrero del Llano*, but the country was already at war by early 1941 when it became an ally of the United States under the banner of inter-American solidarity. Similar to the United States, which had implemented measures that were far from neutral before Pearl Harbor, Mexico's actions against German operations by early 1941 did not signal neutrality. Mexico's cooperation with the United States ended oil disputes by 1941 but dragged Mexico into the war. The German attack on the two Mexican ships, Enrique Krauze and José Agustín have suggested, served as an excuse for Mexico to declare war against the Axis powers.[65] The cooperation of Mexican government representatives did not mean that Mexicans changed their attitudes toward the United States. On the contrary, numerous studies conducted by Rockefeller in 1941 and 1942 indicated that popular opinion in Mexico continued to be predominantly anti-American. In other words, the U.S. government scored a victory in getting the Mexican government to cooperate with the Allies, but the battle to shape Mexican public opinion had just begun.

Newspaper Research and Public Opinion

Determined to change public opinion in favor of the United States, American government officials set out to revolutionize Mexico's communication industry during World War II. They introduced newspaper and radio research aimed at getting a clear understanding of the Mexican audience. They developed an extensive intelligence infrastructure through the OIAA's information and content division to monitor the information disseminated by Mexican media. Most important, they rationalized the production of information. The OIAA used the research results to design anti-Nazi propaganda. Such coordination between audience research and the production of information was a new phenomenon in Mexico. The theoretical approach and research methodology introduced by Rockefeller included conducting field research, compiling statistical data, and studying the media's impact on different sectors of society. The OIAA developed publicity campaigns after carefully examining audience preferences by class, gender, and region. Rockefeller's approach and methodology revolutionized the information and communication industry in Mexico.

The theoretical approach endorsed by OIAA officials ironically reflected models developed by the Frankfurt school. It resembled the works of well-known German exiles such as Max Horkheimer and Theodor Adorno. The head of the OIAA information and content division in Mexico, Harold Elterich, echoed Frankfurt school scholars when he argued that commercial culture and the ideals displayed in film, radio, newspapers, magazines, and other media shaped public opinion.[66] According to Elterich, media and modern technology created a "universal language" through messages and fixed images that shaped public opinion without making distinctions by class, race, or gender.[67] In other words, Elterich perceived newspapers and radio as vehicles for a mass culture that wiped out an individual's ability to think independently. Horkheimer and Adorno described this process as a "culture industry" in modern industrial societies. The culture industry, according to them, obliterated individual thought and imagination; it absorbed the individual through images, gestures, and words.[68] The danger of the culture industry, they argued, was that these expressions were powerful enough to make people accept views, values, and practices that were unethical. Considering the fact that U.S. government officials and exiled German scholars had witnessed the rise of Nazi Germany, this approach made sense. However, as OIAA personnel later learned in Mexico, it mistakenly assumed that audiences would have a single response, instead of many responses, to messages crafted by media personnel. Mexicans often shaped the content of messages by responding positively or negatively to specific issues, strategies, and approaches adopted by the media. Elterich, Don Francisco (the director of the OIAA information and content division), and Rockefeller agreed with the general approach put forth by Frankfurt school scholars. However, they considered evaluating public opinion as well as understanding and incorporating local values, beliefs, and practices instrumental in designing information and messages distributed through the mass media. Therefore, they conducted newspaper research to better understand the connection between the media and people's values and opinions.

The first major study conducted by Rockefeller's OIAA focused on examining the information disseminated by Mexican newspapers. A crew of "information specialists" were assigned the task of reporting on newspaper headlines, editorials, articles, advertising, and the overall content of newspapers in Mexico City. The first report in April 1941 provided a thorough analysis of fifteen Mexican newspapers over a six-week period.[69] The study revealed that major newspapers such as *La Prensa*, *Excélsior*, and *Novedades* expressed unfavorable attitudes toward economic cooperation between Mexico and the United States. It also noted a "decline in the amount of space Mexican newspapers devoted to themes of cooperation with hemispheric defense, American business methods, and the American way of life."[70] Most important, it indicated that Mexican newspapers were devoting an increasing amount of space to discussions of the benefits of a German victory to small nations.[71] Newspaper headlines such as "The United States versus Hitler in Mexico: Mexicans Remember the 'Big Stick' and Remain Suspicious of Yankees" were threatening to the United States.[72] Links between Nazi officials and *Hoy!* led OIAA official John H. Carson to label the magazine pro-Nazi in the June 1941 report. Carson recommended withdrawing U.S. publicity, which he said would "kill the magazine" since U.S. advertising constituted 50 percent of *Hoy!*'s revenues.[73] Rockefeller decided to spare *Hoy!*'s life but instructed Carson to closely observe its operations. Carson monitored *Hoy!*'s editorial content and its advertising, paying particular attention to the placement of ads and checking for pro-Nazi messages.[74]

Pro-Nazi messages in articles, columns, and publicity that also expressed support for the Allies presented a dilemma for U.S. authorities. OIAA officials indicated in their April 1941 report that newspapers that were generally positive toward the United States, such as *El Universal* and *Excélsior*, often included articles, ads, or sections that conveyed pro-Nazi messages. One reason for the problem was that U.S. officials interpreted any criticism of the United States as "pro-Nazi." Their criteria made it difficult to distinguish the extent to which German propaganda influenced the Mexican media since criticism of the United States did not specifically signal Nazi leanings. Rockefeller instructed Carson to conduct a newspaper survey in May 1941 to develop effective strategies for spreading pro-American messages to different Mexican audiences. The survey shed some light on class and gender differences among Mexico's newspaper audiences.

Carson interviewed 290 people for the study. Thirty-one out of the 54 people classified as wealthy were men and 23 were women. Twenty-eight of the upper-class men said they read *El Universal* and *Excélsior* because they liked the papers' business sections and advertising. It is not surprising that the majority of upper-class men interviewed considered advertising and business news the most important features of newspapers. Projecting male dominance over economic forces and national leadership, upper-class men took pride in their entrepreneurial attitude. By contrast, upper-class women claimed to read *El Universal* and *Excélsior* for their social pages, editorials, and religious news.[75] The response among elite women showed that they generally focused on family obligations. Upper-class women were expected to assume a "centralizing" role that kept their families linked to business, social, and family networks.[76] Financial security, business success, and the overall welfare of the family depended on developing friends and contacts and maintaining the support of family members.

Upper-middle-class newspaper readers valued honesty and rejected dramatic political content in newspapers. Forty-two out of the 60 upper-middle-class readers were men. Twenty-eight of them read *El Universal* and *Excélsior*. Fifteen out of 18 upper-middle-class women said they liked *El Universal* because it was sincere and not "alarmist." This response was consistent with upper-middle-class women's reaction to the debate over whether women should participate in the public arena or remain in the private sphere. Upper-middle-class women who supported women's right to vote often cited arguments that reinforced traditional views of women. They maintained that women should participate in politics and get an education in order to be better prepared to raise children. The preference for newspapers that were not "alarmist" indicated that they sought to avoid controversial political issues. Upper-middle-class women also liked *El Universal*'s neutral coverage of news from the United States.

Out of the 50 middle-class interviewees, 41 were men, 22 of whom claimed they read *El Universal* and *Excélsior* because they created no conflict with the government and were "more Mexican." In the midst of the war to sway public opinion during World War II, *El Universal* and *Excélsior* were anything but neutral. Yet the preference for a less politically charged tone among upper-middle-class and middle-class readers suggests a cry for neutral rhetoric. The OIAA realized how serious this middle-class "cry for neutrality" was in 1943, when the Mexican audience forced it to soften its pro-Allies propagandist tone.

Lower-middle-class readers preferred *Novedades* to other newspapers in Mexico City. Forty-one out of the 61 lower-middle-class readers were men, and 20 were women. Fifteen men read *Novedades* for its sports and comics section. Nine read *La Prensa* because they considered it pro-Mexican and thought it had "not sold out to the British."[77] They liked its sensationalism and its monthly raffle. Fourteen men read *El Universal* and *Excélsior* for their classified ads and because they were "read by serious people." Lower-middle-class women were more evenly divided in their preferences for newspapers. Of the 20 lower-middle-class women interviewed, 9 read *Novedades* and 8 read *El Universal* or *Excélsior*. *Novedades* readers mentioned that they enjoyed its beauty section. *Excélsior* and *El Universal* readers liked the housekeeping sections, the prizes they offered in exchange for subscriptions, and the occasional raffles. Raffle prizes often included a house in a middle-class neighborhood. Women who read *El Universal* and *Excélsior* also expressed liking these newspapers because "fine people" read them.[78]

Working-class interviewees preferred to read *La Prensa* and *Novedades*. All of the 65 working-class readers were men. Twenty of them stated that they read *La Prensa* because it was easy to read and featured public scandals. They also liked the newspaper's less pro-Allies tone. This response alarmed U.S. officials. The OIAA did not blacklist *La Prensa* since it had no direct connection with Nazi officials. However, it kept *La Prensa*, as it did *Hoy!*, under close surveillance. Nineteen liked *Novedades* for its sports and variety sections. Only 7 reported that they read *El Universal* and *Excélsior*, and 19 apparently did not read any newspapers. The large percentage of working-class residents who did not read newspapers concerned U.S officials. OIAA officials were instructed to do extensive radio surveys from 1941 to 1943 to find a mechanism to reach people who did not read newspapers.

Ages ranged from eighteen to the late forties among working-class and lower-middle-class readers. These readers favored *La Prensa* and *Novedades* for their sports coverage, comic strips, raffles, beauty pages, and pro-Mexican stance. However, lower-class readers of *Excélsior* and *El Universal* often expressed a desire for upward mobility when they explained that they read these papers because "serious" and "well-respected" people read them. Wealthy and upper-middle-class readers were more business-oriented and seemed to find *El Universal* and *Excélsior* more suitable. Their ages ranged from the upper twenties to over seventy. Research results indicated that middle-class, lower-middle-class, and working-class readers valued entertainment. Therefore, it is not surprising that the OIAA planted pro-Allies messages in the entertainment sections of newspapers. The OIAA made lower-middle-class and working-class residents the primary targets of pro-Allies campaigns based on these reports.

The OIAA also compiled data on newspaper circulation to increase the efficiency of its pro-Allies messages. Data on newspaper circulation was available prior to the 1940s, but it was often exaggerated. A June 1941 OIAA report ranked *El Universal* first in readership with 32 percent of those surveyed and *Excélsior* second with 23 percent. *Novedades* had 21 percent, and *La Prensa* had 12 percent.[79] *El Universal* had a circulation of 80,000 in Mexico, with 48,000 in Mexico City. The OIAA report stated that 40 percent of its readers were wealthy, 25 percent were upper middle class, 15 percent were middle class, and 20 percent were lower middle class or working class. It classified *El Universal*'s content as 50 percent commercial advertising, 17 percent classified ads, 15 percent local news, 6 percent foreign news, 5 percent editorial, and 4 percent news in English. The data for *Excélsior* was similar. The audience for *Novedades* and *La Prensa* was smaller. *Novedades* sold 40,000 issues throughout Mexico, and *La Prensa* sold about 32,000 issues.[80]

U.S. government officials reported that advertising had become a primary source of revenue for Mexico City's leading newspapers. Mexican newspapers had been running commercial advertising since the late nineteenth century, but initially it was only a small part of their revenue. The volume of commercial advertising increased in the late 1910s, and by 1941, OIAA reports showed that commercial publicity constituted up to 67 percent of some issues of *El Universal*.[81] Most important, reports also showed that about a third of the advertising revenues from May to August 1941 came from American companies. *El Universal* received 300,000 pesos in monthly advertising revenues, 90,000 of which came from American advertising.[82] This figure is even more significant considering that it does not include publicity by American companies with subsidiaries in Mexico. *Excélsior* gained 181,000 pesos in monthly revenue from American advertising. *Novedades* received over 50,000 pesos, while *La Prensa* earned only 5,000 pesos. OIAA officials recommended that American companies continue to purchase publicity in *El Universal*, *Excélsior*, and *Novedades* because these news-papers were generally favorable to the United States and in tune with American values. However, they suggested that the U.S. government discourage Ameri-can companies from advertising in *El Popular* because of its anti-imperialist tone. American advertisers contributed only 3,000 pesos to *El Popular*'s 30,000 pesos in monthly advertising revenues—well below the average in other news-papers.[83] But American officials, as Rockefeller learned, did not have the luxury of discouraging American publicity in Mexico by 1942.

Audience Reception, Content, and the Modernization of Radio

Determined to reach Mexicans who did not read newspapers, the OIAA con-ducted extensive radio research on the tastes, habits, and opinions of radio listeners.[84] The first survey in May 1941 gathered general information on how often people listened to the radio, the programs they preferred, and the type of news coverage they trusted. The survey was administered to 3,000 residents of different Latin American countries, and it concluded that listening habits in Latin America "revealed regional differences."[85] This conclusion, while obvious in many ways, was important because U.S. officials in the 1940s did not always acknowledge the vast differences among Latin American countries. The survey led OIAA personnel to pay close attention to the way listeners in different regions responded to their publicity and programs, in effect "localizing" OIAA broad-casting. The OIAA did not fully realize the importance of catering to local values and tastes until 1943, when ratings showed that audiences in Mexico City often criticized radio programs produced in New York. The delayed response by the OIAA radio division was the result of a number of setbacks in radio research and programming.

As the director of the OIAA radio division, Herbert Cerwin set out to make radio a more effective medium for successful communication with the Mexi-can public by conducting a number of surveys (similar to the newspaper sur-veys). Mexicans were hired to conduct telephone surveys, which provided a sample of urban-middle-class and upper-middle-class residents but excluded lower-middle-class or working-class residents who did not have telephones. The OIAA introduced house surveys in poor neighborhoods to get responses from lower sectors of society, but they were not very successful. OIAA inspectors dis-covered that the men they had hired to interview lower-class families had been fabricating the answers instead of conducting interviews.[86] Residents often lied when asked what program they had listened to the previous night or mentioned programs that had not been on the air. Some poor residents refused to answer the questions.[87] To address these problems, OIAA leaders heightened their supervision of the people who conducted the interviews. They also changed their strategy. Instead of interviewing people in poor neighborhoods, they hired people to walk through lower-class neighborhoods and note the radio programs or stations people were listening to. According to Cerwin, the new strategy proved effective for measuring the popularity of specific programs or radio stations but failed to explain why people preferred a specific program or station.

Studies by the Sydney Ross Company in 1942 were more focused and provided information U.S. government officials and corporations could use to develop efficient OIAA broadcasting. The Sydney Ross Company sponsored anti-Axis programs produced by the information and radio division of the OIAA. It began conducting a radio survey in mid-1942 to study Mexico City's audience.[88] Interviewers were instructed to poll merchants, businessmen, and office workers in the downtown area as well as residents of middle-class, lower-middle-class, and working-class neighborhoods. The research indicated that 76 percent of the 5,087 radio listeners interviewed were twelve to thirty years old. Close to 53 percent of the 3,550 women listeners were between the ages of twelve and nineteen, and nearly 27 percent were in their twenties. About 1,500 of the people interviewed were men. Almost 73 percent of the men were between the ages of twelve and thirty. About 79 percent expressed their preference for dramas and ranchera or other types of Mexican music as opposed to American music. The survey also reported that there was an average of seven people per radio in each house.[89]

OIAA leaders were pleased with their progress in urban areas by 1943, but they were concerned about public opinion in provincial areas. The number of people who owned radios was much higher in Mexico City than in provincial areas because residents of urban areas could afford such luxuries. For example, a General Motors survey of 175 employees in early 1943 reported that 47 percent of the 68 unskilled employees in the study owned radios. Of the 86 skilled laborers, 87 percent owned radios, and of the 21 office workers, 71 percent owned radios.[90] Mexico City residents owned over half of the operating radios in Mexico. Such figures presented a challenge to the OIAA's efforts to reach residents in provincial areas. As a result, the OIAA decided to try to reach residents in provincial areas indirectly. It learned that "many farms around towns employed people who got information and formed opinions from contact with the patron or mayordomo who was likely to have a radio."[91] It considered rural upper-income residents important in influencing public opinion since they were likely to own radios.[92] Loudspeakers, restaurants, and clubs that played radios throughout the day could also disseminate pro-Allies messages, according to the OIAA. OIAA representatives believed that pro-American ideals and anti-Nazi propaganda would trickle down to the masses through radio broadcasters and radio owners. The problem with this approach was that it assumed that listeners would automatically absorb the values, beliefs, and practices of radio broadcasters. The OIAA continued to view the impact of the media on Mexican society through the lens of the Frankfurt school and insisted that its radio publicity would shape public opinion in favor of the United States. The task proved to be difficult, however, since few rural residents owned radios, and even those who did would not readily accept ideas or values radiating from Mexico City.

Based on early radio research, the OIAA tried to design programs that addressed regional differences in Latin America by adopting local rhetoric and traditions. However, addressing regional differences by early 1942 meant producing advertising and radio programs in New York and then adapting them to the local conditions of each country. OIAA officials who promoted this approach rejected the "centralized advertising" previously used by U.S. government officials. Proponents of centralized advertising wanted to produce publicity in the United States and disseminate it throughout Latin America with no modifications. They argued that the tremendous success of *Reader's Digest* in Latin America proved that advertising and radio programs did not have to reflect regional traditions.[93] *Selecciones de Reader's Digest* translated articles and publicity from *Reader's Digest* into Spanish. Soon after the journal was introduced in Latin America in the early 1940s, subscriptions skyrocketed. U.S. officials and corporations faced the dilemma of either imposing American values or adopting Mexican culture in their campaign.

The anticentralized camp gained the upper hand in radio programming and advertising strategies by 1942. This is not surprising given Rockefeller's approach and his influence on U.S.–Latin American relations in the early 1940s. OIAA representatives decided to gradually expose Mexicans to values and rhetoric that fostered the American ideals of freedom and democracy. However, they argued that publicity should simultaneously celebrate Mexican traditions. The new OIAA approach by 1942 radically changed previous centralized advertising strategies. It introduced American values and ideals within pre-existing regional traditions. According to the OIAA, the content and rhetoric of advertising and programs by late 1942 had to "draw on characteristics familiar to the local areas, local history, and local legends."[94] The OIAA had decided in favor of disseminating pro-American ideals through "concepts, values, and traditions Mexicans would readily accept as their own."[95] In essence, U.S. government officials syncretized American and Mexican culture, thus forging a middle ground that blurred the lines between "Mexican" and "American." Yet the syncretizing of cultures was a gradual process. The designing of radio programs and advertising was only part of such a process.

The OIAA began producing shortwave drama, music, news, and sports programs in New York for broadcasting in Latin America. It encouraged American companies to sponsor these programs. Advertising through sponsorship of radio programs was already common in Mexico. Ford Motors, General Electric, and El Palacio de Hierro, among other companies, advertised their products by sponsoring music, comedy, and drama programs. By 1943, shortwave NBC programs produced in New York were broadcast throughout Mexico in fifteen-minute or thirty-minute segments. American companies that sponsored shortwave OIAA programs paid for the actual airtime, but the networks produced the programs in collaboration with the OIAA. The companies advertised their products before and after the program. Publicity often consisted of stating that the broadcasting of the program was made possible by the sponsor's support. The programs often linked the consumption of the sponsor's products with pro-American and anti-Nazi ideals. In short, the OIAA tied its anti-Nazi campaign to the consumption of American products and American democracy.

Shortwave programs gained popularity, but the audiences criticized them for not fully acclimating to Mexican culture. Radio programs initially were simply translated into Spanish before being broadcast in Latin America. Although CBS and NBC adapted programs to Latin American audiences, research showed that Mexicans disliked adaptations.[96] According to Cerwin, research on listening habits in Mexico indicated that "one of the great criticisms of NBC and CBS shows in Mexico was that they sounded 'foreign' to the average Mexican audience."[97] He argued that programs produced in the United States would never be as popular as those produced in Mexico City because full acceptance by the Mexican audience required that producers and actors have a mastery of Spanish and an understanding of Mexican psychology. He argued that there was a great deal of difference between Mexican and American psychology, ideals, and ambitions, even though some themes in American programs appealed to Mexicans.[98] Cerwin criticized those who favored centralized advertising. He argued that the lack of originality in shows produced in Mexico would improve once radio producers stopped trying to imitate American programs and started utilizing the artistic talent available in Mexico. As the head of the OIAA in Mexico, Cerwin's comments can be seen as a cry for autonomy from OIAA headquarters in Washington, D.C., and New York. His persistence in supporting a greater Mexican presence in the syncretizing of American and Mexican culture gave Mexicans some agency.

Cerwin's research triggered changes in OIAA operations by 1943. He insisted on designing different programs for different parts of the country since research indicated that Mexico City residents were less critical of American programs than people in provincial areas. The programs Cerwin designed for provincial areas incorporated local traditions. Cerwin supported the use of Mexican music in rural programming and developed fifteen-minute programs of ranchero music that included three minutes of OIAA publicity.[99] OIAA themes also stressed American leadership in democracy, science, and capitalism. Cerwin believed that programs featuring Mexican music would not be as popular in Mexico City since the audience there had a higher social status and was accustomed to drama programs and American culture.[100] The war, conflicts between the centralized and anticentralized camps, and Cerwin's research reports convinced U.S. authorities that OIAA programs should be produced in Mexico with Mexican actors and actresses. As a result, OIAA programs were produced in Mexico instead of New York by 1943. To this end, Mexicans who favored the production of American radio programs in Mexico exercised a form of agency. In the process, they gave a boost to Mexican artists, singers, and actors and actresses. Ironically, such agency depended on the belief that Mexicans were culturally unique while it served U.S. military purposes and gradually syncretized Mexican and American values and practices.

The U.S. and Mexican governments hoped to reach those whom newspapers and radios did not reach through the Catholic Church. U.S. officials learned by the early 1940s that they needed the support of Mexican religious authorities in order to "conquer the sympathy of the masses."[101] Father O'Grady, a personal friend of Roosevelt, was sent to study the Catholic Church in Mexico, but church representatives felt that O'Grady's report misrepresented the church's role in Mexico.[102] Fortunately for U.S. government officials, the relationship between the Mexican government and the church had radically improved as a result of Ávila Camacho's gesture of conciliation toward religious authorities in 1940. Ávila Camacho's predecessors had established a tradition of strictly divorcing themselves from any affiliation with the church as a result of conflicts between the church and the state. These tensions had increased since the 1850s when liberal leaders believed that state legitimacy and secular authority required removing strong colonial institutions like the church from power. Revolutionary political leaders continued to strip the church of its power and authority after 1917, ultimately leading to armed conflict between the church and the state in the 1920s and 1930s. Ávila Camacho's gesture of conciliation toward the church in the 1940s was timely and perhaps strategic. By December 1940, Archbishop Luis Maria Martínez publicly praised Ávila Camacho's gesture and instructed Catholics to obey civil authorities.[103]

Government officials used the spirit of conciliation to ask Archbishop Martínez to assist in the war effort by "instruct[ing] peasants and people who could not read or write to reject the false claims of Nazi propaganda."[104] They urged the archbishop to encourage people to trust government authorities. Ending on a persuasive note, they asked religious authorities to "save humble Mexicans from criminals who lied with false versions of life under Nazi regimes."[105] By 1943, government officials secretly met with Martínez to discuss the church's role in the war effort. Martínez agreed to support public statements that indicated that Catholics, like other Mexicans, were cooperating with the government in the war effort.[106] Their objective was to show unity with the Allies and counteract criticism of Ávila Camacho's involvement in the war. The archbishop also authorized 1,500 members of the Club Fraternal de Radio to use the image of the Virgin of Guadalupe as a representation of the mother of Mexican soldiers.[107]

Rockefeller, Manufacturers, and Advertisers at the Commercial Front

A sharp decline in U.S. exports as a result of World War II triggered a drop in American advertising, despite Rockefeller's effort to encourage businesses to continue publicity in Mexico. U.S. advertising in the automotive, radio, and electrical supply industries dropped about 35 percent between the summer of 1941 and the summer of 1942.[108] This decline limited America's ability to influence public opinion in Mexico. Most important, it left Mexican radio stations, newspapers, and magazines vulnerable to Nazi clients. The U.S. Department of Commerce estimated that newspapers and radio stations in Latin America "had suffered a loss of forty percent of their advertising revenue received from U.S. firms."[109] American firms reduced their export advertising, claiming that it did not make sense to continue advertising when they had no merchandise for sale. U.S. government representatives argued that newspapers and magazines that had previously rejected German advertising as a gesture of solidarity would either go out of business or begin accepting advertising from German firms. Rockefeller considered the decline in advertising "threatening to the very existence of newspapers and radio stations" that were friendly to the United States.[110] He told American manufacturers that "the decline in advertising to Latin America jeopardized the future economic position of U.S. products in rich markets."[111]

Advertising arrangements by American manufacturers were partly responsible for the sharp decline in U.S. commercial advertising in Mexico. According to Elterich, about 75 percent of the advertising of American products in Latin America was done by local companies at the request of retailers and distributors.[112] U.S. government representatives did not have much control over local advertising. As a result, American advertising frequently went unchecked and lacked "the intervention of manufacturers in the United States."[113] Two-thirds of the publicity spent by local retailers on American merchandise advertised products that U.S. manufacturers had stopped exporting to Mexico as a result of the war, such as automobiles, tires, radios, and refrigerators.[114] Rockefeller's OIAA learned that a revision of publicity contracts and, most important, an increase in U.S. advertising were necessary to win the war for public opinion in Mexico.

U.S. government officials tried to gain the support of American companies in their efforts to create a favorable attitude toward the United States. Rockefeller's OIAA worked closely with the Export Advertising Association in New York and the Association of American Advertising Agencies (AAAA). It focused on coaching U.S. businessmen to adopt a "missionary" approach in Latin America. It instilled the belief that American businessmen "represented the United States in the most critical time in history" and that their work was fundamental in gaining the favor of Mexicans toward the United States.[115] The OIAA used Coca-Cola as an example. Coca-Cola increased its expenditures for Latin American publicity from $150,000 in 1941 to $350,000 in 1942, half of which was spent in Mexico (see figure 2.1). It also offered the OIAA full cooperation in the crafting of pro-American messages and requested that newspapers and magazines carrying its publicity reject the advertising of German products.[116] U.S. government representatives also used Sterling Products as an example of commercial cooperation by early 1941.[117] They reported that Sterling executives worked diligently to "knock out their German competition" in the pharmaceutical market in the shortest time possible.[118] Colgate-Palmolive, Kodak, and General Motors, among other American manufacturers, were working with the U.S. government to drive German companies out of Mexico by early 1942. However, the battle to gain Mexican support for the United States required much more than the cooperation of a few American companies.

Determined to increase American publicity in Mexico, Rockefeller intensified his efforts to convince American manufacturers and advertisers that it was in their best interests to continue advertising in Mexico and Latin America. He wrote 500 American manufacturers to request that they cooperate with the information and content division of the OIAA, but only 367 responded. Of the companies that responded, 40 percent reported that they would continue advertising in Mexico despite declining sales.[119] Twenty-five percent announced that they planned to increase their advertising, and only 12 percent claimed they could remain in business only if they reduced or stopped advertising.[120] Rockefeller followed up on manufacturers who did not respond. He asked John Wheaton, vice president of Lord and Thomas Advertising, to urge Armour Company and other clients that had not responded to cooperate.[121] According to Rockefeller, the OIAA strategy was to "introduce appropriate thoughts, slogans, and symbols into advertising and radio programs."[122] Other American advertising agencies also cooperated with the OIAA. Representatives of J. Walter Thomp-

Figure 2.1. Coca-Cola publicity became a model for pro-American advertising during World War II. This 1943 Coca-Cola ad includes a map of the Americas with the statement, "United today . . . United forever." (Author's personal collection)

son released a statement reassuring Elterich that many of their clients had agreed to increase their advertising in Latin America.[123]

Rockefeller and the OIAA used a variety of arguments in their attempt to convince American manufacturers to continue advertising in Latin America. They claimed that American advertisers that stopped publicity in Latin America were making a big mistake because it was "necessary to maintain the trademark and the knowledge of the qualities and virtues of [American] products abroad"— just as American companies were doing in the domestic market.[124] According to them, American companies could lose the reputation and goodwill they had gained for their merchandise if they discontinued advertising, not to mention the loss of support for the war effort. They thought advertising should "explain the shortage of U.S. products" and show that, like Mexicans, other people (including U.S. citizens) were making sacrifices for the Allied war effort. This approach addressed increasing complaints by Mexicans that they were suffering food shortages and price irregularities while their country was exporting products to the United States.[125] This criticism was generally classified as a product of Nazi propaganda. However, the Reciprocal Trade Agreement signed by Mexico and the United States in the summer of 1942 radically increased Mexican exports, providing desperately needed supplies to the United States and raising prices to Mexican consumers. Therefore, the complaint was not simply a product of Nazi propaganda. Mexico's participation in the war, including economic cooperation with the United States, created bread-and-butter issues for Mexican families.

By late 1942, OIAA officials focused advertising on promoting goodwill, maintaining trade, and, most important, explaining delays and shortages of merchandise. They attempted to convince American companies of the long-term benefits of advertising in Latin America. They argued that despite market disruptions during the war, continuing corporate advertising would keep Mexican customers interested in U.S. products.[126] Elterich assured American companies that continuing advertising would "definitely place U.S. firms in a stronger position and help maintain their dominance in Latin America" when international corporations launched their "economic offensive" after the war.[127] Reconfirming Elterich's approach, John C. Rovensky, another OIAA representative, explained that Mexico and Latin America offered great potential for commercial growth and that continuing publicity during the war would guarantee future profits. He argued that population growth and the advancement of Latin American cities offered new "vistas of progress that look toward a greater world of material and cultural value."[128] Rovensky assured American manufacturers that, far from being a waste of money, advertising during the war should be considered postwar corporate planning. The Florida Chamber of Commerce echoed this tone, arguing that advertising was crucial to maintaining consumer loyalty.[129] It also reminded corporate executives that American companies that stopped advertising during World War I learned that increasing competition in the postwar period made it very difficult for them to regain consumers' acceptance. Many of them lost markets they had gained prior to the war.[130] In addition to appealing to patriotism, business sense, and fear, U.S. government officials offered American companies an incentive that was sure to catch their attention—a tax break.

After Rockefeller's announcement of a tax deduction for companies that continued publicity in Latin America in the fall of 1942, the OIAA was flooded with letters from manufacturers and advertisers requesting details on the requirements for receiving tax exemptions. Letters addressed to Elterich raised different questions: "Is radio like newspaper advertising tax deductible? Is advertising expense tax deductible from net or gross income? Do companies that were previously advertising in Latin America qualify for tax deductions?"[131] Elterich responded to each letter, trying to clarify the confusion caused by Rockefeller's announcement. He explained that according to the Office of the Price Adjustment Board, American advertising in Mexico had to be directly linked to the war effort and had to promote sympathy for the Allies in order to qualify for a tax deduction.[132] He also clarified that tax deductions did not apply to domestic advertising. He responded that the amount of money spent on print and radio advertising would be tax deductible from the company's gross income starting from the time the company registered with the OIAA.[133]

The U.S. government and American companies benefited from cooperating during World War II. Elterich and Rockefeller worked closely with well-established advertising agencies. Lord and Thomas Advertising suggested that Rockefeller could help American businesses by making research reports and data available to them. It stated that details on research methods, market data, and the lifestyle of Mexicans would be very helpful to advertising agencies.[134] Lord and Thomas advised Rockefeller that convincing American manufacturers and advertisers to cooperate with the OIAA depended largely on the type of "material they provided for prospective agencies and clients."[135] Hoping to make OIAA research useful to American companies, Rockefeller engaged the Export Advertising Agency to conduct newspaper and radio research. In the era of modern industrial capitalism when business success depended on efficient corporate planning at the production and consumption level, the research provided by Rockefeller's OIAA came in handy to American companies interested in investing in Mexico after the war. OIAA research allowed American companies to coordinate corporate resources in an efficient manner, facilitating their ability to make a profit.[136]

Rockefeller's OIAA, American Businesses, and the Commercialization of the War

OIAA representatives initially adopted slogans promoting cooperation and solidarity in their publicity, but by late 1942, the OIAA questioned the effectiveness of publicity that did not include a substantial pro-American message.[137] In an attempt to create a clearer message, Don Francisco decided that the OIAA should portray the United States as the leader of Western civilization and advertise the American way of life by contrasting it to totalitarian rule under the Germans. He insisted on stressing that, thanks to U.S. love for peace, the greatest advances in "world science, world culture, and world industry had moved westward" from Europe to the Americas.[138] Other OIAA publicity suggested that cooperation would lead to an Allied victory and incorporated slogans appealing to the importance of unity, well-being, happiness, freedom, progress, victory, and prosperity.[139] This publicity championed U.S. neutrality prior to 1942 as a symbol of love for peace. It also associated the United States with scientific and industrial leadership and portrayed German militarism as the enemy of culture and a menace to the achievements of Western civilization.[140] It "humanized" Americans by claiming that, unlike Germans, they "loved their homes, had a sense of humor, and enjoyed art, music, and poetry."[141] Francisco and Elterich explained that their objective was to "saturate the minds of these people with an entirely different conception of the United States" to replace Mexicans' view of the United States as an imperialist nation driven by money and power.[142] They wanted to depict the United States as a more civilized, more practical, and more humanitarian nation than Germany.

Francisco and Elterich idealized class and race relations in the United States to make American society more appealing. They advertised the "American dream" by arguing that "there was no such thing as class distinction in the United States and that any person, from any walk of life, of any race, creed, or religion could rise to unlimited heights through his own initiative and merit and that a humble beginning would not mar anyone's future."[143] In other words, they presented the United States as a nation where capitalist democracy, individual effort, and abundance allowed people to achieve upward mobility. They suggested that social welfare and programs like Social Security indicated that the United States was a society that cared for the disenfranchised. They used the examples of Latin Americans who had gained a high social standing in the United States as evidence that injustice, racial discrimination, and prejudice were not a problem. This strategy was a response to increasing complaints about American prejudice and incidents of brutality against Mexicans by the Los Angeles Police Department. The media reports of police brutality against Mexicans and Mexican Americans during the 1943 Zoot Suit riots in Los Angeles angered Mexicans.[144] Concerned over the negative impact of the riots on Mexican public opinion, OIAA personnel decided to stress racial harmony and the "human side" of Americans. OIAA concerns were legitimate since the rampant beating of Mexicans by U.S. authorities was counterproductive to their mission to gain favorable Mexican public opinion toward the United States.

In cooperation with the OIAA, U.S. companies presented American industrial and scientific superiority as the most effective and humanitarian way of achieving progress. Republic Steel Corporation broadcast a weekly shortwave radio series to Latin America outlining the reasons for its success as a pioneer in American industry. It hoped to build goodwill by demonstrating that the "American way of life allowed companies to produce better goods and peacefully promote commerce."[145] The program told the history of industrial development in the United States. The first episode, "Our Faithful Servant—Industry," emphasized how modern industry had improved the standard of living throughout the world. It contrasted life before and after American technological innovations and featured "the struggles, the disappointments, and the triumphs of well known pioneers in industry."[146] It presented industry not as a product of bloodless machines but as a product of people inspired to improve the world. Humanizing American industry was not a new strategy in American advertising. According to Roland Marchand, corporate advertising had adopted this tactic in the 1920s in order to combat American perceptions of corporations as soulless.[147] Similar to 1920s American advertisers, Republic Steel and the OIAA tried to humanize industrialization and American business through publicity in 1940s Mexico. Every episode in the Republic Steel series presented industry as a liberating force. The series placed men (not women) at the forefront of industrial and technological development as the leaders in the advancement of Western civilization. Themes varied from accounts of men being liberated by the unlimited energy of steam to features on petroleum, farm machinery, food preservation, modern construction methods, machine-made textiles, and steel.[148] OIAA leaders pointed to Republic Steel's campaign as a prime example of how American manufacturers could promote a positive attitude toward American ideals while advertising their merchandise throughout Latin America.

OIAA advertising in Mexico presented the United States as the protector of the Americas. This message was an important aspect of anti-Nazi propaganda since German technology had been highly regarded in Mexico before the war. The advertising of General Motors, General Electric, Coleman, RCA, and other companies attempted to diminish the reputation of German technology by attributing Allied successes to the scientific superiority of the United States.[149] General Electric advertising often stressed that U.S. expertise in the communication industry saved thousands of lives and guaranteed a final Allied victory. According to General Electric, its scientists were working to win the war and to enhance science for the good of Western society as a whole.[150] The healthier, safer, and more comfortable world General Electric claimed its scientists were building would, according to this advertising, benefit humanity.

Trade magazines cooperated with the OIAA by encouraging businessmen to emphasize themes of unity and solidarity in their Latin American advertising.

Such advertising championed U.S. and Latin American businessmen as the leaders of the free world. It suggested that despite language differences, there were "no borders in the minds or the hearts of businessmen because they held the same views, the same ideals, and the same hopes."[151] Some American companies took this approach seriously, one company echoing OIAA representatives by stating that "American businessmen could do a lot to bring about a better understanding between the Americas."[152] Their cooperation fostered Rockefeller's efforts to commercialize the war.

Most American companies cooperated with Rockefeller's OIAA, but some were especially determined to end Nazi influence in Mexico. Sterling Products developed fifteen- to thirty-minute radio scripts that local production managers broadcast in different regions throughout Latin America after adapting them to local conditions in each region.[153] It developed a staff of writers, producers, and directors who produced the programs in Mexico. It sponsored drama and sport programs, quiz shows, letter-writing contests, and musical competitions that encouraged audience interaction.[154] Bristol Myers, Dulcería La Suiza, El Aguila Cigarette, Tangee, and Coca-Cola sponsored sports, music, and comedy shows as well. Tangee and Coca-Cola programs featuring Mexican music were among the most popular radio programs in Mexico, receiving higher ratings than shows airing American music. By December 1943, radio surveys indicated that despite XEW's popularity, "its listening audience dropped to an unusual low" when its programs featured music played by a New York orchestra.[155] Both Tangee and Coca-Cola included war advertising in their programs.[156]

By 1943, magazine and newspaper cosmetic advertising adopted militant OIAA rhetoric along with American symbols that represented Pan-American solidarity. Hinds Cream advised readers that in addition to maintaining their beauty, women should remind their families that a world war threatened their liberty.[157] Cutex nail polish advertisements told women that protecting their beauty was more important than ever since modern women occupied prominent positions in society. Ironically, Cutex flirted with the idea of women's leadership and independence, whereas the OIAA told women to "protect their beauty in order to inspire compatriots who defended the liberty of the Americas."[158] Both Hinds and Cutex promoted Pan-American unity. Each displayed a map of the Americas with the statement, "With unity comes liberty." Tangee lipstick took a more patriotic and paternalistic approach in one advertisement (see figure 2.2). It displayed the Statue of Liberty below the headline, "Tangee will make you victoriously beautiful." A statement next to the Statue of Liberty read, "Beauty—the glory of women. Liberty—the glory of nations. . . . Let's defend them both." This cosmetic advertising reinforced conservative gender norms while endorsing OIAA goals.

Figure 2.2. 1943 Tangee lipstick ad with the message, "Tangee will make you victoriously beautiful." (*La Familia* 198 [March 31, 1943]: 5, author's personal collection)

Colgate-Palmolive Peet Company used its corporate structure to create a militant approach among its distributors. The company wanted to "make Mexicans hate the Japanese and the Nazis."[159] It developed a "Colgate-Palmolive Legion" made up of salesmen with the purpose of militarizing sales and marketing rhetoric in favor of the Allies. Salesmen were given gold stars based on their success in sales to indicate their status within the company's hierarchy, which modeled military ranks. According to John Rebaza from Colgate-Palmolive, the objective was "to inject the military idea into salesmen and to make them very patriotic."[160] OIAA research showed that Mexicans saw the war as an event that did not impact them directly. By mid-1942, the OIAA was designing campaigns to make Mexicans understand the urgency of the war, and Colgate-Palmolive's cooperation aided its efforts to "militarize" the Mexican population.

Colgate-Palmolive carefully orchestrated corporate operations, distribution, and language in its efforts to promote Pan-American unity. It trained salesmen to use militaristic language. For example, they were instructed to say "attack a territory" instead of "cover a territory," to refer to competition as the "enemy," and to say that they had "made a killing" when they had a good business day.[161] The company required salesmen to spread weekly messages that appealed to Pan-American solidarity and convinced consumers that "the only ones to blame for increased prices or increased cost of living were the Japanese and the Nazis."[162] According to Rebaza, Colgate-Palmolive "expected to reach about nine million people with their word of mouth advertising as merchandise flowed from their production centers into the hands of retailers and distributors."[163] Colgate-Palmolive also used its newsletter, "The Palmolive Bulletin," to disseminate anti-Nazi rhetoric. The front page of the newsletter displayed the flags of all countries of the Americas with the Mexican flag, twice the size of the other flags, at the center to illustrate that the stand against the Axis powers was a Pan-American effort. Colgate-Palmolive ads used a similar format (see figure 2.3).

Other advertisers incorporated war slogans and phrases into their advertising. Ford Motors adopted the slogan "He who values freedom will fight for it" under the direction of McCann-Erickson Advertising Corporation.[164] According to Elterich, other companies used a similar slogan, "He who values freedom will protect it."[165] Thompson reported that Royal baking powder would adopt any slogan that would link OIAA war ideals with its product, such as "Maintain the liberty of the Americas by using the resources of the hemisphere wisely" and "Royal helps you use the fruits of your native soil wisely."[166] Royal also changed its recipes, reducing ingredients that were likely to be scarce in Mexico as a result of the war, and it broadcast a radio program on housekeeping in Latin America.[167] Some companies used militant solidarity in favor of the Allies dif-

Figure 2.3. 1943 Colgate-Palmolive ad that includes a border of Latin American flags and displays a map of the Americas with the statement, "Friends forever. Union leads to strength and strength leads to victory." (*La Familia* 196 [February 28, 1943]: 39, author's personal collection)

ferently. For example, an advertisement for Spam displayed images of children exercising and an armed soldier with a statement that read, "Healthy people; strong nation" (see figure 2.4). The ad suggested that adopting a healthy lifestyle, which included eating Hormel products like Spam, contributed to the war effort.

Wrigley chewing gum used nationalist themes to promote its new Aztec gum. The marketing of chewing gum was carried out through "package appeal" at the point of sale and relied on methods that impressed the brand name and packaging on the minds of consumers.[168] Wrigley planned to model the packaging of the gum on that of cigarette manufacturers, which had effectively used cards featuring images of famous athletes, actresses, and national flags in their packaging.[169] Wrigley officials reported that they had used red and green in the gum's packaging in an effort to associate the product with the colors of the Mexican flag.[170] This nationalist spin in marketing was not coincidental. OIAA officials had learned through extensive radio surveys that Mexicans generally welcomed a touch of nationalism in publicity.

Figure 2.4. 1943 Hormel ad suggesting that exercise and a "healthy nutritional regime," which included eating Spam, contributed to the war effort in defense of liberty and democracy. (*La Familia* 196 [February 28, 1943]: 27, author's personal collection)

The Struggle for Power over Mexico's Communication Industry

U.S. government representatives became concerned about the concentration of power in the hands of a few Mexicans who owned the information industry. The concern was not surprising considering the significance the international community had given to the information industry during the 1940s. U.S. officials were specifically concerned about reports that Emilio Azcárraga, who owned most of the information industry, was pro-Nazi. The American embassy quickly responded in his defense, stating that he not only was a good capitalist but also was favorable to the Allies. Azcárraga had apparently offended a representative of the AAAA who submitted a report to the U.S. government that classified him as pro-Nazi. The embassy, OIAA, and AAAA agreed that Azcárraga was a good capitalist who had become "the most powerful man in Mexico by monopolizing the information industry" but that he was not pro-Nazi.[171] One of Azcárraga's radio stations, XEW, controlled 50–75 percent of the radio audience in Mexico.[172] U.S. government and business leaders were irritated by Azcárraga's tight control over the communication industry, as well as the Mexican government's lack of regulation of monopolies. However, the Mexican government had recently entered the war on the side of the Allies, and U.S. officials did not want to lose its support by demanding that it address the issue of monopolies.

Instead of confronting the Mexican government about the problem of monopolies, U.S. officials tried to break Azcárraga's hold on the communication industry. By mid-1943 Walter Longan, executive secretary of the OIAA Coordination Committee for Mexico, reported to Francisco that he planned to launch a program on station XEQ featuring Mexico's leading popular actor, Mario Moreno Cantinflas. According to Longan, "if XEQ could not reduce XEW's audience with shows featuring Cantinflas then it would be safe to conclude that it could not be done at all."[173] Coca-Cola moved its radio program from XEW to XEOY in early 1944 to help break XEW's monopoly but returned to XEW after two months because XEOY's radio audience was too small. Herbert Cerwin reported in March 1944 that a division of the OIAA, the Coordinator Committee for Mexico, had purchased the most airtime on XEW for U.S. government publicity in Mexico since 1942.[174] Azcárraga's monopoly over the communication industry continued throughout the 1940s.[175]

Conclusion

U.S.-Mexican relations had changed substantially by the time the United States dismantled the OIAA as a war emergency agency in 1945. The two countries had finally reached a consensus or middle ground in which mutual respect, cooperation, and dialogue prevailed rather than confrontation and force. This form of diplomacy was central to Rockefeller's Good Neighbor Policy. To this end, Rockefeller laid the foundation for political and commercial relations between Mexico and the United States throughout the 1940s. U.S. government officials headed by the State Department launched anticommunist campaigns in Mexico, similar to World War II propaganda, during the late 1940s and early 1950s as Cold War tensions escalated.[176] American companies such as Thompson and Sears picked up on Rockefeller's cues for doing business in Mexico and Latin America with different degrees of success. Yet both learned that syncretizing rather than rejecting Mexican beliefs and practices was essential to achieving business success in Mexico. Rockefeller's OIAA also laid the foundation for American companies in Mexico by supporting developments in the nation's communication and research infrastructure. The OIAA's gathering of data on potential markets in Latin America was no small contribution to American businesses at a time when market analysis determined corporate planning and a company's ability to compete.

The war accelerated the consolidation of the concepts of Mexico as a nation and the legitimacy of the state—a process that government representatives championed under the banner of the 1917 constitution. This acceleration was propelled by changes in Mexico's communication industry and the country's industrial and commercial growth. The sense of urgency created by the war triggered efforts by the U.S. and Mexican governments to increase the efficiency of Mexico's communication industry, thus reducing the distance between provincial areas and Mexico City. This process was compounded by Mexican nationalism and pro-American rhetoric designed to discredit Nazi influence in Mexico. It portrayed Mexico's industrial capitalism as a mechanism for upward mobility and a product of diplomatic cooperation between Mexico and the United States. It reinforced Mexico's capitalist development, a process Mexicans had pursued since the late nineteenth century.

Prophets of Capitalism: The Growth of Advertising as a Profession and the Making of Modern Mexico

chapter 3

Juanita Guerra Rangel described her experiences as a leading advertising representative in Mexico City in the 1930s and 1940s in a 1987 interview with journalist Amilcar Leis Marquez.[1] Rangel or "little Juana," as she was known in business circles, migrated from Querétaro to Mexico City in the early 1930s with her family at age sixteen. Financial difficulties and her father's illness forced the family to return to Querétaro shortly after their arrival. Rangel convinced her family to let her stay in Mexico City by arguing that she could help the family financially when she finished high school and started working. Rangel found a job in Nestle's sales division shortly after her family returned to Querétaro. She remembered her job interview as a life-changing experience. She said she had mixed emotions when she walked into Nestle's office. According to her, wearing hosiery and high heels for the first time made her feel important since it represented a symbol of success in Mexico City. Excited, uncomfortable, nervous, and uninformed, she walked into Nestle's office in 1931 and asked to see Mr. Nestle. The secretary explained that Mr. Nestle was the founder of the company and had been dead for almost a hundred years. Rangel was hired as a secretary in the sales division and then promoted to head of the new corporate advertising division in 1935. She developed fifteen-minute radio programs hosted by popular singers like Agustín Lara and Pedro Infante. She gained national and international recognition when she became the first woman president of the ANP in 1943. Rangel credited Mexico's industrial capitalism and Nestle for her success.

Similar to Rangel, a generation of advertising agents, copywriters, and publicity personnel climbed the corporate ladder by mastering the field of advertising in the 1920s and 1930s. They came from different backgrounds and performed various tasks. Some of them, such as Eulalio Sánchez, were Mexicans who migrated to the United States, worked for American companies, and then returned to Mexico as advertising agents. Others, like Eulalio Ferrer, were Spanish exiles who migrated to Mexico in the 1930s and achieved wealth and success in Mexican publicity. Like Rangel, Sánchez and Ferrer presented their success as an example of how Mexico's industrial capitalism made it possible for hardworking individuals to climb the social ladder. They defined their work as a profession that served as the force behind modern economic growth, national progress, and individual prosperity. Their efforts to legitimize advertising as a modern profession faced opposition from provincial and small-scale merchants who did not value publicity. They also faced opposition from government officials who acknowledged the value of advertising but refused to recognize advertising agents as "certified professionals." As a result, Mexicans like Rangel became successful in publicity without a college degree, but they were not considered certified professionals. Not having a college degree, the *licenciatura*, excluded advertising personnel from the professional ranks outlined by the federal government.

Determined to define their work as a modern profession that was vital to Mexico's material prosperity, advertising representatives formed their own association, the ANP, and used the reputation of international advertising to legitimize their work. They described themselves as prophets of Mexico's industrial capitalism. The professionalization of advertising required the development of educational institutions to instruct, monitor, and certify advertising representatives. It also required introducing research methods and technological innovations to elevate business practices in Mexico to the level of those in industrialized countries like the United States. To this end, prophets of capitalism borrowed business strategies introduced by American companies and embraced American and international advertising as a model. They modeled the ANP on the AAAA and adopted advertising codes and standards established by other international advertising associations. However, their acceptance of American and international models did not mean they openly embraced foreign business practices. On the contrary, they convinced American companies that business success in Mexico required hiring Mexican advertising agents. The respect that Mexican advertising representatives received from the international community in the 1940s legitimized Mexican publicity as a modern profession.

Capitalist Development and the Growth of Commercial Advertising, 1870–1920s

The title "professional," which postrevolutionary advertising representatives sought so persistently, suggested far more than having a college degree or certificate. It denoted a lifestyle that included appreciation of literature and the arts, academic training, and intellectual mastery over the essence of Western civilization. It represented bourgeois culture and defined urban middle-class residents as *gente decente* or "decent people" throughout the nineteenth century. *Gente decente* were considered the opposites of "common" or "uneducated" people. The term defined status in social and cultural rather than economic terms. It suggested that Mexicans could have "class" and "culture" without having money.[2] Educated middle-class professionals (doctors, lawyers, and dentists, among others) were perceived as *gente decente* and the foundation of "democratic liberalism" during the early nineteenth century.[3] They represented the ideal "enlightened citizens" at the core of the newly independent nation. By the late nineteenth century, Porfirian educated professionals or the "wizards of progress," to use Mauricio Tenorio-Trujillo's phrase, served as the backbone of Díaz's modernizing program. They took pride in their mastery of science and statistics and worked toward placing Mexico within the ranks of Western civilization.[4] Porfirian writers like Federico Gamboa defined professionals as urban residents who worked in an office setting and, unlike aristocrats, lived an honorable, comfortable lifestyle.[5] Characters in Gamboa's works were accountants and hardworking individuals who enjoyed the artistic, intellectual, and commercial aspects of life in the modern urban setting. In sum, professional status implied a prestigious middle-class lifestyle that was characterized by honesty, good manners, and mastery over different aspects of Western civilization and not necessarily by material wealth.

The prestige historically associated with professional status drove entrepreneurs to identify themselves as professional administrators rather than capitalists as they emerged as a powerful force behind Mexico's capitalist development in the late nineteenth century. The emergence of stable institutions, banking networks, foreign capitalization, and a native investing public that "became increasingly attuned to the potential interest and profit to be gained by investing in new enterprises" triggered Mexico's economic growth during the Porfirian era, 1876–1910.[6] By the 1890s, these "investing capitalists" met at cafés in downtown Mexico City to carry out informal financial transactions handled by brokers at the Bolsa, the Mexican trade institution established in 1895.[7] They financed the first joint-stock industrial firms with investments in the textile, tobacco, and brewing industries, among others. The number of these industrial firms grew to twenty-five by the early twentieth century. The growth of these firms led entrepreneurs to define themselves as professional administrators in order to differentiate themselves from other sectors of society.

Entrepreneurs sought to distinguish themselves from capitalists (company owners and large stockholders) because they preferred to identify with the social and cultural status associated with professionals throughout the twentieth century.[8] Even wealthy capitalists who owned large businesses in Mexico, as Flavia Derossi has suggested, encouraged their children to obtain professional training and a college degree because "being professional was more prestigious than being wealthy."[9] By the 1920s, over half of all Mexican entrepreneurs and business administrators had a college degree (although not in business administration since it was not available as a major until the 1950s), and the number increased to 96 percent by the 1930s.[10] They had trumpeted their education and professionalism as a symbol of status since the late nineteenth century. However, by the 1940s entrepreneurs began to present themselves as protagonists of Mexico's industrial capitalism. According to Derossi, entrepreneurs associated education and economic power with their social status in the 1940s as a result of new cultural models emerging from the "coexistence between traditional values and modernization."[11]

Similar to entrepreneurs, advertising representatives flourished as a result of capitalist development during the Porfirian period, but they defined themselves as prophets of capitalism and did not begin demanding recognition as professionals until after the 1920s. The planning, designing, and production of publicity required an unprecedented level of specialization. Increasing demand for specialized advertising personnel transformed Mexican publicity by the turn of the century. During the late nineteenth century, merchants advertised their products and services in local newspapers by giving a description of the product and its price. Merchants negotiated advertising contracts directly with local newspapers.[12] By contrast, large corporations in Porfirian Mexico either imported their advertising from the United States and Europe or had their own personnel handle advertising contracts with newspapers. They advertised in magazines, newspapers, theaters, bull-fighting events, and lotteries.[13] Advertising often included slogans that became popular. Toluca Beer, for example, urged customers to "drink Toluca Beer or not drink at all" in one of its ads.[14] The highly specialized nature of publicity led large corporations to look for alternative institutions to handle commercial publicity.

Contracts between large corporations and specialized publicity personnel gave rise to advertising agencies and offered legitimacy to corporate advertising. Hoping to tap into the increasing demand for specialized publicity services, Gretschell and Bossero Brothers opened the first advertising agency in Mexico in 1905 and a second advertising agency, Maxims Advertising, in 1911. Advertising agencies planned, designed, and produced ads. They also served as brokers between corporate executives and newspapers. Advertising agencies received 15 percent of the fee newspapers charged for publicity.[15] According to Marcos Desideiro, an advertising agent and author of one of the first books on publicity in Mexico, advertising continued to grow throughout the 1910s. He reported that advertising revenues increased from 1 million pesos a year in 1910 to 4 million pesos a year in 1922.[16]

The growth of advertising and large corporations in Porfirian Mexico increased the consumption of brand-name products and marked the beginning of a process aimed at legitimizing publicity as a modern profession. Commercial advertising in Porfirian Mexico gained legitimacy among *gente decente* and the elite. It linked the consumption of brand-name products to specific ideals and forms of expression as it created "an environment that glorified personal and family consumption where definitions of social norms and the ideal image of a modern Mexico centered around the act of consumption."[17] Publicity commercialized lifestyle in specific areas of Mexico, primarily Monterrey and Mexico City. In Mexico City, residents of the western part of the city displayed the latest European and American products as they strolled, visited fashionable cafés like Sanborns, and shopped at elite department stores such as El Palacio de Hierro.[18] Yet small-scale merchants and business owners throughout eastern Mexico City and the rest of the country either were not convinced of advertising's benefits or could not afford to use specialized advertising services.[19] Many who considered advertising an effective tool for increasing sales did not think publicity required paying professional advertising agents. As a result, the commercial activity in eastern Mexico City and provincial areas did not promote brand-name merchandise. Small-scale merchants marketed their clothing, jewelry, candy, and other homemade products door-to-door in Mexico City's working-class neighborhoods.[20] Milk, fish, and ice cream, among other products, were sold from donkeys in working-class neighborhoods on the east side of the city. La Merced market displayed hand-carved toys, shoes, hats, and rebozos for lower-class residents.[21] The prophets of capitalism before 1910 catered to specific sectors and regions of Mexico and had no problem legitimizing advertising among large corporations and stores that catered to the elite. However, commercial advertising and the sale of brand-name merchandise as planned, designed, and handled by advertising agencies remained beyond the reach of provincial merchants and small businesses throughout the country.

Efforts to enhance the reputation of advertising as the engine of modern industrial capitalism led publicity representatives to describe advertising agents as "religious missionaries." Desideiro argued that, like religious missionaries, advertising agents had to learn effective ways to convince the public to purchase advertised products. According to him, advertising agents told merchants that publicity generated faith—not in religion but in the consumption of specific products. Desideiro insisted that the "faith" advertising agents developed in the consumption of a specific product generated wealth and guaranteed the acceleration of capitalist development. He argued that publicity representatives were more effective at stimulating Mexico's industrial capitalism than entrepreneurs, merchants, and investors because they dedicated "all their activity, all their intelligence, and all their imagination to advertising."[22] Their specialized expertise, according to him, gave advertising representatives familiarity with different topics and social environments. It also fostered qualities such as "personal discretion and tact," which according to Desideiro was vital to effective publicity.[23]

Desideiro's work demonstrates the promise of advertising in 1920s Mexico. Desideiro defined advertising as a mechanism that stimulated interest among potential customers. He did not think advertising should be directed at existing customers. He acknowledged the need to use different media, but he considered newspaper advertising the most efficient form of publicity, arguing that people read newspapers regardless of social status, gender, or region. Newspaper advertising continued to be a reliable source of publicity even after radio advertising became popular in the 1940s. However, Desideiro's view of newspapers as a "democratic force" that disseminated information to everyone regardless of class, gender, or regional differences ignored the fact that the majority of newspaper readers in the 1930s were elite and middle-class residents. Illiteracy remained high among urban working-class residents and peasants until the 1940s. Desideiro's perception of newspapers as a "democratic" medium did not translate into his definition of culture and consumption. He delineated a rather rigid hierarchy within publicity. According to Desideiro, the cultural values and products advertised in newspapers were supposed to reflect the socioeconomic status of the audience, thus reducing publicity to class analysis. He urged advertising agents to publicize products that poor families could afford in working-class newspapers such as *El Demócrata*. Middle-class newspapers like *El Heraldo*, according to him, should advertise middle-class merchandise. He believed that the majority of magazine readers were from the elite, and as a result, he recommended that magazine publicity focus on advertising luxury products to wealthy families. In the 1920s and 1930s, magazines such as *Jueves de Excélsior*, *La Familia*, and *Blanco y Negro* targeted a middle-class audience, thus challenging Desideiro's assessment.[24] However, Desideiro's analysis raised issues that were central to the efficiency of advertising and the professionalization of publicity as a field. He advocated coordination between audience and advertising across class lines to increase publicity's efficiency. He encouraged the rationalization of publicity as a field that combined advertising production with reception.[25] He launched a process that defined advertising agents as prophets of capitalism. Other advertising agents continued Desideiro's mission of defining publicity as the engine of modern industrial capitalism throughout the 1920s and 1930s.

The ANP and the Growth of Advertising as a Modern Profession, 1920s–1950

The development of advertising and its significance as a force behind modern capitalism led to the growth of the ANP. Fernando Bolaños Cacho from

Huasteca Petroleum Company and José Pulido from Chapultepec Height Company formed the ANP in 1923 as an umbrella organization to mediate tensions in advertising, establish nationwide publicity standards, and provide a social and intellectual network for discussing different aspects of publicity. Other ANP founders included Juan J. Allard from El Palacio de Hierro (a French-owned department store) and Francisco Sayrols, editor of *La Familia* in the 1930s and 1940s. As an umbrella organization, the ANP provided a network for dedicated individuals who worked their way through the corporate world of advertising, just like Rangel.[26] They became the first generation of "professional" advertisers. ANP membership reached about 100 in 1937 and close to 200 in 1944, representing the publicity departments of different corporations, advertising agencies, and magazines. The ANP began publishing its own journal, *Publicidad: Organo Oficial de la* ANP, in 1938 under the leadership of Humberto Correa (who later became a top advertising agent for J. Walter Thompson). It distributed 1,000 to 1,500 issues of *Publicidad* a month throughout the 1940s.[27]

Tensions between government officials and advertising representatives prevented the ANP from working with the Mexican government to legitimize advertising as a profession. Government efforts to regulate publicity triggered a combative response from advertising representatives and the ANP. Sayrols, Pulido, and other advertising representatives formed a Pro–Visual Advertising Defense Committee (Comité en Defensa de los Anuncios Visuales or CDAV) to stop government efforts to ban mural advertising in the mid-1930s. Committee members argued that murals and other visual ads, such as billboards, "were allowed in every city of the world because they represented the country's economic potential and expressed an artistic tone."[28] CDAV members condemned government regulation of publicity for limiting advertising's potential and urged government agencies to help make advertising a modern profession. According to them, advertising required specialized skills that could only be properly monitored by the establishment of professional guidelines. They asked government institutions to oversee the professionalization of advertising to "elevate the status of publicity and benefit Mexico's industry and commerce."[29] Advertising agents welcomed government intervention if it meant ending irregularities in publicity and making advertising a certified profession. However, the long-awaited constitutional reform of Article 4 of the 1917 constitution, which established guidelines for official professions in 1943, excluded advertising.

Several factors contributed to the tense relationship between the ANP and the government and the exclusion of advertising as a certified profession. The 1943 reform of Article 4 of the 1917 constitution standardized professional training by requiring professionals to earn a four-year college degree or the *licenciatura*. Advertising representatives were well trained and engaged in serious intellectual discussions addressing numerous aspects of publicity. However, many of them did not have the *licenciatura*, which carried the prestige that entrepreneurs and other professionals enjoyed. By 1943, the government made *licenciaturas* the official stamp of professionalism. In stark contrast, the ANP insisted on establishing independent schools and maintaining control over professional training at a time when the federal government tightened its control over professional titles as a result of the 1943 constitutional reform to Article 4. Most important, the ANP saw the government as a negative force that often worked against its interests throughout the 1930s and 1940s. The ANP considered government regulations extremely disruptive to advertisers. For example, according to the ANP, the interference of the government institution in charge of regulating advertising after 1943, the Secretaría de Salubridad, wasted advertisers' time, money, and resources. The ANP complained that "advertising agents spent long hours trying to develop publicity campaigns that occasionally derived from a specific idea, a specific word, or a specific phrase just to have it taken out by a government representative in the Secretaría de Salubridad."[30] As a result, the ANP condemned the government for having "no regard for the inconvenience, delays, and loss of money caused when it rejected phrases or words."[31] It protested the disruptions that government regulations caused in publicity campaigns that were often timely. Government officials explained that restrictions on publicity were necessary in order to protect consumers. However, regulation of advertising was often driven by ideological and moral standards. For example, popular protests headed by conservative sectors (primarily Acción Católica) triggered a 1944 presidential decree that placed certain restrictions on advertising. The Secretaría de Salubridad tightened its surveillance on publicity in an effort to address this wave of conservatism. Government officials often sacrificed the interests of advertising agents in their efforts to protect consumers and pacify conservative sectors. Ironically, government efforts to mediate tensions among different groups served as a source of conflict between the ANP and government agencies. The ANP opted for establishing advertising as a modern profession independently from the Mexican government as a result of such conflicts.

The ANP used the reputation of American advertising and American corporations to elevate advertising to the status of a legitimate profession in Mexico's capitalist development, but it often criticized American influence on Mexican advertising in order to strengthen its position against government regulations. For example, a second wave of conservatism in 1949 led the ANP to play the "nationalist card" against government policies that promised tougher restrictions on advertising. Advertising restrictions were temporarily enforced in the mid-1940s, but loose enforcement in the late 1940s triggered the second wave of conservatism. In response, the government threatened to ban the advertising of alcoholic beverages on radio and fully enforce the publicity restrictions outlined in the 1944 decree.[32] The ANP rejected these policies, arguing that the "advertising of alcoholic beverages should not be eliminated in Mexico simply because the United States prohibited the publicity and sale of alcoholic beverages."[33] Alcohol, according to the ANP, had been advertised in Mexico for years. The ANP's decision to disregard some ethical values promoted by the United States did not mean it divorced Mexican publicity from global debates on the appropriateness of advertising alcoholic beverages. ANP representatives agreed that phrases such as "drink" and "consume" and other expressions that promoted the habit of drinking should not be used in advertising.[34] They also agreed with some of the arguments presented by Mexican government officials concerning the use of women in alcohol advertisements. They established internal mechanisms to regulate publicity and enforce ethical standards, but they rejected strict government control over publicity. Playing the "nationalist card" against policies that attempted to tighten government control over publicity gave ANP representatives some leverage against strict enforcement of government policies. Ironically, the enforcement of regulations and ethical standards that the ANP rejected was fundamental to making advertising a modern profession.

Efforts to transform publicity into a modern profession required the development of training programs and institutions that monitored the pedagogical and practical aspects of advertising.[35] The government was responsible for establishing institutions that provided professional training and certified professionals in the 1940s, but the ANP decided to establish its own mechanisms for training and certification. ANP president Humberto Sheridan tried unsuccessfully to establish an advertising school in 1942.[36] He blamed the failure of the school on World War II, but the barriers to building a professional educational institution were directly linked to lack of funding and lack of support from the Mexican government. As an alternative to the school, the ANP developed a curriculum for use in established educational institutions. Although some schools adopted the curriculum, they had no funding or qualified faculty. By 1945, the ANP had failed once again to establish an advertising school.[37] As a result, it turned to a government institution for assistance, the CNC, which organized courses in advertising under the leadership of Clemente Serene Martínez from 1945 to 1947. Correa, Sheridan, and other advertising agents offered the courses in schools that had been authorized by the ANP and CNC to distribute advertising certificates. The program led to the opening of the National School of Advertising and Sales in 1947, which became the Technical School of Advertising in 1949. The advertising school continued its affiliation with the CNC but remained independent from the Secretariat of Public Education, which had the authority to approve professional titles, until 1964. The ANP thus successfully established an adver-

tising school that offered courses and certificates in advertising independently
from the Mexican government even though it often networked with institutions
affiliated with the government. Its autonomy did not mean that the Mexican
government did not exercise any power over publicity. However, the ANP's autonomy depended on its ability to present advertising as the engine of industrial
capitalism and to cleverly tap into the reputation of international advertising
(particularly U.S. advertising).

The ANP had stressed internal supervision and the enforcement of ethical
standards in publicity since the 1920s even though it opposed strict government
regulations. In fact, when it was founded in 1923, it resolved to end vicious advertising campaigns launched by large corporations against each other. It considered negative publicity campaigns unethical, unprofessional, and unaccept-
able in modern industrial capitalism.[38] The ANP viewed advertising aimed at
discrediting competitors as detrimental to business, publicity's reputation, and
Mexico's capitalist development. It argued that negative advertising made it difficult to portray publicity as an honest, positive force in capitalism. In its efforts
to institutionalize ethical standards, the ANP became a member of the Advertising Clubs of the World (ACW) and adopted its rules and regulations.[39] The
ACW required the ANP to establish an Ethics Committee that would outline advertising principles and report to the ANP's General Assembly.[40] The committee
declared war against fraudulent and inaccurate advertising in 1944, arguing that
the "truth" was central to publicity's reputation.[41] It promised to promote trust,
responsibility, and service as the banner of advertising agencies. The committee
urged ANP members to report advertisers that violated ethical standards. It also
called for ANP enforcement of advertising rules and regulations.[42] Negative publicity declined throughout the 1930s and 1940s, but the ANP still considered it a
problem in 1949 when it launched another aggressive campaign against negative advertising. It based its opposition to negative publicity on moral grounds.
It argued that manufacturers spent a lot of money trying to develop a reputation
for their products and that publicity campaigns that sought to drive hardworking people out of business were inhumane and illegal.[43]

By 1949, Mexican advertising had gained international recognition under the
leadership of the ANP. The ANP organized advertising agencies from Mexico,
Brazil, Uruguay, Cuba, and the United States in the Pan-American Advertising
Federation (PAAF) in early June 1949. The PAAF established technical, pedagogical, and ethical norms that defined advertising as a modern profession. It
hoped to create a technical body to coordinate research and standardize advertising terminology throughout Latin America.[44] The PAAF promoted cooperation among advertising associations and encouraged communication among advertising professionals from different countries. It declared its commitment to

sponsoring advertising conferences and promoting programs for teaching advertising, including the sponsorship of student scholarships. The PAAF was also responsible for resolving conflicts among members.

A dispute between Mexican and Argentine advertising associations tested the PAAF's role as mediator in June 1949. Argentine representatives wanted to host the first PAAF meeting in early June 1949. The AAAA, the Advertising Federation of America, and other associations granted the ANP the privilege of hosting the meeting in Mexico. In protest, Argentine advertising agents did not attend despite pleas from other international associations.[45] However, Mexico received overwhelming support as host of the event from other members of the PAAF. The ANP boasted that its selection as host of the first PAAF meeting represented the importance that Mexican advertising agencies had gained in the international arena. It credited Mexican advertising agents' use of psychology, art, and scientific research with radically transforming advertising into a modern profession. Annual advertising revenues had reached 120 million pesos by 1949. ANP representatives argued that the economic growth they had stimulated had raised the standard of living for millions of Mexicans.[46] PAAF members praised the ANP for elevating the effectiveness and status of Mexican advertising. However, the emergence of advertising as a profession occurred primarily in Mexico City and did not signal nationwide acceptance of publicity.

The Struggle for the Legitimacy of Advertising in Provincial Areas

The success of Mexican advertising among small-scale businesses and in provincial areas was less impressive than the recognition Mexican publicity received from large corporations and in the international arena. Despite the ANP's efforts to consolidate advertising as a modern profession, small businesses in Mexico City and merchants in provincial areas were still skeptical about publicity by the late 1940s. Traditional tensions between Mexico City and provincial areas made efforts to legitimize advertising at the national level more difficult. Frustrated at the low status of advertising outside Mexico City, ANP representatives often revealed their prejudice toward provincial areas by characterizing provincial businesses as backward. They argued that provincial merchants' ignorance of the benefits of advertising practically drove newspapers and small radio stations out of business.[47] Provincial newspapers and radio stations experienced a temporary decline in revenues shortly after the war because U.S. government agencies reduced their advertising. Yet the ANP blamed provincial merchants for the decline. Commercial advertising revenues eventually increased after 1945, but provincial merchants still considered spending large amounts of money on advertising a waste of hard-earned profits.[48]

The ANP's efforts to legitimize publicity nationwide reinforced Mexico City's prejudice toward provincial areas. The ANP, like nineteenth-century liberal leaders and government officials in postrevolutionary Mexico, blamed provincial areas for Mexico's underdevelopment. It argued that provincial merchants' lack of acceptance of advertising and "backwardness" were responsible for poverty. This was not surprising given that most advertising representatives and advertising agencies were based in Mexico City. ANP representatives argued that provincial businessmen lacked creativity and innovation. They claimed that provincial store owners did not give much thought to the name of their store, spent 200–300 pesos on advertising for the grand opening, and then stopped advertising. The ANP argued that store owners who continued to advertise designed their own newspaper or magazine advertisements rather than paying for professional publicity services. Even worse, provincial businessmen, the ANP reported, were openly hostile to advertising representatives. According to the ANP, "professional advertising representatives who worked with provincial businesses often opted for not suggesting improvements in advertising" for fear of angering their clients (see figure 3.1). Another problem was that small businesses continued to use the same ad for years. The ANP underestimated the impact of provincial businesses on Mexico's capitalist development. Although provincial merchants and store owners did not use professional advertising services, they distributed brand-name products that large corporations such as Coca-Cola and Corona publicized on a mass scale. Therefore, they supported market expansion in the interior of the country. Most important, the ANP's prejudice toward provincial merchants obscured the fact that the legitimacy of advertising as a modern profession depended on large corporations more than small businesses.

The ANP faced different problems among small businesses in Mexico City. Small-scale manufacturers and merchants in Mexico City recognized the significance of advertising but believed that advertising campaigns by large corporations harmed their businesses. Small businessmen often turned to the government for protection from large corporate advertising campaigns. Gustavo Barcenas, a small Mexico City cigarette merchant, expressed his concerns to the general director of industry and commerce under President Ávila Camacho. He argued that small cigarette merchants suffered the consequences of bitter advertising campaigns launched by Cigarros El Aguila and La Tabacalera Mexicana. The battle between the giant corporations, according to Barcenas, started shortly after sales for El Aguila's Embajador cigarettes declined as a result of a negative campaign run by La Tabacalera. El Aguila responded by launching a more expensive advertising campaign for Embajador cigarettes and hosting concerts at the Plaza de Toros. The audience could attend the events free of charge if they brought an empty pack of Embajador cigarettes. El Aguila also "distributed 40,000 cigarettes for the audience to start smoking during the concert."[49] Bar-

Figure 3.1. 1949 cartoon depicting a local store owner violently expelling a professional advertising agent from his store. (Rubén Acuña, "Publicidad en la provincia," *Publicidad: Tarifas Oficiales, La Revista de los Ejecutivos de Negocio* 7 [October 1949]: 43, courtesy of the ANP)

cenas urged Ávila Camacho to break El Aguila and La Tabacalera's monopoly on the cigarette industry because it was impossible for small cigarette merchants to compete with their mass publicity. He claimed that mass advertising campaigns were unjust and illegal publicity that "killed small cigarette companies."[50]

Advertising agencies and the ANP launched campaigns to convince metropolitan and provincial merchants of the benefits of hiring professional publicity agents. Publicistas Mexicanos advertised its services by displaying an image of a woman forcing her child to take medicine accompanied by a statement that warned women not to give home remedies to children without understanding the cause of the illness and the possible effects of the remedies.[51] The ad suggested that home remedies were usually ineffective and often counterproductive. Likewise, it stated that "homemade advertising" was sometimes dangerous, could lead to poor results, and was often ineffective against competitors.[52] It urged merchants to turn their publicity over to specialists at Publicistas Mexicanos. Ironically, the ad equated women's performance in the domestic setting with inefficiency and ignorance as it argued that "nonprofessional" advertising was detrimental to businesses. The ad portrayed women as bearers of domestic values and practices that were contrary to progress, professionalism, and efficiency, thus reinforcing conventional gender norms.[53] Other ads portrayed advertising agents as the leaders of progress and capitalist development. For example, an Anunciadora Latino Americana ad argued that Mexican advertising was fundamental to Mexico's progress (see figure 3.2). The ad described publicity as the key to "national greatness" and economic independence. Demonstrating a nationalist and gendered approach, the ad featured the image of an indigenous man rising from a map of Mexico with the caption "Elevation toward Progress." The ad argued that Mexican businesses deserved national publicity. However, the ANP and other advertising agents did not encourage divorcing Mexican publicity from the rest of the world. On the contrary, they suggested that the introduction of new methods and technology used in industrialized countries would modernize Mexican advertising. They emphasized the need to foster the unique aspects of Mexican advertising but welcomed the publicity methods and technology of other countries.

Advertising Methods, Technology, and the Modernization of Publicity in the 1940s

Advertising agents transformed existing forms of publicity in their efforts to modernize Mexican advertising. For example, institutional advertising had been used in Mexico since the late nineteenth century, but it changed dramatically in the 1930s and 1940s. According to Cano Farías, institutional advertising displayed the benefits of shopping at stores that carried patented merchandise.[54] Department stores like El Palacio de Hierro advertised to Mexico's elite from the 1890s to the 1940s through catalogs and *viajeros*.[55] *Viajeros* were young Frenchmen who migrated to Mexico, lived on the upper floor of the Palacio de Hierro building in Mexico City's downtown, and became salesmen for the store after learning Spanish and becoming familiar with the merchandise.[56] According to Margarita Rostan, who migrated to Mexico from France and worked for El Pala-

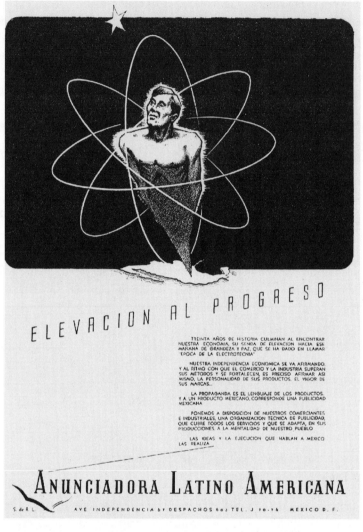

Figure 3.2. 1944 Anunciadora Latino Americana ad publicizing advertising agencies' services as the key to elevating Mexico's status and competitiveness in the international arena. (*Publicidad: Boletín Oficial de la Asociación Nacional de Publicistas* 7 [September 1944]: n.p., courtesy of the ANP)

cio de Hierro from 1929 to 1999, once these young Frenchmen were "Mexicanized," they were sent to different areas of the country to take catalog orders
from provincial merchants.[57] El Palacio de Hierro also received mail and telephone orders from provincial and Mexico City residents and sent store representatives to customers' houses to take orders, deliver merchandise, and provide
some services offered at the store. These forms of publicity continued throughout the first half of the twentieth century and kept the store in business after a
fire destroyed the Palacio de Hierro building in 1914. The store operated out of
its warehouse until a new building opened in 1921. By the 1930s, El Palacio de
Hierro relied heavily on newspaper and magazine advertising. *La Familia* was
among the magazines that carried its advertising. The publicity did not promote the consumption of a specific brand-name product even though it often
featured a particular item. The strategy of institutional advertising, according
to Manuel Muñiz, focused on instructing consumers to purchase merchandise
without mentioning specific brand-name products.[58]

Similar to institutional advertising, collective advertising publicized a particular product without referring to a specific brand name. Collective advertising campaigns were sponsored by multiple manufacturers, retailers, and distributors.[59] Sponsors funded advertising for products linked to their companies
hoping that an increase in the consumption of the products would benefit their
companies indirectly. For example, the National Association of Candy Manufacturers launched an advertising campaign that included sponsorship from sugar
producers, candy manufacturers, and distributors who believed that lack of publicity was responsible for the low consumption of candy.[60] Part of the campaign
focused on presenting candy as a product with great nutritional value, echoing publicity promoting sugar as a great source of energy throughout the early
1940s. The other part of the campaign suggested that thanks to modernization
in the production of chocolate Mexicans could simply grab a delicious chocolate bar.[61] Like other sponsors, candy manufacturers expressed concern that collective advertising did not mention specific brand names or sponsors. As a result, advertising agencies began listing sponsors in ads, which gave a paternalist
and public service tone to collective advertising. They presented sponsors as
public servants who worked collaboratively in order to improve the quality of
products and made the consumption of specific products safer for consumers
through the use of standardized manufacturing techniques. Collective advertising highlighted the sophisticated production of a specific product and stressed
that the highly specialized nature of modern industrial society improved lifestyle by making consumption safe. Most important, it developed networks that
funded large publicity campaigns, thus providing the basis for the rapid growth
of advertising.

The ANP presented mechanical production and innovative packaging methods as essential components of the quality and safety of brand-name merchandise. Manufacturing, according the ANP, provided mass production of brand-name merchandise and eliminated any question about the quality, texture, taste, or amount of the product.[62] It cited the marketing of Milky Way bars as an example, arguing that customers in different parts of the country could purchase Milky Way bars with the same taste, the same amount, and the same quality. In contrast, the ANP claimed that homemade candies were unsafe, low-quality products. The ANP went beyond comparing the consistency and quality of products. It associated manufactured brand-name products with modern industrialized progress that contributed to safety, high quality, and consistency and homemade candy with traditional production methods that required intensive manual labor and produced risky low-quality merchandise.

Advertising representatives focused publicity on specific products and did not invoke personal characteristics, ideals, or dreams in advertising prior to 1940. The *Boletín Mensual de la Cerveza Carta Blanca* in 1935 reported on debates over the proper use of dark and clear bottles for different types of beer. Carta Blanca's advertising personnel argued that it was fine to use dark bottles for dark beer, but light beer should not be sold in dark bottles because it could give the impression that producers were hiding the color of the beer.[63] They believed that the presentation of the product was important because desire for consumption was stimulated by sight.[64] As a result, they argued that Carta Blanca should market its light beer in clear bottles.

The ANP presented innovative marketing strategies as a liberating force made possible by modern industrial capitalism. It argued that standardized manufacturing and packaging methods had radically transformed marketing in Mexico. It credited Nescafé for ending domestic disputes over making coffee with the introduction of instant coffee. Prior to Nescafé, women purchased ground coffee of no particular brand; they had to measure the right amount for the percolator or for boiling water, depending on their social status. Upper- and middle-class women brewed coffee in percolators, while working-class women added coffee to boiling water. According to the ANP, the process of preparing coffee prior to Nescafé "led to fights at home because women never knew whether the coffee was too light, too strong, too sweet, or whether it had enough milk."[65] Neatly packaged Nescafé coffee, according the ANP, was never too light or too strong. It always had the right amount of sugar and milk. Furthermore, husbands, children, and guests could always adjust the flavor at the dinner table. These claims implied that the days when women controlled their families' tastes from the kitchen were gone. Nescafé stressed personal control over individual taste, women's relief at not having to worry about giving homemade coffee the perfect touch, and conflict resolution at home. Nescafé's advertising in the 1940s went beyond stressing individual control in the household setting; it also presented the consumption of advertised products as a way of generating specific qualities among customers.

Advertising agencies introduced other, less common forms of publicity in the 1940s. One of the less common methods, combined advertising, consisted of the advertising of two products in the same ad. For example, automobile advertising often included publicity for a tire company. The tire publicity was secondary to the automobile publicity and simply consisted of displaying the brand name of the tire. Advertising agencies also promoted publicity campaigns that offered discount prices to newspaper readers who completed marketing surveys.[66] The advantage of this type of publicity went far beyond simply making a discounted sale. Receiving data from customer surveys became crucial to advertising agents in the 1940s. The rationalization of advertising, including the coordination between consumer response and production, became vital to advertising effectiveness and efficiency. It characterized the modernization and professionalization of advertising within industrial capitalism.

The ANP valued the rationalization of publicity as the key to efficiency and effectiveness. According to the ANP, rationalization required close coordination between research and production. To this end, the ANP argued that public-opinion research was an important component of designing the language and context of a particular ad.[67] It also insisted that advertising agents incorporate psychological principles and graphic design in their publicity (based on audience research and data).[68] ANP representatives believed advertising required sociological and psychological studies of popular behavior and attitudes.[69] They quoted the works of well-known American scholars such as Elma Lewis and H. D. Kitson who had studied the psychological aspects of publicity.[70] They urged Mexican advertisers to follow Lewis's and Kitson's model for advertising, which involved defining and highlighting the manufacturer's name and then convincing consumers that a particular need could be fulfilled through consumption of the advertised product.[71] According to the ANP, advertising expertise required understanding the impact of color, sound, and written messages on the audience.[72] It argued that a well-designed ad with the right combination of colors had the power to imprint a message on the mind of the viewer.[73] Graphic design and a basic understanding of the psychology of color could be carefully orchestrated to link consumers to a particular brand-name product.

The ANP warned advertising representatives that publicity campaigns that had not applied rationalized procedures had failed because of the lack of intelligent market analysis. Newspaper representatives, small merchants, and salesmen had historically conducted market analysis in Mexico prior to the 1940s.

However, the ANP placed this important component of publicity in the hands of advertising agents in the 1940s. It suggested that effective publicity campaigns required that advertising agents be involved in the research aspects of advertising in order to incorporate research results in the planning, design, and production of advertising. According to the ANP, companies that introduced products without engaging the services of professional advertising agents failed because they did not have the expertise to coordinate market analysis and research data.[74] The ANP cited the examples of a merchant who failed to sell high-quality pliers because clients preferred less expensive pliers and a company that tried to market cheap peanut butter but failed because the public did not like the taste.

ANP representatives developed new methods of gathering data before launching publicity campaigns. They introduced a marketing observation process that utilized different research methods. Marketing observation started with a general review of government documents, commercial directories, and industry reports to get an idea of market conditions.[75] After this review, researchers might conduct bathroom inventories, which consisted of visiting homes in different neighborhoods and creating a list of items stored in the bathroom. The goal was to get a sense of the products used by families from different socioeconomic backgrounds. Another research method consisted of observing traffic in front of a store to study people's reaction to store displays, the merchandise, and the location of the merchandise. The most common form of research consisted of interviews and surveys composed of basic, open-ended questions. A watch company, for example, asked the following questions: "What made you buy your watch? How much did it cost? When did you buy it?"[76]

The ANP provided various forums for evaluating the efficiency of publicity in the 1940s. In addition to organizing events, as it had done since 1923, it introduced columns in its journal *Publicidad* to facilitate a written dialogue on publicity. Many of the topics addressed in the columns were discussed at ANP meetings. *Publicidad*'s "Ads of Yesterday and Today" column provided an analysis of the changes in advertising from the 1920s to the 1940s. For example, a 1949 article compared two ads for Moctezuma beer (see figure 3.3).[77] The image used in the 1920s ad was aesthetically impressive, but the article insisted that good advertising consisted of more than aesthetics. The 1940s ad, although less appealing aesthetically, demonstrated a clever use of language that linked holidays, festivities, and Christmas Eve to Noche Buena, a beer brewed and manufactured by Moctezuma. In addition to suggesting that Noche Buena (the Spanish phrase for Christmas Eve) provided the best quality and taste, the ad implied that although "Noche Buena is already gone," the spirit of Christmas Eve could be recaptured by purchasing Noche Buena beer. The ad also featured

Figure 3.3. Comparison of a 1920s ad (left) and a 1940s ad (right) for Moctezuma beer. (*Publicidad: Tarifas Oficiales, La Revista de los Ejecutivos de Negocio* 6 [September 1949]: n.p., courtesy of the ANP)

Santa Claus drinking beer with one of the Wise Men. The ANP's idea of good publicity in the 1940s constituted encouraging the consumption of a particular product within the context of national and international traditions through symbolic language.

The comparison between 1920s and 1940s Moctezuma publicity reveals the coexistence of conflicting values in 1940s advertising. Making reference to Christmas to encourage alcohol drinking was not in line with the church's observance of Christmas. Moctezuma's advertising turned religious traditions into festive family events. The advertising went beyond syncretizing religious traditions with alcohol drinking. It also placed a nationalist spin on its message by

Figure 3.4. Comparison of a 1920s ad for Sanborn's Margarita face cream (left) and a 1940s ad for Du Barry cream (right). (*Publicidad: Tarifas Oficiales, La Revista de los Ejecutivos de Negocio* 6 [September 1949]: n.p., courtesy of the ANP)

highlighting the name of the manufacturer, Moctezuma, an Aztec emperor. At the same time, it made a direct reference to an American Christmas tradition. The careful coordination and sophisticated design of Noche Buena advertising were not a coincidence. Advertisers and manufacturers consciously forged the coexistence of contradictory values, beliefs, and practices—a middle ground— in order to market products within a context that did not trigger direct opposition. The 1949 Noche Buena ad blended drinking, individual satisfaction, and American commercialization with religious festivities and Mexican nationalism, all of which coexisted harmoniously.

The ANP considered advertising's ability to convince the consumer that using a product would improve the consumer's performance or appearance a vital component of modern publicity in the 1940s. An article in *Publicidad*'s "Ads of Yesterday and Today" column compared 1920s and 1940s facial cream publicity (see figure 3.4). The article argued that modern advertising should persuade consumers that a product would impact personal character. The article examined a 1920s ad for Sanborn's Margarita face cream that featured the image of a woman in a nightgown looking in a mirror with the caption "Your friends use 'Margarita,' the adorable and favorite cream." The article highlighted the simplicity of the ad, criticizing it for focusing on the product and not the individual. In fact, the ad did appeal to personal qualities by presenting Margarita cream as a popular item. The article compared this ad to a 1940s Du Barry cream ad that cleverly orchestrated visual and textual images to construct ideals that promised a complete transformation of individual qualities and appearance. The ad displayed an image of a young assertive-looking woman with short hair wearing fashionable clothes. The ad asked, "Who is she? . . . This can be you if you use Du Barry cream." The ad suggested that women would be so seductive and beautiful after using Du Barry cream that people would not recognize them. The article claimed that the ability to project a change of personality constituted one aspect of modern publicity in the 1940s.

ANP discussions of publicity often echoed broader themes in 1940s Mexico. A writer for *Publicidad*'s "Commenting on Advertising" column, Vir Norman, provided an analysis of recent ads that, according to him, did not meet ANP standards. His analysis represented a conservative stand in the ANP. He criticized a hosiery ad for advertising women's products in an inefficient and inappropriate manner (see figure 3.5). He suggested that hosiery publicity should display women in "normal postures" such as getting out of a car, taking a baby out of a crib, and sitting on a sofa reading a book. According to him, advertising hosiery by displaying women showing their legs in a seductive manner was not good advertising. He rejected references to sexual attraction in hosiery advertising as morally offensive and commercially ineffective, arguing that using a masculine appeal to advertise women's products was poor publicity.

Norman's analysis promoted a conservative view of women's sexual expression. It implied that women would reject the use of feminine sex appeal in an ad that advertised women's products. It denied the possibility that some women might find public sexual expression appealing as a challenge to conventional views of sexuality and gender. In this context, portraying sexual expression while advertising products for women did not necessarily limit the ad's effectiveness. Norman admitted that the hosiery ad had good results, but he believed the results would have been better if the designer had not based it on sex appeal. Other advertising agents did not think that messages encouraging women to be sexually expressive should be excluded from the advertising of women's products. On the contrary, they suggested that advertising should tap into the urban nightlife counterculture that was becoming widely accepted among youth in 1940s Mexico. Similarly, popular movie stars like Tongolele and films such as *Distinto Amanecer* and *Salón Mexico* reinforced the notion that being sexually

Figure 3.5. Two 1949 hosiery ads deemed to be poor publicity by conservative elements of the ANP because of the use of female sex appeal to advertise women's clothing. (*Publicidad: Tarifas Oficiales, La Revista de los Ejecutivos de Negocio* 2 [May 1949]: n.p., courtesy of the ANP)

expressive in public was acceptable among young women. ANP discussions of what constituted good and bad advertising did not offer a single approach or set of values. Although Norman promoted a conservative approach on issues of gender and sexuality in publicity, other ANP members considered Mexico City's booming nightlife counterculture an opportunity to use new technology to appeal to different values.

Technology and the Transformation of Advertising

The introduction of radio as a tool for publicity presented problems in the effort to legitimize advertising as a modern profession. Radio publicity in Mexico was used widely by government institutions and large corporations from Mexico and the United States. However, small businesses and provincial merchants did not consider radio advertising effective. Radio advertising also faced an aggressive campaign that promoted newspaper advertising as the most effective and efficient form of publicity.[78] Newspaper advocates argued that one newspaper could circulate to the entire family as well as customers and coworkers at the office. In an effort to counteract negative publicity, radio advertisers presented radio as a symbol of modernity and a vehicle of commercial publicity that created new consumers by reaching people in remote areas.[79] The ANP took an active role in encouraging the use of radio advertising. It presented radio advertising not as a threat to newspaper publicity but as a complement to other forms of advertising. It argued that radio symbolized the scientific and technological advancements that made publicity more effective but insisted that the effectiveness of radio publicity, like other forms of advertising, depended on the techniques, skills, and professionalism of advertising representatives.[80] Thus, the ANP used the introduction of radio technology and its new forms of publicity to validate the work of its members.

Radio advertising in Mexico supported some of the most successful advertising campaigns by American companies in the 1940s. Coca-Cola sponsored a nightly radio program, *The Coca-Cola Musical Raffle*, on XEW during the peak listening time, 7:45 to 8:15 P.M. Listeners were encouraged to send letters including their name and address and the advertising slogan of the week. Some of the most common slogans were "The only thing equal to Coca-Cola is Cola-Cola" or "Coca-Cola, the pause that refreshes."[81] Four letters with the correct slogan were selected as prizewinners. Prizes included a trip to New York including 3,500 pesos to cover expenses, 100 pesos, 50 pesos, a refrigerator, and a set of dishes. Carlos Rivera del Prado, an agent for D'Arcy Advertising, which directed Coca-Cola's advertising campaign, received 16,000 letters a week from listeners. Coca-Cola announced advertising slogans on radio, on billboards, in newspapers, and in other forms of publicity. The company argued that slogans imprinted the brand name on the audience. According to Coca-Cola, slogans left no doubt that the brand was the best product on the market and made the product inseparable from the brand name.[82] Coca-Cola's success clearly indicated that Mexican audiences were not only listening to radio but also participating in programs.

Other successful radio programs in 1940s Mexico included *Dr. I.Q.*, in which a charming radio announcer, Jorge Marrón, asked a number of questions over the radio. Marrón broadcast *Dr. I.Q.* live from different parts of the country. He awarded prizes for correct answers to the questions, and the value of the prizes varied depending on how many questions audience members answered correctly. Grant Advertising spent an average of 3,000 pesos for each half hour *Dr. I.Q.* was on the air.[83] According to Rubén Acuña, a staff writer for "Hablando de radio," a column in *Publicidad*, *Dr. I.Q.* reached about 70 percent of the national audience.[84] It was introduced in Mexico by Canada Dry Bottling in 1941. Cigarros El Aguila sponsored it from 1942 to 1946, then Mars, the manufacturer of Milky Way and Snickers bars, continued to sponsor it after 1947. The fact that both Mexican and American companies sponsored the program suggested that they had a similar publicity approach. Similar publicity strategies were the result of the fact that Mexican advertising agents and copywriters often worked for foreign agencies. They also suggest that advertising was not limited by national boundaries. Although *Dr. I.Q.* originated in the United States and was produced in Mexico by an American advertising agency, Marrón was Mexican and his charm gave the program a "Mexican flavor."

Radio advertising did not replace newspaper publicity, but it ended other forms of advertising, such as *cancioneros*, small booklets that featured popular music while advertising products. "Cancionero Picot" became one of the most popular *cancioneros* prior to the 1930s under the leadership of Eduardo Cabral (see figure 3.6). It advertised Picot medical products, and according to *Publicidad*, it served as an excellent means to make Mexican music popular outside Mexico before the introduction of radio.[85] Picot *cancioneros* were distributed for free throughout Mexico and the Americas. *Publicidad* reported that Picot *cancioneros* had made over 2,000 Hispanic American songs popular in the United States and claimed that 80 percent of those songs were Mexican.[86] Commercial sponsorship of radio shows made the introduction of popular songs through *cancioneros* irrelevant since an increasing number of families preferred to listen to their favorite songs on the radio rather than having local groups play popular songs featured in *cancioneros*. Radio symbolized a modern medium that linked music and entertainment to commercial advertising, just like Picot had done. Similar to Picot, radio programs sponsored by commercial advertisers were produced in Mexico City and broadcast throughout Mexico and Central America.

The use of radio advertising by large corporations stimulated large profits for some Mexicans in the communications industry. Emilio Azcárraga founded XEW in 1930 and XEQ in 1938 after studying in the United States and working as a travel agent, a representative for shoe stores, and an automobile distributor. He also worked for RCA Victor, established a record company, and edited a catalog of Mexican songs. He benefited from nationalist policies in the 1930s and 1940s that required that radio stations be owned by either the state or Mexican nationals. Neither the state nor private companies could compete with Azcárraga. As a result, publicity and other radio programs had to be filtered through Azcárraga's radio stations. XEW carried advertising for Coca-Cola, El Aguila, General Motors, and other large national and foreign corporations. Azcárraga's success symbolized emerging urban ideas of upward mobility and the advantages of pursuing commercial relations with transnational companies. However, provincial or small-scale merchants, entrepreneurs, and manufacturers felt threatened by the increasing power of large corporations. They feared

Figure 3.6. "Cancionero Picot" distributed Mexican music to people in Mexico, the United States, and Central and South America. (Demoscopia, S.A. de C.V., *Publicidad mexicana: Su historia, sus instituciones, sus hombres* [Mexico City: Valencia, 1971])

mass production and mass publicity campaigns funded by large corporations and considered radio publicity expensive and ineffective.

Radio strengthened the link between Mexico City and provincial areas by disseminating entertainment and publicity throughout the nation. It made it possible for mothers and daughters in Veracruz, Acapulco, Oaxaca, and Monterrey to gather in front of the radio every evening to listen to the *Hora Íntima*, which featured Mexico's most famous romantic composer and singer, Agustín Lara, live from Mexico City.[87] Children throughout the country enjoyed listening to the songs and tales of Gabilondo Soler, known as Crí Crí. Mexicans could remember radio publicity that included phrases, slogans, and narratives a half century later. In an oral interview, Ubaldo Riojas recalled radio slogans of 1940s Mexico, such as "From Sonora to Yucatan, everyone uses Tardan hats," "Corona and Coronita, the big one is just as good as the small one," and "ACE is washing as I am resting."[88] Radio novellas and sports programs were also popular. The opening of Plaza México, the largest bullfighting stadium ever built in Mexico, was broadcast live in February 1946, featuring one of Mexico's most popular bullfighters, Manuel Rodríguez, known as Manolete. The announcement of Manolete's death a year later kept listeners tuned in as they mourned his loss. Radio programs informed, entertained, and disseminated information at a speed and level that Mexicans had never experienced before. Radio made it possible for Mexicans to be informed, entertained, or saddened by events broadcast from Mexico City. Although programs broadcast from Mexico City did not automatically transform the lifestyle of people in provincial areas, they identified Mexico City as the center of information, news, and entertainment and the nation's leader in technology and industrial economic development. As a vehicle of communication that accelerated the flow of information, radio reinforced the supremacy of Mexico City over provincial areas and encouraged modern industrial development.

ANP representatives in the late 1940s claimed that electronic advertising, like radio, signified Mexico's advancement into the modern industrial world. Advertising agencies began using electricity and neon in Mexico City in the early twentieth century. Department stores displayed "flashing colored lights, national flags, and other eye-catching decorations placed in and around the windows."[89] By the 1930s, advertising agencies turned eye-catching electronic advertising into an elaborate form of publicity that, according to the ANP, made Mexico City one of the happiest cities in the world.[90] The ANP argued that advances in electricity had made it possible for advertising agencies to decorate the streets of Mexico City with spectacular electronic advertising by the late 1940s. It described electronic advertising as a form of urban entertainment that delighted residents with aesthetically pleasing displays.[91] According to the ANP, one of the grandest electronic ad residents noticed while driving on Juárez Avenue near the Palacio Nacional de Bellas Artes announced Goodrich Euzcadi tires. Strolling along Juárez, the ANP continued, viewers were bound to be impressed by the numerous lights featuring various colors, phrases, and brand names, but nothing could prepare them for the dazzling experience of seeing the Nacional ad. At thirteen meters high and fifty meters wide, it was the largest electronic ad in Latin America; it read, "Nacional is quality in furniture for your business and your home."[92] Placed on the Nacional building, the ad featured 3,000 meters of flashing neon light tubes in four colors. Antonio Ruíz Galindo of Grant Advertising designed the Nacional ad as well as other electronic ads for companies that had contracts with Grant Advertising. Other Mexican and foreign companies such as Moctezuma, Nestle, General Popo, Ford Motors, and El Aguila blanketed busy streets throughout the city with smaller electronic ads.

Electronic advertising in the 1940s served as entertainment and symbolized an urban lifestyle that portrayed Mexico City as a city of lights and a "city that never sleeps." Advertisers linked the dynamic display of images, messages, and advertising to the urban nightlife that defined Mexico City as a place of excitement. They targeted streets that were known for their nightclubs and entertainment events. Dancing, drinking, and partying became common among Mexico City's youth throughout the 1940s. As a result, it was not difficult to find streets suitable for electronic advertising at night. Not surprisingly, the most popular electronic signs catered to youth, who were likely to walk or drive throughout the city in search of an exciting nightlife. Coca-Cola, El Aguila, Moctezuma, and Berreteaga liquor dazzled Mexico City's youth with the largest number of electronic displays urging them to drink, smoke, and party.[93] They commercialized nightlife entertainment by bombarding viewers with displays that described Mexico City as a great modern industrial metropolis. Salvador Novo's description of Mexico City's metropolitan geography and lifestyle in his book on Mexico City resembles the image that advertising agents and copywriters tried to build. He equates the city's metropolitan lifestyle with the rise of modern buildings, which he describes as symbols of a modern city in the midst of progress and industrial capitalism.[94]

Intellectuals and Mexican Advertising

By the 1940s, the reputation of Mexican advertising triggered intellectual discussions of national identity among publicity representatives. Some advertisers placed a nationalist spin on Mexican publicity. Scholars like Fernando Carrillo argued that "advertisers had to identify values and ideals that were uniquely Mexican" and project them in national advertising.[95] The Mexican audience, according to him, reacted differently to advertising from the United States, and as a result, advertising had to identify Mexican values and lifestyle. Carrillo advocated the need to give advertising a "Mexican flavor," which required that companies turn to Mexican advertising agents. He believed that only Mexican advertisers could effectively capture the "Mexican character and lifestyle that was occasionally humorous and occasionally fatalist."[96] The Mexican experience, according to Carrillo, had developed a unique national identity in which struggle, humor, and fatalism blended and only people of Mexican origin could illustrate this national character through graphics, charts, and text. Interestingly enough, it was this type of national character that writers like Octavio Paz and Carlos Fuentes introduced in Mexican literature.[97] Carrillo's persistence in defining a unique national character served to promote the hiring of Mexican advertising agents. It was also a response to criticism that Mexican advertising had lost its unique character as a result of the changes it experienced in the 1940s. Although some Mexican advertisers believed that these changes had improved quality, design, and artistic presentation, they claimed that Mexican advertising had lost its national heritage as a result of such changes.[98] José Agustín López, known as Caballero López, argued that Mexican advertising had lost its originality and Latin flavor in its effort to "catch up" with international advertising.[99]

Other senior advertising agents like Eulalio Sánchez echoed Carrillo's and López's concerns about the importance of defining the unique character of Mexican advertising. Ironically, some of the people who advocated nationalism in Mexican advertising began their careers in the United States. Sánchez started his career at Maxwell House in Chicago in the early 1930s. He moved to New York to work for the Acme Plastics Manufacturing Company after publishing an *Advertiser's Guide to Latin American Countries* in 1935. He became the director of international operations at D'Arcy Advertising's New York branch for four years. During this time, he was appointed one of the leading crew members charged with opening a D'Arcy branch in Mexico City in 1941. He left D'Arcy in 1945 to work for *El Universal*'s publicity division and open his own advertising agency, Publicidad Interamericana. Sánchez considered his Pepsi-Cola campaigns his most highly regarded work. He stressed the need for "Mexicans to think by themselves instead of copying American publicity methods."[100]

Some advertising scholars attempted to define Mexican publicity further by establishing national boundaries in international advertising. Eulalio Ferrer argued that the character of advertising was inherently different in different countries.[101] According to Ferrer, Americans celebrated size, Europeans valued the past, and Brazilians emphasized exuberance and rhythm. Mexicans, Ferrer argued, celebrated nationalism. Unlike other Mexican advertising agents, Ferrer believed that different countries developed their own styles and traditions by learning from others, but he insisted that this did not mean they copied foreign models.[102] He argued that Mexico's proximity to the United States and the reputation of American advertising made Mexicans gravitate toward American techniques and models. However, the size, history, and influence of the United States, according to Ferrer, were threatening to Mexicans. As a result, Ferrer argued, nationalism in Mexican advertising served as "a defense mechanism geared toward preserving or protecting the national aspects of advertising against foreign influences."[103] Protecting national identity from foreign influences required that advertising agents "revitalize Mexican roots in advertising in order to promote cultural development and national identity."[104]

ANP representatives like Francisco Sayrols were less optimistic about the status of Mexican advertising. Sayrols believed that advertising had reached its highest level in the United States and England. He argued that despite its achievements, Mexican advertising had not advanced as much as it should have considering its proximity to the United States. According to him, Mexican advertising would reach the level of success of U.S. and European publicity once merchants recognized its significance as the engine of capitalism. Fortunately, Sayrols noted, merchants were learning to value publicity even though they still questioned the effectiveness of specific ads or the media. He admitted that gaining widespread recognition for advertising was not an easy process because many merchants "feared spending money on advertising."[105] However, he considered Mexican publicity promising and argued that the acceptance it received in the 1940s moved it in the right direction.

Conclusion

Discussions of the national character of Mexican advertising attributed the success of Mexican advertising agents to Mexico's industrial capitalism. Advertising representatives cited their success stories in publicity as examples of the unlimited opportunities available to every hardworking individual despite his or her background thanks to capitalist development.[106] Juanita Guerra Rangel's success story presented capitalist development as a phenomenon that "liberated" women from traditional domestic roles. In her narrative, she described being a young, single woman living in Mexico City without parental protection as a sign of independence. Such independence represented a break from the traditional view that unmarried women should remain under parental protection within the domestic sphere. Yet Rangel's increasing independence and her success in advertising had limitations when she stepped outside the boundaries generally accepted in the 1940s. For example, Rangel served as ANP president for only one year, whereas male presidents served longer. Also, her efforts to establish a Women's Advertising Club failed in the 1940s, although the club did form in the mid-1950s. The ANP nevertheless insisted that advertising improved the status of women and liberated them from previous forms of oppression. It presented Mexican advertising as a liberating force in its efforts to legitimize advertising as a modern profession that supported upward mobility and urban industrial capitalism. It promoted a type of individual freedom and independence that disregarded, although it did not contradict, the limitations embedded within Mexico's modern industrial capitalism in the 1940s.

Advertising National Identity and Globalization in the Reconstruction of Modern Mexico

An announcement for the 1940 commercial census described Mexico City as the core of a nation that had heroically decided to move forward. It claimed that the "march for progress" and the nation's glorious past placed Mexico at the center of modernity. According to the ad, the constant movement of cars and people throughout the city represented Mexico's cosmopolitan lifestyle and determination to join the international community in the race for modern industrial capitalism. It presented colonial architecture and modern buildings as symbols of Mexico's heritage and commitment to progress. The ad assured Mexicans that their country would defend its heritage but would no longer remain at the margins of capitalist development. It also suggested that Mexico was heading in the right direction at a time when global industrial capitalism offered opportunities for development. It suggested that the entire world looked forward to a promising future despite uncertainties caused by the war.[1] Similar to the census announcement, commercial advertising presented a cosmopolitan lifestyle and the modern industrial setting as symbols of material progress, national prosperity, and civilization. Idealizing the city as the center of civilization, advertising presented science, technology, mechanized means of production, and rationalized procedures as fundamental to Mexico's success. It presented rural life as simple, irrational, and restricted by antiquated traditions. It rejected noncommercial practices and brandless merchandise as signs of poverty and "backwardness."

Commercial advertising presented conflicting images and values that blurred conventional boundaries between traditional or national and modern or global trends. It presented industrial and commercial development as the key to securing an abundance of goods, creating unlimited opportunities, and increasing the standard of living among Mexicans. It suggested that entering the modern industrialized world required that Mexicans welcome some American values and practices. Yet advertising adopted forms of patriotism and nationalism that had emerged since the colonial period. It created a romanticized vision of Mexico's indigenous past and the nation's revolutionary tradition. Advertising syncretized national cultural trends and global cultural trends stemming primarily from the United States. It promoted American industrial capitalism and lifestyle while celebrating anti-American nationalism. It championed prerevolutionary liberal ideals while proudly celebrating Mexico's socialist and revolutionary traditions. Advertising glorified Mexico's indigenous past as well as current folk traditions at the same time that it encouraged Mexicans to move away from rural areas. It reinforced traditional views by showing women how to be obedient daughters and wives while teaching them how to be popular, how to attain beauty, and how to conquer men. Advertising constructed a cultural middle ground in which apparent contradictions embedded within modern Mexico coexisted. This created a sense of ambiguity that allowed Mexicans to embrace revolutionary and nationalist values while welcoming American culture, which they considered necessary for entering the modern industrialized world. From a corporate perspective, portraying conflicting values within a middle ground allowed companies to appeal to different audiences regardless of social status, political ideology, and moral standards. It provided a safety net for companies at a time when Mexico was experiencing social, political, economic, and cultural transformations. The middle ground allowed Mexicans to drink Coca-Cola and shop at Sears while eating tortillas and celebrating the nation's indigenous heritage.

Advertising and the Recycling of Modern Mexico in the Postrevolutionary Era

The reconstruction of modern Mexico after the social and military upheaval of the 1910s recycled processes that had been fundamental to nation building during the period of Porfirio Díaz (1876–1910). As in the late nineteenth century, the pursuit of material progress became central to Mexican society. Advertising tapped into the notion of progress as it presented an image of Mexico as a country that was moving away from a convoluted past toward a promising future in which scientific development and industrial growth provided the basis for a prosperous society. Echoing late-nineteenth-century liberalism, advertising presented cities and a cosmopolitan lifestyle as expressions of progress and modernity. Faith in progress, science, industrial growth, and the image of the city as a symbol of modernity and civilization was central to the making of modern Mexico under Díaz. Advertising adopted these values after the 1920s but presented them with a new spin. It portrayed material progress (the product of scientific achievement and modern industrial capitalism) and the consumption of advertised products as the basis for a new form of democracy, a "consumer democracy."

Díaz's efforts to modernize urban centers further enhanced Mexico City's legitimacy and prestige as a symbol of Western civilization. This image of Mexico City served as a mechanism for nation building and reinforced federal authority over provincial areas as provincial elites championed "'progressive' ideas radiating from the nation's metropolis."[2] The image of Mexico City as a center of progress and modernity similar to Paris and London served as a model for provincial centers. The carefully planned layout of Mexican cities and their commercial businesses, retail stores, electric lights, paved roads, and theaters, according to Alan Knight, turned them into "showpieces of the Porfirian regime" as they symbolized the nation's material progress.[3] Yet since Díaz's agenda defined urban development in provincial areas as part of a modernizing project headed by Mexico City, provincial cities were placed below the ranks of Mexico City. For example, Governor Olegario Molina's effort to "uplift" the appearance of the city of Mérida to meet Mexico City standards won Díaz's enthusiastic support for Mérida as an integral part of Mexico's modernizing project as opposed to a provincial backwater.[4]

Mexico City's image as a symbol of progress, modernity, and civilization championed the lifestyle of wealthy residents on the west side of the city and misrepresented the socioeconomic status of other sectors of society. Díaz's efforts to present cities as centers of modernity and progress, according to Allen Wells and Gilbert Joseph, divided urban residents according to social status and punished those who did not represent modernizing urban principles.[5] Wealthy sectors of Mexican society "moved into new suburbs that lined Reforma, a wide avenue that ran southwest for a mile and a half from Alameda Park to Chapultepec Castle," throughout the Porfirian period.[6] West side residents displayed their wealth as they visited coffee shops, strolled, and paraded in carriages lit with side lanterns in the early evening.[7] American cafés like Sanborn's and European department stores like El Palacio de Hierro and Puerto Liverpool catered to Mexico City's elite. They became symbols of the material progress and lifestyle fostered by Western capitalism. Liberal leaders portrayed precisely this image as a sign of Mexico's progress and civilization, associating modern cities with wealth, abundance, happiness, and comfort and characterizing the countryside as antiquated, poor, backward, and hostile to modernity.

Political leaders during the 1920s and 1930s continued to view Mexico City as a symbol of progress and modernity that would educate and civilize the rest of the country, but they put a nationalist spin on the "civilizing mission" of the city. They organized cultural missions to spread the civilizing aspects of urban culture to the countryside. The objective of these missions was to educate rural residents in subjects such as history, art, and hygiene. Training in "proper" behavior and the celebration of folk and national festivities were central to these cultural missions. This did not mean that urban residents wiped out local values and practices. On the contrary, community leaders throughout the 1920s and 1930s, as Gilbert Joseph and Mary Kay Vaughan suggest, exercised a great deal of agency by negotiating how urban programs and institutions headed by federal authorities were adopted in their communities.[8] However, the negotiation between rural communities and federal authorities had limitations.

The interaction between rural and urban areas blurred the lines between local and national values. For example, rural and *ranchero* folk traditions, *charrerías*, became part of the national culture and were presented as symbols of Mexico.[9] Similarly, provincial songs, *rancheras*, were adopted as expressions of national culture. The development of *charrerías* as urban forms of entertainment and the growth of *ranchera* music as a symbol of Mexico's folk and popular culture celebrated a romanticized version of rural *ranchero* lifestyle. They turned provincial folk values and practices into national symbols and forms of expression. Whereas local leaders resisted or negotiated (at a social and political level) how federal programs were introduced in their communities, they were less likely to challenge urban ideas and practices that were carefully syncretized and presented a romanticized celebration of rural traditions and lifestyles. Negotiating the introduction of urban programs and values required a level of consciousness, a goal, and mechanisms that facilitated such mediation. The flow of information and imagery between urban and rural areas, however, provided no fixed or coherent message other than promoting Mexico's industrial capitalism. For example, the celebration of folk culture and the romanticized image of Mexico's indigenous and peasant heritage (as portrayed in art, music, archaeology, and other cultural expressions) elevated peasant lifestyle to the status of a national cultural icon. However, the representation of peasants or indigenous peoples as "uncivilized" and backward lowered their status.

Commercial advertising in the postrevolutionary period revitalized late-nineteenth-century liberal interpretations of the city, portraying urban centers as symbols of progress, modernity, and civilization. General Popo tire advertising in the 1940s suggested that it was possible to bring rural people to "civilization" thanks to modern developments in transportation. A General Popo ad displayed a boy standing next to his mother waving to a bus on its way to the city (see figure 4.1). Both the child and the mother are wearing traditional peasant clothing. The ad read, "His fathers [ancestors] never had an opportunity to see this. . . . Today, roads open for these children from faraway neighborhoods [the countryside], routes for contact with civilization [the city] for a better culture and better life. . . . These are new forces that unify and contribute to our national march toward progress." The ad constructed a concept of time and space that portrayed Mexico City as the leading "civilizing" region, which, thanks to the advancement of modern technology, was now able to offer greater oppor-

Figure 4.1. 1948 General Popo tire ad suggesting that Mexico's development and future depended on the incorporation of peasants in national development programs headed by urban industrialization. (*Excelsior*, June 1, 1948, n.p.)

tunities than it had in the past. By opening contact with the city, according to the ad, General Popo tires would lead to a prominent future and ultimately to Mexico's progress. In addition to presenting the countryside as "backward" and uncivilized, General Popo promised national unity. It idealized city life and promoted a harmonious relationship between the countryside and the city. General Popo portrayed rural routes as "neighborhood routes" that would unite Mexico by bringing wealth from its tropical jungles to its "higher territorial planes." Advertising presented Mexico City as a symbol that "represented the summation of national progress and dreams."[10]

Postrevolutionary advertising also featured chronological narratives and historical episodes that highlighted Mexico's progress. It appealed to progress and modernity by contrasting products from the past with products from the present. For example, a 1947 Pep orange soda ad compared its soft drinks with the Canica lemonade of 1910. The ad stated, "So many years have passed since the famous 'Canica' lemonade made delicious drinks for our grandparents. . . . Now, everyone in Mexico drinks Pep" (see figure 4.2). The ad associated antiquated lemonade drinks with primitive automobiles as symbols of Mexico's prerevolutionary period and fashionable soft drinks with the latest car models of the postrevolutionary era. The contrast between 1910 and 1947 implied that thirty-seven years of progress had improved the quality of merchandise and enhanced the degree of convenience for Mexicans. It characterized Canica lemonade, old cars, and anything before the revolution as backward and undesirable and identified the origin of Mexico's progress with the beginning of the Mexican Revolution. The association of Pep, a non-Mexican brand, with the latest car models constructed a positive image that suggested Mexico had moved away from a convoluted and impoverished past into a promising era. On a practical level, neither Canica lemonade nor Pep had any relationship to automobiles. However, Pep advertising depicted a relationship between unrelated products to suggest a chronology of national progress brought about by modern industrial capitalism and its transformation of consumer products. Most important, Pep advertising characterized progress and the comfort, satisfaction, and convenience it brought to consumers as consequences of the Mexican Revolution. Other forms of advertising identified different historical eras as the source of Mexico's progress and commercial prosperity.

Advertising misrepresented complex economic and political networks that supported Mexico's progress and industrial capitalism. The success of Celanese, for example, was directly linked to government policies and World War II, but its publicity attributed the company's success to Mexico's indigenous, colonial, and early-nineteenth-century liberal heritage. Small rayon manufacturing plants declined after the government declared rayon a "saturated" industry in 1937. The decline escalated during the war when the number of small rayon manufacturing plants fell from 250 in the late 1930s to 140 in 1945. This drastic decline facilitated the opening of Celanese Mexicana de América, a 20 million peso joint venture funded by Mexican and American capital, by the mid-1940s. According to Sanford Mosk, the close cooperation of an American company with Mexican investors and the Mexican government raised concerns about foreign investment.[11] The company's publicity sought to counteract such concerns by

Figure 4.2. 1947 Pep orange soda ad associating Pep drinks with the latest automobiles and Canica drinks with primitive automobiles. (*Excelsior*, June 4, 1947, n.p.)

claiming that Mexican clothing had been impressing the world since the pre-Columbian era (see figure 4.3). Other Celanese ads argued that Europeans had enriched the rayon industry during the colonial period, thus making Mexican fabrics globally known.[12] Other ads honored early-nineteenth-century Mexican liberals like Esteban de Antuñano for creating the first modern factories. These ads portrayed liberal leaders as the founders of Mexico's industrial and commercial progress. They suggested that Celanese produced high-quality fabrics that were equal or superior to those imported from other countries thanks to the work of leaders like Antuñano.[13] Other Celanese ads implied that Miguel Alemán's protectionist economic policies served as the engine of Mexico's industrial and commercial success. They suggested that 1947 marked a watershed for Mexican textile industries as Celanese began to provide 100 percent Mexican fabrics.[14]

Postrevolutionary advertisers, like scholars of Mexico, did not agree on the

Figure 4.3. 1950 Celanese ad tracing the origin of the Mexican textile industry to the pre-Columbian period. (*La Familia* 361 [June 15, 1950]: n.p., author's personal collection)

origin of Mexico's industrial and commercial prosperity. Publicity for companies like Pep associated modernity and progress with the Mexican Revolution.
This approach represented the "official history" endorsed by government authorities after the revolution. Various scholars of Mexican history supported
this interpretation. They argued that government expenditures, state politics,
and an industrial revolution supported by political leaders served as the engine of Mexico's industrial and economic success after the Mexican Revolution.[15] Unlike Pep advertising, Celanese advertising linked the industrial and
commercial progress of early-nineteenth-century liberalism to the protectionist
economic policies of the late 1940s at the same time that it glorified Mexico's
pre-Columbian and colonial heritage. The company's decision to highlight a particular strand of early-nineteenth-century liberalism and 1947 protectionism was
not coincidental. The company benefited from the 1947 import-restriction policies implemented by Alemán. Celanese identified the work of prominent early-
nineteenth-century liberal leaders like Antuñano as the foundation of industrial
success, the origin of national prosperity, and the precursor of 1947 protectionist
policies. Antuñano, according to Jesús Reyes Heroles, considered national industrial growth and material prosperity central to progress.[16] Alemán's ISI policies offered a similar form of protection to new industries in the late 1940s.
Antuñano proposed one of two strands of liberalism. He supported the temporary protection of national industries because he viewed industrialization (as
in England and the United States) as fundamental to the growth of a middle
class, which he considered a requirement for the success of liberal laws and
democracy.[17] The other strand of early-nineteenth-century liberalism rejected
government protection and encouraged free trade. Reyes Heroles, Arnaldo Córdova, Charles Hale, and Andrés Molina Enríquez, among other scholars, suggested that the Díaz administration abandoned fundamental liberal principles,
including the protection of national industries and the middle class. According
to them, the 1917 constitution recycled those principles as it selectively revitalized aspects of nineteenth-century liberalism.[18] Celanese's publicity echoed this
interpretation to the extent that it idealized economic and industrial development platforms promoted by early-nineteenth-century liberals and Alemán's industrial development policies in 1947 as the backbone of its corporate success.

Celanese, like other companies, avoided associating Díaz with Mexico's progress and prosperity. No ads in major newspapers or magazines identified the
Porfirian period as the origin of the nation's prosperity and progress. Commercial publicity in the postrevolutionary era rejected Porfirian Mexico and opted
for presenting either one of the strands of early-nineteenth-century liberalism or
the 1910 revolution as the origin of Mexico's industrial and commercial progress.
The rejection of Díaz in commercial publicity reinforced the message that politi-

cal leaders wanted to imprint on public consciousness after the 1920s: that the Mexican Revolution had been a war in defense of the masses against Díaz and his alliance with foreign companies and the national elite. However, the rejection of Díaz's government did not prevent postrevolutionary advertising from appealing to vital aspects of Porfirian liberalism, such as faith in science, industry, and technology as the basis of national development; the view that material prosperity was the foundation of Mexico's progress; and the creation of a sense of national "originality" within a global context.

Science, Industry, and Technology as the Basis of Mexico's Progress

Postrevolutionary advertising insisted on locating the roots of industrial and commercial prosperity within Mexico, but it also presented Mexico's achievements in science, technology, and industry as part of a global process and the advancement of Western civilization. The challenge of identifying a "unique" national character in the midst of a global movement that required mastery over science, industry, and numerous corporate laws led advertising agents, business executives, and political leaders to broadcast conflicting messages that syncretized national and global values. Efforts to define a unique Mexican identity within Western civilization dated back to the colonial period. According to David Brading, Mexican Creoles (Mexicans who could trace their family background to Iberian Spain) in the seventeenth century established a unique identity through literature, math, science, and iconic symbols like the Virgin of Guadalupe.[19]

Creole patriotism continued during the eighteenth and nineteenth centuries within certain tenets of liberalism. It assumed different forms of expression in Porfirian Mexico. Liberals under Díaz tried to place Mexico within the ranks of the modern cosmopolitan world by portraying an authentic Mexican character at world's fairs. Efforts to depict both a glorious past and an image of Mexico as a country that welcomed modern science, industry, and technology created a sense of ambiguity. Mexican liberals, or the "wizards of progress," to use Mauricio Tenorio-Trujillo's phrase, understood science as a universal form of knowledge that increased efficiency and provided the basis of progress. To this end, Mexico's success in a modern capitalist world required the mastery of science at the national level. However, placing Mexico on the global map of science required originality. According to Tenorio-Trujillo, Díaz launched a campaign to develop a sense of "national originality" in his efforts to create a form of nationalism in the late nineteenth century. Exhibits such as the Aztec Palace at the 1889 World's Fair presented Mexico as a "national entity with a glorious past but ready to adjust" to a modern cosmopolitan lifestyle.[20] In other words, Creole patriotism during the colonial period and Díaz's "wizards of progress" gave Mexico a sense of originality. However, the point of reference had changed. Creole patriotism during the colonial period expressed a sense of optimism and defined New Spain (Mexico) as a unique and prosperous country within the ranks of Western civilization. The "wizards of progress" operated under the assumption that northern Europe and the United States had taken the lead in Western science and industrial capitalism. They suggested that Mexico had fallen behind but could ultimately achieve progress if it established legitimate institutions, transformed its population, and applied universal scientific laws fundamental to success in global capitalism.

Echoing the "wizards of progress," postrevolutionary advertising suggested that cooperation with the leaders of Western science, technology, and industry was necessary in order to achieve progress. To this end, advertising argued that Mexican companies must cooperate with leading American companies. Advertisers demonstrated how urban leaders and corporations had worked with international companies to bring progress to Mexico. They promoted the message that cooperation with American companies would improve the quality of products and lifestyle of Mexicans. For example, General Popo advertising argued that the quality of products available to Mexican consumers had improved thanks to the cooperation of Mexican and American companies. One ad pointed out that in addition to its own scientists, its associate, General Tire and Rubber Company (GTRC), had employed scientists from the Carnegie Institute. According to the ad, Standard Oil of New Jersey had developed a formula for making synthetic rubber that was later granted to GTRC. GTRC then worked on improving the quality of synthetic rubber. This type of cooperation, according to the ad, "demonstrated the prestige and capability of El Popo to produce the best tires of synthetic and natural rubber to better serve Mexican consumers."[21] The ad suggested that because Americans had taken the lead in scientific development, Mexicans had to adopt American science in order to move forward in Western capitalism.

Other ads located the origin of certain products in Mexico and suggested that advances in Western civilization had improved the quality of such products. For example, Larín insisted that its Bambú chocolate dated back to pre-Columbian Mexico. It explained that "Nahoa Indians referred to it as 'Cholalt,' the Europeans called it 'chocolate,' and today people recognize it as 'Bambú.'"[22] Given the origin of chocolate as a native American product, advertisers could have used a nationalist appeal in Bambú's publicity. However, they chose to present Bambú as an indigenous product that was enhanced by Western civilization. They stressed both the national origin and the universal perfection of the prod-

Figure 4.4. 1950 Bambú chocolate ad suggesting that progress was the result of the historical dialogue between Mexicans and the rest of the world. (*La Familia* 357 [April 15, 1950]: 3, author's personal collection)

uct as they equated the history of chocolate with Bambú. One ad insisted that "Mexico had given the world chocolate . . . and Larín now gave Mexico the best chocolate" (see figure 4.4). It displayed people from different parts of the world enjoying a cup of Bambú chocolate and argued that Larín had elevated Mexican chocolate to its highest quality. Bambú presented its chocolate tablets as an innovative phenomenon that had increased the convenience and comfort of consumers. In other words, postrevolutionary publicity portrayed an interplay between the national and the global as it appealed to the indigenous or national origin of certain products and suggested that the scientific advancement of Western civilization enhanced the quality of such products. Thus, advertising for General Popo and Bambú sought some consensus between the national and the global.

Some postrevolutionary advertising disregarded national appeal altogether as it defined the United States as the leader of Western science. This type of publicity was used widely as anti-Nazi propaganda during World War II. It was designed to address concerns about the high regard for German technology and products in Mexico before the war. The advertising of General Motors, General Electric, Coleman, and RCA, among other companies, repeatedly attributed the success of Allied battles to the scientific advancement of the United States. General Electric advertising highlighted how its scientific developments had made it possible for the Allies to win air and water battles.[23] General Electric advertising often claimed that expertise in the communication industry not only saved thousands of lives but also guaranteed victory. According to General Electric, its scientists were not just working to win the war; they were also working "to make sure that advances in the electronic industry guaranteed a healthier and safer place with more comfort" that would benefit all humanity.[24] Yet General Electric's portrayal of science and technology as a "civilizing" force characterized indigenous, peasant, and working-class lifestyles and traditions as backward. In one ad, modern electric washing machines were compared to primitive clothes-washing methods (see figure 4.5).

Advertising stressed the qualities that Western science could endow in an object and a consumer. One ad for Alamo wine compared Alamo with an automobile, portraying both as the "maximum expression . . . and progress" Mexicans could enjoy thanks to scientific advances that had perfected the making of wine and automobiles.[25] This comparison of two objects that required different levels of complexity in manufacturing stressed consumption rather than production. Automobile production required a much greater level of industrial and technological complexity than wine production. However, at the level of consumption, both automobiles and Alamo, according to the ad, symbolized progress and scientific development. Drinking Alamo, just like driving an automobile, was an expression of being in tune with the modern world and distinguishing oneself from ordinary Mexicans. By the late 1940s, advertising suggested that science could endow consumers with personal qualities instead of simply improving the quality of the object being advertised. It even associated science with women's lingerie as it suggested that the scientific design of Seduction bras would make women seductive.[26] Cerveza Moctezuma advertised its Noche Buena beer by

Compare!...

ese NIDO DE MICROBIOS que es el lavadero anticua-
do y bárbaro, DIFICIL DE LIMPIAR, con la porcelana
INMACULADA de la LAVADORA GENERAL ELEC-
TRIC, reluciente, con sólo pasarle un trapo húmedo!...

COMPARE LA GENERAL ELECTRIC CON CUALQUIE-
RA OTRA MAQUINA, EN VENTAJAS Y FUNCIONA-
MIENTO Y PRECIO, Y TENDRA QUE SUSTITUIR LA
QUE TENGA, POR UNA G-E...!

GENERAL ⊛ ELECTRIC

ARTICULO 123 Y SAN JUAN DE LETRAN. — MEXICO, D. F.

GUADALAJARA.   MONTERREY.

Figure 4.5. 1941 General Electric ad contrasting modern electric washing machines with primitive clothes-washing methods. (*La Familia* 164 [October 31, 1941]: 7, author's personal collection)

stating that its "experienced chemists and experts continuously monitored the making of Moctezuma beer."[27] Thanks to this ongoing inspection, according to the ad, Moctezuma had acquired a unique quality that made it the most popular beer among beer connoisseurs.

Advertising also portrayed science as a vital force in industrial development and commercial prosperity. One ad for Corona beer depicted an industrial setting in the background as it read, "Mexico progressively marches toward a prom-

Figure 4.6. 1948 Corona beer ad suggesting that the consumption of Mexican beer contributed to Mexico's march toward progress and modern industrial capitalism. (*Excelsior*, June 2, 1948, n.p.)

inent future and along with Mexico, Corona beer" (see figure 4.6). The ad presented the consumption of Corona and Negra Modelo beer as part of Mexico's industrialization. It celebrated industrial development as a victory and a product of a collective national effort. It suggested that Corona and Negra Modelo were contributing to Mexico's industrialization and progress. In this context, drinking Corona and Negra Modelo allowed the consumer to be part of a collective process leading to modern industrial development. The ad avoided an emphasis on alcohol consumption since drinking alcohol was associated with laziness and backwardness. Mechanically manufactured beer served in industrially manufactured beer bottles distinguished modern beer from old-fashioned *pulque*. Similarly, the first Children's Toy Exposition in Mexico City in 1945 was announced as a symbol of the collective achievement and developments in the production of toys; "it is of vital importance for the toy industry to develop strong roots so that it can sustain its [national] progress."[28] Like the Corona publicity, the advertising of the toy exposition stressed collaborative work and production as a civic action leading to modern progress and national industrial development.

Advertising suggested that Mexico was making progress in its race to "catch up" with countries like the United States thanks to its commitment to industrialization. One General Motors ad stated, "Industrialization—a vital factor for Mexico" (see figure 4.7). General Motors argued that industrialization had generated economic growth and was contributing to the free and peaceful society that Mexico and most of the world were finally achieving by 1945. It claimed that industrialization would direct Mexico toward economic independence in the international arena.[29] Projecting masculine leadership in Mexico's industrialization, the ad contrasted the image of a man's hands holding an engine in the air with the image of a horse-powered well. The emphasis on the engine highlighted the superior power of mechanical force compared to the antiquated physical labor illustrated by the rural scene. The ad presented a bleak picture of Mexico's traditional tools and labor resources as it credited men with intelligently guiding Mexico toward prosperity. The images it presented promoted independent national development as well as integration into the international arena. According to General Motors, the consumption of its products was a step toward achieving a vital national goal, industrialization, as well as the introduction of liberty and freedom, all of which were described as requirements of a progressive modern world. The modern industrialized world, according to this advertising, would bring qualities that Mexicans could enjoy. In other words, General Motors was selling more than automotive merchandise. It was serving as an agent of U.S. foreign policy and a missionary of American culture, including America's "consumer democracy."

Scholars have interpreted the portrayal of the United States as a leader in science and modern industrial capitalism as an effort to spread the "American dream" and "Americanize" Mexico. According to Emily Rosenberg, the "American dream" championed the United States as a pioneer in technological and scientific achievements and a leader in large-scale industrial production for mass consumption.[30] Scientific and technological advancement was associated with

Figure 4.7. 1945 General Motors ad declaring that industrialization was important for Mexico's progress. (*Excelsior*, December 2, 1945, n.p.)

mass production and abundance. The "American dream" included liberal developmentalism, which Rosenberg described as the belief that other nations should adopt America's development strategies, faith in free enterprise, and support for free access to investment and trade. It used, according to Rosenberg, a "free market" metaphor or the belief that everyone was equal in the world market. To this end, the market broke barriers, eliminated differences in class and nationality, and created conditions whereby producers were judged on the merits of their products.[31] Ironically, the United States promoted free markets abroad but protected its home market. According to Thomas W. Zeiler and Alfred Eckes Jr., the United States did not accept free trade until "free traders" linked trade to political ideology and foreign diplomacy in the 1930s.[32] Similar to Rosenberg's approach, Thomas F. O'Brien suggests that the introduction of

American companies, business practices, and corporate reformers in the 1920s and 1930s led to the "Americanization" of Mexico. According to O'Brien, this Americanization included the introduction of welfare capitalism as practiced by companies like Phelps Dodge and corporate reformers who hoped to transform the "dirty, drunken, dissolute Mexican" into a clean, sober, productive worker.[33] Similar to Rosenberg and O'Brien, Fredrick B. Pike suggests that efforts to transform or "uplift" Latin Americans included the expansion of American principles of labor discipline and managerial planning.[34]

American political and economic leaders acted as emissaries of progress on a mission to transform Mexican society by spreading American values, beliefs, and practices. However, the popular nationalism that forced the nationalization of American oil companies in 1938 led many American companies to appeal to Mexican values and practices in their advertising. It forced advertising agents, business executives, and retailers to filter advertising through different forms of nationalism. Publicity for soft drinks and alcoholic beverages appealed to a radical form of nationalism as a political, national, and ideological tool. By contrast, cosmetic advertising endorsed a nonpolitical form of nationalism that aimed at identifying Mexico's "originality" within a global context. Cosmetic advertising echoed the patriotism described by Brading and the subtle nationalism described by Tenorio-Trujillo. The simultaneous display of different forms of Mexican nationalism and the spread of American values and ideals made it difficult to make a distinction between "Mexican" and "American."

Mexican Nationalism and the Search for Identity in the Western World

Nationalism in postrevolutionary Mexico transformed previous forms of Creole patriotism into popular rhetoric and ideology that appealed to the mestizo and radical forms of nationalism. Mexican intellectuals defined the mestizo as the "true" symbol of Mexico. Rejecting Díaz's preference for Creole and foreign traditions, Molina Enríquez defined Mexico's mestizos as the only group capable of leading the effort to achieve national and religious unity in Mexico in 1909. According to him, "Mestizo traditions and culture should prevail in Mexico because they represented the common experience" of Indians and Creoles.[35] The social and political upheaval of the 1910s triggered an indigenous movement, but this movement did not succeed in establishing the Indian as the true expression of Mexico.[36] It defined Mexico's indigenous heritage as a vital part of Mexican culture. Molina Enríquez's preference for the mestizo as a true representation of Mexico's racial makeup prevailed. As a leader of the mestizos, an intellectual, and a politician, José Vasconcelos recycled Molina Enríquez's approach as he defined Mexicans as a "cosmic race" that placed the mestizo at the center of Mexican identity and Mexico at the center of world civilizations. He viewed Mexico as the place where all races, Western and non-Western, came together to form the mestizo.[37] According to Nancy Leys Stepan, Vasconcelos's approach endorsed the international eugenics movement. It praised racial hybridization as a way of elevating the Indian to the superior standards of the European. Mexican eugenics as defined by Vasconcelos, which acquired a unique spiritual character, tapped into previous debates about how the Indian population could become integrated into the nation and how the health of the poor could be improved.[38] According to Stepan, "Centering national identity on Mestizo meant the depreciation of the Indian as an acceptable part of the national fabric."[39] The glorification of the mestizo included Indians as long as they adapted to modernity and adopted the materialism and rationalism of the Mexican state. In other words, Molina Enríquez and Vasconcelos turned colonial and nineteenth-century Creole patriotism, as described by Brading, into a mestizo form of nationalism by the 1920s.

Creole patriotism and nationalism were not limited to elites and intellectuals prior to the 1920s. Indians and Creoles, regardless of their social status, had united behind patriotic symbols such as the Virgin of Guadalupe since the colonial period.[40] Insurgents headed by Miguel Hidalgo in 1810 raised the image of the Virgin of Guadalupe as their banner for independence from Spain. Defining the image as a religiously patriotic but politically neutral symbol, Díaz mitigated bitter church-state tensions by allowing a month-long celebration of the crowning of the Virgin in 1895. Giving the Virgin a more radical nationalist tone, peasant followers of Emiliano Zapata carried her image as they walked through the streets of Mexico City in 1914 during the Mexican Revolution.[41] The Virgin also became the symbol of the Cristeros, who launched a religious war against the state in the late 1920s and mid-1930s. It was precisely this type of radical nationalism that was often used as a political tool by government officials, advertising agents, and business executives in the 1940s.

Like Hidalgo, Zapata, and the Cristeros, Palmolive soap raised the banner of the Virgin of Guadalupe in its publicity in 1945 as it tried to counteract an anti-Palmolive campaign launched by a small group of conservative Catholics who did not have the support of top religious authorities.[42] These protesters condemned a private donation to Protestant mission organizations made by a high-ranking Palmolive representative. The protest spiraled into a popular anti-imperialist rejection of Palmolive. Flyers describing Palmolive as a Protestant imperialist company and urging people to not buy Palmolive soap began to circulate in Mexico. Posters read, "With gringo money, anti-Catholics are attacking our faith."[43] Palmolive representatives asked Herbert Cerwin, a former OIAA representative in Mexico, to meet with Archbishop Luis María Martínez on their behalf. Cerwin's meeting with Martínez was very successful. The archbishop apologized for the anti-American campaign. He explained the difficulties of controlling and mediating tensions between different factions of the church and confessed, "We are handicapped by our clergy because they are not always well trained or as learned as your own; our people are too fanatically inclined and it does not help the Church."[44] The next morning, the archbishop published a manifesto on the front pages of Mexico City's newspapers urging the protesters to stop attacks on U.S. companies. Palmolive focused on restoring the company's public image as a "Catholic-friendly" company. It promised to include a colored image of the Virgin of Guadalupe on every package of three Palmolive soap bars (see figure 4.8). Using one of the most popular religious symbols of Mexican Catholic faith and nationalism to market its products changed Palmolive's image. Palmolive syncretized its corporate identity and popular nationalism by forging a middle ground between the two.

Efforts to operate within a middle ground led some companies to adopt different forms of nationalism in their advertising. Publicity appropriated rhetoric that promoted pride in Mexico's history, folk traditions, film industry, territory, and even female bodies. For example, Corona beer stated that there was only one Mexico and only one Mexican beer—Corona. The ad displayed a picture of Xipe, a Toltec god, whose monument was found in Tenochtitlán Museum in the state of Mexico.[45] Other Corona advertising spotlighted folk products like *zarapes* or traditional games while stating that like these folk traditions, Corona and Negra Modelo "symbolized a truly Mexican tradition and industry."[46] Similar to Corona, an ad for Gauge hosiery linked an erotic image of a woman's legs with "national pride" by stating, "These are the only ones in Mexico!" In the background, the ad displayed public buildings and monuments in Mexico City, including the independence monument.[47] A Belmont cigarettes ad associated the cigarettes with another "true" Mexican product—the Mexican film industry; it read, "Our national film industry has achieved great triumphs, not only at a national level, but also worldwide."[48] The ad suggested, "Our national films and the incomparable red cigarette box of Belmont proudly represent the stamp of 'Hecho en México.'"[49] The Mexican film industry served as a symbol of national pride during its Golden Age in the 1940s.[50]

The advertising of American products replaced themes of pro-Allied solidarity with rhetoric that "Mexicanized" American products during the postwar period. Coca-Cola emphasized its "Mexicanness" by identifying its alliance with Mexican industry: "Coca-Cola bottling is under contract with Coca-Cola de México through the Bottling Industry of Mexico."[51] A 1950s ad illustrated the "Mexicanizing" of Pepsi-Cola by depicting two huge hands placing a trac-

Figure 4.8. 1945 Palmolive soap ad displaying the image of the Virgin of Guadalupe. (*La Familia* 260 [December 1945]: 139, author's personal collection)

tor on a map of Mexico with the caption, "Pepsi-Cola Bottling Company from the Republic of Mexico is for the Mexican industry, for the Mexican people, and for the progress of Mexicans" (see figure 4.9). Other soft drink brands, such as Mexi-Cola, could not compete with the massive advertisement of Pepsi-Cola and Coca-Cola. The selective use of language in the advertising of American brand names not only defined American products as participants in Mexico's industrial capitalism but also blurred the political or economic distinction between what was "Mexican" and what was "foreign."

Figure 4.9. 1950s ad illustrating the "Mexicanizing" of Pepsi-Cola.
(*Siempre!*, ca. 1950s)

While Nacional furniture appealed to nationalism, national sovereignty, and national unity, Cervecería Cuauhtémoc chose to "Americanize" its products. Nacional described its corporate growth as a collective effort that supported Mexico's patriotism, economic growth, and autonomy. It argued that the company was formed by Mexicans and had been faithful to its patriotic duties by providing civic service at a time when Mexico called for national unity and sovereignty. By contrast, Cuauhtémoc advertised its beer as an international product consumed in "ultracivilized" cities like New York. One ad described

Figure 4.10. 1940 Cervecería Cuauhtémoc ad suggesting that Mexican beer was the preferred drink among people in "ultracivilized" society. (*Excelsior*, June 1, 1940, n.p.)

the New Yorker Hotel as the most beautiful hotel in an "ultramodern" environment (see figure 4.10). The ad suggested that Carta Blanca had conquered the taste of hotel guests. Nacional and Cuauhtémoc advertising illustrated the two dominant trends in Mexican publicity after the 1920s: one appealed to different forms of Mexican nationalism and insisted on "Mexicanizing" American or global products and culture and the other stressed American and global leadership while encouraging the "Americanization" or "globalization" of Mexico.

Advertising and the commercialization of public space during the 1940s blurred the lines between the national and the global. Industria Electrica de México (IEM), a subsidiary of Westinghouse, for example, urged Mexicans to "invest millions of pesos in the purchase of Mexican products" (see figure 4.11). IEM advertising insisted that IEM was an independent company and declared that it contributed to industrial development and the progress of Mexico. IEM used patriotic and nationalist rhetoric while presenting its alliance with West-

Figure 4.11. 1949 Industria Electrica de México ad supporting nationalist "buy at home" campaigns, even though the company was a subsidiary of Westinghouse. (*La Familia* 344 [September 30, 1949]: 9, author's personal collection)

Figure 4.12. Street advertising promoting the consumption of
Mexican and American products. (*Revista de Revistas* 10 [June 10,
1951]: n.p., author's personal collection)

inghouse as the key to the company's success and Mexico's progress. Street publicity also portrayed a mixture of Mexican and American or global trends. By the
early 1950s, Mexican brand-name products like Corona echoed nationalist rhetoric, asking Mexicans to drink "the beer of Mexico," while transnational companies like Westinghouse blanketed the streets with ads for American brand-name
products (see figure 4.12). Publicity's appeal to national and global brand-name
products and trends revealed processes that, at least at the level of consumer
culture, erased political borders.

Cosmetic Advertising and the Interplay between National and Global Beauty

Cosmetic advertising during the 1930s and 1940s defined beauty as a global rather than a Mexican phenomenon, but the "globalization" of beauty did not stop some cosmetic companies from flirting with Mexican beauty in the 1940s. Cosmetics generally embraced a universal concept of beauty throughout the 1920s and 1930s by making reference to European and American celebrities and portraying white Anglo-Saxon women as the ultimate expression of beauty. Companies like Max Factor and Ponds endorsed the white European and American concept of beauty up to the 1930s, but they began to feature Mexican celebrities and occasionally appealed to Mexican beauty in the early 1940s after Nelson Rockefeller urged American companies to incorporate Mexican culture in their publicity. Their definition of Mexican beauty adopted Mexico's mixed heritage of the the the mestizos as the model of feminine beauty, echoing Vasconcelos's view of Mexico as a place where all races had come together. Other cosmetic advertising was more dismissive and made no effort to associate Mexican women with its definition of beauty. Lipstick advertising, for example, defined feminine beauty as a universal Anglo-Saxon phenomenon. It tried to incorporate a Pan-American concept of beauty as a result of Rockefeller's plea for pro-Allied solidarity from 1942 to 1945. However, the tasteless patriotic messages attached to lipstick advertising did not diversify its concept of beauty across race or ethnicity. In contrast to Ponds, Max Factor, and lipstick advertising, Palmolive, which had earned a reputation in cosmetics, celebrated Mexican beauty.

Columnists for *El Universal* associated American values and practices with a global concept of beauty. Similar to lipstick companies, Ponds, and Max Factor, they showed less concern for Mexican beauty than Palmolive or *La Familia* columnists. *El Universal* featured beauty lessons by American actress Claudette Colbert in 1940 in its "Taking Care of Your Beauty" column.[52] The column changed its title to "Feminine Beauty" and featured articles by American women: Ginny Simms in 1945 and Lois Leeds in 1949.[53] Articles by U.S. women spread American ideals and notions of beauty to Mexico. Echoing America's work ethic, Colbert told Mexican women that hard work instead of wealth was the key to acquiring beauty. She claimed that obtaining the "chic" look required a tremendous amount of effort. Colbert also echoed aspects of America's consumer democracy as she insisted that race and class were not barriers because any woman could acquire beauty by using inexpensive methods or products.[54] Ironically, the model beauty described by columnists excluded the majority of Mexican women. Sections of Ginny Simms's column on special care for golden-skinned, blond-haired women catered more to an Anglo-Saxon American audience than to the primarily mestizo and indigenous population of Mexico. Simms also suggested that Hollywood celebrities had made certain cosmetics fashionable and that Mexican women should imitate them in order to acquire the beauty men desired.[55] Cosmetic advertising endorsed Colbert's individual work ethic and democratizing approach as well as Simms's "cinematic" take, but it also introduced new venues for obtaining beauty.

Similar to newspaper articles, commercial advertising featured endorsements by international figures that encouraged a global concept of beauty. It urged Mexican women to achieve glamour by adopting the beauty regimens of American beauty experts like Dorothy Gray and Helena Rubenstein.[56] It instructed women to consult beauty departments for more information on beauty methods.[57] According to Margarita Rostan, upper-middle-class and elite Mexican women developed an interest in beauty methods like those of Gray and Rubenstein. She reported that El Palacio de Hierro's beauty department offered popular beauty classes that provided instruction on the latest beauty methods and cosmetics coming out of Europe and the United States.[58] Other stores in Mexico either provided lessons from beauty experts or celebrities from Europe or the United States or disseminated beauty tips through advertising.

Max Factor gave a Hollywood spin to global beauty by urging women to adapt their appearance to different activities. It instructed women to seek a discreet, moderate, and harmonious look at the office and a glamorous, vivid, and inviting appearance for nightlife.[59] Its advertising included endorsements by Hollywood celebrities or wives of movie stars. Similarly, Ponds advertising demonstrated how to make simple and fast beauty masks that, according to statements from celebrities, would give Mexican women a special touch of beauty.[60] Lipstick advertising also stressed a global beauty as it suggested that beauty was perfected in Hollywood and disseminated throughout the world. Tangee, Michels, and Zande adopted a global discourse without expressing much concern for local reception. Zande, for example, suggested that its lipstick was preferred throughout the world because it gave the "chic look" of Paris, the "good tone" of London, the "elegance" of Rio, and the "fascination" of Geneva. The ad did not mention Mexico, thus suggesting that Zande would bring its global qualities to Mexican women. As lipstick advertising often did, Zande localized global beauty instead of globalizing Mexican beauty.[61]

Ponds developed a tradition of advertising cosmetics as universal products that appealed to international rather than local trends. It argued that its cosmetic advertising campaigns "tried to show that since beauty was universal, so was its care, and naturally Ponds products were preferred by beautiful women in all parts of the world."[62] Ponds international publicity was produced in New York by its advertising agency, J. Walter Thompson, and adapted to local conditions in each country. Ponds had earned a reputation for conducting successful endorsement campaigns since the 1920s. These campaigns included the testimony of royal European women who claimed that their beauty depended on Ponds. Countess Howe and the Duchess of Leinster of England, both in their thirties, stated that thanks to Ponds they looked like they were in their early twenties.[63] In its 1930s publicity, Ponds told Mexican women that the feminine beauty Ponds provided could "make them internationally famous" like Lady Rachel Sturias and Lady Gladys Jessel.[64] The ad included statements from these women confirming that Ponds had contributed to their success. Using variations of the same strategy, Ponds advertising included instructions by popular figures such as American actress Geraldine Spreckels on how to use Ponds cream and beautifying masks.[65] Ponds ads also included endorsements by Mexican and Latin American celebrities by the early 1940s.[66] The company did not completely exclude Mexican celebrities from the "universal" beauty it wanted to project.

Thompson monitored the production of all Ponds advertising in New York. It worked with local branches throughout the world, providing assistance in the preparation and placement of advertising. The success of an advertising campaign relied on the local agency. The Thompson office in New York acted as a "control center."[67] In addition to providing assistance, Thompson personnel in New York designed international Ponds advertising, then sent the ads to regional branches that had the option of rejecting, accepting, or modifying them. The Thompson branch in Mexico City decided to use the New York advertising format after 1943, but it often replaced international celebrities with Mexican or Latin American actresses. Thompson tried to blend international beauty trends with Mexican popular culture.[68] Most important, this advertising strategy placed Mexican women and beauty at an international level while giving Ponds advertising a "Mexican flavor." However, both Ponds and Thompson insisted on maintaining beauty as a universal phenomenon and thus used internationally famous American and European figures. Whereas Ponds looked at beauty through a global lens, other companies presented beauty through a Mexican lens.

Unlike Ponds, Palmolive publicity strategies from the 1930s to 1950 adopted a "Mexican spin." The company did not reject global discourses on beauty, but it featured ideals and subjects that were more in line with the daily experience of the majority of Mexican women. It presented a global notion of Mexican beauty rather than a "Mexicanized" version of global beauty. Early 1930s Palmolive advertising boasted that the most beautiful women in Mexico had patronized the Godefroy Salón in Mexico City for years and that the salon recommended Palmolive soap. Ads suggested that years of experience showed that Palmolive was the best soap for preserving beautiful skin, and as a result, it was the preferred soap in the entire world.[69] Palmolive sponsored a weekly radio program on Mexico's leading station, xɛw, featuring popular Mexican singers such as the Aguilar Sisters.[70] In the late 1930s, the program commonly aired *ranchera* music, which called to mind traditional rural lifestyles. This music complemented the company's publicity strategy, which highlighted Palmolive's ability to preserve natural beauty. In the 1940s, music selections featured Mexican music with a cosmopolitan twist that alluded to life in the urban industrial setting rather than the rural setting. Popular singers such as Agustín Lara became regular guests on the program.

Palmolive's publicity and business approach during the 1930s set the stage for Rockefeller's Good Neighbor Policy activities during the early 1940s.[71] The company welcomed U.S. government efforts to promote Pan-American solidarity and "friendship" during the war. However, Palmolive's cooperation was not a result of orthodox anti-Nazi militancy. The company perceived Rockefeller's work as complementary to the marketing strategy it had pursued in Mexico since the 1930s: the translation of Mexican values, beliefs, and practices into effective publicity. The portrayal of beauty and happiness in cosmetic advertising at a time when Mexico was subject to different moral, ethical, and ideological currents illustrates Palmolive's sophistication in marketing. It also shows the significance Mexican women gave to beauty in the 1940s.

Beauty, Cosmetic Advertising, and "Traditional" versus "Modern" Values

In a letter in *La Familia*, a young woman asked for advice on her relationship with her boyfriend. She reported that her boyfriend was constantly looking at other women. According to her, his behavior was understandable because she was not pretty. The letter was addressed to Juana Inés, the correspondent for *La Familia*'s "Tell Me Your Problem" column, and it was signed, "Yours truly, Sadness." Inés instructed the reader to stop worrying about her looks because physical appearance was less important than character. Inés recommended ending the relationship since the boyfriend was clearly interested in other women. She advised "Sadness" to visit friends, read, and attend parties as alternative methods of attaining happiness. This letter suggested that Mexican women associated beauty with happiness. Similar to "Sadness," beauty columnists and advertisers (including Palmolive) agreed that beauty and personal appearance were central to a woman's happiness and success.[72] Contrary to Inés, they argued that every Mexican woman could attain beauty and happiness simply by following certain beauty regimens and learning the impact of cosmetics on their bodies. This was not easy, according to them, since various products had different results depending on each person's body and features.

Columnists and cosmetic advertising linked women's happiness to different beauty products and methods. Their concept of beauty embodied conflicting values, beliefs, and practices from the 1930s to 1950. They encouraged the use of natural noncommercial beauty methods as well as the consumption of the latest commercially manufactured cosmetics. The conflicts revealed by columnists and cosmetic advertising extended the boundaries of the definition of beauty and expanded the methods that produced the different forms of beauty. They created a "middle ground" or neutral setting where cosmetic advertising could market natural and commercial forms of beauty, appeal to traditional and modern notions of gender, and project universal beauty without implying that Mexican women were ugly. From a corporate point of view, advertising cosmetics within a middle ground offered the opportunity to market products to Mexican women with different backgrounds, moral values, and ideological standards. Beauty columnists and cosmetic advertisers recognized fewer gender boundaries than scholars have identified in Mexican art, literature, film, and comic books.

Scholars of Mexico have generally used two models to discuss women in Mexico. One model, often classified as a traditional discourse, suggests that Mexican women are submissive and the guardians of public life and the nation. According to this discourse, women resemble the image of the Virgin of Guadalupe, and as a result, they are expected to remain pure and assume moral responsibility over the family and the nation. According to studies by Jean Franco, nineteenth-century liberals recycled this discourse from the colonial period and made women's roles as mothers and guardians of public life central to nationhood.[73] The other model, represented by "La Malinche," portrays Mexican women as "whores" who betrayed Mexican society and, as a result, deserve no trust. Franco argues that these representations of women became important in the emergence of two responses by late-nineteenth-century liberal leaders to new trends and attitudes. She suggests that while "moralist liberals traditionally criticized women's fashion as indulgence and the index of social decay, many of the progressive intelligentsia saw fashion as the positive symbol of modernity."[74] One response interpreted new values and practices as a decay of moral standards, and the other either welcomed or tolerated them as part of progress and "modernity." The pre-existing interpretations of women as either virgins or whores justified these two responses to new beliefs and forms of expression by the late nineteenth century.

The same trend continued in postrevolutionary Mexico, according to Anne Rubenstein. She suggests that socially conservative sectors defended a discourse of tradition, conservatism, rural life, and Catholicism, while nonconservatives promoted "ideas, arguments, attitudes, and metaphors related to modernity, progress, industrialization, and urbanity."[75] According to Joanne Hershfield, the

portrayal of women in 1940s Mexico echoed pre-existing trends in which conflicting discourses portrayed women as virgins or whores and nurturing mothers
or "femmes fatales."[76] Both Hershfield and Rubenstein show how film and comic
book producers who depicted an interplay between modern versus traditional
values projected a sense of ambiguity in their works.[77] A similar ambiguity was
also conveyed in the artistic expressions of Frida Kahlo, according to Claudia
Schaefer.[78] It was precisely this ambiguity that cosmetic advertisers created by
displaying mixed messages and constructing a middle ground. This middle
ground allowed advertisers to market cosmetics to different audiences at a time
when values, beliefs, and practices were in constant flux as a result of Mexico's
modern industrial capitalism.

Beauty columnists and cosmetic advertising used artificial distinctions between traditional and modern methods and forms of beauty. Traditional methods appealed to natural beauty, encouraged the use of natural products, and
promoted homemade cosmetics and beauty regimens. The emphasis on nature,
tradition, and "purity" in cosmetics was dominant in 1930s Mexico. Modern
methods of beauty encouraged the use of the latest manufactured cosmetics,
sanctioned a cosmopolitan lifestyle, and commercialized beauty. A commercialized cosmopolitan form of beauty prevailed by the 1940s, but advertising added
a "nature spin" by marketing cosmetics as products that would discover, un-
cover, or elevate already-existing beauty. This advertising also promised women
an artificial beauty that did not exist but that cosmetics could produce thanks to
scientific perfection and the progress of civilization. Both discourses coexisted
in the 1930s and 1940s, forming a middle ground where neither traditional nor
modern cosmetics and forms of beauty were completely rejected. Advertisers
and columnists did not respect the boundaries between traditional and modern
or between national and international forms of beauty.

Palmolive capitalized on its brand name as it marketed natural beauty to
Mexican women in the 1930s. Ads included statements by popular celebrities
suggesting that beauty should be acquired naturally rather than through the use
of manufactured cosmetics. Without completely disregarding the mechanical
production of soap, Palmolive insisted that its product was a mixture of natural
palm and olive oils that produced soft and attractive skin.[79] Appealing to natural
beauty as a publicity strategy made good business sense in 1930s Mexico. Although Mexican women welcomed the latest methods and products to enhance
beauty, the belief that beauty was a natural phenomenon was widely accepted,
especially among the lower sectors of society. Mexican women had traditionally used noncommercialized natural methods of acquiring beauty. As late as
1937, magazines targeting urban middle-class women such as *La Familia* still
published articles instructing women on how to acquire beauty through natural

means. *La Familia* told women to place slices of fruits and vegetables on their faces for ten to fifteen minutes twice a day to acquire young, soft, attractive skin. It recommended cucumbers, although it said peaches, oranges, and avocados would also work.[80] The article insisted that well-known figures had used this method to enhance their beauty. Palmolive advertising replaced slices of fruits and vegetables with a "natural" combination of palm and olive oil as it presented its manufactured soap as a natural cosmetic. Palmolive's publicity blurred the lines between natural and mechanically produced items. Most important, it created a brand name for its soap in the cosmetic industry by carefully tapping into pre-existing notions of beauty in Mexico.

La Familia continued to encourage the use of noncommercial homemade cosmetics until the late 1940s. A 1943 article on how to fight against an "enemy of beauty," body hair, gave detailed instructions on how to prepare a depilatory cream and how to use it to remove unwanted hair. It promised results within five days.[81] The article described this process as a natural method in contrast to commercial hair-removal products.[82] However, it was neither natural nor Mexican, since there is no indication that Mexican women were accustomed to removing their body hair prior to the 1940s. By 1946, *La Familia*'s beauty column, "Pages of Beauty," featured articles offering women advice on preserving healthy and beautiful hair by using homemade products and methods. These articles recommended the use of rum, chicken bouillon, and oil, among other ingredients, to prevent hair loss and a mixture of alcohol, oil, acid, carbonated soda powder, and menthol to promote clean healthy hair.[83] Articles on skin care offered similar instructions. One article in 1946, for example, recommended using a mixture of egg whites, vinegar, cinnamon, and talcum powder, among other ingredients, for a soft, tender, beautiful face.[84] Other articles covered topics such as how to prevent wrinkles and the importance of a woman's nose or hips to her appearance.[85] The detailed instructions that magazine columns offered turned the acquisition of beauty into a process that required discipline and knowledge about numerous ingredients and methods. They promoted a type of beauty that women could achieve through the use of noncommercial products and processes. However, they also encouraged the use of other products and methods.

La Familia's beauty column appealed to a cosmopolitan lifestyle and concept of beauty. A May 1939 column advised women to wear discreet swimsuits and other casual attire. The article suggested that selecting a swimsuit was not an easy task since a swimsuit that looks perfect on a slim young woman would look repulsive on an older heavy woman. It also recommended the use of moderate makeup for beach vacations.[86] Similarly, an October 1941 article on dental beauty warned Mexican women that not having the proper dental care could be devastating to their appearance. It argued that good nutrition and hygiene were crucial in maintaining beautiful teeth. It offered detailed advice on how to preserve beautiful teeth.[87] A dramatic Colgate toothpaste ad accompanied the article. The ad presented scenes of a woman losing her boyfriend because she has bad breath. After a doctor convinces her to begin using Colgate toothpaste, she celebrates "reconquering" her boyfriend. The boyfriend's statement, "Now nothing will separate us," ends this ad linking beauty, attraction, and love to Colgate and "dental beauty," which according to the column was crucial to a woman's overall beauty.[88] Articles in *La Familia*'s beauty column were often accompanied by ads that reinforced the beautifying processes that the articles described. Other beauty columns such as *Blanco y Negro*'s "Among Us Women" and *Maruca*'s "Is This Your Problem?" used a similar strategy of commercializing beauty methods.

Advertising continued to feature the interplay between natural and commercially manufactured beauty throughout the 1940s, but the emphasis on nature declined. Following general trends in Mexico, Palmolive dropped its natural-beauty angle as the primary marketing pitch by the early 1940s and adopted a scientific spin in its advertising by the late 1940s. One late 1940s ad argued that according to medical research "two out of three women acquired a marvelous skin in only fourteen days thanks to the Palmolive method."[89] Palmolive's beauty method consisted of using a gentle "friction massage" with a wet hand towel and Palmolive soap. However, the process differed according to skin type. Women with oily skin were instructed to do the massage each morning, afternoon, and night, but women with dry skin were advised to massage their skin only in the morning and at night.[90] The use of endorsements by medical authorities to legitimize Palmolive's effectiveness in beauty was not a new strategy, but its emphasis on science was a late 1940s phenomenon. The company's publicity had included statements from specialists and doctors recommending that women and children use Palmolive for soft and beautiful skin since 1935.[91]

Palmolive's appeal to science and medicine as proof of its soap's ability to "beautify" women was part of a discourse that presented science and medicine as factors that contributed to Mexico's progress. It was also a clever marketing pitch that promised to keep Palmolive soap in the ranks of cosmetics. As a company selling soap, Palmolive found it difficult to compete with the massive advertising for conventional cosmetics (lipstick and face creams, among other products) in the 1940s. Palmolive soap maintained its reputation as a cosmetic by legitimizing its "beautifying" qualities through science and medicine. Yet the company did not drop the "nature spin" that defined its soap as a cosmetic during the 1930s. On the contrary, Palmolive appealed to both nature and science to differentiate itself from other cosmetics. Its publicity suggested that Palmolive would give women a natural beauty, in contrast to the artificial beauty other products provided. Most important, the natural beauty Palmolive provided, ads insisted, was scientifically and medically tested. In other words, late 1940s Palmolive publicity blurred the lines between science and nature as it appealed to both natural and modern forms of beauty in order to preserve Palmolive's reputation as a cosmetic item.

Cosmetic advertising portrayed an interplay between pure and seductive forms of beauty from the 1930s to 1950, even though it emphasized specific forms of beauty at different points. In the 1930s, advertising appealed to pure and innocent beauty, which complemented the emphasis on nature. Advertising for Tangee, Max Factor, Michels, Nivea, and Ponds, among other cosmetic companies, stressed an enchanting, delicate, and indisputable beauty throughout the 1930s.[92] Ads that did not refer directly to a pure form of beauty but implied it urged women to "intensify natural colors and elevate their beauty without leaving tasteless artificial qualities."[93] Some products went so far as to put a religious spin on beauty as they described their methods as "rituals of beauty."[94] The same products also spoke of cosmetics as conquering and seductive.

Cosmetic advertising emphasized seductive beauty during the 1940s without completely abandoning the sense of purity it had previously promoted. Tangee advertising began to capitalize on seduction in the late 1930s. It emphasized different forms of seduction and tried to balance seduction and purity until the early 1940s. Its advertising spoke of a natural seductive beauty as a quality needed to conquer men until the mid-1940s, but it dropped its natural spin by the late 1940s. The company referred to a seductive global beauty more often in the late 1940s.[95] Advertising for other products followed a similar pattern. A 1945 ad promised women that Michels would "make vibrant colors and generate a delicate and seductive effect on their enchanting lips."[96] Colgate urged women to always be beautiful and seductive in 1947. It claimed that the seventeen exotic essences in its fragrant talcum powder would make women 50 percent more beautiful and seductive.[97] Similarly, Ponds lipstick suggested in 1948 that the "radiant and seductive beauty" women acquired by using its products would last for hours.[98] However, late 1940s cosmetic advertising created a sense of ambiguity by displaying mixed messages. For example, Tangee's publicity in 1946 promised an enchanting beauty thanks to the "purity of the ingredients" in its products, yet it also claimed that its modern tone would give women a seductive beauty.[99] In other words, cosmetic advertising added a touch of nature to the seductive global beauty it stressed by the late 1940s.

The seductive beauty that was promoted in cosmetic advertising during the 1940s was both sensual and explicit as ads often included images of half-dressed women. However, the sensual imagery of cosmetic advertising and its reference to an innocent form of sexual seduction did not fit within the boundaries defined by the virgin and whore dichotomy described by some scholars.[100] Cosmetic advertising reinforced the image of a cosmopolitan, independent, and sexually revealing *chica moderna* that comic books described in their narratives.[101] Rubenstein and Hershfield suggest that comic book and film producers had a choice: seduction, sexual independence, and new values and practices could be portrayed as either good or bad. Stories of *chicas modernas* and sexually adventurous women, such as those portrayed in *Distinto Amanecer* or *Salón México*, among other films, could have a happy ending, end ambiguously, or end in disaster. While comic book narratives predominantly endorsed the lifestyle of the *chica moderna*, Mexican films during the 1940s disapproved of women who were sexually independent. Comic book narratives appealed to a counterculture, but films favored a conservative approach, as Rubenstein and Hershfield suggest, even though comic book and film producers flirted with ambiguity.

Unlike comic books and films, cosmetic advertising always presented seduction and sensuality as positive traits, synonyms of happiness, and qualities women should pursue. As a result, cosmetic advertisers were left with only one choice: to present conflicting values and flirt with ambiguity, hoping to operate within a middle ground that would allow them to market products to diverse audiences regardless of their social, ideological, and moral standards. In the process, their appeal to seduction and sensuality expanded the boundaries of what became socially acceptable in 1940s Mexico. Most important, it provided an alternative to traditional gender roles. Women, according to cosmetic advertising, could be sensual, independent, and even seductive without being classified as whores or social deviants. However, cosmetic advertising commercialized values and practices and made the relationship between beauty and happiness vague. Was the ability of the letter writer "Sadness" to conquer men because of her beauty the solution or the cause of her problems in achieving happiness?

Advertising "Consumer Democracy" in Modern Mexico

Commercial advertising and columnists defined beauty as a type of happiness that women could achieve through consumption, and they presented this process as a form of democracy embedded within Mexico's industrial capitalism. They suggested that the urban industrial setting offered endless forms of entertainment, an abundance of products, and happiness, which Mexicans could enjoy as individuals, in a family setting, or as a group whenever they pleased. Advertising portrayed the freedom to choose from a variety of brand-name products as an exercise in democracy. It presented individual control over physical appearance and personal success as a product of consumption. In other words, advertising sold more than merchandise; it sold "consumer democracy."

Advertising linked the consumption of products to different forms entertainment, popular events, and concepts of happiness. It described Berreteaga as the ideal drink for celebrating New Year's Eve in an urban setting.[102] Coca-Cola also offered happiness; one ad stated, "Family memories . . . honeymoon at the beach . . . among those unforgettable moments, the refreshing and delicious Coca-Cola was there. . . . Yesterday, today, and tomorrow, [Coca-Cola] is as gratifying as those special occasions you celebrate."[103] One ad suggested that Coca-Cola was the ideal complement to the excitement and emotion of a bullfight. A Cordon Blue champagne ad stated that Cordon Blue was the champagne that accompanied every special occasion, stating, "Here is the bachelor. . . . Here is the bachelor's party. . . . And here is the champagne to celebrate!"[104] It reminded readers that champagne had always been a symbol of festive events. Deportes Martí advertising urged readers to "have fun at home!"[105] It claimed that Ping-Pong was an inexpensive home sport that entertained every family member. Advertising also promised to prevent family unhappiness. A Listerine ad, for example, featured a family drama, stating "Rosita, the happiest girl in school, bitterly cried in a corner of her house" after her father abandoned her mother.[106] Rosita, according the ad, was not aware that "her mother had repeatedly offended her father every day, not with words or thoughts, but with negligence of her hygiene, such as bad breath." Rosita's mother, the ad continued, could have prevented her husband's departure by using Listerine, which guaranteed fresh breath as well as happiness for every family member.[107] Ironically, the ad implied that women were responsible for breaking up the home and bringing unhappiness to their families.

Advertising promised to "liberate" women while reinforcing conventional gender norms. An ad for Tappan ovens, for example, included a sketch of a woman sitting in a living room next to the kitchen and the statement that Tappan brought beauty to the kitchen and happiness to women.[108] The advertising of other kitchen products in the late 1940s implied that modern technology made domestic work easier for women. Kemagas suggested that thanks to its stoves women could cook without having to bother with cleaning or getting rid of unpleasant cooking odors.[109] According to a General Electric ad, "Women were no longer house slaves" (see figure 4.13). It suggested that women felt happy when all domestic work was done by mid-morning. According to the ad, General Electric irons and washing machines would "free women" from difficult and time-consuming housework. The concept that home appliances "liberated" women simply meant that appliances made domestic work less labor-

Figure 4.13. 1941 General Electric ad declaring that women were no longer slaves to housework. (*Excelsior*, December 7, 1941, n.p.)

intensive for women; it did not change gender roles or domestic duties. On the contrary, advertising strengthened the notion that women's happiness was linked to the family, home, marriage, and even pre-existing gender roles. Advertising offered women mixed messages about finding happiness. While the advertising of home appliances repeatedly suggested that a woman could find happiness only at home serving traditional domestic and gender roles, cosmetics advertising located women's happiness at the individual level. The advertising of women's cosmetics linked women's happiness to a variety of products and ways of changing their appearance. Its appeal to seductive beauty contradicted the notion that women's happiness could be found in traditional family and gender roles, as the advertising of home appliances suggested. The conflicting messages over what constituted women's happiness coexisted within a cultural middle ground to the extent that women could pursue happiness either within the family or at the individual level depending on their upbringing, age, social status, or desire to "rebel" against conventional gender norms.

Reinforcing pre-existing gender norms, advertising offered men individual control over when and how to achieve a neat, elegant, professional appearance. Chesline, for example, suggested that neat and well-combed hair was a sign of distinction for men whether in the country or in the city.[110] Willdrop was more assertive in stating that having neatly combed hair was not just a sign of distinction; it was a vital quality to modern men.[111] Other products such as Tap shoes suggested that "it was a duty for men to improve their appearance before their girlfriend, their wife, their son, their friends, before the entire world because appearance was a decisive factor in success."[112] Thanks to Tap shoes, according to advertising, men could look taller and more attractive and be successful at anything they wanted to do.[113] The ad suggested that having individual control over appearance was a crucial factor in individual success. Advertising described a variety of ways through which Mexicans could change their physical appearance. It presented the consumption of advertised products as a way of obtaining success, happiness, excitement, and beauty. Since all Mexicans were free to acquire specific qualities or transform their appearance through consumption (if they had the money), consumption appeared to be "liberating" and capable of granting "freedom." In other words, advertising suggested that freedom was achieved not through political and social action but through consumption. In this context, even the advertising of products such as shoes and cosmetics was linked to broader issues such as political stability and consumer democracy.

Advertising associated Mexico's industrial capitalism with democracy. It suggested that, as the basis for mass production, industrialization had lowered the price of merchandise that was previously considered a luxury, thus allowing middle and lower sectors of society to purchase products they could not have afforded in the past. As a result, industrial capitalism, according to advertising, "democratized" consumption. Advertising also associated abundance, variety, and individual choice with modern industrial capitalism. For example, an early 1940s Maiden Form ad reported that "there was a Maiden Form bra for every figure and every shape with different dimensions."[114] Such rhetoric increased in the late 1940s. As early as 1944, newspaper headlines announced that there would finally be enough automobiles to meet the increasing demand as a result of a decline in labor demands for war products.[115] Majestic declared that its first postwar radios had just arrived in Mexico and that in addition to high quality

Figure 4.14. 1948 American Beauty iron ad selling the concept of consumer democracy. (*El Universal*, December 1, 1948, n.p.)

they offered a wide variety of styles and models.[116] It claimed that any product that people wanted was now available and that the only difficulty was knowing how to select the proper merchandise to purchase.[117]

Postwar prosperity and the belief in material abundance prompted newspaper columns and advertising to instruct consumers in how to select merchandise. Ginny Simms, a columnist for "Belleza Femenina" in *El Universal*, urged her readers to send written requests for instructions on how to choose the perfect perfume.[118] American Beauty irons advertising urged Mexicans to compare products before deciding which one to buy. The ad displayed a sketch of an overweight, short, older woman next to a tall, slim, younger woman. It stated, "The opportunity to compare is the only means in life that allows people to choose the best" (see figure 4.14). It claimed that consumers would choose American Beauty irons over all other irons. Exercising one's judgment and choice in selecting from among a variety of products gave the sense that Mexicans had individual freedom at least at the level of consumption.

Conclusion

Advertising images bridged conflicting values in Mexican society in the 1930s and 1940s. They drew on different facets of Mexican history and the history of the Western world to create a setting in which the national and the global coexisted. This strategy allowed American and Mexican companies to market their products to a diverse audience in a society where values, beliefs, and practices were rapidly changing. In other words, advertising did not present 1930s and 1940s Mexico as divorced from its past or the global setting. Advertising images reinforced the belief that Mexico was moving from a heroic but convoluted past toward a modern industrial capitalist society that offered happiness, excitement, and self-realization through consumption. To this end, advertising attached the notion of "consumer democracy" to basic physical qualities, such as female beauty. It reconstructed Mexican identity to the extent that it portrayed the 1940s as a period of transition when Mexicans were moving toward a modern industrialized world where democracy, abundance, and opportunities for upward mobility would prevail. Most important, advertising suggested that such an achievement was possible because of the resilience of the Mexican people, which it illustrated by referring to historical events, episodes, and figures.

5 J. Walter Thompson and the Negotiation of Mexican and American Values

At a 1961 board of directors meeting, J. Walter Thompson executives recalled the problems Thompson faced when it first opened in Mexico in November 1943. They identified the company's ignorance of Mexican values and practices as one of the main reasons for its failure during its first five years in Mexico. For example, shortly after Thompson opened in Mexico, one of its top executives adopted the practice of publicly embracing clients. The executive began "hugging clients in the office, in the elevator, on the street, or in other public places."[1] He was apparently trying to blend into Mexican society by using a local form of greeting. Mexican men often embraced each other with an *abrazo*, but these hugs only took place in specific contexts and were always followed with a firm handshake, which reaffirmed masculinity. The Thompson representative did not follow through with a handshake. As a result, his hugging of male clients hinted at homosexuality. Puzzled at complaints from clients, Thompson learned that embracing a business client was inappropriate unless a person of higher rank initiated it.[2] Implying that American advertising agents had a higher status than their Mexican business associates was not an effective business strategy. Thompson also learned that the *abrazo* was used to congratulate someone for a marriage, a birth in the family, a promotion, or obtaining a job. Most important, it discovered that hugging was never appropriate unless you had a close business or personal relationship with the person you greeted.[3] Instead of instructing its American personnel to become friends and close associates of their Mexican clients, which was required in establishing good business relationships in Mexico, Thompson ordered employees to stop hugging clients and greet them the American way—with a forced smile and a handshake. The misunderstanding caused by the hugging was not surprising given Thompson's corporate approach to its international operations.

Thompson's self-proclaimed status as the biggest and best American advertising agency led to misunderstandings, conflicts, and the failure to generate profits until 1948, five years after its arrival to Mexico. As a company that took pride in providing innovative and high-quality advertising to large corporate clients, Thompson entered the Mexican market to serve transnational U.S. clients. The New York management expected its international employees to have some familiarity with Mexican culture, but it projected an imperialist "stick to American business" attitude. It expected Mexicans to follow Thompson's lead. The U.S. clients Thompson served in Mexico were initially unprofitable, and the company could not secure lucrative local accounts until it learned the rules for doing business in Mexico. Thompson was forced to deal with Mexican businessmen even when handling large American corporate accounts because Mexican subsidiaries of American companies customarily handled publicity in Mexico. Despite its initial failure to generate profits and establish cordial business relations, Thompson introduced innovative research methods and built its corporate advertising infrastructure from 1943 to 1948. Company profits and corporate success in Mexico after 1948 turned the Mexico City branch into an international division in 1950 when operations for the El Salvador and Caribbean branches were turned over to the Mexico City office. Thompson's 1925 formula for expanding operations proposed that the company transplant its U.S. operations abroad. Entering the Mexican market required that Thompson acclimate to Mexican culture.

Thompson as a Commercial Missionary for Transnational Corporations

Thompson's international operations adopted a self-righteous attitude because of its reputation as the leading U.S. advertising agency. J. Walter Thompson established the company in 1878 and made his initial profits by introducing magazine advertising and gaining a monopoly as a space broker for magazine publicity during the 1880s.[4] Thompson controlled 80 percent of magazine advertising space in 1889.[5] It remained one of the strongest competitors in the field from 1890 to the 1920s, a period that marked the transformation of American advertising into a modern profession.[6] Thompson's role as an advertising broker ended by the 1890s when magazines and newspapers began hiring their own brokers. Thompson then turned to new areas of advertising, such as designing advertisements, conducting marketing research, and offering business planning. Thompson also decided to specialize in working for large corporations in the early 1900s, but it continued to handle small accounts as well until 1916 when Stanley Resor, Henry Stanton, and James Webb Young purchased Thompson for half a million dollars.[7] This new management team chose to focus on large, profitable corporate accounts.[8] Servicing corporate accounts, according to Resor, required conducting intensive research in every phase of the client's business—production, packaging, distribution, pricing, and competition—a com-

mitment that demanded a great deal of specialization. Allocating time, resources, and expertise to small accounts, according to Resor's rationale, limited
Thompson's efficiency and service.[9] Thompson's business objective of providing
highly specialized service for large corporations pushed its international expansion after 1925. Thompson executives believed the company could serve transnational clients better by opening branches abroad and developing a large international publicity division.

Resor's commitment to providing service to large corporations led to the
introduction of highly specialized publicity methods in Mexico during the 1940s.
As an advocate of scientific management and research, Resor remained at the
forefront of Thompson's marketing and statistical research from the time he
joined Thompson in 1908 to the mid-1950s, when he retired. As president and
chairman, he established Thompson's research department, which was divided
into planning and statistical investigation sections in 1919.[10] Resor hired world-
renowned experts, including J. B. Watson (a leading behavioral psychologist),
and marketing professors from the Harvard Business School.[11] Resor continued
to hire leaders in American publicity in the 1940s and 1950s such as Don Francisco, whom he hired as vice president. Francisco had served as Rockefeller's
right-hand man in the radio, information, and content division of the OIAA during World War II. He oversaw Thompson's international operations in the late
1940s when the company finally learned how to do business in Mexico. Thompson's commitment to providing the best marketing research, business advice,
and publicity service was not simply rhetoric. The company had earned its reputation as the best advertising agency in the world by the 1920s, and its ability to
attract large transnational corporations such as Ponds, RCA, and Kodak was not
coincidental. However, Thompson's success story prompted the self-righteous
approach and organizational structure the company adopted in international
operations. This approach and organization might have worked in England,
Argentina, and Brazil during Thompson's expansion from 1925 to the 1940s, but
it clashed with Mexican culture and irritated Mexican clients.

Thompson hoped to transplant its expertise and domestic operations abroad
through a hierarchical organization centered in New York. Its New York international division directed company operations throughout the world. It consisted of close to 1,000 employees who were directly monitored by the vice president. According to Samuel W. Meek, head of Thompson's global operations in
1957, this centralized structure was necessary to manage international offices.
He argued that establishing standardized procedures on a global scale required
"very close supervision from the New York headquarters."[12] In its efforts to standardize company operations abroad, Thompson developed a policy of employing only American citizens as managers of international offices.[13] It trained all

U.S. employees in Thompson's research methods, advertisement production, and business planning. The company sent experienced managers to foreign branches. These managers served as "commercial missionaries" who spread America's business formula abroad. Thompson claimed that managers of international branches had a great deal of autonomy, but representatives from the New York headquarters frequently visited local branches to make sure that international operations met company standards. The company also required managers in different countries to report local problems to the planning board of the international division in New York. The board included representatives of different domestic departments who were trained in U.S. publicity. Thompson's tight control over international operations was not surprising considering the company's organization. The president of each international branch was stationed in New York. Samuel Meek was appointed president of the Mexico City branch in 1943.[14] The vice president resided in Mexico City and could advocate certain strategies, but decisions regarding local concerns were ultimately made by the president of the Mexican branch in New York.

Neither the international division nor the planning board at the New York headquarters had adequate knowledge of local conditions in foreign countries to deal with problems abroad. Like other Thompson employees, representatives of the international division in New York were required to take a two-year course that covered all aspects of Thompson operations.[15] Most of the training focused on Thompson's operations. Training in international operations gave only a "rudimentary knowledge about foreign markets."[16] Courses in international operations included educational films and reading on the different countries where Thompson operated. As a result, Thompson's international division personnel in New York were ignorant of the history, culture, and local conditions of foreign countries. Yet Thompson's international organization placed the responsibility for finding solutions to the challenges faced by foreign branches on employees at the New York headquarters. Thompson clearly valued the advertising expertise of its personnel in New York more than the actual conditions at its foreign branches. It was precisely this corporate strategy that led to Thompson's growing pains in Mexico.

Thompson's Failure to Acclimate to Local Conditions in Mexico

The difficulties Thompson encountered in Mexico were inevitable considering the company's expansion strategy. Thompson decided to open a branch in Mexico City partly as a result of World War II. The company had handled advertising for U.S. clients in Mexico prior to 1943. Its international division in New York designed the ads and developed contracts with Mexican newspapers and magazines. It translated the ads into Spanish for distribution in Mexico and other parts of Latin America. Promises of tax breaks from the U.S. government in 1942 and the desire to cooperate with the war effort renewed efforts by American manufacturers to increase their advertising expenditures in Latin America. Rockefeller's OIAA studies conducted prior to 1943 suggested that appropriating local traditions, values, and practices made advertising more effective. Many U.S. manufacturers, including Thompson clients, accepted Rockefeller's approach. They argued that a Thompson branch in Mexico City would provide an in-depth analysis of the market and conditions in Mexico, an area that looked promising for postwar expansion.[17] Ponds, J. B. Williams, RCA Victor, Parker, Gillette, Standard Brands, and *Reader's Digest* requested that Thompson open a branch in Mexico City. Thompson agreed and gave John Adams Kuneau the responsibility of opening the branch in mid-summer 1943.

Kuneau's actions as head of the Mexico City branch set the tone for Thompson's operations during the company's first five years in Mexico, which were characterized by corporate failure and frustration combined with a promise of future success. Kuneau arrived as a tourist in Veracruz with his wife and unlicensed dog, disregarding Mexican law, which required that executives obtain visas authorizing their residence in Mexico. Thompson asked Kuneau to find a location, hire advertising personnel, and open the agency. Kuneau began by hiring two of the leading Mexican advertising agents, Eduardo Correa and Humberto Sheridan. This was a big accomplishment considering the shortage of experienced Mexican publicity personnel. Both Correa and Sheridan knew of Thompson's reputation in the United States and welcomed the opportunity to work for such a prestigious organization. After hiring Sheridan, Kuneau reported to the New York headquarters that he had hired "one of the most competent men in Mexican advertising with over twenty years of experience in the field."[18] Sheridan's talent and experience led him to become president of the ANP in the early 1940s. Correa was also a prominent ANP representative and was the founder and editor of *Publicidad y Ventas*, the leading advertising journal in Mexico. Both Sheridan and Correa were members of the generation of Mexican advertising agents that had given Mexican advertising a respectable reputation by the 1940s. Thompson welcomed their experience and reputations but not enough to assign them top management positions or change its corporate expansion formula. Sheridan and Correa held high positions in different departments, but their activities were subject to close supervision by Kuneau and the New York headquarters.

Kuneau was less successful in areas other than hiring. The Mexican branch was scheduled to open in September 1943, but it opened two months late. Newspaper advertising operations presented no problems, but radio advertising operations were more difficult to begin. The company initially sent for Holly-wood-trained radio personnel, but they arrived too late to meet the advertising deadlines. Radio advertising for Parker pens started in December 1943, three months after its scheduled date, and Goodrich and Ponds had to wait until 1944 for radio advertising.[19] Problems continued even after radio operations started. For example, Carnation milk distributors in Mexico filed a complaint against a radio commercial that, according to them, had a sexual connotation. The incident revealed Thompson's poor management and service in Mexico. Thompson hired a professional singer to record the Carnation milk commercial, but miscommunication between the agency and the singer forced Thompson to ask an employee in its accounting department to do the commercial. The lyrics of the commercial stated, "I am the milk-giving cow. . . . Listen to my bell. Milk from a satisfied cow."[20] The announcer was supposed to end the song with a motherly "moo," but Thompson decided to use a recording of a bull that was played before bullfights. The client argued that lyrics that referred to a "satisfied cow" followed by a masculine "moo" had a sexual connotation.[21] Upsetting clients as a result of poor management and the lack of cultural literacy did not help Thompson's performance during its first few years in Mexico, especially at a time when radio advertising was not very profitable in the first place. It was also counterproductive to the company's rationale for expanding abroad: the commitment to providing the most effective and efficient service for large transnational corporations.

Thompson's international operations and organization were responsible for its lack of profits during the first five years in Mexico. For example, its commission on RCA Victor's fifteen-minute radio program early in 1944 added up to only seven pesos and fifty cents a day.[22] Even worse, RCA required Thompson to reject lucrative contracts with competitors such as Philco, General Electric, and Phillips, all of which spent much more money on Mexican advertising than RCA. Thompson continued to handle RCA advertising in Mexico despite the low profits because RCA was a very important account in the United States and other parts of the world. RCA advertising expenditures increased after 1944, but Thompson did not begin making profits until 1947, when it earned close to 1 percent profit from the total amount billed to all its Mexican clients, a figure that was still below company expectations.[23] Thompson's billings represented the operating cost, and the company required a minimum of 2 percent of the total billings to consider any international branch profitable, a status the Mexican branch reached in 1948.

Thompson lost some of its accounts as a result of its failure to understand Mexican business culture. Reports of poor advertising results were common. Thompson representatives blamed the poor results on Mexican business practices. They argued that they would never have launched some of the advertising campaigns if their clients had shared valuable marketing and sales information with Thompson. They complained that Mexican "clients guarded sale figures very closely and did not disclose information to advertising agencies."[24] Mexican businesses were reluctant to share information that, according to them, might give competitors an advantage, and they were not accustomed to providing extensive company information to outsiders who had not earned the trust of top executives. Thompson was an outsider to clients in Mexico, and Mexican businesses resented Thompson's interest in closely reviewing their records. They were not accustomed to working closely with agencies like Thompson that were almost obsessed with statistical analysis and marketing research. Unfortunately for Thompson, its executives failed to understand that the company's status, position, and reputation were very different in Mexico than in the United States. They recognized the differences between Mexican and American businesses, but they failed to understand the implication of those differences. Many Mexican businesses were family partnerships rather than publicly held corporations.[25] Family partnerships often formed commercial networks or *grupos comerciales* that maintained strong family or friendship ties. Their business operations (including credit, management, and business contracts) revolved around circles of trust composed of family, friends, and close associates.[26] As a result, they were determined to guard market information and company records closely. Their approach was reasonable: for example, why should a Ford dealer share detailed information about his business with Thompson when the agency also provided advertising service to all other Ford distributors in Mexico?

Thompson failed to understand that obtaining the information it needed to carry out its publicity required establishing a sense of trust, developing networks, and participating in different social, political, and corporate settings. Participation in merchant, manufacturing, and advertising organizations such as the ANP provided a forum for the discussion of different business issues and a setting for networking. Thompson showed no interest in participating in national organizations or networking in Mexican society. Frustrated at its inability to get data from clients, the company complained about the lack of professionalism among Mexican businessmen. Thompson's frustration was understandable given that planning advertising campaigns and developing business strategies were difficult without the appropriate information or data. However, blaming Mexican clients for their poor performance did not benefit the American advertising agency. On the contrary, it created a tense and frustrating business relationship. This relationship did not benefit Thompson clients either, but at least they could turn to other advertising agencies. By contrast, Thompson did not have the luxury of losing clients. Unlike its U.S. operations, Thompson de

México needed both small and large accounts in order to reduce company losses. Conflicts between the company's personnel and its Mexican clients led to the loss of customers. The agency reported that at least four clients decided to terminate their contracts by 1946 because they had no confidence in the general manager.[27]

Thompson tried to understand Mexican culture and lifestyle when it entered Mexico, but the vast differences between Mexican and American business practices made its first five years in Mexico frustrating. Language presented Thompson's first major challenge. In the United States, the company's official name was J. Walter Thompson. The "J" did not work for Thompson in Mexico because it had a homosexual connotation if slightly mispronounced.[28] Kuneau feared that Mexicans would read the company's name as *Joto* (the Spanish word for a gay man) as opposed to *Jota* (the pronunciation of the letter "J") Thompson. As a result, the company dropped the letter "J" and opened as Thompson de México. Also, Thompson argued that the hiring of predominantly Mexican personnel would give its advertising a "Mexican flavor." However, the agency insisted on transplanting its American advertising methods in Mexico. Frustrated at their lack of success in fitting into the Mexican business world, Thompson's personnel became defensive and focused on trying to explain their failure rather than learning Mexican business practices.

Thompson agents pointed to Mexican nationalism as one of the main reasons for their failure, arguing that many executives preferred to be represented by Mexican advertising agencies.[29] They complained that personal friendships carried a lot of weight in Mexican business, which placed Thompson at a disadvantage when competing against Mexican advertising agencies. Mexicans, they argued, "develop strong political, family, and school ties that often translate into business preference for friends, relatives, or classmates."[30] As a result, Thompson reported that the success of advertising agents depended on how many influential friends and relatives they had and not on the quality of their work. Yet Thompson did not use its influential and skilled Mexican personnel wisely. Correa and Sheridan were very well known and had a well-developed network of media and business associates. However, the company insisted on hiring American managers who did not have the knowledge of Mexican culture or the contacts that would have increased their clientele. To this end, Thompson wasted Sheridan's and Correa's expertise, contacts, and ability to connect with Mexican businesses.

Thompson's decision to limit Sheridan's and Correa's responsibilities did not make sense within the business context in Mexico, but it did make sense within an American corporate context. Neither Sheridan nor Correa had a college degree, which was not unusual in Mexico since most Mexican advertising agents were not college graduates. By contrast, Thompson took pride in hiring the best researchers and graduates from top universities in the United States. Why should Thompson assign Mexican advertising personnel with little or no college education to head its branch in Mexico when the company hired college graduates as publicity experts in New York? Thompson valued Sheridan's and Correa's experience enough to state that its Mexican branch hired some of the best publicity agents in the country. Company reports detailed the impressive records of the top Mexican employees.[31] They boasted that educational institutions in Mexico requested that Sheridan and Correa teach courses in advertising. However, Thompson believed that its extensive training in elaborate and sophisticated publicity methods in New York was the best advertising training in the world. To this end, Thompson suggested that even the best Mexican advertising agents barely reached mediocre standards when compared to New York Thompson personnel. Unlike other American companies, Thompson did not think its top Mexican executives merited training in its U.S. facilities. Instead, it brought Americans to Mexico.

Mediating Tensions and Learning by Confrontation

Thompson's international organization and operations triggered conflicts over workers' expectations and disagreements among Thompson personnel in 1946. A request for a Christmas bonus for Mexican employees heightened tensions between Thompson's American management in Mexico and the New York headquarters. Donald Thorburn, Thompson's top executive in Mexico City, approved a Christmas bonus budget that amounted to over 17,000 pesos. Donald Foote from the New York headquarters initially rejected the proposed budget. He argued that the Christmas bonus was based on yearly profits in each branch and was designed as compensation for low-income employees. Foote stated that he "could not justify before the board of directors a bonus to Mexican employees that was higher (in terms of percentage) than the amount received by employees in New York at a time when the Mexican branch continued to report losses for a third consecutive year."[32] Thorburn replied that because Thompson had set a precedent by giving employees a Christmas bonus in 1945, he was forced to approve a 1946 bonus because "under Mexican law, equal payments must be made for equal services granted by an employee," and such payments included both regular pay and bonuses.[33] Thorburn argued that Mexican employees at Thompson saw their Christmas bonus as part of their income as opposed to a gift. Not approving the proposed bonus, according to Thorburn, would mean reducing their income.

Thorburn spoke on behalf of Mexican employees in his efforts to convince the New York headquarters to approve the proposed employee bonus. He argued that Mexican employees had, in good faith, agreed to forego a raise during the previous years. However, he feared that "a deviation from previous policy would have some extreme adverse effects" and might even lead to the loss of some "key" employees. He warned Foote and the New York headquarters that it would be very difficult to replace people like Sheridan and Correa. He concluded: "You see, these people do not really know Thompson except as it has operated in Mexico. They do not have the sense of security that all of us who have worked with the parent company have. They do not see Thompson as a solid paternalistic organization that grows."[34] The New York headquarters approved Thorburn's proposed budget with the condition that the bonus would not increase for the next two years. The Christmas bonus incident of 1946 led Thompson's headquarters to implement a profit-sharing program in Mexico. Foote recommended introducing profit sharing in Mexico because, according to him, it offered the "best way of compensating workers based on the financial performance of the local branch."[35] Thompson (like Sears) had implemented profit sharing in the United States, but the company did not consider it appropriate for Mexican employees until Foote suggested that it would encourage the Mexican branch to perform better, reduce tensions over the annual bonus, and ultimately project a sense of corporate paternalism. According to Carol Wilson, a Thompson representative in the New York international division who frequently visited the Mexican branch, profit sharing led managers and employees at foreign branches to take a "personal interest in the financial success of their own office."[36]

Thompson clients in Mexico often forced the company to respond to their demands. For example, Mexican Ford dealers were not pleased with the advertising representative Thompson assigned to handle their account. At a meeting between Thompson and Ford dealers, Thompson's general manager noticed that the facial expressions and body language of the dealers suggested that they disapproved of the agent. The manager asked for their opinion after the agent left the room, and the Ford dealers unanimously rejected him. They forced the general manager to appoint another agent for their account.[37] The general manager suggested that appearance was the reason for the Ford dealers' disdain. One report claimed that the dealers disliked the Thompson representative because he did not wear "a white handkerchief in his breast pocket."[38]

The rejection of the Thompson representative by Mexican Ford dealers showed that Mexicans expected business associates to respect certain business traditions and notions of proper public behavior. The business etiquette expected by Mexican Ford dealers did not develop overnight; it was deeply rooted in Mexico's social and business practices. According to geographer Michael

Johns, appearance became crucial in indicating class and regional distinctions in Mexico City during the late nineteenth century. Wealthy residents living on the west side used practices such as bathing, wearing a handkerchief, and maintaining clean parks, streets, and shopping areas to distinguish themselves from residents living on the east side of the city.[39] They described residents living east of the Zócalo downtown plaza as "dirty, insolent, unruly, uncivilized, and even as 'human waste' of the city."[40] Mexican Ford dealers knew the Thompson representative did not, by any means, resemble Mexico City's poor. However, dealers were apparently disturbed at his lack of manners. The response of the Ford dealers suggests that Mexican businessmen judged Thompson advertising agents according to the standards, practices, and personal manners they had previously learned. The dealers' rejection of the advertising representative indicates that Mexican businessmen were not willing to accept people they did not consider *simpáticos* or well liked. Most important, it suggests that being *simpáticos* required more than simply celebrating Mexican culture at a rhetorical level. It required proper personal and business manners.

Tensions among Thompson employees also contributed to the company's inability to work as a team and make profits in a country where clients had different business practices and expectations than those of clients in the United States. According to a company report, a top American executive at Thompson made remarks to one of his young female employees that were taken out of context and misinterpreted as sexual harassment. The woman mentioned the remarks to her brother, who went to the office the next day, met the American executive in the "hall in front of the elevator and without mentioning his sister punched him in the nose, knocked him down, and stepped on him a bit, and then left."[41] The report described the incident as an example of how family ties in Mexico interfered with effective management. It characterized this type of action as barbaric and irrational.[42] It also described the calm and rational manner in which American management dealt with this type of incident while simultaneously implying that Mexicans were driven by emotion. Months later, when the woman asked for a salary increase, the report continued, the general manager made her promise that she would not allow her brother to manhandle Thompson personnel. Thompson apparently did not consider the possibility of misconduct on the part of its American personnel even though the woman and her brother had no doubt that the remarks were sexually explicit.

Learning the Rules of the Game: Innovating Mexican Advertising, 1943–1948

Thompson personnel at the New York headquarters insisted on making the Mexico City branch profitable despite its initial failure. They recognized that it had a great deal of potential and could provide substantial profits. As a result, they focused on building the company's advertising infrastructure and learned to think of their first four years in Mexico as a learning experience. Thompson was particularly impressed with Mexico City's commercial art. It reported that "the layout and design performed by Mexican artists could equal work done anywhere else in the world."[43] It was very pleased with the work of Alfonso Ortíz, the director of the commercial art department. Ortíz had worked as a cartoonist for *El Universal* for twelve years prior to his arrival at Thompson in 1943. Thompson claimed that the over 450 printing shops, 50 lithograph plants, and 12 large offset-printing plants in Mexico City offered a dynamic infrastructure for advertising production. It reported that Mexican photo-engraving companies were "of such excellence that several of them have customers in the US and Latin America."[44] Thompson was equally impressed with the media in Mexico. It reported that a talented group of professional radio announcers, producers, scriptwriters, sound engineers, and other technicians were a great asset to radio advertising and enriched "the color, the folklore, the sentimentality, and native artistry of the country."[45] Thompson also praised the status of the print media in Mexico. It enthusiastically reported that there were 9 morning papers, 2 afternoon papers, 8 papers in different languages for foreigners residing in Mexico, 9 general-interest magazines, 7 women's magazines, and over 25 trade magazines.[46] Thompson was also pleased with the work done by its personnel in the media and checking division. These divisions researched and monitored the circulation rates, typography, and press work of newspapers and magazines. They were also responsible for handling the placement and scheduling of advertising.

The talent of its Mexican personnel, the high quality of different aspects of advertising, the media infrastructure, and the potential for continued growth made the Mexico City branch promising. Taking advantage of the infrastructure for advertising production in Mexico, Thompson decided to produce advertising for Central America, the Caribbean, and northern South America in Mexico. By the late 1940s, company executives believed that the branch in Mexico City could do a better job of producing advertising for other parts of Latin America than the New York headquarters. In other words, although the Mexican branch did not generate profits for Thompson at the beginning, it provided the infrastructure for producing publicity in a large part of the Americas. Thompson capitalized on the promise of future success even though the promise started to fade by 1946 as tensions and corporate growing pains escalated. Company operations received a boost in 1946 when Don Francisco became vice president of Thompson. However, during the 1940s, Thompson was learning to negotiate the boundaries that defined the rules of the game for doing business in Mexico.

Francisco did not radically transform Thompson's business approach as vice president, but he injected America's advertising giant with a shot of Rockefeller's

Good Neighbor Policy. His emphasis on establishing good corporate public relations and his commitment to defining publicity as a democratic force caught Rockefeller's attention during World War II. As president of Lord and Thomas Advertising in the 1930s, Francisco had defended social welfare as a vital component of American democracy and capitalism. He argued that selling good merchandise at low prices was not enough and that American businesses had to win the approval of consumers and the general public by demonstrating that they were servants of American society.[47] His approach echoed Rockefeller's Good Neighbor Policy. As a result, Rockefeller hired Francisco to head the radio information and content division of the OIAA during the war. Francisco's experience in the OIAA turned him into a "commercial diplomat" and an advocate of America's consumer democracy abroad by 1947. As Thompson's vice president and overseer of the company's international division, Francisco encouraged Thompson to establish good international relations and commercial ties with the countries where the company operated. He presented advertising as a symbol of economic freedom. According to him, economic liberty implied the freedom of every individual and every enterprise to seek markets for their services. It also included the "right of every individual as a consumer to satisfy his wants, to buy what he wants, and to reject what displeases him."[48] Such freedom, Francisco argued, was the basis of American democracy and industrial capitalism, which according to him advertising agencies had to spread throughout the world. In other words, he championed the spread of America's consumer democracy outlined by the Good Neighbor Policy. To this end, Thompson's international operations under the leadership of Francisco sought to accomplish much more than making profits abroad. Thompson, from Francisco's perspective, served as a commercial diplomat instead of a "commercial missionary" as it initially had done.[49] Being a commercial diplomat required participating in a dialogue that included acclimating to foreign values and practices, as well as introducing Thompson's expertise as America's leading advertising agency. It rejected America's and Thompson's "missionary" approach of simply spreading American business culture and lifestyle.

Thompson introduced its marketing research methods in Mexico, hoping to gather information that would facilitate its service to large transnational corporations. It considered market data vital to business and corporate planning. The company had earned a reputation as the leader in statistical and marketing research in American advertising since the early twentieth century. It published the first market analysis for business planning, the *Population and Its Distribution*, before World War I.[50] Thompson continued to study population trends and consumption and living standards for clients.[51] It also established a panel in 1939 to research the consumer habits of over 5,000 families across the United

States. The families answered questionnaires about the products they purchased throughout the year.[52] Thompson introduced extensive marketing research in Europe and Latin America after 1944. Mexican advertising offered excellent graphic design and media resources prior to Thompson's arrival, but it did not emphasize research. In 1944, Thompson became the first advertising agency to establish a research department in Mexico.[53] Mexicans reacted positively to Thompson's research. The weekly newsletter of Mexico's National Chamber of Commerce classified Thompson's *Mexican Market*, a publication providing detailed statistical data on the Mexican market in the 1950s and 1960s, as "the most effective study that exists in the field of marketing research in Mexico."[54] Similarly, *Novedades* commented that the report reaffirmed Thompson's "supremacy in the field of marketing research, which is science and art since it finds, analyzes, and interprets facts for use by businessmen."[55]

Thompson's research in Mexico focused on understanding the different factors that determined consumer preference and the selection of specific brand-name products. The company conducted surveys from March to June 1947 in its effort to evaluate market conditions for its client, Squibb toothpaste, and its leading competitors. It also provided comparative data on market conditions for toothpaste in Mexico, Argentina, and Cuba.[56] The comparative aspect of the research was not surprising given Thompson's emphasis on understanding international trends and its publicity strategy of developing advertising that could be used in different countries. The research focused on shopping practices, perceptions of dentifrice, and the qualities customers preferred when selecting a dentifrice. Thompson divided the survey in two sections: a customer questionnaire and a dealer survey. It also compared the responses of high- and low-income families. Fifty-two percent of the 434 Mexico City families interviewed were considered low-income families, a category that included residents who did not own their own house, did not have a car, could not afford to purchase refrigerators or electric stoves, and did not have maids or servants. Forty-eight percent of the respondents were considered high-income families who enjoyed a comfortable lifestyle.[57]

In an effort to identify the appropriate target of dentifrice advertising, Thompson's survey requested information on who selected products. Forty-three percent of the 419 families who answered this question reported that the wife was responsible for purchasing toothpaste. Thirty percent reported that a servant purchased dentifrice. Only 13 percent of the families responded that the husband purchased toothpaste.[58] Thompson learned through research what Mexican advertising agents considered basic information: Mexican women and servants were responsible for performing domestic and family duties, which included raising and educating children, cooking, cleaning, and shopping. Yet

Thompson's research facilitated the development of advertising strategies that targeted specific sectors of Mexican society. Thompson promoted close coordination between research findings and the production of advertising to increase the efficiency of publicity. Such coordination was new in Mexico.

Thompson's research also provided data on different aspects of the consumer selection process. The company learned through its research that Forhan's and Colgate were the most popular brands of toothpaste in Mexico City. Thirty-five percent of the families interviewed responded that they used Forhan's, and 28 percent indicated that they preferred Colgate.[59] They ranked taste as the most important quality in their toothpaste and cleaning effectiveness as the second most important aspect.[60] However, Thompson and other advertising agencies focused on advertising the medicinal aspects of dentifrice instead of its taste. Toothpaste advertising featured shocking accounts of tooth decay caused by not using the proper dentifrice. These ads often included detailed explanations by experts of how the advertised product prevented serious dental and medical problems. Why did Thompson use educational advertising to market dentifrice when research showed that consumers ranked taste and foaminess as the most important features in their dentifrice?

Thompson used educational advertising to capitalize on the public relations angle. It argued that educational advertising was necessary because schools were not teaching children the significance of dentifrice. Only 5 percent of the respondents indicated that their children had been instructed in the need for dentifrice at school.[61] Schools had traditionally assumed the responsibility for educating the public about hygiene. Teachers during the Cárdenas administration, for example, had organized "sanitary brigades" to introduce basic hygiene and health care in the countryside.[62] Thompson's educational advertising for dentifrice reinforced government efforts to educate the public on hygiene. This educational campaign was not simply a measure to convince the public of the health benefits of dentifrice since 95 percent of the families interviewed reported that they used dentifrice. Using educational advertising was a strategic move that suggested that toothpaste protected consumers' health. Yet Thompson's strategy went beyond an effort to project a paternalist public relations approach or be on good terms with the Mexican government. It was a response to other results in the survey. Seventy percent of Mexican families in the survey indicated a preference for toothpaste made by a manufacturer with a reputation for producing drugs.[63] Of these respondents, 30 percent mentioned Squibb as having a reputation in drug manufacturing, and 42 percent knew of no dentifrice brand with a reputation for manufacturing medicine.[64] Thus, Thompson decided to advertise Squibb toothpaste as a medicinal product because it hoped to capitalize on the large number of Mexicans who valued toothpaste as a medicinal product or believed that no dentifrice had a reputation in drug manufac-turing. Yet Thompson's educational dentifrice advertising indirectly reinforced the paternalism of government institutions as it promoted health care, hygiene, and Western medicine as mechanisms for protecting the population.

Thompson's 1947 research also included a comparison of dentifrice markets in different parts of Latin America. This comparative research indicated that Thompson took an interest in learning regional differences in Latin America. Prior to 1947, Thompson opted for transplanting American advertising strategies abroad, though it allowed regional branches to adapt its international advertis-ing. Thompson targeted Mexico City, Buenos Aires, and Havana for its compara-tive research because it claimed capital cities represented the largest market and provided an accurate sample of the population of each country. It distrib-uted the dentifrice survey it used in Mexico City to 504 families in Havana and 1,149 families in Buenos Aires. The results showed substantial regional differ-ences in the purchase and consumption of dentifrice. For example, 51 percent of the families in Mexico indicated a preference for foamy toothpaste, but that figure skyrocketed to over 81 percent in Argentina and 81 percent in Cuba.[65] In Mexico City, only 43 percent of housewives purchased toothpaste compared to 75 percent in Buenos Aires and 66 percent in Havana. Thirty percent of the fami-lies in Mexico had servants purchase toothpaste, but that percentage dropped to 8 percent in Argentina and 1 percent in Cuba.[66] There were also clear differ-ences in the locations where Latin Americans purchased dentifrice. While over 90 percent of Mexicans purchased toothpaste at drugstores, only 29 percent of Argentineans and 44 percent of Cubans did so. Twenty-nine percent of Argen-tineans purchased dentifrice at cologne and accessories stores (*perfumerías*), but only 1 percent of Mexicans and no Cubans did so. Twenty-five percent of Cubans purchased toothpaste at variety and department stores, but the figure dropped to only 16 percent in Argentina and 4 percent in Mexico.[67] Thompson's research indicated that the agency could not use one advertising strategy to market toothpaste in all of Latin America. Thompson proved through its market-ing research what Rockefeller had told American businesses in the early 1940s: Latin Americans from different regions were very different, and American diplo-mats and corporations had to develop regional strategies in order to reach them effectively.

Consumer responses suggested that Mexico City residents were ambiguous about the qualities they valued in toothpaste. Mexico had the highest turnover rate in brand-name preference, with 47 percent of interviewees indicating that they had used their current dentifrice for less than three years.[68] By contrast, over 70 percent of the respondents in Argentina and Cuba said they had used the same toothpaste for over three years. Advertisers and dentifrice manufacturers saw Mexico City's high turnover rate as an indication that Mexico was fertile ground for increasing the influence of their product. They took research findings very seriously as they developed advertising strategies and approaches. Perhaps Thompson representatives overlooked the possible benefits of highlighting taste and foaminess in toothpaste advertising. Mexican consumers might have thought of dentifrice as a medicinal item, but advertising toothpaste as a personal health-care product with a pleasing taste and foaminess might have given the advertised brand an advantage over its competitors.

Thompson's research in Mexico during the 1940s was innovative for Mexican publicity, but it fell short of reaching the level of sophistication and quality of advertising in the United States. Thompson did not establish a consumer panel in Mexico as it had in the United States in 1939. It acknowledged the significance of general regional differences in Latin America by 1947, but its personnel continued to lump diverse areas together in research and market analysis. For example, Thompson's research in consumer habits in Mexico, Central America, and the northern region of South America was centered in Mexico City from 1943 to 1950. This strategy changed in 1950 when satellite centers in Central America and the Caribbean operated under the supervision of the Mexico City branch. Thompson defended its Mexico City–based research and advertising production strategy by arguing that Mexico City provided a good sample of the entire population of Mexico. Its approach ignored the differences between Mexico City and rural lifestyles as it disseminated Mexico City values, beliefs, and practices throughout the nation. But thanks to the introduction of Thompson's marketing research methods, the hiring of Don Francisco, and the ongoing misunderstandings and conflicts that Thompson encountered, Thompson was gradually learning the rules of the game for doing business in Mexico and Latin America. In the process, it was tempering the self-righteous attitude it had when it entered Mexico in 1943. By focusing its research and publicity on Mexico City's lifestyle, Thompson reinforced what Mexican liberals and politicians after the 1910 revolution had tried to achieve since the nineteenth century: a social, political, economic, and cultural mechanism that supported Mexico City's supremacy over provincial areas.

Thompson representatives claimed that the company's expertise, international reputation, and experience during its first five years in Mexico facilitated the introduction of innovative and effective marketing strategies in 1947. This claim was not just self-promotion. Thompson introduced marketing strategies that were very successful. It created a market advantage for the distribution of Clarafan, a clear packaging material made by Calanese Mexicana. Mexican supermarkets had traditionally sold rice and beans in paper bags.[69] Thompson argued that if these products were sold in clear packaging, consumers would be able to see if they were of inferior quality. Thompson also transformed the marketing of Clarafan dog food by recommending packaging the food in single portions. The company launched an advertising campaign with the slogan, "Let's take a look at your product through Clarafan," to address complaints that supermarkets misrepresented the quality and quantity of the merchandise.[70] It attached discount coupons and surveys to the newly packaged Clarafan products. It received 700 responses in support of its marketing techniques. Thompson also conducted a study to boost napkin and toilet paper sales by Scott Paper Company, which signed a contract with Industrial de San Cristóbal as a joint venture. Research reported that "even among high-income groups in Mexico City, more than fifty percent [of Mexicans] did not use toilet tissue."[71] Based on research results, Thompson launched "promotional advertising methods designed to change people's habits and to sell the public on the idea of using toilet tissue."[72] However, the company did not focus solely on changing habits in Mexico. Its publicity also flirted with international trends by the late 1940s.

Thompson used paternalism in its advertising of food products to tap into values and issues that were central to Mexican society. Its publicity suggested that American food products would end social ills and poverty in Mexico. It handled publicity for Lechería Nacional, a subsidiary of Kraft. Lechería Nacional imported Kraft powdered milk from the United States, rehydrated it, and purified it in a six-step process.[73] Consumers purchased the rehydrated milk in sealed bottles at local stores. Thompson's marketing strategy transformed the sale and distribution of milk in Mexico. Local milkmen distributed milk door to door before the late 1940s. Milk was scarce and complaints about diluted milk were so common that they found their way into films featuring Mario Moreno Cantinflas. For example, in a scene in one of Cantinflas's most popular films, *El Gendarme Desconocido*, Cantinflas arrests a store owner for allegedly diluting milk. When the store owner asks if he is being arrested for adding water to the milk, Cantinflas responds, "No sir, I am arresting you for adding milk to the water, which is something different." The scene ends with Cantinflas tapping the store owner on the head with his hat while reminding him about the shame of diluting milk.

Numerous complaints of milk dilution in working-class neighborhoods were reported to various government institutions. The National Health Laboratory reported in 1958 that 24 percent of the pasteurized milk sold in Mexico City was diluted.[74] Thorburn referred to the import of powdered milk as "one of the greatest contributions to the advancement of Mexico" and claimed that it would end widespread malnutrition.[75] Advertising also focused on discrediting local milkmen and building customer trust in Lechería Nacional. Thompson argued that the collaboration between Lechería Nacional and Kraft would end the irregularities in milk distribution and offer wholesome milk. It ran full-page ads in newspapers and broadcast a husband-wife radio program, *Breakfast with Dalia and Juan*.[76] It trumpeted the significance of purchasing pasteurized milk from manufacturers who carefully monitored its processing and guaranteed quality instead of from local milkmen who lacked hygiene and tampered with the quality of the milk. In the process, Lechería Nacional was gradually displacing milk distributors who could not compete with a Mexican subsidiary of an American corporation. Thompson presented the standardized production and marketing of Kraft milk as a process that protected the Mexican public. It promised the same consumer protection that government officials provided when they enforced government regulations.

The 1947 import restrictions imposed by the Mexican government forced Thompson to examine local conditions closely in order to develop effective strategies for meeting its clients' demands. The government's decision to prohibit the import of luxury items prevented the import of Parker pens that included a gold cap. As the publicity agent for Parker, Thompson introduced the Lady 51 pen in its effort to maintain profits despite the decline of the gold cap pen.[77] Shirley Woodell, a Thompson employee who frequently inspected operations in Mexico and Central America, recommended the introduction of the Lady 51 model since fountain and Sheaffer Parker pens were popular among Mexican women.[78] The strategy behind the marketing of the Lady 51 pen suggested that Thompson developed publicity for its Mexican clients within the boundaries established by local conditions. Woodell's reports included recommendations aimed at securing profits for Thompson clients in the midst of economic protectionism.

Conclusion

Thompson became one of the most successful advertising agencies in Mexico by the 1950s, but its success depended on its understanding of Mexican values, beliefs, and practices. Its reputation as a leading American advertising agency gave it both an advantage and a disadvantage when it entered the Mexican market. Thompson already had a number of well-known clients as it entered Mexico, including RCA, Standard Brands, Aqua Velva, Gillette, and J. B. Williams. The opening personnel were able to hire some of the most qualified Mexican advertisers as a result of Thompson's reputation in the United States. Thompson conducted detailed marketing surveys to measure public opinion and collect data, which it considered instrumental in developing effective advertising campaigns. It tapped into Mexico's solid printing and communication infrastructure. Mexico City became the advertising capital of Mexico, Central America, and part of

South America. Yet Thompson's performance during its first five years did not meet company expectations. Poor planning; a lack of understanding of Mexican values, culture, and lifestyle; and Thompson's international organization prevented the company from making profits until 1948. The lack of profits, miscommunication, and failure to understand Mexican laws and culture created tensions between the company's personnel in Mexico City and its headquarters in New York. However, these tensions never escalated to the point that Thompson considered closing the Mexican branch. On the contrary, the company's headquarters acknowledged the potential of its Mexico City branch despite its losses. The first five years of operation in Mexico taught Thompson that doing business in Mexico required acclimating to Mexican culture and operating within a middle ground rather than simply transplanting American values and practices.

6 In Search of Markets, Diplomacy, and Consumers: Sears as a Commercial Diplomat in Mexico

Sears launched its grand opening festivities in Mexico City in February 1947 with a religious ceremony performed by the nation's top religious authority. Store management and the opening crew asked Archbishop Luis María Martínez to initiate the celebration with a religious procession to the department store a few days before the opening. The procession included craftsmen, construction workers, and employees. A Sears publication reported, "The archbishop went from department to department blessing the workers' achievements."[1] Sears organized the religious procession after learning that 95 percent of Mexicans were Catholic.[2] Religious celebrations had traditionally preceded grand openings in Mexico, but they were restricted to the private sphere as a result of bitter conflicts between the church and state during the Cristero revolts in the 1920s and 1930s.[3] Fortunately for Sears, these church-state tensions had declined by the early 1940s, and the political climate under Ávila Camacho promoted conciliation rather than confrontation.[4] Archbishop Martínez (1937–56) cleverly used the climate of conciliation to revitalize the power and public presence of the church. He started making public appearances in the early 1940s even though the 1917 constitution restricted such events.[5] In 1945 he organized a week-long religious ceremony to commemorate the fiftieth anniversary of the crowning of the Virgin of Guadalupe as a Mexican patron.[6] He invited the Canadian cardinal and high-ranking American priests to the ceremony, in which a new crown was placed on the statue. According to Archbishop Martínez, the original crowning on October 12, 1895, symbolized the Christian confirmation of Mexico's national soul and the unity of its people as descendants of the Virgin of Guadalupe.[7] The 1945 anniversary ceremony included religious processions headed by the Canadian cardinal. The cardinal visited stores in Mexico City's downtown and publicly blessed businesses and employees. Customers dining at Sanborn's "dropped to their knees as the Cardinal entered." Surprised at the large number of participants and the various public ceremonies, an American priest reported to Herbert Cerwin, Rockefeller's right-hand man in Mexico's OIAA, that the week-long celebration was "not Catholicism, it was a religious orgy."[8] Similar to Archbishop Martínez, Sears used Mexico's Catholicism and the country's nationalist and revolutionary heritage as a marketing tool for introducing a department store that had earned a reputation as a symbol of America's middle class and a hallmark of welfare capitalism in the United States.[9]

The use of a religious procession in Sears's grand opening in Mexico City was also controversial among Sears stockholders and the American business community. U.S. newspapers had given substantial coverage to the introduction of Sears in Mexico and Latin America since 1945 as Sears sought to prove that its dramatic expansion prior to 1940 would continue abroad in the postwar era. Sears opened over 600 stores from 1925 to 1940, but the war interrupted the company's expansion. After the war, Sears's headquarters in Chicago referred to the Mexico City operations as a "commercial laboratory" for further expansion into Latin America. The religious procession was one of the first events preceding Sears's grand opening day. U.S. newspaper headlines reporting on the religious ceremonies raised concern, criticism, and uncertainty in the U.S. business community.[10] Some critics argued that they understood the need to adopt local cultural practices in other countries, as promoted by Rockefeller and Sears's top executives. However, they argued that mixing business and religion was too great a departure from American business culture, in which the church and the corporate sector were separate entities. The opening staff responded that a religious ceremony was necessary because Mexicans would not enter the store until a religious figure blessed the building.[11] Reports of shopping-crazed mobs, lucrative profits, and Sears's success quickly ended criticism of the company's business strategy. The frenzy lasted for "three full weeks as cargo planes shuttled to and from the United States bringing fresh merchandise to keep shelves from becoming completely bare."[12] Sales surpassed $1 million two weeks after opening day.[13] The quick end of criticism of Sears's business formula suggested that Sears's ability to make profits in Mexico prevailed over ethical judgments that had historically separated business and religion in the United States.[14]

Sears's grand opening illustrated the company's business approach and established the basis of its corporate success in 1940s and 1950s Mexico. On the marketing level, the company operated within the boundaries established by Mexican culture, even if this meant radically departing from American corporate culture. To this end, Sears filtered its operations through Mexican nationalist and revolutionary rhetoric. It presented its compliance with Mexican government policies and regulations as an indication that it respected, understood, and was in tune with Mexican society. It introduced its U.S. welfare capitalist services (discounted lunch programs, paid vacations, and profit-sharing) as products of the Mexican Revolution. It claimed that its highly regarded in-house training programs, its high salaries, and the prestige associated with working at Sears served as mechanisms for upward mobility into the ranks of Mexico's middle class—a process that the company and Mexican political leaders defined as a vital aspect of the 1910 revolution. Most important, Sears presented its well-established U.S. reputation as a middle-class retailer as a powerful force that would "democratize" consumption in Mexico by delivering high-quality merchandise to Mexico's middle class. Sears portrayed its American notion of "consumer democracy" as a product of Mexico's industrial capitalism.

Sears did not hesitate to present its corporate operations as a product of American capitalism despite its flirtation with Mexican nationalism and the revolution. Projecting a belief in American superiority in business, Sears translated manuals that transplanted American procedures, standards, and even corporate language to its Mexican stores. Company manuals, training programs, and exams required Sears de México employees and manufacturers to adopt standards established by the U.S. headquarters. Sears's willingness to operate within the boundaries established by Mexican culture and its corporate leadership made company operations in Mexico successful despite tensions. Government policies aimed at protecting national industries under ISI forced Sears to make major changes in corporate planning by the summer of 1947. Misconceptions about Mexico's middle class, a limited understanding of social conditions in Mexico, and the appointment of a president who did not operate within the boundaries of Mexican culture triggered a restructuring of the company by late 1949. Yet Sears's profits and the company's expansion in Mexico and Latin America continued at an impressive rate despite these setbacks. The company's corporate identification with welfare capitalism and its diplomatic expansion strategy, which differed from Thompson's "missionary approach," were vital to its success in the Mexican market.

Sears as a Commercial Diplomat to Latin America

The opening of Sears de México marked the continuation of an aggressive expansion campaign the company had initiated in the United States under the leadership of Robert E. Wood, known as General Wood, in the mid-1920s. Richard W. Sears and Alvah C. Roebuck started Sears as a mail-order retailer in the 1880s. Sears sold watches and trinkets until a Chicago clothing merchant, Julius Rosenwald, joined the company in the 1890s and turned it into a retailing giant by the early twentieth century. By 1906, Sears's central mail-order plant in Chicago ranked among the largest in the world, occupying ninety acres of floor space.[15] Changes in American society, such as the growth of the urban population, led Sears to open its first department store in 1925. Acknowledging that city residents would rather shop in stores than order from catalogs, Sears decided to open department stores in cities throughout the nation.[16] Its expansion took place at such a rapid pace that there were over 300 Sears department stores by 1929. Sears opened an average of one store every other business day during a twelve-month period in the late 1920s.[17] The Great Depression did not stop Sears's expansion. Sears executives cut hundreds of ribbons at opening ceremonies throughout the 1930s, and by 1940, there were over 600 Sears department stores.

Although the Great Depression did not stop Sears's expansion, World War II did. Sears was forced to close some of its existing stores, and it only opened two new stores during the war, one in Hawaii and the other in Havana. The Havana store was not very successful because of the war, but Wood developed plans to open a store in Mexico City immediately after the war ended. Plans to open new stores throughout Latin America were already under way in 1946 when construction of the Mexico City store began. However, Wood decided to test Sears products in Mexico before finalizing contracts to open a store in Brazil. Success in Mexico City assured stockholders that Sears stores could successfully market American brand-name products and make profits south of the border. Sears opened seven stores in Mexico by 1952. Sales from these operations exceeded $15 million a year.[18] Sears became the second largest retailer in Mexico by the early 1950s, and fifty-nine Sears stores were operating throughout Latin America by 1959. According to John F. Gallagher, the vice president of the Sears Latin American division in Chicago, Sears's expansion in Latin America was funded by reinvesting about 50 percent of its profits in the opening of new stores.[19]

Sears established a more centralized management structure in Latin America than it had in the United States, but it still allowed room for regional autonomy. Wood had developed a decentralized corporate structure in the United States in the late 1920s that consisted of five divisions with headquarters in Los Angeles, Dallas, Chicago, Atlanta, and Philadelphia. Each division operated with a great deal of autonomy from the headquarters in Chicago. District managers in each of the five divisions reported directly to the president in Chicago. The decentralized structure of Sears was based on Wood's philosophy that efficient management and corporate success required tapping into local resources and allowing district managers to develop efficient retail strategies at the regional level. His approach partly explains why Sears decided to begin its grand opening festivities in Mexico with a religious procession.

Wood rejected centralized management in the United States because he believed it established rigid procedures and prevented individual thinking, which led to poor decision making at the local level. According to him, corporate decisions were too removed from local areas and could decrease rather than increase efficiency. As a result, Sears maintained a highly decentralized empire in the United States in the late 1940s.[20] Each district operated as a "minicorporation" within the corporate structure. In Mexico, however, the Mexico City headquarters maintained substantial control over provincial stores. The Mexico City management was involved in the planning, design, and opening of provincial stores.[21] Employees of provincial stores had to complete a month-long training program in Mexico City. Provincial stores had to use the publicity produced in Mexico City even though they could produce a limited amount of publicity at the local level. The publicity department in Mexico City served as the central publicity unit for the entire nation. Store managers in provincial areas reported to the president in Mexico City, who submitted monthly reports to the Latin American division at Sears's headquarters in Chicago. The president of the Latin American division received reports from all Sears operations in Latin America. He reported directly to Sears's top authority, Wood.[22] Sears's Latin American operations were thus more hierarchical than its U.S. operations.

The centralized structure of Sears in Mexico suggests that the management in Chicago preferred to keep the Mexican personnel (particularly the management of provincial stores) on a "shorter leash" than the U.S. personnel. This reinforced the belief prevalent among American executives that provincial residents did not have adequate academic and technical training. Yet Sears's management cleverly avoided suggesting that provincial Mexicans were "backward." Instead, Sears gave a very clear message to its Mexican employees: follow Sears guidelines but use your personal judgment because you know local conditions better than the management in Chicago. This proved to be a successful business and management formula. Keeping managers in provincial stores on a "shorter leash" did not mean Sears abandoned Wood's preference for encouraging local and individual business leadership. According to Jorge Bonilla and Ernesto Zatarain, who worked for Sears in the 1950s and 1960s, Sears manuals and management instructions urged managers in Mexico City and provincial areas to follow management decisions but also to use their personal judgment based on local conditions.[23] In other words, Sears tried to find a middle ground in its management and retained elements of Wood's approach. This strategy, Bonilla argued, boosted the self-esteem of Mexican employees.[24]

Political conditions in Mexico gave Sears management greater autonomy over some operations than the level of autonomy exercised by regional districts in the United States. For example, the Chicago headquarters conducted purchasing for all Sears stores in the United States. The objective was to be able to gain lower prices on large-volume purchases from suppliers. Sears initially considered supplying merchandise for the Mexico City store an expansion of its purchasing operations in the United States. The Chicago headquarters made purchasing arrangements with suppliers in Houston and instructed them to export merchandise to Mexico City. However, Sears de México established its own purchasing division in July 1947 when the Mexican government prohibited the import of close to 80 percent of Sears's merchandise. After 1947, personnel in provincial stores placed orders from the central buying office in Mexico City. Local branches were allowed to base their purchasing decisions on local demand. This gave stores in Mexico greater autonomy in making purchasing decisions than stores in the United States. It was generally agreed that local "buying experts" knew more about prices and production in Mexico than the purchasing department in Chicago. The central buying office in Mexico City was referred to as a "miniature" of the purchasing division in Chicago.[25]

Wood's concerns about the limits placed on the U.S. economy as a result of disruptions in supply and demand drove Sears's expansion in Mexico and Latin America. Wood was no stranger to Latin America. He had commanded military units in the Caribbean during the Spanish-American War and had been stationed in Panama during the construction of the Panama Canal. Wood stated in 1948 that he had learned about Latin America's desperate need for innovative retailing while in Panama. Disregarding Latin America's commercial diversity and historical changes, he argued that retailing in 1945 Mexico was no different from retailing in Panama in 1905, when retailers earned profits through small-volume sales at high prices. Echoing his militant tone in commercial terms, he argued that Sears would "conquer Latin America" by selling high-quality merchandise at low prices, the retailing formula Sears had used in the United States.[26] Wood's "conquering" of the Americas provided a different diplomatic formula for dealing with Latin America than the aggressive approach of the U.S. government prior to the 1930s.

Wood endorsed Rockefeller's approach under the Good Neighbor Policy as a corporate initiative. He insisted on respecting the political and cultural boundaries established by Mexicans. He believed that the introduction of welfare capitalism in Mexico would benefit both Mexicans and Sears. Wood, like Rockefeller, encouraged commercial relations that promoted a higher standard of living and political and economic stability in Mexico as diplomatic tools for preventing the rise of communism and supporting America's capitalist expansion. As a politically conservative businessman and former military leader, Wood stressed the need to spread America's commercial abundance as an anticommunist strategy. According to him, America's corporate sector had the potential to build "international good will and do more for the prestige and influence of the United States than all the diplomats of the world."[27] He believed that Latin America offered great potential for Sears despite the low purchasing power of its working class. According to him, raising the standard of living among Mexicans through welfare capitalism would increase the purchasing power of lower sectors of society, thus providing opportunities for further expansion of Sears in Mexico.[28]

Like other American retailers, Sears developed welfare capitalist programs in the early twentieth century such as free lunches and free or low-cost medical care in response to criticism of debilitating working conditions in department stores.[29] Sears also offered paid vacations by the early twentieth century. It introduced such programs under the leadership of Julius Rosenwald, who was replaced in 1928 by Wood. Rosenwald established "one of the nation's most generous and publicized profit-sharing" programs at Sears in 1916 in response to an embarrassing accusation that young single female employees were paid unfair wages.[30] Sears's profit-sharing pension fund allocated close to 10 percent of net profits to employees.

Sears followed a corporate formula that had been central to the expansion of American capitalism. According to Alfred Chandler, the emergence of modern mass retailers in the United States during the late nineteenth century led to the standardization of commercial processes. Retailers developed a business strategy that guaranteed profits by accelerating the distribution of merchandise from producers to consumers. To this end, department stores aimed at maintaining a high volume of sales and high turnover of merchandise by selling at low prices and low profits.[31] Thus, Sears's corporate success depended on extracting low profits from a large volume of sales rather than making large profits from a small number of sales. Coordination in administration and the development of a corporate managerial hierarchy became essential to guarantee the fast and efficient flow of goods from suppliers to consumers.[32] Sears, like other American retailers, believed that speed and efficiency in the flow of merchandise would make the store, to use the company's rhetorical banner, a "merchant to the millions" and make the company profitable.

Sears championed welfare capitalism as a strand of U.S. corporate culture when it expanded to Latin America. Scholars of U.S. history such as Roland Marchand have identified two dominant strands of U.S. corporate culture. According to Marchand, one strand consisted of a masculine "stick to business" attitude by the 1920s.[33] This approach prevailed among advisers who counseled Latin American governments on financial planning as part of dollar diplomacy up to the 1930s.[34] The other trend in America corporate culture, according to Marchand, was exemplified by businesses that "employed new, more 'feminine' practices, consciously catering to public opinion, adopting show-business techniques of display and publicity, and institutionalizing welfare and public relations programs."[35] This strand promoted welfare capitalism as a business strategy that responded to popular criticism that corporations were indifferent to workers' concerns. Welfare capitalism emerged in American corporate culture in the nineteenth century, but concerns introduced by modernization made it a viable corporate strategy for many companies in the United States by the 1920s.[36] According to Marchand, American corporations like General Motors responded to accusations that they were "soulless" and insensitive to workers by launching advertising campaigns that defined them as "human" rather than corporate institutions.[37] These corporations adopted welfare capitalism to "find a corporate soul as company executives spoke of the company's goal of achieving something higher than profits."[38] Their publicity stressed their support of welfare initiatives, leadership in society, and contribution to the nation. By the 1920s, publicity for companies that adopted welfare capitalism championed service first and the ability to generate profits second. Some scholars of U.S. history, including Marchand, suggest that the 1930s ended many welfare capitalist programs and that by the end of World War II, business executives had adopted a "stick to business" mentality.[39] However, studies by Sanford Jacoby demonstrate that American companies such as Sears and Kodak modernized and developed a new form of welfare capitalism during the 1930s.[40] Mexicans had seen the two faces of America's corporate culture by the 1940s. Some American companies that entered the Mexican market before the 1940s, such as Phelps Dodge in 1918 and Ford Motors in 1925, had introduced American welfare capitalism in Mexico.[41] By contrast, American oil companies and other U.S. corporations that entered Mexico during the Díaz administration adopted America's "stick to business" approach.

As an American retailer that supported welfare capitalism and was strongly committed to the Good Neighbor Policy, Sears became the model for a new type of commercial relations between Mexico and the United States. Both Rockefeller and President Miguel Alemán cited Sears's success as an example of how the new commercial relationship between Mexico and the United States benefited both nations. Rockefeller considered Sears a "commercial diplomat" that would spread America's democracy by encouraging consumption. His definition of democracy was grounded in America's consumer culture, which associated material abundance and the ability to choose from a wide variety of merchandise with individual freedom.[42] It was part of a broader policy within the United States that used the contrast between America's abundance and "consumer democracy" and totalitarian authority, scarcity, and lack of freedom as a political tool against the Nazis and communists during the 1940s.[43] According to Seth Fein, films shown by the U.S. State Department mobile motion picture unit spread similar anticommunist propaganda in provincial areas in Mexico during the early 1950s.[44] Sears representatives championed America's consumer democracy as they argued that the freedom of consumers to choose from a variety of goods provided the basis for a democratic political structure in Latin

America.[45] In the words of John Gallagher, "Economic growth in a free society takes place at an accelerated rate where there exists some freedom of choice to purchase from a wide variety of consumer goods. I believe that the free play of the market in consumer goods—which provides the individual with the opportunity of making a choice—can be the basis from which will come a democratic political structure."[46] Sears argued that it provided Mexican consumers with variety and choice. It served as a commercial diplomat claiming to present material abundance and consumption as an alternative to communism.

Similar to Wood, Rockefeller and other U.S. diplomats supported welfare capitalism and a higher standard of living among Latin Americans. Rockefeller suggested that rapid economic and industrial growth made the United States and Latin America interdependent. He argued that as Americans "we can no longer pretend to be self-sufficient and [that we] don't need underdeveloped areas or that it is simply out of kindness of our hearts that we want to help."[47] He advocated the need to work with Latin Americans to raise their standard of living. He insisted that a higher standard of living among Latin Americans would guarantee the economic expansion of the United States and secure the comfortable lifestyle that Americans enjoyed. What will happen, he asked rhetorically, echoing concerns about the legacy of the Great Depression, if the United States reaches overproduction? According to Rockefeller, postwar economic stability required that U.S. companies find markets abroad.[48] Rockefeller claimed that the United States had to help Latin America "create a vast pool of consumer purchasing power for our business men, workers, and farmers to prosper, for they will be selling more [and] . . . helping to stabilize employment, farm prices, and profits."[49] Most important, the economic well-being of Latin Americans, according to Rockefeller, would provide American citizens with employment and "an assurance of an ever higher standard of living."[50]

Rockefeller supported U.S. cooperation with Latin America's industrial capitalism. He advocated an economic-development model similar to ISI as he concluded that the introduction of industrial machinery would increase the number of jobs and raise wages among Latin Americans, making it possible for them to purchase new products. Rockefeller argued, "As men unite their efforts with machines, they sell each other their needs. With the new buying power, they reach out into a circle—expanding production, creating a market as they become one themselves reaching . . . to the farthest concerns of the world to purchase materials and goods."[51] In other words, industrialization would trigger upward mobility and increase purchasing power in Latin America, which would allow the expansion of American companies. Sears initially agreed with this rationale for Latin America's capitalist development. In July 1947, however, aggressive Mexican protectionist economic policies challenged Sears operations in Mexico and ended the company's honeymoon.

Economic Nationalism and Sears Marketing

The shopping frenzy that characterized Sears's grand opening was a result of an aggressive advertising campaign (see figure 6.1). The advertising office in Chicago began advertising Sears's opening early in 1946 while construction for the Mexico City store was under way. It published editorials and ads introducing Sears to the Mexican people. According to Sears representatives, their initial advertising focused on "introducing the owners of Sears" to "show that the company was owned by common people: the butcher, the baker, the candle stick maker."[52] According to this advertising, Sears's decision to come to Mexico City had been carefully planned based on interviews with Mexican women. It described Sears's arrival in Mexico as a "match that fit in perfectly—just like the perfect dress would fit a well-figured woman."[53] Sears's advertising also claimed that Mexico had earned the privilege of being a "window to Latin America" because of its leadership in industrial growth, marketing, and banking and that it had earned an international reputation thanks to its rich historical tradition, prosperity, and potential.[54]

Sears's preopening publicity focused on building customer acceptance. Sears sponsored half-hour radio programs that consisted of accounts of the growth of Sears in the United States and its introduction in Mexico. The programs told the audience that the Mexico City Sears store was a store of and for the Mexican people and that it would benefit Mexican consumers and employees and stimulate national commercial growth. Sears advertised in the leading Mexico City newspapers: *Excélsior*, *El Universal*, *Novedades*, and *La Prensa*. It ran ads on Fridays, Sundays, and Wednesdays because marketing experts considered Saturdays, Mondays, and Thursdays the "best shopping days" in Mexico City.[55] Sears also placed billboards in strategic locations such as the four main entrances to Mexico City and the airport to "direct tourists and native motorists to Sears."[56] Publicity described Sears products as high-quality merchandise with low prices. According to company representatives, publicity focused on "building customer acceptance, which would become apparent only when every [trade]mark is synonymous to Sears."[57] According to the director of preopening publicity, Marvin Lunde, Sears's reputation as a distributor of high-quality products with low prices became so widespread in Mexico that it turned into word-of-mouth publicity, creating some misunderstandings. Publicity mentioning that refreshments would be served during the grand opening led some people to believe that Sears

Figure 6.1. Sears ad announcing the grand opening of its Mexico City store in February 1947. ("Sears, Roebuck de México: La institución que conquistó a México en tres dias," *Publicidad: Tarifas Oficiales, La Revista de los Ejecutivos de Negocio* 3 [June 1949]: 13, courtesy of the ANP)

was going to give free merchandise to customers as part of its grand opening celebration.[58]

The massive publicity campaign conducted prior to Sears's opening led to four months of dramatic business success. Mexico's ANP said Sears had "conquered Mexico in three days" (see figure 6.2). It claimed that Sears had launched the most successful preopening advertising campaign up to that time. The shopping frenzy declined after the first three days, but impressive sales continued.

By April 1947, some Sears executives reported that they expected the store's "honeymoon" to end soon, but high-volume sales continued. To their surprise, the honeymoon ended as a result of government intervention in the economy and not as a result of natural market conditions.

President Alemán ended Sears's initial success in July 1947 when he signed a presidential decree that raised tariffs and prohibited the import of luxury items. Alemán's protectionist policy was a response to fluctuations in the international market and part of the nation's desperate effort to industrialize. It offered a practical solution to Mexico's adverse trade balance immediately after World War II. Mexico had accumulated a $300 million trade surplus thanks to its increased exports to the United States during the war, but it had reached a deficit of $130 million by 1946.[59] Alemán's policy sought to develop national industries through ISI in order to manufacture products previously imported from abroad, reduce Mexico's dependence on industrialized countries, create jobs, raise the standard of living of urban residents, and ultimately allow Mexico to "catch up" with industrialized countries.[60] To this end, the Mexican government encouraged national and foreign investment in sectors that supported industrial growth.[61] Ironically, Alemán's ISI encouraged economic nationalism as a development strategy while simultaneously placing the United States as a model of the type of modern industrial prosperity Mexicans could achieve.[62] ISI sup-

Figure 6.2. Headline describing Sears as "the institution that conquered Mexico in three days." ("Sears, Roebuck de México: La institución que conquistó a México en tres dias," *Publicidad: Tarifas Oficiales, La Revista de los Ejecutivos de Negocio* 3 (June 1949): 12, courtesy of the ANP)

ported policies that seemed politically and economically nationalist, but its ultimate goal was to make it possible for Mexico to achieve a level of industrial and
economic development equivalent to that of the United States.[63] However, ISI
encouraged new forms of investment. It encouraged investment in manufacturing (instead of oil, mining, and transportation) in the form of joint ventures.[64] In
other words, Alemán's ISI policies were not threatening to Sears, but they established clear ground rules for how Sears should operate in Mexico: Sears could
not import its merchandise from the United States if the merchandise could be
manufactured in Mexico. Sears learned to deal effectively with Mexican policies, but not before trying unsuccessfully to change them. It initially perceived
Alemán's ISI as hindering its operations. Its personnel believed that Mexican
manufacturers could not compete with American suppliers.

Sears expressed its objection to ISI in June 1947 by presenting itself as a defender of Mexico's middle class. Wood wrote to Mexico's minister of commerce
urging him to lift import restrictions for the sake of Mexico's middle class. He
argued that Sears used to sell a particular refrigerator in Mexico City for 1,100
pesos prior to import restrictions but was forced to sell "an inferior model from
local manufacturers for nineteen hundred pesos after the embargo."[65] Sears's
petition addressed the vulnerability of Mexico City's middle class and its dependence on larger issues, such as Mexican exports, monetary instability, and
competitiveness in the international market, which neither the minister of commerce nor President Alemán could easily control. Mexico's adverse currency and
trade balance created uncertainties and threatened consumers, whose standard
of living declined as the prices of products increased. The standard of living
among middle-class residents, according to Theodore Houser of the Sears Latin
American division in Chicago, could not be maintained in Mexico because increasing prices made the cost of living very high.[66] Lower incomes and inflation
forced middle-class families to choose old-fashioned iceboxes and hire maids
instead of purchasing refrigerators and washing machines. ISI went far beyond
slowing Sears's dramatic beginning in Mexico; it reminded Sears that the international market and national economic policies affected the purchasing power
of the emerging Mexican middle class. Sears was not able to persuade Alemán to
rescind ISI and was forced to carry out retailing differently than it had originally
planned.

Sears used its compliance with Mexican law to strengthen its public image
as a company that supported Mexican patriotism. A 1929 constitutional decree
required retailers to display "Made in Mexico by the Mexican people" tags on
Mexican merchandise.[67] Sears welcomed the idea of identifying its corporate
operations with Mexico's revolutionary and nationalist heritage. It presented
Sears as a Mexican company that respected Mexican values and encouraged

economic and industrial growth in Mexico. It "stressed its involvement with Mexican nationalism rather than exhibiting aloofness," as previously displayed by oil companies.[68] Sears's publicity reminded customers that most of its merchandise was made by local manufacturers. By 1948, the company also highlighted the local origin of its merchandise even when the products were U.S. brands. It argued that locally manufactured American brand-name products "conformed to U.S. standards of quality and styling," which guaranteed the best quality in Mexican manufacturing.[69] The company's persistence in illustrating American "superiority" in quality reflected research findings that suggested that Latin Americans wanted "mass produced merchandise and preferred anything with U.S. labels."[70] However, stating that American merchandise was better than Mexican products was not politically or commercially appropriate since it might trigger anti-American nationalism. To this end, appropriating policies and practices that demonstrated the company's "patriotism" to Mexican law while simultaneously highlighting the American quality of its merchandise forged a middle ground in which the suggestion that Mexican merchandise was inferior to American brand names coexisted with nationalist rhetoric. Most important, the company's publicity implied that Sears would elevate Mexican manufacturing to American standards and quality.

Sears used welfare capitalism to identify Sears as a Mexican company that fostered the nation's social democratic ideals, which, according to Sears, Mexicans had heroically achieved through the revolution. It introduced low-priced lunch programs, paid holidays, medical services, scholarship programs, and a profit-sharing plan. Profit-sharing served as a political tool in Mexico. Sears advertised its profit-sharing as an example of the achievements made by the Mexican Revolution. Coincidentally, Sears's profit-sharing implemented some of the most radical aspects of the 1917 constitution, the hallmark of the revolution.[71] Sears complied with Mexican labor policies and established programs that (at least symbolically) resembled radical constitutional reform. Sears employees welcomed the company's programs. According to Jorge Bonilla, "Profit-sharing was Sears's most effective management strategy primarily because employees actually felt that they owned part of the company."[72] Similarly, Ernesto Zatarain stated that profit-sharing especially benefited Mexican employees who had their shares of the company's profits automatically deposited into Sears's stock holdings.[73] Sears also sponsored sporting events, such as baseball tournaments, and social events among employees. These events created an environment in which, according to Bonilla, employees and management considered themselves members of the "Sears family."[74] According to Bonilla, the environment of the company was so amiable that "you actually felt a member of a big family."[75] Wood represented the paternal figure of the "Sears family." Ironically, the corporate paternalism centered on Wood represented a shift from the popular paternalism associated with Cárdenas during the 1930s.[76]

Sears's welfare capitalism did not mean that Mexicans controlled Sears, but it reflected the company's efforts to establish good relations with Mexican employees and to operate within a cultural middle ground. It offered a corporate strategy that political leaders found useful in the late 1940s because it made the corporate sector instead of the state directly responsible for the well-being of Mexican workers. It provided a formula that President Alemán found particularly useful for ending state subsidy of social programs that provided assistance to the working class. Alemán distanced his administration from the belief that the state was directly responsible for the basic economic necessities of the people. Instead, he encouraged the corporate sector to assume such responsibilities and promised state assistance to businesses in exchange.[77] It is not surprising that Alemán used Sears as a model for Mexico's industrialization and as an example of a new formula for commercial relations between Mexico and the United States. According to Rockefeller, Alemán responded to merchant complaints against Sears by stating, "You people go back to study the methods used by Sears and adopt those methods in your own industries. It is the greatest thing that has happened to Mexico."[78] Alemán's approach was not coincidental. Sears created a space for Mexico's middle class through consumption, and its corporate operations after July 1947 became a model for Alemán's industrial capitalism. Sears's marketing strategy and corporate identification with the middle class tapped into the political agenda of the Mexican government in the 1940s. The Alemán administration made the growth of the urban middle class a top priority. Alemán, like other political leaders in the 1940s, presented upward mobility into the ranks of the middle class as the ultimate goal of the Mexican Revolution and the nation's industrial capitalism.

America's Middle-Class Retailer and Import Restrictions in Mexico

Industrial and commercial growth modeled on ISI led to the expansion of Mexico City's middle class despite Sears's initial judgment that protectionist policies would have an adverse effect on the middle class. Mexico's middle class grew from 12.5 percent of the population in 1940 to 25 percent in 1950.[79] An increasing number of jobs in store management, office employment, medicine, education, and civil service supported upward mobility into the ranks of the middle class. In the meantime, leisure activities expanded as urban residents found new ways to enjoy their middle-class lifestyle. Mexico City's middle-class residents began touring different parts of the country and attending nightclubs and sporting events, among other forms of entertainment. Tourism became a "rite of passage" into the middle class.[80] The growth of the middle class also created markets for industries such as radio, film, and printing.[81] Clothing, stoves, refrigerators, and other products were available to middle-class residents at shops on the city's west side and in the downtown area. The location of one's residence also served as a symbol of class status. The middle class moved away from the downtown area to the periphery of the city in the 1920s and 1930s. By the 1940s, Mexico City's middle class lived in areas like the southern part of Colonia Roma, Colonia Polanco, La Condesa, and Hipódromo and in the southern *colonias* of Del Valle and Tlacopac.[82] Economic growth and the emergence of different forms of entertainment expanded the definition of middle-class status by the 1940s beyond the previous bourgeois attitude that reduced the middle class to *gente decente* and professionals living in urban areas.

Sears introduced two definitions of the middle class in Mexico: one rationalized the socioeconomic status of Mexicans and was used as a tool for corporate planning; the other was a cultural definition that established middle-class status through consumption and transplanted Sears's corporate identity in Mexico. A customer survey conducted by Sears during its first two months of operation in Mexico reported that 35 percent of the 207 people interviewed were "well-to-do" individuals who bought some luxury goods, owned an old car, and rented an apartment. Fifty-seven percent of the customers were middle-class people who had the basic necessities, some comforts, but few luxuries.[83] They could educate their children and subscribe to the daily paper. In terms of occupation, 37 percent of the people interviewed were government employees and professionals such as doctors, lawyers, teachers, and police officers. Based on the survey, Sears considered business executives, plant managers, and other professionals the nucleus of a rapidly expanding middle class that had buying power to form the backbone of Sears's clientele.[84] Sears used a socioeconomic definition of Mexico's middle class for market analysis and corporate planning, a process that was vital to the company's success and, according to Chandler, to American capitalism.[85]

In its publicity, Sears classified its customers as middle class regardless of their socioeconomic status. It portrayed a romanticized image of Sears as an agent of consumer democracy that made merchandise that was previously a luxury of the elite available to the masses. Middle-class Mexicans, according to Sears, had two options prior to its arrival. They could purchase their merchandise from small shops or street vendors who "hawked their myriad wares to crowds and to whom the practice of haggling over price was considered a fine art," or they could buy goods at luxurious retail stores that sold merchandise at prices most Mexico City residents could not afford.[86] Retail stores were mainly "large department stores of pre-1910 French vintage, whose iron balconies rose in the skies like nineteenth century opera boxes and whose merchandise policies seemed to be of the same vintage."[87] According to Sears, other department stores catered to high-income groups, offered no variety, and sold in small volume at high prices.[88]

The marketing pitch that Sears was a "democratic" force compared to elite department stores was not new to America's retailing giant. Sears had used mass marketing as a democratizing process since the early twentieth century. Its concept of mass marketing and consumption as a democratizing force was part of America's corporate culture. The introduction of Sears as a synonym of consumer democracy and middle-class status revealed Sears's imperialist side since it spread concepts that were deeply rooted in American society.[89] Sears's advertising defined democracy strictly at the level of consumption. In the process, it blurred the lines between income or occupation and the cultural aspects of middle-class status. Although social status was largely determined by income, purchasing at Sears marked, at the level of consumption, upward mobility into the ranks of the middle class. In this context, middle-class status depended on the store's ability to attract customers from diverse socioeconomic levels, which was determined by its response to local challenges.

Sears held up middle-class status as a model for its customers and employees. As an employer, it defined the middle class in economic terms by suggesting that Mexico City residents could pull themselves up the social ladder by working at Sears. It claimed that the company created professional and technical jobs that allowed employees to maintain a middle-class lifestyle. Sears suggested that it offered Mexican employees and manufacturers opportunities for upward mobility by stimulating industrial and economic growth.[90] As an American department store, Sears provided a space and merchandise that offered a cultural definition of the middle class through consumption.[91] It presented shopping at Sears as a public expression of a person's social status. Expressing one's social status through shopping was not a new phenomenon in Mexico City. Shopping at exclusive department stores like El Palacio de Hierro served as a public expression of upper-middle-class and elite status in Mexico City prior to the 1940s. However, associating middle-class status with a department store like Sears was new. By presenting itself as a middle-class department store, Sears created a space where Mexico City's middle class could publicly buy merchandise and interact in the public sphere. However, Sears's commitment to remaining a middle-class store after the summer of 1947 required that the company change its original marketing approach in Mexico. Most important, it forced Sears to acclimate to local conditions.

Local Solutions to Local Problems, Import Restrictions, and Mexican Manufacturing

Sears responded to the July 1947 import restrictions by tapping into local suppliers and developing an industrial infrastructure that provided the benefits of vertical integration without the corporate risk. Instead of developing manufacturing plants or moving into industries that supplied merchandise, Sears provided loans to small manufacturers who agreed to supply the store with specific product lines. Manufacturers paid off the loans with merchandise, but the contracts did not require Sears to purchase the merchandise.[92] Thus, Sears took a very small financial risk in exchange for receiving a steady supply of merchandise. Unlike other companies that vertically integrated the manufacturing of different product lines, Sears was risk-free at the production level. This was no small achievement. Sears was able to secure a steady supply of merchandise in a country where the industrial infrastructure was not able to keep up with demand. Loans to Mexican manufacturers also gave Sears some control over production. Sears considered monitoring the production and quality of merchandise a crucial component of its retailing. The company took pride in maintaining customer satisfaction, and this commitment required keeping suppliers, especially Mexican suppliers, on a "short leash." Sears supplied manufacturers with instructions for manufacturing and required that they receive training in production and quality-control methods.[93] Experts from Chicago frequently visited shops in Mexico City. They monitored manufacturing procedures and tested the merchandise to make sure that Mexican production met American standards. Sears's loans also gave small-scale manufacturers in Mexico the opportunity to expand their businesses. For example, a rack manufacturer expanded his business dramatically as a result of a loan he received from Sears and eventually sold to other department stores after he finished paying off the loan.[94]

Sears's ability to make lucrative profits throughout the 1940s despite protectionist policies was impressive, and its corporate strategy offered a good example of the ways in which commercial relations between Mexico and the United States were changing in the late 1940s. By 1949, Sears was purchasing about 75 percent of its Mexican merchandise from local manufacturers.[95] According to Flavia Derossi, other forms of business interaction between Mexico and the United States besides the introduction of companies like Sears also increased after World War II. She reported that 67 out of the 100 Mexican entrepreneurs she interviewed had traveled to the United States on business trips. One entrepreneur claimed that "Sears taught Mexicans" effective retailing strategies and then Mexican businessmen had perfected them.[96] He reported that Sears had also taught Mexican consumers to demand quality. Sears took pride in publicizing quality as a hallmark of its merchandise. In addition to its close monitoring of suppliers, it conducted thorough testing of random samples of merchandise to make sure that products met Sears's standards. It is ironic that Sears entered Mexico because the U.S. government was pushing exports to the Mexican market immediately after the war and that Sears then undercut U.S. exports by improving the quality of Mexican manufacturing as a result of Alemán's protectionist measures. Sears's strategy of purchasing merchandise from local manufacturers proved successful, and the company transplanted the corporate approach it learned in the "commercial laboratory" of Mexico as it rapidly expanded to other parts of Latin America. By 1949, Sears managers were convinced that "the success of Sears [in Mexico and Latin America] depended on the successful establishment of a source relationship, on the efficiency of local manufacturers, and on the indoctrination of local manufacturers in the principle of mass production at a low unit profit."[97] Sears's objections to ISI ended by 1949. The company's advertising presented its contracts with Mexican manufacturers as an indication that Sears was a Mexican company that supported Mexico's industrial capitalism, which according to Sears would offer Mexicans upward mobility into the ranks of the middle class.

Innovating Mexican Retailing

Sears's efforts to remain competitive in the Mexican market in the midst of protectionist policies forced Sears to develop effective marketing and advertising techniques. It presented itself as an innovative force that would use the latest and most sophisticated U.S. merchandising methods to improve Mexico's industrial capitalism even though Sears's marketing approach was driven by Mexican government policies, local conditions, and popular values and practices. Import duties, for example, made imported cookware too expensive for Mexican consumers by 1949. It seemed nearly impossible for Sears to compete against local vendors, who sold cookware at much lower prices. Sears initially tried to work with local manufacturers to develop special cookware models in the hopes of becoming competitive, but it "could not sell enough cookware products to make designing new models worthwhile for manufacturers."[98] Determined to increase its cookware sales, Sears asked manufacturers not only to produce new models but also to design better-quality cookware. It attempted to raise the quality of its local cookware products to meet U.S. standards to give them an advantage over the poorly manufactured low-quality merchandise its competitors sold in Mexico. Sears introduced "new methods of enameling, a complete revision of merchandise styling, and a much more rigid system of factory inspection" in its efforts to increase sales.[99] The strategy worked, and Sears became a successful retailer of cookware in Mexico.

Import restrictions made Sears de México a competitive middle-class retailer of soft-line or small-ticket items, which consisted of clothing, shoes, and other apparel-industry products. Sears introduced blue jeans, sports shirts, and other ready-to-wear clothing for men and women.[100] It increased its sales of shoes, one of its most popular soft-line products, by providing a "broader assortment in teenage and sports styles with special promotions on nurse's shoes, comfort shoes, play shoes, and slippers."[101] Sears de México made 44 percent of its sales on soft-line items by spring 1949. By 1954, it "increased its ready-to-wear business four to five times from its initial volume" as the demand for ready-to-wear clothing, shoes, and other soft-line items increased.[102] Sears's emphasis on marketing soft-line products introduced American fashion and clothing styles to Mexico's middle class. Its soft-line products catered to a younger audience and encouraged new consumer habits. The company's compliance with Mexican government policies gradually made Sears de México a large distributor of soft-line products while its parent company in the United States continued to earn its well-established reputation as a hardware or big-ticket-item retailer to America's middle class. Sears's soft-line merchandise represented only 20 percent of company sales in the United States.[103] The emphasis on marketing soft-line products along with other innovative measures kept Sears de México profitable in the midst of economic nationalism.

Sears's marketing revolutionized the apparel industry in Mexico. Before Sears, Mexicans typically bought yard goods (cloth) and hired seamstresses to make their clothing. Even elite department stores like El Palacio de Hierro offered custom-made clothing until the 1940s. El Palacio de Hierro hired Margarita Rostan in 1929 to head its fashion department. Rostan traveled to France and New York to purchase fashions, which she brought to Mexico for display. She greeted women customers, helped them pick out dress designs, took their measurements, and then had the dresses made for them.[104] Sears changed dressmaking with the introduction of ready-made clothing. According to a reporter for the *Chicago Sun Times*, Mexican women could not resist purchasing the dresses neatly displayed at Sears.[105] Ready-made dresses became the most popular item in the store by 1951. Sears displayed dresses on the first floor in order to give them "a prime location."[106] Swimsuits and sweaters were also sold on the first floor throughout the year.

Adding to the innovation of ready-made clothing, Sears allowed customers to touch the merchandise, a practice that no other Mexican department store allowed prior to Sears. El Palacio de Hierro sold ready-made swimsuits before Sears's arrival, but Sears was able to market such products at lower prices. Catalina swimwear and sweaters were so popular that Sears maintained its low sale prices throughout the year in order to attract customers. Brightly colored swim trunks and jackets were introduced in 1951, but only for boys because, according to Sears representatives, "Mexican men dressed conservatively . . . [and] were more restrained than men in the United States."[107] Sears introduced ready-made suits of 13 ounce rayon at 26–40 pesos each. These suits were not of the highest quality, but they were less expensive than the $65–85 wool suits that competitors customarily sold. Rayon suits were mid-level products in terms of quality compared to wool suits. They accounted for an increase in sales of about 30 percent in the men's clothing department within a four-month period early in 1951.[108] Sears also added wool and leather items to its clothing department. Its U.S. stores did not carry wool products and sold very little leather clothing. According to a reporter for the *New York Daily News Record*, the Mexico City Sears store sold about twenty-five leather sports coats a year for $35 each while few, if any, leather jackets were sold in the United States.[109] Sears's introduction of leather clothing represented a new phenomenon in Mexico.

Sears also introduced an innovative credit program in Mexico that allowed customers to purchase products they could not afford otherwise. Customers who could not afford a 1,500 peso refrigerator could make monthly payments for up to three years without having to pay interest. Close to "one third of Sears sales were done on credit, [and] almost half of credit sales were 'big ticket' items."[110] Sears also introduced a coupon credit plan in an effort to increase sales on small-ticket items. Customers could purchase a coupon that gave them up to 250 pesos in credit. They made a 25 peso deposit in order to activate their personal credit line and then made monthly payments once they started charging items. This credit plan worked like a credit card, and it allowed customers to increase their purchase of shoes, clothing, and other smaller items. Sears's credit plans conveniently hooked customers on the store as they coached Mexicans on financial planning. Sears's credit programs provided Mexicans with a mechanism that directly allocated personal income to the purchase of specific items before such income made it into personal or family savings. Large retailing stores like El Palacio de Hierro had credit plans for customers, but they sold very little on credit because they marketed to upper-class and upper-middle-class residents who considered purchasing on credit a sign of lower social status. Other stores that sold on credit placed many restrictions on credit as a result of numerous difficulties they encountered collecting monthly installments. They hired a person to collect monthly payments from house to house. Credit approval was a complicated process, and department stores were very strict in verifying an applicant's assets. As a result, very few customers purchased on credit before Sears.

Sears eventually expanded its credit system and asked customers to make monthly payments at the store. Credit customers generally responded well and not only paid their monthly installments on time but also ended up browsing and purchasing new merchandise. Some customers kept their credit at the maximum limit despite making monthly payments because they could not resist making new purchases on credit as they brought their monthly installments to the store. Sears's credit plan secured "repeat sales" and maintained a pool of loyal customers. Customers who did not qualify for credit or had reached the maximum credit limit could purchase new merchandise through Sears's layaway system. According to this program, Sears would hold an item for up to six months as long as the customer paid 20 percent of the cost up front and then paid the remaining amount in six months.[111] Store personnel contacted customers who did not pay for the merchandise in six months and returned the initial deposit.

The lack of sales resistance from Mexican customers who entered the store to make credit payments and ended up either adding purchases to their credit line or putting products on layaway was not coincidental. Sears's interior architecture and space arrangement were designed to seduce customers into shopping. The store had earned a reputation in American retailing for its ability to carefully plan interior architecture and orchestrate space and displays in a manner that tactfully encouraged shopping. Sears established the store-planning and display department in 1932 in an effort to build new stores "inside out." Sears carefully designed displays and space arrangements to direct customers through each sales department. Retailers traditionally fit merchandise into buildings prior to 1932, but Sears changed this process by the 1930s. Sears "built the store around the merchandise" after 1932.[112] The new store-planning and display department made sure that each store had the "proper tables . . . proper fixtures . . . proper space for different departments . . . [to secure] the flow of customers from one part of the store to another."[113] The same building design and merchandise display were introduced in Mexico in the 1940s.

Sears also hoped to stimulate interest and seduce potential customers to come into the store through its window displays. Large retailing stores such as El Puerto Liverpool introduced window displays in Mexico in the early twentieth century.[114] Window displays became popular, especially at shoe stores throughout Mexico City. However, the display of merchandise was not very sophisticated. Retailers and department stores believed in three basic rules when it came to window displays by the late 1940s: displays had to have a theme; they had to present the merchandise in an attractive manner and multiple displays had to match; and they had to be interesting enough to make viewers stop, observe, and be seduced into entering the store.[115] Sears became a leader in designing window displays by the late 1940s by introducing elaborate themes. It

Un primer premio de $2,500.00 obtuvo este Aparador de Sears Roebuck de México, en un concurso que Philco organizara entre sus distribuidores de la República. El mundo gira en un sentido y los radios en el contrario; efectos de luz complementan el efecto. Diseñado por Luis Reynoso, director de decoración de S & R.

Figure 6.3. 1949 Sears window display advertising Philco radios. (*Publicidad: Tarifas Oficiales, La Revista de los Ejecutivos de Negocio* 6 [September 1949]: n.p., courtesy of the ANP)

won first prize in a 1949 competition for a display featuring Philco radios with the caption, "The world rotates one way, but radio rotates in the opposite direction" (see figure 6.3).[116] Luis Reynoso, the director of the decoration and display division at Sears, designed the display. Reynoso won many display competitions and gave Sears a reputation for being a leading window display advertiser in Mexico. Sears's personnel used success stories like that of Reynoso to promote Mexican nationalism and show the public that Sears was a Mexican store run by Mexicans for Mexicans. Ironically, the themes outlined in its displays often dealt with issues of globalization and the revolutionizing aspects of Western technology.

Sears introduced innovative retailing in Mexico by simplifying the purchasing process. Other stores generally kept merchandise locked in showcases and drawers, out of the reach of customers. To purchase an item, a customer had to endure a complicated process, which Sears considered off-putting to customers. A customer had to get a receipt for the item he or she wanted to purchase from the salesperson. The customer would then take the receipt to the cashier and pay for the item, getting another receipt that proved that he or she had paid. Both receipts were taken back to the sales clerk, who would give the customer the merchandise. In contrast, Sears displayed the merchandise for customers to see and touch and clearly marked the price. Customers could browse freely through the merchandise at Sears. Sears believed that customers would be more likely to make purchases if they could handle the merchandise.[117]

Sears considered accurate labeling of merchandise very important in gaining the trust of its customers. It discovered that Mexican stores (particularly small stores) often used labels that were misleading. For example, "if an item looked like wool, it was often labeled as a one hundred percent wool item even if it contained forty percent rayon."[118] Sears took pride in declaring that "if an item was fifty percent rayon and fifty percent wool, it was clearly marked as such, delighting customers who felt certain that the item was just as good as what they had been told elsewhere was one hundred percent wool."[119] Sears also introduced fixed marked pricing of merchandise. El Palacio de Hierro and other department stores had used fixed marked pricing since the late nineteenth century, but price haggling was very common throughout Mexico City among small shops that catered to Mexico's middle class. Sears managers, however, reported that "the crowning touch was a simple sign above the entrance of the Mexico City store which read 'satisfaction guaranteed or your money back'; no one else had told Mexican customers this before. . . . No other policy did so much to insure the success of Sears in Mexico—and throughout Latin America for that matter."[120] Guaranteeing customer satisfaction clearly indicated a shift in what retailers valued. It transformed retailing from the simple distribution of merchandise to a profession that valued customer service and satisfaction. Sears promised to satisfy its customers as a systematic method of marketing its merchandise. Rather than simply making a sale, it wanted to develop a relationship of trust to gain repeat business. Sears leaders advertised their retailing practices as innovative. They effectively presented these practices to the Mexican public as proof that Sears was a modern store that was different from its competitors.[121]

Although Sears successfully acclimated to local conditions and used innovative marketing strategies, it experienced difficulties in other areas. Sears's mail-order retailing failed in Mexico. It introduced mail-order sales by sending 20,000 catalogs to Mexican families in provincial areas. The first catalogs produced a total of 800 orders in 1947, but the number increased to about 400 a month by January 1948. The distribution of a second catalog in May 1948 boosted business to about 1,000 orders a month, and the third catalog in November 1948 increased the figure to about 1,400 a month.[122] Sears had opened four mail-order houses in Mexico by November 1948, including one in Torreón and another in San Luis Potosí. It used Mexican women to model dresses and coats in the first few catalogs. The models were women who worked for Sears in secretarial positions or the sales department.[123] The catalog designers apparently did not consider Mexican women good models for selling lingerie. Describing the Sears catalogs in Mexico, a reporter for *Women's Wear* in New York stated, "For the bra and underwear section, typical American girls smiled broadly in comparison with the sour look of most of the swarthy Mexican girls."[124]

Failing to generate profits in its mail-order department, Sears tried to boost mail-order sales in 1949 by increasing publicity. It distributed circulars at the post office urging customers to pick up a Sears catalog, and it advertised its mail-order service in phone directories, newspaper ads, and flyers in different cities. These aggressive publicity methods, according to Sears representatives, were feasible because advertising costs were "unbelievably low" in Mexico.[125] However, although aggressive advertising had created the shopping frenzy Sears experienced during its grand opening, in 1949 it did not save Sears's mail-order department. Instead, it increased operating costs without radically increasing sales, which contributed to the closure of the mail-order department.[126] Publicity in itself did not guarantee Sears's success despite the ANP's claims that advertising had made it possible for Sears to "conquer Mexico in three days."

A number of factors led to the failure of Sears's mail-order department. Wood did not fully understand the complexities of 1940s Mexico. He often compared conditions in 1940s Mexico to conditions in the United States in the 1890s when Sears's catalog sales boomed and made the company a retailing giant. Unlike Americans in the 1890s, however, provincial middle-class Mexicans were not accustomed to purchasing merchandise by mail. El Palacio de Hierro had marketed its merchandise to Mexico's provincial elite during the early twentieth century through catalogs.[127] However, catalog sales were sluggish, and El Palacio de Hierro apparently discontinued its mail-order operations by the 1920s. *Negro y Blanco y Labores*, as well as other magazines, developed a small mail-order market among middle-class women in provincial areas, but it advertised different products from the type of merchandise Sears sold in catalogs. Women readers of *Negro y Blanco* wrote letters about personal issues and asked for suggestions from magazine columnists. Many of the letters requested tips on ways to enhance beauty or improve home decorating, among other concerns. The columnists responded to such letters by suggesting items women could purchase by mail. *Negro y Blanco* apparently had a contract with El Atoyac department store.

Negro y Blanco mail-order sales had a "touch of intimacy" as magazine executives publicized personal accounts as an effective marketing tool.[128] *Negro y Blanco* had no publicity or catalog production and mailing expenses. Most important, the magazine had an audience of about 200,000 subscribers throughout the country. Thus, *Negro y Blanco* had a comparative advantage over Sears in the mail-order business, a form of retailing that was not widely accepted in Mexico in the first place. To make things worse, Sears failed to understand this aspect of Mexican society. Sears executives repeatedly blamed illiteracy and poor mail service for their failure in mail-order sales. Illiteracy remained high among peasants and working-class Mexicans, but it was not a problem among the urban middle-class residents who represented Sears's mail-order market. The mail-order department continued to function until 1951, even though it was clear by 1949 that mail-order business in Mexico would not work. Sears remained profitable despite losses in its mail-order division. To this end, the failure to capitalize on mail-order sales was simply part of the company's learning process in Mexico.

Nationalism, Employee Resistance, and Corporate Restructuring

Relations between Sears's top American management in Mexico and its employees had deteriorated by early 1949. The first president of Sears in Mexico, Walter Reed, established a friendly and paternalistic relationship with Mexicans in 1947. However, tensions between Mexican employees and American management emerged when N. A. Barron replaced Reed as president. Employees formed the Sears Projustice Committee, which became an "anti-Barron" organization, shortly after Reed's departure. Tensions between Mexican employees and Barron mounted in the spring of 1949. Employees sent a letter to Adolfo Ruiz Cortines, head of Mexico's Secretaría de Gobernación, Wood, and Barron that accused Barron of "despotism and discrimination against Mexicans."[129] The letter denounced Barron as racist for publicly stating that it would be impossible for Mexican workers to replace the "American brains" working at Sears. According to the letter, Barron's statement clearly revealed his disregard for Mexican intelligence and his lack of appreciation for the contribution of Mexicans to Sears. Most important, Sears employees reminded Ruiz Cortines that "the discriminating attitude of Mr. Barron is contrary to the nationalist sentiment of our government."[130]

Like their managing personnel, Sears employees did not hesitate to use Mexico's nationalist and revolutionary heritage to their benefit. They hoped Ruiz Cortines would intervene and force Barron to promote qualified Mexicans to positions left vacant by American employees. They accused Barron of denying Mexicans promotion by filling vacancies in top management positions with more Americans. They complained that "North Americans, with equal or less responsibility and capacity than many Mexicans, earned double or triple the salaries earned by Mexicans."[131] They argued that Barron's attitude was an affront to the hospitality Mexico had offered Sears and contrary to Wood's ideal that Sears and its employees were mutually beneficial. They reminded Wood that at his inauguration in February 1947 he had promised the Mexican people that Sears "would be a company of and for Mexicans and that trained and capable Mexicans would occupy important positions." Workers claimed that unlike Reed, Barron had not complied with these promises. Barron, according to them, had "imported a large number of North American 'extras,' taking away the opportunity for promotion from many hardworking, honorable, and very skilled Mexican citizens."[132]

Sears employees urged the Mexican government to use immigration laws to fight Barron's policies. They asked Ruiz Cortines not to allow American employees to remain in Mexico after their visas expired so that "Mexicans [could] occupy the positions left vacant, which was and is the wish of General Wood."[133] In response to the letter, Wood instructed Barron to reduce the number of American employees and ordered that no Mexican employees be fired. Mexico City's exclusive Bankers Club denied Sears membership in its prestigious organization and protested the comments, attitude, and actions of Barron.[134] Club leaders warned Wood that Barron did not represent Sears's original philosophy in Mexico. They stated, "We do not feel the present policy of your local management will produce the results you desire and expect."[135] The Bankers Club admitted Sears into the club when Wood replaced Barron with a new president, George Lynch, in August 1949.

Relations between Sears management and Mexican employees improved after Lynch became president. However, some of the tensions between Barron and Sears employees were the result of changes in the policies of the Mexican government and an increasing awareness among Mexican employees that they were receiving lower wages than American workers. As a result, Mexican employees did not stop at Barron's removal. They attempted to shape company operations in Mexico and even the personal behavior of American personnel. Sears management learned from Barron's experience that becoming *simpático* was instrumental for success in Mexico. The Chicago headquarters instructed Lynch to learn Spanish immediately and show courtesy toward Mexican government officials, professionals, businesspeople, and employees.[136] Wood, like Rockefeller, had stressed the significance of such personal and business manners since the early 1940s.

Mexican government officials and Sears leaders changed their personnel and operations to ease tensions among Sears employees. By 1949, the Mexican government enforced immigration policies "to force branches of American-owned Mexican companies to employ, insofar as possible, Mexican citizens."[137] It reduced the number of visas it granted to American employees, but it did not deny "visas for employees whose positions could not be filled by qualified Mexicans."[138] Sears stopped requesting visas for American trainees because they "created suspicion among the employees that they were going to stay and block the way for promoting [Mexicans] when and if a qualified personnel developed."[139] American employees slated for jobs in Latin America received training in Mexico from 1947 to 1949. The labor tensions of 1949 forced Sears to begin using Havana instead of Mexico as a training ground for Americans.

Labor tensions also led to an increase in the number of Mexican employees. Although the proportion of American employees had remained just below 3 percent throughout the 1940s, it declined after 1949. In 1947 2.2 percent of the Sears employees in Mexico were American, and in 1948, the proportion increased to 2.7 percent.[140] As a result of the labor tensions, the proportion of Americans employed by Sears in Mexico dropped to 1.7 percent in 1949. Only 1 percent of Sears employees were American by 1951.[141] Despite the restructuring, American employees continued to hold the top management and training positions. The decline in the number of American personnel after 1949, however, led to more consistent efforts to train Mexican personnel. Mexican workers began receiving training in Chicago and other cities in the United States. Jorge Bonilla visited the Chicago headquarters for training in company operations.[142] Promising Mexican students like Ernesto Zatarain received full scholarships from the Sears Scholarship Fund in the 1950s. According to Zatarain, Sears made it possible for him to study accounting at the Universidad Autónoma de Guadalajara. Sears later hired Zatarain at the Mexico City corporate office in the purchasing division. Zatarain believes that, considering his modest family background, his success would not have been possible without Sears's assistance, and as a result, he considers himself a "son of Sears."[143]

Sears considered training fundamental to the company's efficiency. It required that every employee undertake a thirty-day training program. New employees were given a training manual outlining their responsibilities and the operations of their department.[144] Bonilla translated manuals and questionnaires from English into Spanish in the Sears Latin American Translating Unit. Employees were required to pass an exam at the end of the program.[145] Sears reserved the right to dismiss employees if their performance was not satisfactory within thirty days. Training became institutionalized into what became known as the Sears Seven-Phase Training Program. The program included studying a seven-booklet series. Employees were required to take an exam at the end of each booklet. Of all the booklets he translated, Bonilla recalls "Getting Acquainted with Your Merchandise" as one of the most important in the training program. The booklet described the merchandise in each department. Another manual described different types of customers, stressing the importance of "silent customers," or people who do not complain even if they are not satisfied with the service or the merchandise they purchase. The booklet warned that these customers were the biggest threat to the store's success because they shared their negative experience with family members and friends.[146]

Sears's training program included familiarizing Mexican employees with basic corporate operations and language. Store management asked Bonilla to develop a dictionary of English terms used for basic Sears operations with detailed descriptions of the concepts. Each new employee received a dictionary. The company expected employees to learn terms like "pull stock," "shipping department," and "big- or small-ticket item."[147] According to Zatarain, Sears's effort to familiarize employees with its corporate language created a form of "Spanglish." He remembers employees commonly making statements such as "Voy al [I am going to the] 'shipping department.'"[148] Sears's commitment to training Mexicans in its corporate language and its instructions to American employees on the importance of being *simpático* in Mexico suggest that Sears insisted on educating Mexican and American employees in binational "cultural literacy."

Sears's training stressed commitment to complete customer satisfaction. Instructors began the training program by relating a classic story about customer satisfaction. According to the story, an elderly woman visited the president's office at the Chicago headquarters on a daily basis. She refused to talk to lower-level officials and claimed that she would continue coming to the president's office until she was allowed to talk to him. When the president finally agreed to talk to her, the woman complained that customer service representatives had refused to exchange a toothbrush she did not like after having used it for about a week. She argued that based on Sears's policy of "complete satisfaction or your money back," the customer service representatives should have returned her money. The woman said she had to use the toothbrush for a few days before deciding whether she liked it.[149] The narrative ended with a very clear lesson in customer service: the president gave the woman her money back in exchange for the toothbrush. Sears's commitment to "complete satisfaction or your money back" became a hallmark of the company and revolutionized Mexican retailing, according to Bonilla and Zatarain.[150] The policy was not a new phenomenon in the Mexican retail industry. El Palacio de Hierro's exclusive service to Mexico's elite promised customer satisfaction. However, Sears introduced this policy to nonelite sectors of Mexican society. Small shops and other department stores did not offer this guarantee. Sears also used "complete satisfaction or your money back" as an advertising pitch and presented the return of merchandise as a normal part of shopping. Sears also introduced warranty and repair services for its big-ticket items (refrigerators, stoves, washing machines, etc.). Sears guaranteed its merchandise for up to three months and gave customers the option of purchasing extended warranties for three- to five-year periods. Customers who purchased the extended warranties had Sears technicians perform repairs.[151]

Training manuals also outlined strategies for making the most profitable sales. For example, they instructed sales personnel to use a "trade up" or "trade down" system depending on the customer they assisted. Sales personnel were taught to "trade up" or direct customers to the most expensive merchandise if they did not show concern about cost. Manuals instructed personnel to "trade down" or direct customers to the least expensive merchandise if they expressed concern about cost.[152] The system required sales personnel to use their judgment in determining whether to trade up or trade down while answering questions and educating customers on the merchandise. In other words, Sears manuals gave specific instructions to personnel but allowed room for them to evaluate each situation and develop practical steps to increase the store's profits. The corporate training Sears provided made working at America's leading retailer in Mexico prestigious, according to Jorge Bonilla and Ernesto Zatarain.[153] In other words, Mexicans could acquire a sense of "professionalism" by going through Sears's corporate training programs and working for the company, even without a *licenciatura* or college degree. Bonilla and Zatarain had college degrees, but most Mexicans working at Sears did not. Mastering specific skills and procedures at Sears gave them a sense of legitimacy as "professionals."

The changes Sears implemented in its training programs and corporate structure after 1949 restored its public image as a mechanism for upward mobility. Mexicans were not hired simply because they knew local conditions better than Americans. They were expected to learn the skills that would allow them to hold top-level management positions in Mexico. However, Sears's efforts to create more equitable opportunities for American and Mexican employees did not mean the status of Mexicans automatically rose to that of American managers or employees. Only a few Mexicans had the privilege of receiving training in the United States, and those who did went back to Mexico after their training. Considering Sears's philosophy of "acclimating to local conditions," some Mexicans who were trained in the United States should have been sent to open stores in Latin America because they understood Latin American culture better than American employees. Instead, American employees trained in Latin American business culture in Havana had the opportunity to gain prestige and recognition, as well as upward mobility, by heading new store operations in Latin America. These employees were also guaranteed high-ranking positions at the Chicago headquarters once they returned to the United States.

Reports in 1949 created concerns about Sears's ability to remain a competitive middle-class retailer in Mexico. Lynch reported to Wood that the popular perception of Sears as a distributor of high-quality low-priced merchandise had changed.[154] According to him, Sears was now considered one of the most expensive stores in Mexico.[155] Lynch blamed previous management for abandoning comparative price advertising after 1947, when Sears gained a reputation as the store with the lowest prices in Mexico. He reported that competitors had given Sears bad publicity during the peso devaluation in late 1947 and 1948, which made imported American merchandise more expensive. Most important, competitors, according to Lynch, had blasted Sears by comparing only their lowest-priced merchandise with Sears products.[156] Lynch accurately evaluated some of the challenges Sears encountered in its first two years in Mexico. However, he did not fully understand that its biggest challenge was the fact that the Mexican middle class as defined by Sears had a much lower purchasing power than the U.S. middle class.

Lynch hoped to revitalize Sears's reputation and competitiveness in Mexican retailing by restructuring its operations and management. He changed Sears's publicity strategies. Before Lynch, Mexican personnel did not break down the advertising budget by division. As a result, according to Lynch, the divisions with large production and sales capacity did not receive special attention from the advertising department.[157] Lynch argued that the lack of departmentalized advertising prevented Sears from strengthening its position on items that could become the most competitive. He complained that the average newspaper ad was a "hodgepodge of largely unrelated merchandise."[158] He pointed out that there was no liaison between the advertising department and each division head. Another problem was that advertising was planned a month in advance, and there was no coordination between stock levels in the store and publicity. The store "grouped its merchandise by divisions, by related departments, by item, and by price, but there was no knowledge of promotional finesse in the store."[159] According to Lynch, Sears personnel did not handle inventories properly prior to his arrival. He argued that "budgets were made at the beginning of each season and were never readjusted to changing trends."[160] Sears could do better than its Latin American competitors in this area, according to Lynch, because Latin Americans were not concerned about inventories and budgets and believed that you "keep on buying, and keep on selling, and the good Lord will take care of you somehow."[161]

Lynch attempted to restore Sears's reputation as a low-priced distributor and take Sears back to the pre–June 1947 days when people said, "Shop at Sears and save."[162] He innovated Sears advertising. According to the *Wall Street Journal*, Sears became "the biggest newspaper advertiser in Mexico."[163] Lynch worked closely with the advertising division to coordinate advertising among division heads, buyers, and top management. He reestablished the connection between Mexico City's advertising division and the publicity personnel in Chicago. Advertising was analyzed by division in order to identify the markets that Sears management wanted to strengthen. Lynch revitalized Sears's window display publicity. He asked the publicity department to closely coordinate newspaper advertising with window displays. Lynch reinstated price-markdown promotions in order to accelerate the flow of merchandise from producer to consumer. Mexican retailers did not mark down their products, and as a result, the merchandise moved out of their stores at a slow pace. The manager of the Mexico City store reported in 1951, "Goods were marked down after six months until they moved out of the store."[164] Sears introduced a three-day clearance sale at the end of each month and used promotional advertising in its efforts to regain a reputation as a retailer of high-quality merchandise at low prices.

Sears held promotional events as part of the restructuring headed by Lynch after 1949.[165] It introduced a January white goods sale, sporting goods week, and hardware week. It coordinated its advertising displays with publicity for promotional events. It also utilized local advertising practices to publicize its promotions. For example, the Monterrey store hired an airplane to drop 60,000 sale circulars throughout the city.[166] This type of promotional advertising would have triggered fines for littering if Sears had attempted it in the United States. Sears also introduced promotional advertising around Mexican holidays, including Mother's Day. Sears offered packaged merchandise for customers to purchase as gifts. It decided to honor the entire family by introducing gifts for Father's Day, Valentine's Day, and Baby's Week. For Father's Day, "all Sears stores in Mexico were decorated with 'Father's Day' streamers and gifts were featured in newspaper advertisements."[167] A reporter for the *New York Daily News Record* stated that Sears marketing was focusing on making Father's Day popular in Mexico. According to him, Sears displayed posters advertising Father's Day gifts that read, "Father hopes for something from Sears" or "Let's understand father on Father's Day."[168] Window displays featured Father's Day gifts for wives and daughters to purchase.

Although observing Mother's Day conformed to Mexico's tradition of honoring mothers for their work in the domestic sphere, celebrating the father's role in the family was not a traditional practice. The father was seen as the breadwinner and the family member who was active in the public sphere. Sears's Father's Day promotions celebrated male participation in the domestic sphere, focusing on men's sensitive or soft side rather than their honor and pride.[169] According to anthropologist Matthew Gutman, traditional male codes of conduct changed in Mexico City after the 1960s, and men began sharing domestic household and family duties.[170] Gutman's account illustrates the extent to which Mexico City men participated in the domestic sphere, but it is not conceptualized within a historical context. Perhaps events that championed men's soft side had some impact on men's participation in the domestic sphere.[171] Ironically, Sears introduced events that did not reflect traditional Mexican male roles while it claimed to be an American store firmly grounded in Mexican values and practices.

Sears introduced other less conventional promotional events, including the Sears employee sale and the Sears fair. During the Sears employee sale, employees ran the store for an entire day with minimal supervision from management. Employees were allowed to work in different departments and were supervised by employees who assumed management roles in each department. They were given promotional vouchers to distribute among friends and family members. Customers were apparently receptive to the sale and used the event to flirt with Sears employees. For example, Bonilla recalled a common joke among male customers during the Sears employee sale. Male customers would come up to him and ask, "Excuse me, sir. Is this the Sears employee sale?" "Yes, it is," Bonilla would respond. "Can I have this gorgeous woman?," they would ask, pointing at a female employee.[172] The Sears fair included a dart-throwing competition and children's games. Sears employees wore traditional Mexican clothing and decorated the store with balloons and other adornments. Both promotional events attracted floods of customers, according to Bonilla.[173] They made Sears's publicity in Mexico different from publicity in its U.S. branches.

Sears used a more American form of publicity in its Christmas promotions. It installed a mechanical Santa Claus whose laughter could be heard from far away in mid-November of 1947. Christmas sales apparently skyrocketed until January 6, the end of the Christmas season in Mexico.[174] The Santa Claus apparently generated a great deal of interest and attracted people to the store. According to Ubaldo Riojas, who lived in Mexico City in the 1940s, visiting Sears and other department stores served as a form of entertainment throughout the year, and the latest innovations, like the Santa Claus, were the highlight of such visits.[175] Similarly, Homero García Loranca remembers traveling with his parents from Puebla to Mexico City (before a Sears branch opened in Puebla) to see the Sears Santa Claus.[176] Bonilla noted that the Santa Claus was very popular among children.[177] Santa Claus, however, was not popular among some political leaders. After seeing the Santa Claus at Sears in 1952, former president Lázaro Cárdenas complained that American influence in Mexico was transforming the way Christmas was celebrated in Mexico.[178]

Conclusion

The lack of upward mobility for Mexicans working at Sears, the continued placement of Americans in top positions, and Barron's attitude were contrary to the nationalist rhetoric and protectionist policies the Mexican government had adopted and Wood had accepted in 1947. Mexico's revolutionary and nationalist experience in the 1930s set the boundaries, the Mexican government set the terms and conditions through ISI, and Sears's opening crew set the grounds on which successful business relations depended in the late 1940s. Stepping outside these boundaries triggered adverse results. Unlike Mexican opposition to American oil companies in 1938, which included popular demands for the nationalization of American companies, resistance to Sears in 1949 was expressed through employee discontent, a decline in sales, and a growing perception of Sears as an expensive "upscale" store. This resistance undermined the company's original goals and marketing identity. As a result, the company was forced to restructure and to revitalize its reputation as a middle-class retailer.

Sears used the same grand opening and marketing strategies it had used in Mexico in 1947 when it opened in São Paulo and other parts of Latin America, hoping to generate the same hype and shopping-crazed mobs. Although successful, the results in São Paulo did not compare to Sears's explosive beginning in Mexico. Lower results in new stores throughout Latin America did not stop Sears from continuing to use its Mexico City store as a "commercial laboratory." Even after 1949, some operations of the Latin American division remained in Mexico City even though the Sears headquarters in Chicago considered operations in each country autonomous. Most important, problems that arose in the Mexico City branch often shaped the Latin American division's policies toward other stores in Latin America.

Sears managers expected a decline in sales after Sears's initial triumph in Mexico City, but they did not anticipate that government policies and labor tensions would force the company to restructure its operations. ISI blocked Sears's initial objective of importing low-priced high-quality merchandise from the United States. It hindered Sears's idealistic efforts to appeal to a primarily middle-class clientele in ways that had worked in the United States. Unlike the American middle class, the Mexican middle class was at the mercy of Mexico's economic growth and its volatile role in the international market. Mexico's economic status and its performance in the international market often determined the type of merchandise Mexico's middle class could afford. Considering the purchasing power of Mexico's middle class compared to that of the U.S. middle class, it is not surprising that Sears de México ended up with far stronger sales in soft-line products. Sears's initial failure to understand the socioeconomic status of Mexico City's middle class increased corporate difficulties after June 1947. The adversities Sears encountered, however, were part of the learning process for doing business in Latin America, a process Sears mastered after its 1949 corporate restructuring under Lynch.

The organizational changes and restructuring that Sears implemented during its first three years in Mexico revolved around retailing principles that the company upheld throughout the 1940s. Despite its ups and downs, Sears maintained its identity as a middle-class retailer and its commitment to allowing the coexistence of conflicting values by operating within a middle ground. It hoped to generate profits while cultivating good public and commercial relations with customers, the Mexican public, and government officials. Sears served as a goodwill ambassador. It found local manufacturers in response to the bold economic policies of the Alemán administration. The benefits, training, recreation, and paternalism it offered employees resembled both Mexican and American political notions of being a good neighbor. Sears also decided in favor of Mexican employees when they demanded that Barron be removed. It feared actions that might trigger the "commercial nationalism" directed at American companies during the 1930s. In this context, Mexican government officials, employees, and customers (through their response to Sears marketing) shaped Sears's operations. However, the influence Mexicans had on Sears depended on Sears's commitment to operating within a middle ground and learning profitable business practices for further expansion. As a result, the ability of Mexicans to shape Sears's business approach and operations was not fixed or static. It depended on the company's legitimacy, reputation, interest in Latin America, and corporate leadership in Chicago and Mexico.

7 Industrial Capitalism, Antimodernism, and Consumer Culture in 1940s Mexico

In a letter published in *La Familia,* Enrique wrote his girlfriend that they were finally going to make their dreams come true because he had achieved what, until recently, had seemed impossible: he had found a job that would allow them to buy their own house and live a comfortable, although not luxurious, life together. Explaining that the job was the product of hard work and years of struggle, Enrique said they had found the key to happiness. Enrique stated that his new job would make it possible for him to offer her a white dress and beautiful flowers for their wedding. He described poverty as painful and characterized his new job as the key to "reaching the stars."[1] Other Mexico City residents felt differently about life in modern industrial capitalism. In a letter to a friend published in *La Familia,* Alberto complained that his job chained him down to a dull, hopeless routine. Describing himself as a "machine operated by foreign forces," Alberto explained that his life consisted of walking to work, getting to the office on time, performing the same task all day, and stopping at the same café to have a drink and smoke a cigarette on his way home. He said the lack of variety in his life had dehumanized him to the point that he had no goals, no plans, no emotions, and no hope that things would be better in the future. He acknowledged that taking a break from his daily routine and visiting other places would help but admitted that financial restraints did not allow him to do so.[2]

Mexicans like Enrique and Alberto saw material wealth as a scale that measured their individual qualities, personal accomplishments, and prosperity. They judged individual success or failure by their degree of access to material products and their ability to climb the social ladder in the urban industrial setting. They defined their status in society through the lens of "consumer culture." Like Enrique, some Mexicans welcomed Mexico's industrial capitalism as the key to economic freedom, better social conditions, happiness, and the well-being of their families. They embraced life in the urban industrial setting because they believed it liberated them from traditional norms and the sense of backwardness they associated with traditional lifestyles. They considered a rural lifestyle uneventful and a barrier to upward mobility and happiness. Yet for people like

Alberto, neither a technocratic job nor the promises of a dynamic urban industrial setting offered personal satisfaction or comfort. According to Alberto, his daily routine in Mexico City led to boredom and hopelessness. He detested the standardized procedures of modern industrial capitalism at the production level, but he welcomed the comfort, satisfaction, and self-gratification it offered at the level of consumption. In other words, Mexicans had mixed reactions to modern industrial capitalism, but they did not entirely reject it. Instead, they tried to shape the changes triggered by modern industrial capitalism and learn to cope with them. Most important, they learned to use both established mechanisms (such as the church) and new avenues to voice their concerns or shape the changes taking place in 1940s Mexico. Yet the intensity of modern industrial development and the changes of the 1940s created a sense of uncertainty and "weightlessness" that proved to be overwhelming. Some sectors of society reacted by challenging the power of consumption, arguing that it corrupted spiritual and moral values. They formed religious organizations, such as Acción Católica Mexicana, and led moralization campaigns from the 1930s to the 1950s.

Mexicans wrote letters to magazine columnists and religious authorities expressing different reactions to modern industrial capitalism. Magazines like *La Familia* began publishing personal letters in the 1940s. Some letters appeared in its "Cartas que se extraviaron [Letters that got lost]" column. *La Familia* received these letters from readers who mistakenly received letters addressed to other people. The magazine also hired women columnists to address readers' concerns in its "Cuénteme su problema [Tell me your problem]" section (see figure 7.1). Through this section, readers and columnists developed a rather intimate relationship at a time when magazine distribution skyrocketed and life was becoming more impersonal. *La Familia*'s distribution increased from 59,000 issues in 1941 to 150,000 issues in 1946. Archbishop Luis María Martínez also received letters from people who blamed modern industrial capitalism for their personal problems. Martínez did not respond to every letter, but a number of initiatives of the church during the 1940s (including religious radio programs) addressed the type of concerns expressed in letters. Echoing Martínez's approach, Acción Católica launched aggressive publicity campaigns to revitalize Christian values and help Mexicans balance spiritual and material concerns. Magazine columnists and religious authorities provided a form of "therapy" as they helped Mexicans deal with emotional, spiritual, and material concerns at a time when society was rapidly changing as a result of industrial capitalism.

Neither magazine columnists nor church representatives rejected industrial and commercial growth, but their advice often challenged the changes that modern industrial capitalism brought to Mexican society. They criticized the

Figure 7.1. 1945 "Cuénteme su problema" column in *La Familia* featuring a woman reading a book entitled "Fear of Living." (*La Familia* 242 [February 1945]: 12, author's personal collection)

fast pace and mechanical aspects of production and the corruption of moral values brought about by consumption. Their objections to specific changes in Mexican society represented, to use U.S. historian T. J. Jackson Lears's term, a form of "antimodernism." Lears defined antimodernism in the United States as a response to the spiritual dislocation and "collective nervousness" caused by modern industrial capitalism (1880–1920) that offered emotional comfort and eased America's "transition from a protestant to a therapeutic world view."[3] Modern industrial capitalism raised similar concerns in 1940s Mexico, and the "therapy" provided by columnists and religious authorities echoed a form of antimodernism that eased emotional distress and helped Mexicans cope with the rapid changes of the 1940s. Columnists, religious authorities, and the population in general looked for a sense of balance or middle ground that would help them cope with the economic, emotional, spiritual, and ethical displacement caused by modern industrial capitalism.

Modern Industrial Capitalism, War, and Emotional Displacement in 1940s Mexico

The changes Mexicans experienced in the 1940s as a result of modern industrial capitalism, Western science, and international conflicts led to a sense of emotional distress and displacement despite the promise of upward mobility and different forms of happiness. Expressing concern about people like Alberto, *La Familia* explained that modern life had certain elements, such as office work, that made people feel emotionally displaced.[4] According to *La Familia*, people found themselves unable to keep up with the accelerated pace of life. It argued that Mexicans were becoming "increasingly impatient with living and finding themselves unable to make their hopes and dreams" come true as time raced forward.[5] It suggested that the accelerated pace of life also affected nations as their "desire for progress, dominance, and power led them to constant activity, continuous agitation, and an endless struggle."[6] *La Familia* denounced World War II as "poison for moral values," insisting that it caused people to abandon their moral, social, and intellectual principles.[7] The results of the "emotional weightlessness" caused by modern society were alarming. Mexico City newspapers reported an increase in the number of suicides, which they blamed on an overall "moral bankruptcy" of Mexican society. *La Familia* described the desire to commit suicide as a "moral and physical imbalance that dominated spiritual strength" among people who lacked intellectual preparation and had an inferiority complex.[8] It reported that 80 percent of the people who committed suicide did so as a result of disillusionment in a relationship. These reports supported antimodernist criticisms of industrial capitalism.

Modern industrial capitalism brought prosperity and upward mobility to some sectors of Mexican society, but it also triggered economic and social displacement. Some immigrants from provincial areas, such as Juanita Guerra Rangel, who was discussed in chapter 3, made their dreams come true by climbing the social ladder in Mexico City, but many found themselves in the slums. Anthropologist Oscar Lewis described the violent, destructive, and disturbing behavior of residents in poor neighborhoods as a "culture of poverty" harbored by urban industrial capitalism.[9] According to Lewis, this culture of poverty had a "structure, a rationale, and defense mechanisms . . . passed down from generation to generation along family lines."[10] Lewis argued that the culture of poverty bred alcoholism, the use of physical violence toward family members, early initiation into sex, and a fatalist attitude. Lewis's approach echoed the antimodernist concerns of the 1940s, which is not surprising given that he conducted most of his research in 1940s and 1950s Mexico. However, he reduced antimodernist concerns to class analysis. The changes caused by modern industrial capitalism, such as massive rural to urban migration, the accelerated pace of life, the growth of urban nightlife and other forms of entertainment, and the increasing commercialization of life, did not produce a single form of behavior or subculture along class lines. To suggest that modern industrial capitalism caused destructive, violent, and pessimistic behavior among the urban poor (as Lewis stated) or in urban society in general (as antimodernists argued) oversimplifies the changes of 1940s Mexico and reduces the multiple responses to such changes to either class or technological determinism.

Antimodernist concerns about the corruption of society by consumer culture and modernity were not new in 1940s Mexico, but the displacement of the urban middle class as the guardian of moral and ethical standards was new. Mexico's urban middle class had established itself as the guardian of good manners and respectable behavior in the nineteenth century. It claimed an educated, bourgeois, genteel lifestyle as it made decency a hallmark of middle-class identity. It associated a middle-class lifestyle with an elite notion of culture expressed through art, literature, and music, among other things. In other words, Mexico's middle class in the early nineteenth century developed a "cultural hierarchy" as it defined *gente decente* lifestyle as "highbrow" culture, to use terms coined by U.S. historians. Lawrence W. Levine suggests that this cultural hierarchy emerged in late-nineteenth-century America as society labeled operas and other cultural performances as highbrow culture because they provided artistic and spiritual elevation and simple forms of entertainment as lowbrow culture.[11] Levine's concept suggests that America's cultural hierarchy was not exclusively a socioeconomic phenomenon. Mexico's middle class had a well-established identity as *gente decente* in a cultural hierarchy that began to crumble in the late nineteenth century and took new forms after the 1910 revolution. Mexico's urban middle class in the nineteenth century considered its intellectual participation in public debates (which U.S. historian Joan Shelley Rubin defines as "middle brow culture" in American society), its cultural practices aimed at artistic and spiritual elevation, and its bourgeois or *decente* attitude the foundation of its identity.[12] It also claimed moral authority over the nation as it criticized aristocrats for their obsession with material wealth and protected *gente decente* from the plebian behavior of the lower classes. Nineteenth-century literature spoke of the challenges that well-mannered, educated urban middle-class residents faced as they tried to preserve Christian and ethical standards in a society that placed too much value on material wealth and nonspiritual forms of entertainment. It criticized people for becoming too concerned with physical appearance and enjoying mundane activities, such as dancing, that did not offer any spiritual reward.[13] Mexico's urban middle class began to lose its highbrow cultural status as modern capitalist programs in Porfirian Mexico (1876–1910) introduced new forms of entertainment.

The 1910 Mexican Revolution and the aggressive modern industrial development introduced by political leaders after the 1920s popularized and commercialized the middle class. Government officials, business leaders, renowned artists like Diego Rivera, and advertising agents, among others, promoted a democratized notion of middle-class identity that they associated with the Mexican Revolution, modern industrial development, and the belief in upward mobility. Government representatives allocated resources, created institutions, and headed cultural projects that aimed at popularizing the image of a revolutionary government that was "Mexicanizing" art, music, and theater and proudly celebrating Mexico's indigenous, mestizo, and revolutionary heritage. Their initiatives, while legitimizing state authority, provided a more democratic notion of culture. Their modern industrial capitalist programs and persistence in making Mexico competitive in the international market also triggered changes that redefined middle-class identity. Advertising, new forms of entertainment, and American companies like Sears defined middle-class status through consumption, which according to antimodernists was the reason for the decay of moral and spiritual values. In other words, modern capitalism defined Mexico's middle class through consumption and took the "decency" out of Mexico's middle class. The decline of the middle class as the guardian of moral and ethical standards increased concerns among people who longed for a romanticized notion of the past.

The devastation of World War II and specifically the atom bomb intensified criticism of the destructive nature of modernization in Western societies, including Mexico. Commenting on the destruction of the war, José Vázquez Amaral argued that, as the leader of Western civilization, Europe had placed the world back in the Middle Ages and shown that there was no distinction between civilization and barbarism. He questioned the existence of moral and ethical values and concluded that they were worthless even if they did exist. According to him, the highly specialized nature of scientific and bureaucratic development in the midst of international political tensions had created conditions in which individuals had "value only as statistical figures at the service of killing machines."[14] Concerned about emotional distress, some people defined religious faith as the common denominator of humanity, the source of greatness and strength, and the quality that separated men from beasts.[15] They rejected reason because it was the product of the Enlightenment and the foundation of modern science and idealized a premodern lifestyle when religious faith reigned. Others, like

Miguel Leal, favored a balanced approach toward science. Defining greed and power as the problem, Leal insisted that science itself was not destructive and that people had to give meaning to it by using it to serve society rather than destroy it.[16] Yet neither faith in religion nor faith in science could stop Mexicans from fearing the level of destruction the world had reached by the mid-1940s.

Magazine articles addressed concerns about the decline in moral values and the emotional weightlessness in Mexican society throughout the 1940s. Responding to collective fear about the destruction of World War II, *La Familia* reported that, according to psychologists and other experts, fear was one of the most common human emotions. The article reassured readers that even the bravest people experienced fear at some point in their lives.[17] It also urged Mexicans to care for their "souls" by devoting more time to the spiritual aspects of life, insisting that "taking care of their soul was just as important as taking care of their physical appearance."[18] *La Familia* did not define "attending to the soul" exclusively in religious terms. It mentioned listening to music as a way to nurture the soul. Yet *La Familia*'s efforts to provide a form of "therapy" to deal with the emotional weightlessness triggered by modern industrial capitalism did not end emotional distress in the midst of escalating international rivalry.

Concerns about the destructive capacity of modern science continued into the 1950s as nuclear testing increased as a result of the Cold War. A 1950 issue of *Revista de Revistas* included a cartoon of a woman representing humanity riding backward on a donkey that was wearing blinders (see figure 7.2). The cartoon caption read, "Where are we heading?" The woman was facing toward an open, natural space that apparently represented the countryside. Since women were traditionally portrayed as the bearers of moral values, the woman in the cartoon held the moral authority to question humanity's destiny. The donkey was trotting toward the entrance to a city; a sign over the entrance read, "World War III." This cartoon projected the sense of ambiguity that characterized the emotional displacement or weightlessness of 1940s Mexico.

Economic difficulties and life in the urban industrial setting also made Mexicans feel emotionally distressed. Catita confessed that she suffered from depression in a letter in *La Familia*'s "Cuénteme su problema" column. She said her depression was a result of not being able to have the comfort and luxury that some people enjoyed. It bothered her that she could not afford items that other people purchased. Consuelo, one of *La Familia*'s columnists, advised Catita to appreciate what she had and stop comparing her lifestyle to that of other people. She argued that privileged people got what they had because God gave each person what he or she deserved. Consuelo instructed Catita to think of herself as fortunate because she had much more than some people did.[19] Consuelo's advice reinforced religious values as she suggested that people got what they deserved

Figure 7.2. 1950 cartoon in *Revista de Revistas* illustrating a sense of ambiguity about the future of humanity. (*Revista de Revistas: El Semanario Nacional* 2090 [August 13, 1950]: n.p., author's personal collection)

from God rather than from determination and hard work. In other words, she endorsed antimodernist values. Similar to Catita, Ana María reported in a letter to a friend published in *La Familia* that she was tired of the degeneration, rancor, hatred, and ambition of people in the city. She feared that city life would make her blind to the pain, ambition, and selfishness that characterized modern industrial capitalism.[20] She described the city as a congested place with sick children, homeless people eating from garbage cans, and greedy residents eager to trick anyone for money. Ana María linked her anger to her disappointment over her breakup with her boyfriend, who had apparently deceived her. However, she interpreted her romantic misfortune as a consequence of the values cultivated by modern industrial capitalism. She did not blame her boyfriend for deceiving her; she blamed the values of the urban industrial setting and capitalism for corrupting him. Ana María decided to seek refuge temporarily in the countryside to remove herself from the degradation of urban life and purify her soul and spirit. Neither Consuelo nor Ana María proposed complete rejection of modern industrial capitalism. They merely advocated measures to cope with the weightlessness caused by life in the modern capitalist setting.

Seeing the countryside as a safety net and a "therapeutic" remedy for economic and emotional displacement was not uncommon. In a letter to Alicia published in *La Familia*, her boyfriend asked her to move with him to the countryside. He argued that his savings were not enough to buy a home in the city at a time when the value of Mexican currency was drastically declining. His letter revealed inner conflicts that were central to male identity. A man's identity had traditionally been defined by his ability to serve as the family's breadwinner in Mexico. Alicia's boyfriend refused to reject such a hallmark of male identity and asked her to move to the countryside, where he could comfortably perform his role as breadwinner. He saw the countryside as a place of comfort and safety from the economic displacement caused by modern industrial capitalism. Similar to Ana María, he expressed his discomfort at not being able to meet traditional expectations in an antimodernist and anticapitalist manner. He said he was very disappointed to have to mix money and love but explained that modern industrial capitalism did not allow people to separate the two. He defined love as a spiritual concept that was superior to material wealth and blamed money for making people ambitious, cruel, and selfish. Moving to the countryside, he stated, would allow them to preserve their love and maintain a good standard of living. He argued that a return to a serene natural setting would add happiness to their marriage and offer them the opportunity to enjoy tropical plants, exotic birds, beautiful flowers, and enchanting sunsets.[21]

Other personal accounts in *La Familia* defined love as a value that was stronger than misfortune and economic displacement. Carlota described city life as "harsh and cruel" in a letter to a friend. She explained that she had learned a valuable lesson from the scene of a homeless mother aggressively defending her two children against strangers. Carlota stated that the determination of the mother to protect her children against the chaos and dangerous conditions of city life made her realize that material wealth and comfort were meaningless compared to the love of a mother.[22] She concluded that love was the basis of happiness in the urban industrial setting, not money. Carlota's conclusion was "classcentric," and it reflected the different forms of displacement in urban Mexico. Speaking as a privileged middle-class resident, Carlota did not consider economic stability and access to basic necessities such as food, shelter, and clothing priorities. "Love" might have provided a solution to poverty in her analysis, but the picture of the homeless mother trying to protect her children suggests that the priorities for the economically displaced might have been different. Industrial and commercial growth triggered different forms of displacement that led to different interpretations of what constituted happiness.

Mexicans who welcomed modern industrial capitalism found comfort and a form of happiness through consumer culture and illusions about the possibility of becoming wealthy. An editorial writer in *La Familia* reported that one of her friends had recently been excited about the possibility of winning 2 million pesos in the national lottery. She was shocked when her friend showed no disappointment when she did not win the lottery after three weeks of hype and excitement. Her friend explained that, at least for a few weeks, she had enjoyed fantasizing about the things she would purchase and the trips she would take if she won the lottery. Her friend considered the money she spent on the lottery ticket a good investment because it provided the self-gratifying "illusion of waiting for lottery officials to announce the winner."[23] The writer concluded that the emotional state of mind generated by the purchase of a lottery ticket was an effective formula for ending the sadness, hopelessness, and emotional displacement she often experienced. She argued that people would be happier if they changed their outlook and trained their minds to look at the bright side of things. However, she acknowledged that such a task required people to rise above the daily routine and explore new avenues of thought and action. The writer's conclusion promoted enjoying life through illusions generated by consumption. Her claim reinforced the message endorsed by supporters of Mexico's industrial capitalism. It suggested that depression triggered by the changes in 1940s Mexico could be cured through the consumption of products, ideals, images, and even illusions.

Consumer culture also triggered memories of past experiences among Mexicans in the 1940s. In a letter to Manolo published in *La Familia*, María Eva reported that the window displays of big shops and department stores in Mexico City reminded her of the time she had spent with him in Mazatlán.[24] After having a romantic encounter with Manolo on a trip to Mazatlán, María Eva had not seen him for ten years. She recalled strolling with him through the streets looking at window displays. Store displays (a form of publicity and tool of consumer culture) generated a form of happiness for María Eva because they reminded her of her happy experience with Manolo. However, as the cases of Catita, Ana María, Alicia's boyfriend, and Carlota illustrate, Mexicans associated different emotions with consumer culture and rationalized its impact for different purposes. Publicity (as a tool of consumer culture) had the potential of triggering mixed emotions among consumers.

Consumer culture (and the values associated with it) also served as a tool to explain personal failure and "unhappiness." In a letter to Archbishop Martínez, Emilio Escalante blamed consumer culture and the nation's economy for his failed marriage.[25] Escalante wrote that his wife left him after fifteen years of marriage because he could not afford to support her extravagant lifestyle. He reported that supporting his wife was not a problem immediately after their marriage in 1925 because his work in the insurance industry provided enough income. However, after economic conditions worsened in the 1930s, he said, marital tensions increased because his wife refused to change her lifestyle. He accused his mother-in-law of adding more pressure to the relationship by encouraging her daughter to continue her extravagance and blaming him for not providing adequate financial support.[26] Escalante argued that he was forced to beat his wife in order to control her consumer habits. He asked the archbishop to help him get his wife back to "preserve the sacred bonds of marriage outlined by church doctrine" in the midst of a materialistic society that had corrupted his wife.[27] In other words, Escalante blamed economic conditions and consumer culture rather than his temper for his failed marriage. His wife's obsession with shopping apparently added financial stress to an already tense relationship. He appealed to conventional gender norms and antimodernism in his efforts to get his wife back.

Mexico's elite did not escape the power and seduction of consumer culture. According to Margarita Rostan, elite Mexican women were often caught shoplifting at El Palacio de Hierro. She recalled an incident when a mink stole fell from under a woman's clothing as she was leaving the store.[28] Rostan remembered another woman who wrapped merchandise in baby blankets and was pushing the stolen goods through the store in a baby carriage.[29] According to Rostan, when women shoplifters were apprehended, store personnel called the male head of the household listed in the customer account. In some cases, the husband would pay for the merchandise. In other cases, the husband came to the store to pick up his wife and publicly humiliate her. However, humiliation for elite women only went as far as labeling them "kleptomaniacs," or women whose obsession with merchandise became a disease that drove them to shoplifting. Middle-class women who shoplifted had been described as kleptomaniacs by U.S. department stores since the late nineteenth century, but in Mexico, the term was apparently used to describe only elite shoplifters.[30] Even Sears de México refused to use the term to describe middle-class shoplifters. In other words, department stores considered Mexican elite women who shoplifted sick whereas they considered middle-class shoplifters criminals. Incidents of middle-class and elite shoplifting reinforced the antimodernist view that modern industrial capitalism had corrupted the moral framework of Mexican society and that this corruption did not respect class differences. However, department stores did not entirely disregard class differences. Elite women who shoplifted at El Palacio de Hierro, for example, preserved the "decency" that had traditionally defined middle- and upper-class culture, but middle-class shoplifters did not.

Capitalism, Modernity, and Balance between Material and Spiritual Life

Mexicans considered economic stability and upward mobility crucial to success in modern industrial capitalism, but concerns about obsession with material wealth led people to search for balance in life.[31] Searching for balance meant striving for material success and upward mobility without disregarding spiritual life or love and nature. For example, in a letter to his girlfriend published in *La Familia*, Leopoldo described himself as a person who considered work important because it provided economic security and guaranteed a comfortable lifestyle. The pursuit of happiness in modern industrial societies, according to him, was impossible without economic security. Yet he apologized to his girlfriend for spending an excessive amount of time at his job whereas his attention and commitment to their relationship had declined. Apparently responding to his girlfriend's decision to break up with him, Leopoldo promised to devote more time to her and balance his life better. He acknowledged that it was counterproductive to value work and material wealth more highly than their relationship; it did not make sense for him to work hard for their economic security as a couple when overcommitment to work put them at risk of a breakup. In other words, he suggested that a balance between love, work, and material wealth was fundamental to happiness in a modern industrialized society.[32]

Searching for balance in the urban industrial setting meant coming to terms with both modern and traditional values. This task was not easy for some women. In a letter to her grandmother published in *La Familia*, Graciela described herself as a "modern woman" who was raised in a materialistic society with values that were very different from those of previous generations. She said she was an "independent woman willing to confront life face to face."[33] She criticized people who perceived "modern women" as insensitive individuals who placed superficial and mundane aspects of life above everything else. According to Graciela, she was a sensitive woman who had fallen in love with a serious, well-mannered, educated man who upheld traditional values.[34] Graciela did not use the term *gente decente*, probably because Mexicans rarely used the term by the 1940s, but her description of the man she loved resembled the image of the nineteenth-century *gente decente*. She classified these manners and values as "traditional," which according to her conflicted with her modern, materialistic, and assertive upbringing. She considered this conflict a big problem because she felt out of place and became shy in the presence of the man she loved. She sought advice from her grandmother in how to attract the romantic interest of and declare her love to a "traditional" man. Graciela wanted to find a balance or middle ground between traditional and modern values so she could feel comfortable and at ease. Her perception of herself as a modern, assertive woman who found herself speechless, confused, and unable to communicate her love for a respectable "traditional" man was the result of conflicts triggered by Mexico's transition to a modern industrial society. It was another form of emotional displacement that characterized 1940s Mexico.

La Familia columnists encouraged a sense of balance as they advised women on traditional and modern gender norms, but their advice generally followed conservative lines. They instructed women to perform duties that were placed on them by society, such as doing housework and being obedient to parents and husbands.[35] Juana Inés instructed Emma to be understanding, sweet, loving, and caring and not to question her husband about other women because, according to her, men often dated other women if their wives were jealous.[36] Consuelo's take on gender roles was not much different. She reassured readers in her response to Conchita's letter that the most appropriate professions for women were those that required their feminine qualities, such as teaching and medicine. The columnist also reported that new areas of law were very appropriate for women, especially defending juvenile delinquents and protecting women and children.[37] Ironically, the conservative discourse that stressed the need for women to preserve traditional gender norms also encouraged women to enter the public sphere and pursue top professions in the urban industrial setting. Columnists also told women to become independent, confident, and assertive because these qualities were vital to personal success. Juana Inés advised one of her readers to boost her confidence and self-esteem in order to face the challenges of the urban industrial setting.[38] She instructed another reader to stand up for her rights and demand that her brother stop threatening to beat up her boyfriend.[39] She characterized the brother's attitude as a barbaric and antiquated tradition that women had to end. Juana Inés told Rosa to defy her parents by marrying the person she loved despite their objection.[40] Yet magazine columnists did not openly embrace a radical change in traditional gender roles. They created a middle ground as they urged women to search for leadership roles in the professional arena, become assertive, and stand up for their rights while stressing the significance of preserving traditional gender norms, which historically had linked women to either their parents or their husbands.

La Familia columnists instructed readers to preserve marriage but also suggested that divorce was necessary in some cases in order to protect the family. They described marriage as a sacred institution that was central to the Mexican family and women's self-realization. Unfortunately, they argued, modern industrial capitalism had brought substantial changes to the concept of family and marriage, and as a result, many women married for the wrong reason. They claimed that many young women married older men for money and ended up being extremely unhappy because even millions of pesos could not bring happiness unless there was love and mutual understanding in a relationship.[41] Personal letters confirmed *La Familia*'s conclusion. In a letter to Irene, her friend reported that some of the people she knew were very unhappy because they had married for money.[42] *La Familia* columnists argued that the increasing number of women who married for the wrong reason required changes in marriage, including divorce. Consuelo instructed Teresa to divorce her husband, arguing that a seventy-two-year-old man was too old for a twenty-one-year-old woman.[43]

Consuelo's position on divorce challenged the authority of the state as she reassured Teresa that getting a divorce was not a problem because "civil marriage did not count in comparison to religious marriage."[44] Thus, Consuelo's take on divorce strengthened the power of the church at the political level. The church had exercised a great deal of power over marriage and family decisions throughout the colonial period.[45] However, nineteenth-century liberals established civil marriage as a legitimate process. The church lost a substantial amount of power to the state as a result of church-state tensions from 1850 to the 1930s, but it retained moral authority over marriage and the family. Ironically, Consuelo's advice on divorce, while strengthening the political power of the church, challenged the church's moral authority over marriage. The church's position on marriage was very clear: marriage was permanent. Consuelo's pro-divorce stance in her response to Teresa was not an isolated incident. She instructed another reader to leave her husband and go to her brother's house until she got a job and became economically independent. She encouraged the reader to find a husband she could live with in the future.[46] Despite the pro-divorce stand, *La Familia* columnists did not encourage a radical feminist approach. On the contrary, they offered practical solutions through conservative means.[47] They perceived divorce as an option that could help women better perform their duty as mothers. Church authorities chose to offer other alternatives to marital difficulties and the changes in 1940s Mexico.

Restoring Moral Boundaries, the Church, and Moralization Campaigns

Mexicans relied on the church to either preserve or push the boundaries of moral values as they looked for a sense of spiritual and emotional comfort in a modern industrial capitalist society. José Valencia Alvares wrote Archbishop

Martínez asking him to help save his marriage. He explained that his wife had become irresponsible toward him and their six children. According to Alvares, she was preoccupied with her physical appearance and only cared about going out with friends. She spent most of her time at beauty salons and movie theaters.[48] Alvares argued that his wife had abandoned the noble sentiments of Mexican mothers and wives even though he had fulfilled his role as the breadwinner of the family. He asked the church to enforce its moral authority in order to save his marriage and preserve traditional marital and gender norms. Other couples urged religious authorities to accept more flexible moral norms and bend the ground rules on marriage. Guadalupe Hernández, for example, asked Martínez to clarify her marital status in 1946 after her separation from her husband, Placido Jiménez. She urged the archbishop to annul their marriage because unfortunate circumstances had forced her to marry him. She claimed that Placido had "dishonored" her after she confided in him about the abuse she received from her father. Guadalupe argued that she was forced to marry Placido after she discovered that she was expecting his baby at the age of sixteen. She said she left Placido in the early 1930s and that her father's abuse had ruined her life and made her "sexually sick."[49] She had apparently been sexually active with different men after leaving Placido. She insisted that her misfortune had led to her improper behavior and that she deserved a chance to live a good Catholic life with a man she loved.[50]

The church did not grant divorces except under very unique circumstances. It authorized the divorce of couples like Gabriel Romero and Alejandra Pérez, who were both already married when they married each other under different names.[51] Their first spouses apparently requested the annulment of their marriage. The church approved their request, but it is unclear whether they returned to their first spouses.[52] Unfortunately for Guadalupe, the church did not consider her request "unique." The requests of people like Alvares and Guadalupe, who turned to religious authorities for spiritual and emotional comfort, strengthened the moral power of the church. However, the "corruption" of Alvares's wife by consumer culture and Guadalupe's unfortunate but "sinful" sexual practices illustrated what antimodernists feared: that the church was fighting a losing war against consumption, corruption, promiscuity, and the moral degradation that accompanied modern industrial capitalism. In an effort to fight this corruption, the Catholic Church launched moralization campaigns headed by different branches of Acción Católica.

Acción Católica and the Union of Catholic Women in Mexico (Unión Femenina Católica Mexicana or UFCM) organized numerous programs and activities in their effort to fight the war against corruption and restore moral values. The UFCM was founded in 1912 by Archbishop José Mora del Río and it became an autonomous branch of Acción Católica in 1930. It administered 39 schools, 92 sites that distributed clothing to the poor, 40 literacy centers, and 139 children's programs, and it published a journal with a circulation of 30,000 issues a month.[53] Similarly, the youth division of Acción Católica (Acción Católica Juvenil Mexicana) included over 1,000 parochial groups and 18,000 members throughout the country by the 1950s. Efforts to restore Christian family values under the umbrella of Acción Católica began in the 1930s and gradually led to well-organized moralization campaigns by the 1940s and early 1950s. Acción Católica mobilized these campaigns in response to a letter signed by at least twenty of the top religious authorities in the country, mainly archbishops and bishops. The letter condemned the decline in moral values in Mexico. The problem, according to the letter, was that life in the modern urban setting promoted the decay of Christian family values. It blamed women for dressing inappropriately and thus causing temptation among men. It also denounced dancing and female sports (gymnastics and swimming, among others) because they seductively exhibited the female body in public and even encouraged sexual intercourse. The letter argued that newspaper and magazine ads, postcards, and commercial advertising also encouraged sex.[54] According to religious authorities, commercial publicity saturated the social and cultural environment with immoral values to the point that people lost the ability to distinguish between decent and indecent behavior. As a result, they decided to fight the war against corruption and promiscuity with their own publicity.

Acción Católica set out to modernize its publicity during its fourth national assembly in 1938 to spread the word of God and revitalize the Christian way of life. It established the Advertising and Census Central Commission (Comisión Central de Censo y Publicidad or CCCP) to conduct extensive research on public behavior and contribute to the dissemination of ethical and moral standards.[55] The CCCP opened a national religious advertising school and the Diocesan School for Directors of Acción Católica that provided training for religious advertising agents and boards of directors.[56] It coordinated nationwide publicity with publicity divisions in local churches. It claimed that advertising agents served as "apostles" who spread the word of God.[57] As a result, according to the CCCP, they needed systematic training that cultivated discipline, humility, intelligence, and the ability to connect with people.[58] Religious authorities favored the standardization and professionalization of advertising, but they preferred to implement their own training rather than having government institutions certify religious publicity agents.

Religious authorities took moralization campaigns from the church walls into the public and commercial sphere in the 1940s despite restrictions outlined in the 1917 constitution. In the 1930s, moralization campaigns consisted of posting banners, signs, and flyers in churches. A typical banner read, "The church is the house of God and women need to dress properly and modestly."[59] Flyers and newsletters published by the Mexican Decency Legion were also distributed, and religious ceremonies that involved dancing were banned because dancing often included suggestive movements. Efforts to restore moral values entered the commercial sector in 1939 when a moralization campaign was launched against swimsuits. Religious leaders headed by the UFCM visited stores to request that they stop selling swimsuits. Stores that refused were the targets of protests and boycotts by the UFCM.[60] The UFCM did not oppose industrial capitalism; it simply rejected the advertising and marketing of products it considered immoral. However, it voiced its opposition in an antimodernist and anticapitalist manner. Other campaigns headed by Acción Católica took a similar approach.

A campaign to restore the religious aspects of Christmas in the 1940s reinforced consumer culture even though it flirted with antimodernism. The CCCP, which changed its name to the Central Commission for Advertising and Statistics (Comisión Central de Publicidad y Estadistica or CCPE) in 1942, launched a campaign to promote the Christian celebration of Christmas, arguing that commercial culture had corrupted Christmas festivities. It distributed 100,000 flyers in 1943 urging Mexicans to reject the non-Christian aspects of Christmas.[61] It condemned people who considered Christmas an opportunity to drink, dance, and seek personal rather than spiritual fulfillment. The CCPE increased the intensity of the pro-Christian Christmas campaign from 1944 to the late 1940s. It adopted a campaign model that the Chihuahua branch of Acción Católica had used that included organizing wealthy church members to bring food to poor families on Christmas Eve and take their children to toy stores to pick out their own gifts. Participants justified the commercial aspects of this program by declaring that the "joy and happiness that Christmas brought to children depended on their ability to choose and enjoy their own toy."[62] The pro-Christian Christmas campaign did not reject the commercialization of Christmas. On the contrary, CCPE representatives asked store owners to post pro-Christian messages during their Christmas sales and urged them to include Christian decorations in their window displays. They also requested that the store owners not display images of Santa Claus, which represented the commercialization of Christmas—the very cause that had led them to organize in the first place.[63]

Acción Católica's moralization campaigns of the early 1940s led to the passage of legislation that protected the public from the immoral values and practices promoted by the media, but these laws were rarely enforced. A presidential decree signed by Ávila Camacho in 1944 addressed antimodernist concerns voiced by Acción Católica and anxiety about the decay of moral values. According to Anne Rubenstein, Ávila Camacho signed this decree in an effort to increase the power of the state and had no intention of enforcing it[64] Alarmed at the lack of enforcement of the 1944 decree, Acción Católica renewed its activism and launched a more aggressive moralization campaign in the late 1940s that lasted until the mid-1950s. It characterized the 1944 government restrictions on film, radio programs, magazines, and advertising as worthless. It declared that its new "war against immoral values" required social activism and direct action against radio stations, film producers, advertising associations, and government officials.[65]

Acción Católica defined "action" not as violent confrontation but as careful planning and networking and coercing people, institutions, and organizations into supporting its cause. It convinced the local government of Oaxaca to limit the hours local bars could remain open and sanction parents who acted irresponsibly toward their children. It distributed 250,000 flyers in Guanajuato with statements such as "Stop enriching merchants who have no scruples; do not listen to their publicity!" and "Your home is a sacred place; keep immoral publicity and inappropriate products out!"[66] Acción Católica publicized the declaration of 600 women who promised to refrain from immoral activities and wear decent clothing. It had its female division visit stores, evaluate the clothing on display, and provide store owners with a list of immoral merchandise.[67] Acción Católica representatives visited directors of the entertainment industry in Mexico City and urged him to force theater and movie producers to include moral messages in their plays and films. They also launched radio announcements that claimed that the corruption of moral values led to the weakness of the nation.[68] They asked store owners to display signs that read, "This house supports the national campaign in defense of morality."[69] A network of newspaper journalists cooperated with Acción Católica by printing statements such as "Christian norms and ways of life are being destroyed," "The structure of the Mexican family is on shaky ground," and "The religious heritage of our people is being threatened."[70] The fanaticism of some Acción Católica members intensified to its highest level in the early 1950s when these members suggested that all public announcements that they considered immoral be destroyed.[71] Fortunately, this level of radicalism was quickly silenced since church-state relations remained fragile. Archbishop Martínez's commitment to maintaining a consensus with government authorities suggests that he may have prevented radical factions of Acción Católica from vandalizing private property.

Acción Católica's moralization campaigns raised enough awareness to affect the marketing strategies of some companies by the late 1940s. A member of the board of directors of Cervecería Modelo, Juan Sánchez Navarro, responded apologetically to a letter that Acción Católica had sent to companies whose publicity its "surveillance crew" considered immoral. Navarro explained that Modelo's publicity was handled by advertising agencies, but he reported that the company had established a rigorous censoring mechanism to make sure that its publicity did not include indecent or immoral content.[72] Acción Católica, the UFCM, and Archbishop Martínez were also successful at stopping a Miss Mexico beauty contest in 1949.[73] In 1954 they prevented Celanese from sponsoring a swimsuit exhibition on television by asking contacts at Mexico's National Bank, which owned large holdings in Celanese, to "stop Celanese from using half-dressed women for advertising swimsuits."[74] It also asked National Bank executives to stop the television broadcast of the 1954 Miss Universe pageant hosted by the United States.

Acción Católica was apparently successful at coercing some companies to adopt "acceptable" moral standards because one of its members (whose name was not disclosed) was a high-ranking official at the National Bank. It was also successful at getting the ANP, the Mexican Association of Advertising Agencies (Asociación Mexicana de Agencias de Publicidad), and the Society of Authors and Composers of Mexico to sign the Pact of Honor in 1950. According to the pact, these agencies agreed to allow the Ethics Commission, which had been formed as part of the 1944 presidential decree, to review books, scripts, and commercial advertising whenever it chose.[75] It declared that marriage and the family could not be depicted negatively and that family themes should encourage unity and integrity. Sex could not be promoted, and the advertising of sexual hygiene products and contraceptives was prohibited. The agreement also encouraged advertising agents to use clear and simple language, and it banned the use of foreign words or phrases unless there was no equivalent word in Spanish to refer to the product.[76]

Other sectors of the church besides Acción Católica were also involved in efforts to restore a Christian lifestyle in 1940s Mexico. Religious leaders within the hierarchy of the church hosted a radio program titled *La hora guadalupana* on XEB and XEBT. The program consisted of dramatic stories in which the Virgin of Guadalupe saved innocent, humble people from death in natural disasters or accidents. For example, one of the programs highlighted the story of Concha and Antonio, a married couple who lived in the provinces. Concha complained repeatedly about Antonio's inability to make higher profits from the cows, milk, property, and other products he sold to local town residents. Concha also complained that Antonio paid his workers more than they deserved. Her greed came to a end one day when a massive storm struck the region. Radio listeners could hear the storm approaching in the background as Concha was demanding that Antonio not pay his workers because they had not worked much in the last six months as a result of a drought. Distracted by the deafening sound of the storm,

Concha and Antonio looked outside the window to see waves of water and mud heading straight toward their house as the river flowed down the mountain dragging trees, horses, cows, and houses. Concha and Antonio managed to escape just as the river ferociously dragged the house into its current. When they realized they had left their baby in the house, they prayed desperately to the Virgin of Guadalupe to save him as they tried to make their way back to the floating house. To their surprise, they found their son floating on peaceful waters just outside the torrential current. They thanked the Virgin of Guadalupe for the miracle, and Concha acknowledged that concerns about material life were secondary to the love and well-being of her family.[77] Ironically, the church, much like Palmolive and Sears, used the Virgin of Guadalupe to promote its own version of capitalism, which entailed a balance among material wealth, the spiritual aspects of life, and commitment to social well-being.

Other *La hora guadalupana* programs had commercial themes that featured families selling their products at the Sunday marketplace or salespeople at bullfighting events selling candies, snacks, and nonalcoholic drinks.[78] Advertisements for a variety of products and brand names offered by the sponsor, Mueblerías MYR, interrupted the most dramatic moments of the programs. Ironically, *La hora guadalupana* stressed the need to value love, family, humility, compassion, and faith while its sponsor encouraged listeners to seek luxury, prestige, and self-realization through material consumption. The content of the programs left radio listeners with a very clear message: work to pursue a comfortable standard of living but avoid obsession with material wealth because it leads to greed and promotes nonspiritual values.

The church's position on spiritual versus commercial aspects of life may seem contradictory, but it was not. The church coached Mexicans on specific ways of balancing life in a modern industrial capitalist society with spiritual life. It offered an educational radio series that encouraged Mexicans to pursue upward mobility and a better standard of living through hard work.[79] One program described money as a representation of commercial and social values that measured people's work and could be used to purchase merchandise that satisfied personal needs. People could consume as much as they worked for. The ability to purchase products, the church argued, would generate happiness, comfort, and well-being. However, according to church officials, work and money were beneficial but greed was not.[80] They argued that it was important to manage the product of people's work by saving money to provide a sense of protection for the family in case of emergencies. Radio programs suggested that modern industrial capitalism required saving money and that saving money required discipline. They argued that radio listeners had to restrain themselves from buying everything they saw in stores, prioritize their needs, and most important, refrain from luxury.[81] According to them, purchasing expensive products and luxury items could lead to economic ruin. Church officials prescribed a balance or middle ground as they instructed Mexicans to seek economic well-being and material comfort without becoming obsessed with wealth and forgetting about their spiritual commitment to God.

Conclusion

Antimodernist efforts to restore moral, spiritual, and ethical values found fertile ground among Mexicans who felt emotionally distressed as result of the changes triggered by modern industrial capitalism, the destruction of World War II, and nuclear testing during the Cold War. In this context, Mexicans sought support and comfort from magazine columnists, religious leaders, and consumer culture as they tried to cope with the changes of 1940s Mexico. The increasing lure of a secular lifestyle worried religious authorities and triggered criticism of modern industrial capitalism among antimodernists. Yet letters sent to religious leaders by people seeking spiritual comfort, the success of moralization campaigns by Acción Católica, and the participation of religious leaders in a public dialogue that defined moral standards suggest that the Catholic Church maintained a considerable amount of power and moral authority in 1940s Mexico. However, the task of guarding moral values was impossible in a society that was moving toward modern industrial capitalism at an accelerated pace. *La Familia* admitted in the late 1940s that following proper moral codes was challenging because industrial capitalism "accelerated the pace of life to a point where the human soul seemed to disappear" as people looked for personal satisfaction and pleasure.[82]

La Familia echoed the church's concerns about the decline in moral values as it sought to restore Christian values among Mexican families. It served as a vehicle for religious authorities to reach the Mexican people. One editorial argued that "Mexicans had to elevate themselves above material life into the spiritual aspects of life in order to reach emotional comfort."[83] However, its antimodernist stand often stressed civic and commercial rather than religious values. For example, it published Tampax advertising, which conflicted with the church's "war" against the publicity of immoral values by encouraging women to insert tampons into their vaginas (see figure 7.3).[84] Other *La Familia* ads contradicted the magazine's concern for the decline in moral values. Life Bra told women that its Formfit style would elevate their breasts, making them "young and seductive."[85] Ironically, Acción Católica considered *La Familia* an "ally" in its moralization campaign since the overall content of the magazine encouraged Catholic and family values. The values displayed in the media did not convey a unified message. *La Familia* might have had the agenda of encouraging moral values

Figure 7.3. Tampax advertising in *La Familia* that challenged Acción Católica's moralization campaign. (*La Familia* 359 [May 15, 1950]: 14; 360 [May 30, 1950]: 104; and 361 [June 15, 1950]: 27)

and providing a mechanism for moralization campaigns launched by church institutions, but its advertising and columns often promoted values, beliefs, and practices that seemed contradictory to this agenda. The mixed messages displayed in *La Familia* and other forms of media, publicity, and government or religious initiatives contributed to the formation of a middle ground. This middle ground created a cultural space where people in modern industrial Mexico syncretized traditional values and the new beliefs and lifestyle encouraged in the commercial setting.

Conclusion

The reconstruction of modern Mexico consolidated the Mexican state under the banner of modern industrial capitalism from the 1920s to 1950. The pursuit of modern industrial capitalism, as this book illustrates, became synonymous with the belief that industrial and commercial growth would bring Mexicans upward mobility, material prosperity, and a form of democracy through consumption. Yet the pursuit of industrial capitalist development served other purposes. It helped political leaders consolidate state legitimacy and authority under the banner of the 1910 Mexican Revolution and the 1917 constitution. Political leaders and government institutions maintained that government intervention in commercial issues and policies that supported capitalist development were efforts to implement revolutionary ideals. Similarly, advertising agents portrayed publicity as the engine of modern industrial capitalism as they insisted on gaining recognition for their work as a modern profession that was vital to Mexico's economic prosperity. They presented publicity as a mechanism for upward mobility and consumption and life in the urban industrial setting as symbols of prosperity and democracy. U.S. government officials and business executives also capitalized on Mexico's pursuit of modern industrial capitalism. They introduced anti-Nazi and anticommunist campaigns that depicted the United States as a partner in Mexico's pursuit of capitalist development.

Mexico's commitment to modern industrial capitalism was not a new phenomenon in the postrevolutionary period, but the popular nationalism and revolutionary rhetoric unleashed by the 1910 revolution gave Mexico's search for industrial capitalist development a new spin. The radical and nationalist aspects of the revolution advocated by leaders such as Emiliano Zapata and Francisco "Pancho" Villa did not find their way into the leadership of government officials after the 1920s, but neither Mexican nor U.S. political and economic leaders could ignore the impact of Mexican nationalism and revolutionary rhetoric. Instead, Mexican and American political leaders and businesses redefined different forms of nationalism and revolutionary rhetoric as they pushed for political, ideological, diplomatic, and commercial objectives that recycled strands of nineteenth-century liberalism. Mexican presidents, advertising agents, and Sears employees, among others, appealed to Mexican nationalism and pointed to the legacy of the revolution in order to increase their diplomatic leverage, define advertising as a profession, and request opportunities for upward mobility. Similarly, U.S. diplomats and business executives hoped to curb anti-

American nationalism by tapping into Mexican nationalist and revolutionary rhetoric while consciously syncretizing Mexican and American values, beliefs, and practices. The syncretizing of Mexican and American culture by U.S. political leaders and business executives represented a new form of diplomacy toward Mexico in the late 1930s.

The reconstruction of modern Mexico, international events such as the Great Depression and World War II, and the emergence of different forms of foreign policy in the United States established new diplomatic boundaries between the United States and Mexico. Echoing American self-righteousness and a blatant imperialist attitude, one form of diplomacy disregarded local conditions, portrayed Mexican culture and society as backward and inferior to American society, and vigorously promoted the spread of American culture and way of life. The other form of diplomacy stressed the need to acknowledge local conditions and adopt local values, beliefs, and practices. It encouraged the syncretism of Mexican and American culture while insisting that the goals of the Mexican people, as laid out by the 1910 revolution, were not incompatible with those of American political and business leaders. This form of diplomacy tapped into the reconstruction of modern Mexico (a process headed by Mexican political leaders) and contributed to a process that redefined national identity in Mexico. It presented modern industrial capitalism as a patriotic duty and a product of the revolution that would bring national prosperity, upward mobility, and a new form of democracy that Mexicans could experience through consumption. Ironically, this form of diplomacy responded to Mexico's revolutionary and nationalist rhetoric and was grounded in anti-imperialist tendencies in Latin America and the United States during the 1920s. Most important, it was a reaction to anti-American sentiment among Mexicans in the midst of the international crisis of the 1930s and 1940s.

Both forms of diplomacy supported the uplifting of Mexico, but one approach was more inclusive and more respectful of Latin American society and culture. America's "progressive diplomacy" acknowledged the need to promote upward mobility and a higher standard of living among Mexicans. Sears's Robert E. Wood and others who supported this form of diplomacy did not think America's commitment to raising the standard of living among Mexicans and Latin Americans should be made out of charity. They considered improving conditions in Latin America fundamental to American capitalist expansion and an effective diplomatic strategy to counteract Nazi and communist influence south of the U.S. border. Mexico's proximity to the United States and anti-American nationalism in the midst of international economic and political crisis made Mexico a potential threat to U.S. national security and a top priority. To this end, Mexicans gained some leverage in their negotiations with the United States. Mexico acquired this leverage at a time when the Mexican state was becoming increasingly powerful after a century of social and political chaos since the country's independence from Spain in 1821. Ironically, the United States supported modern industrial capitalism in Mexico after the 1920s. Industrial capitalist development fostered the creation of a strong Mexican state, which in turn promoted nationalist and revolutionary rhetoric and policies that increased Mexico's leverage in negotiations with the United States.

The new relationship between Mexico and the United States was the product of binational efforts to reconstruct modern Mexico and make the country's industrial capitalism work for both Mexico and the United States. U.S. and Mexican political leaders, business executives, and advertising agents associated Mexico's pursuit of modern industrial capitalism with upward mobility, self-realization, and consumer democracy. They drew on historical processes (nineteenth-century liberalism, the Mexican Revolution, and different forms of Mexican nationalism), as well as American leadership in science and technology, to reconstruct modern Mexico after the 1920s. Yet they introduced development programs, strategies, and policies as products of the revolution and measures that promoted modern industrial capitalism. In other words, they defined the revolution as a heroic struggle for justice within the nation's capitalist development. Most important, national and foreign efforts (by political leaders and corporate executives) to support Mexico's capitalist development were presented as paternalistic measures to carry out revolutionary ideals. Some American companies, like J. Walter Thompson, did not understand the nature of Mexico's capitalist development, but Sears and other companies did.

The case studies of Thompson and Sears offer two business models and corporate strategies for the introduction of American companies in Mexico. Thompson's initial approach endorsed a form of arrogance and self-righteousness that echoed early-twentieth-century American imperialism as the company insisted on transplanting its U.S. corporate culture and operations in Mexico. Thompson gradually learned that the rules for doing business in Mexico required familiarity with local conditions and culture. By contrast, Sears entered the Mexican market with a strong commitment to acclimating to local conditions and filtered its marketing and corporate operations through Mexican nationalist and revolutionary rhetoric. Sears introduced profit-sharing, a pension plan, low-priced meals, and other services in Mexico as an example of its support of revolutionary ideals. Sears's strategy echoed the "progressive" form of diplomacy championed by Nelson Rockefeller and a cadre of U.S. diplomats. The experience of Rockefeller's OIAA and the examples of Thompson and Sears in Mexico suggest that

Mexicans responded positively to a progressive and culturally sensitive form of diplomacy. They rejected American arrogance and the disregard for Mexican culture and social conditions.

_____ In the 1940s, the OIAA, Thompson, and Sears learned the ground rules for operating in Mexico by becoming familiar with Mexican culture and learning to operate within a cultural middle ground that required the syncretizing of American and Mexican values and practices. Unfortunately, some American companies did not learn these lessons as they entered the Mexican market or catered to the Latino community in the United States. Their disregard for local culture and language differences led to some embarrassing marketing efforts after the 1940s. For example, General Motors sent the wrong message when it marketed its Nova car model. In Spanish, "Nova" literally means "It doesn't go." Popular jokes about Novas did not bode well for company profits in Latin America. An even more embarrassing incident led to tasteless jokes that ridiculed American Airlines executives. The company translated its "Fly in Leather" campaign in Mexico as "Vuela en Cuero," which Mexicans interpreted as "Fly Naked."[1] Other publicity has been more cautious and sensitive to cultural and language differences. The California Milk Processor Board, for example, detected the problems of launching a Spanish version of its popular "Got Milk?" publicity in late 1993. As hilarious as "Got Milk?" commercials were to an American audience, this marketing pitch would not have worked for a Mexican or Latino audience. First, "Got Milk?" translates into "Are you lactating?" Second, among Latinos, for whom poverty and scarcity have often been a reality, the idea of running out of milk is not funny. Instead of the "Got Milk?" slogan, the California Milk Processor Board ran the "¿Y usted les dio suficiente leche hoy?" or "Did you give them enough milk today?" pitch after 1994.[2] It recently revised its marketing slogan to "Familia, amor, y leche" or "Family, love, and milk." The mixed results of the different publicity strategies of American companies suggest that U.S. corporations are still trying to find the most effective formula to reach the Mexican and Latin American market. The issue has become a priority in the U.S. corporate sector as a result of increasing trade because of the North American Free Trade Agreement (NAFTA), plans to develop a Free Trade Area of the Americas, and 2000 census data identifying the Latino community as the second largest minority group in the United States.

NAFTA and the wave of neoliberal economic policies the Mexican government has pursued since the 1980s and 1990s have almost ended Mexico's economic nationalism as outlined under ISI during the 1940s. While Mexico's economic-development formula triggered sustained economic growth from the 1940s to the early 1970s, economic crisis during the late 1970s and early 1980s sent the

Mexican economy into a tailspin. Economists designated the 1980s a "lost decade" for Mexico's and Latin America's economy. Politicians, business executives, and different sectors of society proposed neoliberal economic policies, including privatization, as the solution to economic problems in Latin America.
In Mexico, President Carlos Salinas de Gortari (1988–94) aggressively pushed
privatization and moved away from nationalist economic polices that characterized 1940s Mexico in his efforts to prepare Mexico for the signing of NAFTA. The
manner in which Mexico privatized benefited certain groups and individuals in
the early 1990s. Grupo Carso and its leaders, like Carlos Slim, became powerful
figures in the Mexican economy by the mid-1990s as a result of privatization.
Grupo Carso purchased over 80 percent of Sears de México in 1996, leaving
the Sears headquarters in Chicago with only 15 percent of the company. While
Grupo Carso's purchase marked the "Mexicanization" of Sears at an economic
level, at a cultural level, it is still difficult to classify Sears as either a Mexican or
an American store. To this end, the blurring of national boundaries that Sears
introduced in the 1940s continues today despite the fact that the ownership of
the company has changed from primarily American to primarily Mexican investors. Grupo Carso has also invested in other American companies, and its
investments illustrate the extent to which the Mexican and U.S. economies have
become interdependent. Neither Mexico nor the United States can disregard the
economic status and performance of each country as NAFTA has accelerated already existing trade between the two nations.

Newspaper reports of Mexicans committing suicide by jumping in front of
Mexico City's metro because of their inability to pay off loans in the mid-1990s
illustrate the ongoing saga of Mexico's industrial capitalism. On the one hand,
the promise of upward mobility into the ranks of the middle class was fulfilled
for many Mexicans as the nation's economic growth from the 1940s to the early
1970s triggered the growth of the middle class. Modern industrial capitalism
made Mexico one of the most industrialized countries in Latin America, and
to this end, Mexican political leaders (including Salinas de Gortari) have often
suggested that Mexico is just one step away from reaching the ranks of countries
like the United States. However, economic crisis during the 1980s weakened the
status of Mexico's middle class and exacerbated poverty in the lower sectors of
society, forcing millions of Mexicans to migrate to the United States in the hope
of finding better conditions. Mexicans became optimistic about the economy
and their social conditions during the early 1990s when the movement toward
privatization and discussions of NAFTA promised to revitalize Mexico's economy
and push the country and its population toward the "First World." However,
optimism turned into disappointment by the mid-1990s when Mexico's economy
nosedived as a result of political corruption, economic mismanagement, a mili-

tary uprising in southern Mexico, and impatient U.S. and Mexican investors who withdrew their investments and cash. President Bill Clinton's quick response to the crisis illustrates the interdependence between Mexico and the United States by the late 1990s. U.S. and Mexican efforts to stabilize the Mexican economy worked to the extent that the economy experienced steady growth throughout the late 1990s. Yet the crisis of the mid-1990s reminded Mexicans of their economic and social vulnerability. It also made them more cautious and suspicious of promises of social and economic prosperity. While the election of President Vicente Fox in 2000 fostered a certain degree of optimism, Mexicans quickly reminded him of the political cost of not delivering campaign promises, which included continued growth, when his popularity declined substantially shortly after he took office. In other words, Mexicans have learned to accept modern industrial capitalism as the key to economic prosperity and upward mobility, which political leaders, business executives, and advertising agents promoted from the 1920s to 1950s as part of the reconstruction of modern Mexico. However, eighty years of unfulfilled promises, along with an opening of the political process, have led Mexicans to hold politicians accountable for their promises and performance.

Politically, the governing formula established by the PRI worked until 2000, when the party lost the election to the PAN, the conservative party that emerged in opposition to the PRI after the 1940s. Using a "carrot and stick" approach, the PRI managed to maintain political stability from the 1930s to the 1990s at a time when the rest of Latin America was subject to social and political chaos. The PRI curbed political opposition through the electoral process and repression of radical leaders, although it did not resort to the level of repression used by other Latin American governments during this period. Defining itself as the heir of the 1910 revolution, the PRI conveniently used social programs, institutional policies, and the belief that Mexico's industrial capitalism was the key to upward mobility to further cement political stability. However, growing opposition since the 1960s, increasing accusations of corruption, and party divisions debilitated the PRI to the point that Mexicans ended the seventy-one-year PRI reign in the 2000 election. The decline of the PRI has brought substantial changes to Mexico's political process, but the country continues to support the creed that modern industrial capitalism is the key to uplifting Mexicans into the middle class—a creed that became synonymous with the reconstruction of modern Mexico in the aftermath of the 1910 revolution.

Notes

Abbreviations

AEBLT	Archivos Económicos de la Biblioteca Lerdo de Tejada, Mexico City
AGN	Archivo General de la Nación, Mexico City
AHAC	Archivo Histórico de Acción Católica
AHAM	Archivo Histórico del Arzobispado de México, Mexico City
AHUIA	Biblioteca Francisco Xavier Clavigero, Acervos Históricos, Universidad Iberoamericana, Mexico City
HCAMR	Hartman Center for Sales, Advertising, and Marketing Research, Duke University, Durham, North Carolina
IOF	International Office Files
JWTCA	J. Walter Thompson Company Archives
RG	Record Group
RUA	Rockefeller University Archives, New York
SRA	Sears Roebuck and Company Archives, Chicago
USNA	U.S. National Archives, College Park, Maryland

Introduction

1. Jerry Jeran to T. V. Houser, March 2, 1947, SRA, 100.15 IOF, box 52.
2. "Foreign Procedures," report no. 3, SRA, 100.15 IOF, box 1.
3. "Latinoamérica—Oportunidades y responsabilidades: Discurso pronunciado por John F. Gallagher, vice presidente a Cargo de Latinoamérica," December 5, 1960, SRA, 100.15 IOF, box 49.
4. American companies such as N. W. Ayer and J. Walter Thompson opened branches in Latin America in the 1920s but decided to stay out of Mexico because they considered investments in Mexico too risky. Some American companies, however, as shown in O'Brien, *Revolutionary Mission*, entered the Mexican market in the 1920s and 1930s despite occasional tensions with Mexicans.
5. "Boicot contra las mercancías Americanas: El gobierno no volverá a comprar en los Estados Unidos mercancías de ninguna clase," *El Universal*, May 15, 1927, n.p., AEBLT, "Boicot, México, 1927–1982," L06590.
6. "Más quejas se han recibido en Ciudad Juárez, el Partido Nacional Revolucionario presta todo su apoyo al Alcalde Flores, aprobando su actitud," *La Prensa*, February 12, 1931, 2, AEBLT, "Boicot, México, 1927–1982," L06590.
7. Hearst Newsreel Footage, Mexico, 1938–46, University of California at Los Angeles Film Archives, CS559, Mexone 40020000, program 1, tape 2.

8. Townsend, *Lázaro Cárdenas*, 270.
9. "Sears Roebuck's Mexican Revolution," *Harper's Magazine*, April 1964, n.p., SRA, 100.15 IOF, box 1.
10. "Yankees Don't Go Home!," *Saturday Evening Post*, n.d., SRA, 100.15 IOF, box 1.
11. Leach, in *Land of Desire*, states that the emergence of middle-class consumer culture in late-nineteenth-century America created a sense of democracy that equated consumption and abundance with "democratized individual desire—rather than wealth or political or economic power" (7–8). Abundance in terms of territorial (westward) expansion or mass consumption also became instrumental in defining American democracy and identity. See Frederick Jackson Turner, "The Significance of the Frontier in American History," in *The Frontier in American History*, and Potter, *People of Plenty*. Abundance and mass consumption were not static in American society. As Heinze, *Adapting to Abundance*, has shown, they were so much a part of American society that they provided the context through which Jewish immigrants "Americanized" and shaped the commercial process that supported their adaptation to American society. Among other studies of U.S. history, Bushman, *Refinement of America*, suggests that aristocratic values gradually found their way into different aspects of American culture between 1700 and 1800. To this end, the diffusion of aristocratic values through consumption served as a "democratizing force." Cohen, in "Class Experience of Mass Consumption," disagrees with scholars who suggest that consumers in twentieth-century America achieved equality through consumption. She argues that "even when participating in mass consumption, workers in the 1930s did not find themselves unconsciously incorporated into the middle class society" (138).
12. According to Cosío Villegas, "La riqueza legendaria de México," in *Ensayos y notas*, 56–61, the myth of Mexico's wealth conveniently justified the belief that Mexicans were poor because they were lazy.
13. According to Brading, *First America*, 5, 368–69, Creoles succeeded in creating an intellectual tradition that was original, complex, and distinct from any European model and referred to New Spain as a "paradise."
14. Travel accounts by Von Humboldt in *Political Essay on the Kingdom of New Spain* reinforce the perception of Mexico as a wealthy region during the early nineteenth century.
15. Tenorio-Trujillo, *Mexico at the World's Fairs*, 52–53, uses the term "wizards of progress" to refer to Mexican elites who wanted to create an image of Mexico that could be easily grasped by both nationals and foreigners. They produced that image through maps, photographs, albums, almanacs, and statistics. See Topik and Wells, *Second Conquest of Latin America*, and Haber, *How Latin America Fell Behind*, for analyses of how export markets and institutions supported Mexico's notion of progress and modern capitalist development.
16. Among other scholars, Córdova, in *La formación del poder político en México*,

64–68, suggests that modern industrial capitalism became a banner of the Mexican Revolution after Cárdenas.

17. Numerous scholars have written about the use of the revolution and/or its nationalist and revolutionary rhetoric to promote specific social, political, economic, or cultural agendas. See, for example, Krauze, *La presidencia imperial*, 83–85; Benjamin, *La Revolución*, 21, 66–73, 96, 116–20; O'Malley, *Myth of the Revolution*, 4–6, 51–70; and Aguayo Quezada, *El panteón de los mitos*, 63, 77. For a historiographical point of view, see Florescano, *El nuevo pasado mexicano*, 71–152.

18. See Peter Smith, "Mexico since 1946"; Camp, *Entrepreneurs and Politics*; Cline, *Mexico*; Hansen, *Mexican Economic Development*; Wilkie, *Mexican Revolution*; Granados Roldán et al., *México: 75 años de revolución*; and Reyes Heroles, "Función social de las obras públicas."

19. See Joseph and Nugent, *Everyday Forms of State Formation*, and Vaughan, *Cultural Politics of Revolution*.

20. See Cosío Villegas, "La leyenda legendaria de México" and "La crisis de México," in *Ensayos y notas*, 39–72, 113–51; Knight, "Revolutionary Project, Recalcitrant People"; Carlos Monsiváis, "La cultura mexicana en el siglo XX," in Wilkie, Meyer, and Monzon de Wilkie, *Contemporary Mexico*, 624–70; and Krauze, *La presidencia imperial*.

21. My definition of ideology is based partly on LaClau, *Politics and Ideology in Marxist Theory*, which suggests that an economically defined social class articulates an ideological framework and worldview that are not representative of the relationship of workers to the means of production. My view of ideology, however, centers more on issues of national identity and "myths" of Mexico's nationalist and revolutionary heritage and the relationship of different regions to the nation than on class or the means of production.

22. This is partly based on Krauze, *La presidencia imperial*, which suggests that different sectors of Mexican society forged a political consensus during the 1940s.

23. See Peter Smith, "Mexico since 1946"; Camp, *Entrepreneurs and Politics*; and Cline, *Mexico*.

24. See Monsiváis, *Mexican Postcards* and "La cultura mexicana en el siglo XX"; Agustín, *Tragicomedia mexicana*; Hamilton, *Limits of State Autonomy*; Aguilar Camín and Meyer, *In the Shadow of the Mexican Revolution*; Knight, "Revolutionary Project, Recalcitrant People"; Cosío Villegas, "La crisis de México"; and Tzvi, *El sexenio Alemanista*.

25. See Schuler, *Mexico between Hitler and Roosevelt*. Schuler's approach echoes the works of other scholars, such as Katz, in *Secret War in Mexico*, and O'Brien, in *Revolutionary Mission*, who suggest that Mexicans (whether political leaders, workers, or consumers of electricity or other products) often shaped policies and processes by either playing imperial powers off one another or actively finding new forms of resistance against specific American companies.

María Emilia Paz, *Strategy, Security, and Spies*, and Spenser, *Impossible Triangle*, provide a similar interpretation of U.S.-Mexican relations in the 1920s and early 1940s.

26. See Seth Fein, "Everyday Forms of Transnational Collaboration: U.S. Film Propaganda in Cold War Mexico," in Joseph, LeGrand, and Salvatore, *Close Encounters of Empire*, 400–450. Fein, like other authors in Joseph's edited volume, successfully "moves beyond questions of ideology and representation to implementation and reception" through the lenses of Pratt's "contact zones" (403). According to Pratt, *Imperial Eyes*, "Contact zones are social spaces where disparate cultures meet, clash, and grapple with each other, often in highly asymmetrical relations of domination and subordination," causing a transcultural phenomenon in which "subordinated groups select and invent from materials transmitted to them by a dominant or metropolitan culture" (4–6). She suggests that "while subjugated people cannot readily control what emanates from the dominant culture, they do determine to varying extents what they absorb into their own, and what they use it for" (6). In other words, the people in the "contact zone" have agency only to the extent that they respond to a dominant power.

27. See White, *Middle Ground*, 51.

28. Ibid. According to White, finding the middle ground is the "attempt to understand the world and reasoning of the other and to assimilate enough of that reasoning to put it to [one's] own purposes."

29. I think of finding the middle ground as the process of learning the boundaries of what it takes to successfully do business or design images that blend or syncretize values, beliefs, and practices. The syncretizing of images may be a conscious effort on the part of advertisers, broadcasters, or editors, but the audience does not necessarily perceive it at a conscious level. Nor is there any guarantee that it will have the results, expectations, or impact originally intended. It does not necessarily imply that there is a political or economic message that will create either a true or a false consciousness. It translates an experience within boundaries accepted at a conscious level by the viewer. It is the identification by advertisers of the boundaries for making images, messages, values, and rhetoric acceptable in a specific context. It suggests that "agency" exists in a specific multifaceted context in which power, agency, and ideology become muted in a "hypereal," to use Baudrillard's phrase, to the extent that, at the cultural level, the lines between Mexican and American, as well as the hierarchical imperial power structure, become blurred. See Baudrillard, *Selected Writings*.

30. See González y González, *San José de Gracia*.

31. See Vaughan, *Cultural Politics of Revolution*.

32. See Sands, *Charrería Mexicana*; O'Malley, *Myth of the Revolution*; and Agustín, *Tragicomedia mexicana*.

33. See Rosenberg, *Financial Missionaries*, and O'Brien, *Revolutionary Mission*.

34. See Aguayo Quezada, *El panteón de los mitos*, 73–74, 83–85.
35. See Simpson, *Many Mexicos*.
36. Mexican scholars have shed some light on this issue. See Córdova, *La formación del poder político en México* and *La ideología de la Revolución Mexicana*; and Florescano, *El nuevo pasado mexicano*.
37. See Knight, "Racism, Revolution, and Indigenismo"; O'Malley, *Myth of the Revolution*; and Stepan, *Hour of Eugenics*.
38. See Cosío Villegas, *Ensayos y notas*; and Novo, *Apuntes para una historia de la publicidad* and *Seis siglos de la ciudad de México*.
39. This is a similar approach to the one presented in Joseph and Nugent, *Everyday Forms of State Formation*.
40. I borrowed concepts and methodological strategies from Marchand's *Advertising the American Dream* for this chapter.
41. My approach and methodology in this chapter are based on studies that use images as a historical lens. See Tenorio-Trujillo, *Mexico at the World's Fairs*, and O'Malley, *Myth of the Revolution*.
42. See Agustín, *Tragicomedia mexicana*.
43. My approach and methodology in this section resemble Lears's in *No Place of Grace*.

Chapter One

1. Pérez Jiménez, *Vigencia del pensamiento político, económico, y social*, 200–201, 220, 221.
2. Chandler, *Visible Hand*, 1, 485.
3. Reyes Heroles, *El liberalismo mexicano*, 470, 483, 506, 526.
4. Reyes Heroles, *La historia y la acción*, 13; Córdova, "El pensamiento social y político de Andrés Molina Enríquez," in Molina Enríquez, *Los grandes problemas nacionales*, 19–20. See also Córdova, *La ideología de la Revolución Mexicana*, 87, and Camp, *Entrepreneurs and Politics*, 15.
5. According to Topik and Wells, *Second Conquest of Latin America*, 1, 13–14, nineteenth-century Latin American liberals based their principles of free trade and comparative advantage on the views of classic European economists such as Adam Smith and David Ricardo.
6. Some scholars have described Mexico's integration into the world economy as a "second conquest" (ibid., 1).
7. Camp, *Entrepreneurs and Politics*, 15.
8. Mexican historians have long debated what this social democratic process meant and who led it. Knight, *Mexican Revolution*, vol. 2, characterizes it as a revolutionary process driven by the masses. Córdova, *La ideología de la Revolución Mexicana*, describes it as a movement headed by middle-class leaders who endorsed economic ideals of material progress prior to the revolution but objected to the Díaz administration by the early 1900s.

9. Joseph and Nugent, *Everyday Forms of State Formation*; Benjamin and Wasserman, *Provinces of the Revolution*; and Vaughan, *Cultural Politics of Revolution*, have shown how political bosses and community leaders interacted and shaped the ways in which government programs and institutions were received at the local level. These studies give "agency" to regional politicians and community leaders and challenge interpretations by other scholars, such as González y González, in *San José de Gracia*, who suggest that federal authority and culture radiating out of Mexico City absorbed local politics, culture, and lifestyles.

10. Hale, *Transformation of Liberalism*, 3–4, 31–33.

11. Ibid., 3; Reyes Heroles, *La historia y la acción*, 140; Córdova, *La ideología de la Revolución Mexicana*, 87.

12. According to Krauze, *La presidencia imperial*, 23–27, 83–84, the Mexican Revolution as myth became a powerful mechanism for the legitimization of the state and the centralization of power in the hands of the federal government and specifically the presidency.

13. Although works like Aguilar Camín and Meyer, *In the Shadow of the Mexican Revolution*, classify Cárdenas as socialist, others like O'Brien, *Revolutionary Mission*, have demonstrated that Cárdenas was procapitalist and did not object to American investments in Mexico despite the popular nationalism expressed during the nationalization of American oil companies in 1938.

14. Influenced by French positivism, political leaders under Díaz endorsed an organic view of society in which the state would serve as one of the organs of the body or society. It would work in conjunction with other organs but would not necessarily be the driving force. See Hale, *Transformation of Liberalism*.

15. "El bloque de la Cámara de Diputados determinó ya la reglamentación del artículo cuatro," *El Nacional*, October 11, 1940, 8, AEBLT, "Profesionistas, reglamentos, México, 1931–1993," G05099.

16. Ibid.

17. "El ejercicio de las profesiones: La reglamentación del artículo 4 necesaria," *El Nacional*, March 3, 1943, n.p., AEBLT, "Profesionistas, reglamentos, México, 1931–1993," G05099.

18. Lic. Paulino Machorro Narváez, "La reglamentación de profesiones," *El Universal*, November 13, 1943, 9, AEBLT, "Profesionistas, reglamentos, México, 1931–1993," G05099.

19. "Reformas que se harán al artículo cuatro," *El Nacional*, January 14, 1941, 8, AEBLT, "Profesionistas, reglamentos, México, 1931–1993," G05099.

20. "La depuración profesional, el dictamen contra los charlatanes, hoy será discutido en la cámara el proyecto de reformas," *El Nacional*, March 14, 1941, 8, AEBLT, "Profesionistas, reglamentos, México, 1931–1993," G05099.

21. "El bloque de la Cámara de Diputados determinó ya la reglamentación del artículo cuatro," *El Nacional*, October 1, 1940, 8, AEBLT, "Profesionistas, reglamentos, México, 1931–1993," G05099.

22. Rubén Zalazar, "Charlatanismo y cultura," *El Universal*, November 11, 1943, 9, and Francisco Carreño, "Las reformas de la constitución en materia de profesiones," *El Universal*, March 2, 1941, 9, AEBLT, "Profesionistas, reglamentos, México, 1931–1993," G05099.

23. Pogolotti, *La clase media en México*, 24–27, 75, 102.

24. "Flores de sinople en campo de trigo," *El Nacional*, February 27, 1941, 8, AEBLT, "Profesionistas, reglamentos, México, 1931–1993," G05099.

25. Francisco Carreño, "Las reformas de la constitución en materia de profesiones," *El Universal*, March 2, 1941, 9, AEBLT, "Profesionistas, reglamentos, México, 1931–1993," G05099.

26. Ibid.

27. "Congreso sobre el artículo cuarto constitucional, serán convocados todos los profesionistas titulados de la república," *Excélsior*, October 28, 1933, n.p., AEBLT, "Profesionistas, legislación, 1929–1934," G05224.

28. "Precisa determinar la socialización de las profesiones, las respuestas enviadas a la Cámara de Diputados lo dan a entender," *El Nacional*, February 13, 1943, 8, AEBLT, "Profesionistas, legislación, 1929–1934," G05224.

29. "El Gral. Cárdenas acabará con el charlatanismo, el estado debe federalizar la ley de profesiones a fin de no dejar campo abierto a los charlatanes sin escrúpulos," *La Prensa*, October 14, 1934, n.p., AEBLT, "Profesionistas, legislación, 1929–1934," G05224.

30. "Precisa determinar la socialización de las profesiones, las respuestas enviadas a la Cámara de Diputados lo dan a entender," *El Nacional*, February 13, 1934, 8, AEBLT, "Profesionistas, legislación, 1929–1934," G05224.

31. "La reforma del artículo cuarto constitucional," *El Universal*, March 20, 1937, 9, AEBLT, "Profesionistas, reglamentos, México, 1931–1993," G05099.

32. "Estudio para la reglamentación del artículo cuarto," *Excélsior*, June 1, 1937, 10, AEBLT, "Profesionistas, reglamentos, México, 1931–1993," G05099.

33. "El artículo cuatro constitucional, su reglamentación y la Asociación Nacional de Abogados," *El Universal*, April 29, 1943, 9, AEBLT, "Profesionistas, reglamentos, México, 1931–1993," G05099.

34. "Reglamentación de las profesiones," *El Universal*, May 17, 1937, 9, AEBLT, "Profesionistas, reglamentos, México, 1931–1993," G05099.

35. "En contra del charlatanismo, el Sindicato de Abogados del D.F. propugnará por que se federalice la ley reglamentaria para ejercer," *El Universal*, October 4, 1934, 9, AEBLT, "Profesionistas, legislación, 1931–1993," G05099.

36. "Reglamentación de las profesiones," *El Universal*, May 17, 1937, 9, AEBLT, "Profesionistas, reglamentos, México, 1931–1993," G05099.

37. "Anteproyecto de ley reglamentaria de los artículos 4 y 5 de la constitución política de los Estados Unidos Mexicanos en lo que se refiere al ejercicio de las profesiones técnico-científicas del Distrito Federal y Territorios Federales," *El Nacional*, November 16, 1943, 8, AEBLT, "Profesionistas, reglamentos, México, 1931–1993," G05099.

38. Ibid.

39. "El reportero preguntón," *Novedades*, March 25, 1941, 15, AEBLT, "Profesionistas, reglamentos, México, 1931–1993," G05099.

40. Ibid.

41. Ibid.

42. "Surgen las opiniones sobre las reformas al artículo cuarto," *El Universal*, n.d., 9, AEBLT, "Profesionistas, reglamentos, México, 1931–1993," G05099.

43. "La publicidad y la crisis," *Excélsior*, February 6, 1933, 1, AEBLT, "Publicidad: Propaganda, aranceles, relaciones públicas, comunicación de masas, México, 1925–1945," C07040.

44. According to Hale, *Transformation of Liberalism*, 4, constitutionalism, individual freedom, and a vision of social progress through economic development were the key ingredients of nineteenth-century liberalism in Mexico.

45. "La publicidad y la crisis," *Excélsior*, February 6, 1933, 10, AEBLT, "Publicidad: Propaganda, aranceles, relaciones públicas, comunicación de masas, México, 1925–1945," C07040.

46. "El aumento del consumo, los productos de mercancías deben hacer una intensa propaganda dice el Departamento de Economía," *El Universal*, September 1934, 9, AEBLT, "Publicidad: Propaganda, aranceles, relaciones públicas, comunicación de masas, México, 1925–1945," C09040.

47. "Un eficiente instrumento de trabajo, la secretaría de economía ha fundado una Oficina de Propaganda y Publicidad," *El Nacional*, October 19, 1935, 8; "Educación y propaganda," *El Universal*, July 21, 1943, 9; and "El nuevo reglamento de anuncios," *El Universal*, October 23, 1938, 9, AEBLT, "Publicidad: Propaganda, aranceles, relaciones públicas, comunicación de masas, México, 1925–1945," C07040.

48. "El aumento del consumo, los productos de mercancías deben hacer una intensa propaganda dice el Departamento de Economía," *El Universal*, September 1934, 9, AEBLT, "Publicidad: Propaganda, aranceles, relaciones públicas, comunicación de masas, México, 1925–1945," C07040.

49. "Intensa propaganda en los países extranjeros se hace a los productos nacionales," *El Nacional*, July 5, 1934, 8, AEBLT, "Publicidad: Propaganda, aranceles, relaciones públicas, comunicación de masas, México, 1925–1945," C07040.

50. "La publicidad debe ser aplicada a los negocios en general, recomienda la secretaría de la economía nacional a los comerciantes el anuncio," *El Nacional*, December 13, 1933, 8, AEBLT, "Publicidad: Propaganda, aranceles, relaciones públicas, comunicación de masas, México, 1925–1945," C07040.

51. "Se celebra mañana el día del anuncio, trascendental iniciativa a la industria y al comercio," *El Nacional*, April 22, 1935, 8, AEBLT, "Publicidad: Propaganda, aranceles, relaciones públicas, comunicación de masas, México, 1925–1945," C07040.

52. Ibid.

53. Ibid.

54. "Fructífera difusión de los negocios por radio, la secretaría de economía considera que esa propaganda producirá en breve un resultado satisfactorio," *El Universal*, April 30, 1935, 8, AEBLT, "Publicidad: Propaganda, aranceles, relaciones públicas, comunicación de masas, México, 1925–1945," C07040.

55. "La publicidad es la fuerza motriz del comercio moderno," [early 1930s], AEBLT, "Publicidad: Propaganda, aranceles, relaciones públicas, comunicación de masas, México, 1925–1945," C07040.

56. "La producción nacional y la falta de publicidad," *Excélsior*, December 12, 1934, 9, AEBLT, "Publicidad: Propaganda, aranceles, relaciones públicas, comunicación de masas, México, 1925–1945," C07040.

57. "Educación y propaganda," *El Universal*, July 21, 1943, 9, AEBLT, "Publicidad: Propaganda, aranceles, relaciones públicas, comunicación de masas, México, 1925–1945," C07040.

58. Ibid.

59. "Concurso de escaparates de productos nacionales más de doscientas industrias del país están representadas, fue ayer inaugurado," *El Universal*, March 3, 1931, 9; "Todo está listo para inaugurar la hermosa feria del escaparate, entre las exhibiciones hay verdaderas maravillas que serán sorpresa para quienes dudan de nuestro país," *Excélsior*, February 3, 1931, 10; and "Una revelación de lo que es México, fue inaugurado el concurso de los aparadores y altos funcionarios del gobierno dieron realce a la apertura de la feria," *Excélsior*, March 8, 1931, 10, AEBLT, "Publicidad: Propaganda, aranceles, relaciones públicas, comunicación de masas, México, 1925–1945," C07040.

60. "Grande interés por el concurso de escaparates, el certámen nacionalista llama a un público numeroso y entusiasta, no hay jurado aún pero el espectáculo de unión y cooperación ha sido soberbio y unico," *Excélsior*, March 10, 1931, 10, AEBLT, "Publicidad: Propaganda, aranceles, relaciones públicas, comunicación de masas, México, 1925–1945," C07040.

61. "Quienes vencieron el concurso de escaparates, la importancia de los productos fue la base principal," *Excélsior*, March 14, 1931, 10, AEBLT, "Publicidad: Propaganda, aranceles, relaciones públicas, comunicación de masas, México, 1925–1945," C07040.

62. "En los estados deben hacerse concursos de escaparates locales, en la presidencia de la república se recibe esta sugerencia," *Excélsior*, March 19, 1931, 10, AEBLT, "Publicidad: Propaganda, aranceles, relaciones públicas, comunicación de masas, México, 1925–1945," C07040.

63. Ibid.

64. "Comienza la semana del consumo nacional," *El Nacional*, May 4, 1931, 8, AEBLT, "Publicidad: Propaganda, aranceles, relaciones públicas, comunicación de masas, México, 1925–1945," C07040.

65. These promotional events were known officially as the "Semana Blanca" and the "Semana del Calzado" or "Semana Especial del Calzado." See "La venta

de productos nacionales, hay que seguir nuevos sistemas a fin de ensanchar el consumo, el ejemplo de la Semana Blanca, baratas que abarquen toda la república ofrece baratas especiales, reducción de precios y propaganda," *El Universal*, June 8, 1933, 9, AEBLT, "Publicidad: Propaganda, aranceles, relaciones públicas, comunicación de masas, México, 1925–1945," C07040.

66. Ibid.

67. "Se recomienda una acción eficaz para impulsar las ventas de mercancías que están almacenadas," *El Economista*, February 23, 1933, 2, AEBLT, "Publicidad: Propaganda, aranceles, relaciones públicas, comunicación de masas, México, 1925–1945," C07040.

68. Ibid.

69. "La venta de productos nacionales, hay que seguir nuevos sistemas a fin de ensanchar el consumo, el ejemplo de la Semana Blanca, baratas que abarquen toda la república ofrece baratas especiales, reducción de precios y propaganda," *El Universal*, June 8, 1933, 9, AEBLT, "Publicidad: Propaganda, aranceles, relaciones públicas, comunicación de masas, México, 1925–1945," C07040.

70. Mosk, *Industrial Revolution in Mexico*, 46, 97, 133.

71. Chandler, *Visible Hand*, 224, 236.

72. "Se recomienda una acción eficaz para impulsar las ventas de mercancías que están almacenadas," *El Economista*, February 23, 1933, 2, AEBLT, "Publicidad: Propaganda, aranceles, relaciones públicas, comunicación de masas, México, 1925–1945," C07040.

73. "En memoria del anuncio volante," *El Nacional*, January 15, 1932, 8, AEBLT, "Publicidad: Propaganda, aranceles, relaciones públicas, comunicación de masas, México, 1925–1945," C07040.

74. Secretaría de la Economía Nacional, *Ley de patentes y de marcas*, 83–87, 109.

75. "Al fin se pone 'Hecho en México,' los artículos nacionales, se ha estimulado notablemente su consumo," *El Universal*, November 30, 1932, 9, AEBLT, "Publicidad: Propaganda, aranceles, relaciones públicas, comunicación de masas, México, 1925–1945," C07040.

76. "El nuevo reglamento de anuncios," *El Universal*, October 23, 1938, 9, AEBLT, "Publicidad: Propaganda, aranceles, relaciones públicas, comunicación de masas, México, 1925–1945," C07040.

77. "Educación y propaganda," *El Universal*, July 21, 1943, 9, AEBLT, "Publicidad: Propaganda, aranceles, relaciones públicas, comunicación de masas, México, 1925–1945," C07040.

78. "El nuevo reglamento de anuncios," *El Universal*, October 23, 1938, 9, AEBLT, "Publicidad: Propaganda, aranceles, relaciones públicas, comunicación de masas, México, 1925–1945," C07040.

79. Ibid. See also "Educación y propaganda," *El Universal*, July 21, 1943, 9, AEBLT, "Publicidad: Propaganda, aranceles, relaciones públicas, comunicación de masas, México, 1925–1945," C07040.

80. "Una inmoral propaganda, protesta enérgicamente contra ella el Comité Nacional de Lucha Contra el Alcoholismo, algunos fabricantes de bebidas embriagantes hacen uso de una publicidad que debe ser penada," *El Nacional*, May 24, 1930, 8, AEBLT, "Publicidad: Propaganda, aranceles, relaciones públicas, comunicación de masas, México, 1925–1945," C07040.

81. Ibid.

82. Ibid.

83. Ibid.

84. "La comercialización del dolor," *La Prensa*, July 6, 1933, 2, AEBLT, "Publicidad: Propaganda, aranceles, relaciones públicas, comunicación de masas, México, 1925–1945," C07040.

85. Ibid.

86. "¿Qué vio usted ayer?," *El Universal*, April 8, 1931, 9, AEBLT, "Publicidad: Propaganda, aranceles, relaciones públicas, comunicación de masas, México, 1925–1945," C07040.

87. Ibid.

88. "Los fraudes de la publicidad: Iniciativa presentada al consejo consultivo para salvaguardar los intereses de los comerciantes, agentes que cobran por adelantado," *El Universal*, November 19, 1931, 9, AEBLT, "Publicidad: Propaganda, aranceles, relaciones públicas, comunicación de masas, México, 1925–1945," C07040.

89. Ibid.

90. "Se combatirán las formas de anunciar fuera de la ética," *El Universal*, July 7, 1935, 9, and "Educación y propaganda," *El Universal*, July 21, 1943, 9, AEBLT, "Publicidad: Propaganda, aranceles, relaciones públicas, comunicación de masas, México, 1925–1945," C07040.

91. Ibid.

92. "Formas de publicidad que resultan nocivas, la confederación de cámaras de comercio está haciendo labor de saneamiento," *El Universal*, July 7, 1935, 9, AEBLT, "Publicidad: Propaganda, aranceles, relaciones públicas, comunicación de masas, México, 1925–1945," C07040.

93. Ibid.

94. Cámara Nacional de la Industria de Transformación, *Selección, registro y uso de marcas*, 7–8, 11–13, 22.

95. Ibid., 29.

96. "El timbre comercial ha reportado enormes ventajas al comercio y a la industria, en diez años de funcionamiento, el público ha llegado a conceptuarlo ya como un sistema indispensable, en todas las grandes capitales del mundo este sistema forma parte de las transacciones del comercio civilizado, opinión de las señoras de México," *El Universal*, November 15, 1934, 9, AEBLT, "Publicidad: Propaganda, aranceles, relaciones públicas, comunicación de masas, México, 1925–1945," C07040.

97. Ibid.

98. Ibid.

99. "Oneroso gravámen pesa sobre los comerciantes, el llamado 'timbre comercial' es una gabela perjudicial para el consumidor," *El Nacional*, October 22, 1931, 8, AEBLT, "Publicidad: Propaganda, aranceles, relaciones públicas, comunicación de masas, México, 1925–1945," C07040.

100. "Monopolio que debe ya cesar, el comercio habla de los engaños al público por medio del timbre comercial; enérgica protesta ha sido enviada al ejecutivo de la unión, adelantado maniobras de la empresa," *Excélsior*, October 6, 1931, 10, AEBLT, "Publicidad: Propaganda, aranceles, relaciones públicas, comunicación de masas, México, 1925–1945," C07040.

101. Ibid.

102. "Autorización para los cupones y rifas, se reglamentará este sistema comercial en beneficio del consumidor," *El Universal*, November 1, 1931, 9, AEBLT, "Publicidad: Propaganda, aranceles, relaciones públicas, comunicación de masas, México, 1925–1945," C07040.

103. "Manifestación contra el timbre comercial, numerosos comerciantes entrevistaron al señor presidente de la República," *El Universal*, December 14, 1934, 9, AEBLT, "Publicidad: Propaganda, aranceles, relaciones públicas, comunicación de masas, México, 1925–1945," C07040.

104. "El criterio de la secretaría en materia de bonificación al público," *El Nacional*, November 20, 1934, 8, AEBLT, "Publicidad: Propaganda, aranceles, relaciones públicas, comunicación de masas, México, 1925–1945," C07040.

105. "Estudio jurídico de sorteos comerciales, la secretaría de gobernación va a resolver acerca de la nota de economía," *Excélsior*, November 2, 1934, 10, AEBLT, "Publicidad: Propaganda, aranceles, relaciones públicas, comunicación de masas, México, 1925–1945," C07040.

106. "Se forma un reglamento, se trata del que servirá para hacer las ventas por medio de sorteos, estudios en la secretaría de la economía nacional," *El Universal*, October 26, 1934, 9, AEBLT, "Publicidad: Propaganda, aranceles, relaciones públicas, comunicación de masas, México, 1925–1945," C07040.

107. Ibid.

108. "Los víveres se cotizan a muy altos precios," *La Prensa*, October 5, 1930, 2, AEBLT, "Comisión Nacional de Precios—México, 1931–1981," A03305.

109. "Para contrarrestar el alza de los precios," *El Nacional*, October 29, 1934, 8, and "Escandalosa alza de los precios de muchos artículos," *El Día*, October 4, 1935, 101, AEBLT, "Comisión Nacional de Precios—México, 1931–1981," A03305.

110. Ochoa, *Feeding Mexico*, 32–33.

111. "Bans Price Boosting, Mexican Federal District to Close Shops Guilty of Profiteering," *New York Times*, August 17, 1931, 20, AEBLT, "Comisión Nacional de Precios—México, 1931–1981," A03305.

112. "La Cámara Nacional de Comercio vs. La Distribuidora y Reguladora," *El Uni-*

versal, January 30, 1930, 9, AEBLT, "Nacional Distribuidora y Reguladora, S.A. de C.V., 1941–1954," A03193.

113. Ochoa, *Feeding Mexico*, 83.

114. "Ya no hará favoritismos la Nacional Distribuidora pide se le envíen cotizaciones de todos los productos, en sobre cerrado y sellados," *Excélsior*, January 13, 1945, 10, AEBLT, "Nacional Distribuidora y Reguladora, S.A. de C.V., 1941–1954," A03193.

115. "Protestan contra la demagogia los almacenistas, el libre comercio frente al papel de la distribuidora," *Novedades*, November 20, 1944, 15, AEBLT, "Nacional Distribuidora y Reguladora, S.A. de C.V., 1941–1954," A03193.

116. "Las tiendas populares dejan de ser servicio social, ahora puro coyotaje, ya no pueden vender todo, sólo productos de empresas sospechosamente favorecidas," *Excélsior*, January 11, 1945, 10, AEBLT, "Nacional Distribuidora y Reguladora, S.A. de C.V., 1941–1954," A03193.

117. Ibid.

118. "Unión Nacional de Comerciantes en Víveres, nota a los comerciantes en víveres del país y a la opinión pública en general," Mexico City, January 18, 1945, AEBLT, "Nacional Distribuidora y Reguladora, S.A. de C.V., 1941–1954," A03193.

119. "Ofensiva contra la reguladora, algunas casas comerciales intentan tener el control de los artículos de primera necesidad para especular," *El Nacional*, July 10, 1945, 8, AEBLT, "Nacional Distribuidora y Reguladora, S.A. de C.V., 1941–1954," A03193.

120. "De acertas orígenes la reguladora, tienden a abaratar las subsistencias que está vendiendo," *Excélsior*, January 24, 1945, 8, AEBLT, "Nacional Distribuidora y Reguladora, S.A. de C.V., 1941–1954," A03193.

121. "Las tiendas populares dejan de ser servicio social, ahora puro coyotaje, ya no pueden vender todo, sólo productos de empresas sospechosamente favorecidas," *Excélsior*, January 11, 1945, 10, AEBLT, "Nacional Distribuidora y Reguladora, S.A. de C.V., 1941–1954," A03193.

122. "De acertas orígenes la reguladora, tienden a abaratar las subsistencias que está vendiendo," *Excélsior*, January 24, 1945, 8, AEBLT, "Nacional Distribuidora y Reguladora, S.A. de C.V., 1941–1954," A03193.

123. "Sólo aquello que convenga al pueblo, la reguladora aceptará lo mejor en precio y calidad," *Excélsior*, January 27, 1945, 10, AEBLT, "Nacional Distribuidora y Reguladora, S.A. de C.V., 1941–1954," A03193.

124. Ibid.

125. "Comités de vigilancia de precios en todo el país," *El Nacional*, June 14, 1946, 8, AEBLT, "Nacional Distribuidora y Reguladora, S.A. de C.V.," A03194.

126. "Estudio sobre la venta de víveres por la reguladora," *Excélsior*, October 20, 1946, 10, AEBLT, "Nacional Distribuidora y Reguladora, S.A. de C.V.," A03194.

127. "Importamos leche de los Estados Unidos, la Nacional Distribuidora cambiará

sus sistemas en la paz," *Excélsior*, August 17, 1945, 10, AEBLT, "Nacional Distribuidora y Reguladora, S.A. de C.V., 1941–1954," A03193.

128. "Abrirá expendios de leche la Nacional Distribuidora," *Novedades*, September 26, 1946, 9, AEBLT, "Nacional Distribuidora y Reguladora, S.A. de C.V.," A03194.

129. "Cámara Nacional de Comercio vs. Distribuidora y Reguladora," *El Universal*, January 30, 1945, 9, AEBLT, "Nacional Distribuidora y Reguladora, S.A. de C.V., 1941–1954," A03193.

130. Ibid.

131. "20 millones de capital para la distribuidora, debe tenerse en cuenta este factor para evitar mayor desajuste," *Novedades*, November 15, 1944, 5, and "Qué se aumente el capital a la Nacional Distribuidora, trescientos millones pide la CTM para dicha institución reguladora," *Novedades*, January 14, 1945, 15, AEBLT, "Nacional Distribuidora y Reguladora, S.A. de C.V., 1941–1954," A03193.

132. Ibid.

133. "La Nacional Distribuidora invade la órbita del comercio organizado," *Excélsior*, January 18, 1945, 10, AEBLT, "Nacional Distribuidora y Reguladora, S.A. de C.V., 1941–1954," A03193.

134. Ibid.

135. Ibid.

136. "La Reguladora, ámbito en el mercado de los comestibles, no desaparecerá la organización y las tiendas populares podrán competir," *Excélsior*, January 1, 1946, 10, AEBLT, "Nacional Distribuidora y Reguladora, S.A. de C.V., 1941–1954," A03193.

137. "Otra etapa de la Nacional Reguladora: Va a iniciar en su organización el Sr. Gerente Cinta," *El Nacional*, December 17, 1946, 8, AEBLT, "Nacional Distribuidora y Reguladora, S.A. de C.V.," A03194.

138. "Urge reorganizar la Nacional Reguladora," *Excélsior*, January 12, 1947, n.p., AEBLT, "Nacional Distribuidora y Reguladora, S.A. de C.V.," A03194.

139. "La Reguladora ha vendido al comercio libre para combatir el mercado negro," *El Nacional*, October 21, 1947, 8, AEBLT, "Nacional Distribuidora y Reguladora, S.A. de C.V.," A03194.

140. Ochoa, *Feeding Mexico*, 99–104.

141. "Nacional Distribuidora y Reguladora, S.A. de C.V.," *El Nacional*, March 23, 1948, 8, AEBLT, "Nacional Distribuidora y Reguladora, S.A. de C.V.," A03194.

142. Benjamin and Wasserman, *Provinces of the Revolution*, offers a good account of how political leaders during the 1920s revitalized processes of political centralization as they worked toward legitimizing federal and state institutions.

143. According to O'Malley, *Myth of the Revolution*, Mexican presidents from 1920 to 1940 established their administrations around the myth of specific revolutionary leaders in order to consolidate a specific political agenda and ideology.

144. "Boicot, contra las mercancías Americanas, el gobierno no volverá a comprar

en los Estados Unidos mercancías de ninguna clase," *El Universal*, May 15, 1927, n.p., AEBLT, "Boicot, México, 1927–1982," L06590.

145. "Más quejas se han recibido en Ciudad Juárez, el Partido Nacional Revolucionario presta todo su apoyo al Alcalde Flores, aprobando su actitud," *La Prensa*, February 12, 1931, 2, AEBLT, "Boicot, México, 1927–1982," L06590.

146. "Boicot en contra de los comerciantes de El Paso," *El Universal*, March 13, 1931, 9, AEBLT, "Boicot, México, 1927–1982," L06590.

147. "Más quejas se han recibido en Ciudad Juárez, el Partido Nacional Revolucionario presta todo su apoyo al Alcalde Flores, aprobando su actitud," *La Prensa*, February 12, 1931, 2, AEBLT, "Boicot, México, 1927–1982," L06590.

148. "Boicot en contra de los comerciantes de El Paso," *El Universal*, March 13, 1931, 9, AEBLT, "Boicot, México, 1927–1982," L06590.

149. "Graves ataques a comerciantes, se inició ayer en Veracruz una grave ofensiva contra los Chinos y Españoles, actos de sabotaje, los directores de la llamada Liga de Empleados impiden el libre comercio," *Excélsior*, September 1, 1932, 10, AEBLT, "Boicot, México, 1927–1982," L06590.

150. Ibid.

151. "No tiene garantía el comercio en el puerto de Veracruz," *Excélsior*, September 30, 1932, 10, AEBLT, "Boicot, México, 1927–1982," L06590.

152. "Boicot obrero se agrava en Veracruz," *El Heraldo de Cuba*, October 2, 1932, 4, AEBLT, "Boicot, México, 1927–1982," L06590.

153. "Serios perjuicios por el boicot en Córdoba, se pide la intervención de las altas autoridades a fin de que temine," *El Nacional*, December 28, 1932, 8, AEBLT, "Boicot, México, 1927–1982," L06590.

154. Ibid.

155. "Suspensión del boicot, garantías al comercio de Córdoba, instrucciones al C. Jefe de la guarnición, entrevistan los comerciantes al Sr. Presidente," *El Nacional*, December 30, 1932, 8, AEBLT, "Boicot, México, 1927–1982," L06590.

156. Ibid.

157. Ibid.

158. According to Schuler, *Mexico between Hitler and Roosevelt*, escalating tensions between Nazi Germany and Allied forces gave Cárdenas an unprecedented amount of flexibility and power to carry out policies that otherwise would not have been allowed. Cárdenas, Schuler argues, cleverly played the United States and Germany off each another in order to increase the diplomatic power of the Mexican state in the international arena.

159. Aguilar Camín and Meyer, *In the Shadow of the Mexican Revolution*; Tzvi, *El sexenio Alemanista*; and Agustín, *Tragicomedia mexicana*, among others, define the Cárdenas administration as socialist and truly nationalist.

160. O'Brien, *Revolutionary Mission*, 304–9.

161. According to Castañeda Ramos, *La empresa mexicana*, 60, 87, the leadership of the nation's industrial capitalism assumed by the state marked a break from

nineteenth-century liberalism outlined in the 1857 constitution. He argued that, according to the 1857 constitution, the private sector was defined as the vehicle of Mexico's economic development.

162. Camp, *Entrepreneurs and Politics,* 230.

163. According to Tzvi, *El sexenio Alemanista,* 117–22, Alemán's protectionist policies continued throughout the 1940s even though he became less protectionist from 1949 to 1951, when Mexican exports increased.

164. Camp, *Entrepreneurs and Politics,* 17–18.

165. Nacional Financiera, *Nacional Financiera, 1934–1984,* 36–37.

166. Ibid., 41–48.

167. Ibid., 47, 51–52.

168. Mosk, *Industrial Revolution in Mexico,* 136–37.

169. Derossi, *El empresario mexicano,* 126, 139.

170. Mosk, *Industrial Revolution in Mexico,* 176.

171. Camp, *Entrepreneurs and Politics,* 59–60, 78.

172. Derossi, *El empresario mexicano,* 63.

173. Mosk, *Industrial Revolution in Mexico,* 26–29.

174. Derossi, *El empresario mexicano,* 54.

175. Castañeda Ramos, *La empresa mexicana,* 94–95.

176. Mosk, *Industrial Revolution in Mexico,* 63–67.

177. Ibid., 33.

178. According to Derossi, *El empresario mexicano,* 31, the emphasis on modern industrial growth made industrialists less critical of their role in society as they mistakenly implied that there was no difference between the goals of industrialists and the goals of the state and society as a whole.

Chapter Two

1. Transcriptions, [late 1942], USNA, RG 229, OIAA, General Records, Information, Radio, box 344.

2. Lorenzo Meyer, *México y los Estados Unidos,* 407–16, 428–29.

3. María Emilia Paz, *Strategy, Security, and Spies,* 4, 32–34.

4. Lorenzo Meyer, *México y los Estados Unidos,* 400–406, 447.

5. Eckes, *Opening America's Market,* 144–48; Zeiler, *Free Trade, Free World,* 3–4, 8–9, 47.

6. María Emilia Paz, *Strategy, Security, and Spies,* 104–6.

7. Ibid., 122.

8. Lorenzo Meyer, *México y los Estados Unidos,* 462–63.

9. Nelson Rockefeller, chairman of the International Development Advisory Board, address before the Conference of National Organization, Atlantic City, New Jersey, July 9, 1951, 3–7, RUA, Nelson Rockefeller, Washington, D.C., Files, RG 4, series O, subseries 9, box 9, Nelson A. Rockefeller Personal, folder 312.

10. According to Spenser, *Impossible Triangle*, 137, Hoover christened the view that democracy was incompatible with intervention and that cooperation was a better diplomatic tool than force as the "Good Neighbor Policy."

11. Ruiz, *From out of the Shadows*, 13, 68; Sánchez, *Becoming Mexican American*, 56. According to Sánchez, public baths were among the most humiliating experiences of border crossing into the 1920s. U.S. authorities' rationale for forcing Mexicans to bathe and disinfect their clothes was their belief that Mexicans were dirty. In fact, "dirty Mexicans" became a common derogatory term for both Mexicans and Mexican Americans. Mexican immigrants who entered the United States before the 1930s often shared stories of humiliation by American authorities with their friends and family in Mexico. As Balderrama and Rodríguez, in *Decade of Betrayal*, 7, have shown, an estimated 1 million Mexicans migrated to the United States before 1930, and by 1930 about 10 percent of the Mexican population lived in the United States.

12. According to Lorenzo Meyer, *México y los Estados Unidos*, 470–72, international events such as World War I and World War II gave the Mexican government some leverage in negotiating with the United States.

13. Rosenberg, *Financial Missionaries*, 89–91.

14. O'Brien, *Revolutionary Mission*, 251, 264.

15. Spenser, *Impossible Triangle*, 1, 2, 24, suggests that the Mexican government considered establishing relations with the Soviet Union to reaffirm a sense of autonomy as well as the country's nationalist and revolutionary rhetoric.

16. Ibid., 75–83.

17. Rosenberg, *Financial Missionaries*, 141–43.

18. Spenser, *Impossible Triangle*, 24, 85, 93–94, 149.

19. According to Rosenberg, *Financial Missionaries*, 139–46, anti-imperialists have mistakenly been categorized as "isolationists" by scholars of U.S. history.

20. Range, *Franklin D. Roosevelt's World Order*, 53–58.

21. Pike, *The United States and Latin America*, 262.

22. Sklar, *Corporate Reconstruction of American Capitalism*, 62–81.

23. Rosenberg, *Financial Missionaries*, 1–3.

24. Ibid., 6–9, 192. See also O'Brien, *Revolutionary Mission*, 29.

25. O'Brien, *Revolutionary Mission*, 6, 28.

26. Ibid., 31–32.

27. Marchand, *Creating the Corporate Soul*, 14, 44–45, 114–15.

28. Jacoby, *Modern Manors*, 31–35, 95–142.

29. Rosenberg, *Financial Missionaries*, 6–9.

30. Tannenbaum, *Mexico*, represents the increasing interest in Mexico's revolution and the nation's history in the 1920s and 1930s.

31. Delpar, *Enormous Vogue of Things Mexican*.

32. Cronon, *Josephus Daniels in Mexico*, 18–21.

33. Josephus Daniels to Franklin Roosevelt, April 19, 1933, in Kilpatrick, *Roosevelt and Daniels*, 136–38.

34. Cronon, *Josephus Daniels in Mexico*, 12–17.

35. Lorenzo Meyer, *México y los Estados Unidos*, 374–80, 416–27.

36. Ibid., 435–37, 113–15.

37. Ibid., 374–80, 416–27.

38. According to O'Brien, *Revolutionary Mission*, 305–7, Cárdenas protected Phelps Dodge from attacks by radical nationalist labor forces shortly after he nationalized American oil companies. O'Brien argues that Cárdenas also accused radical organized labor of being antinationalist for taking actions that prevented Mexican economic development.

39. Tischendorf, *Great Britain and Mexico*, 138.

40. Ibid.

41. "Report Drafts: Phase I, 1944," n.d., RUA, Nelson Rockefeller, Washington, D.C., Files, Personal Files, folders 84–91, CIAA Report Drafts/Transportation, RG 4, series O, subseries 11, p. 3, folder 85, box 1.

42. Ibid.

43. Von Mentz, Radkau, Spencer, and Pérez Montfort, *Los empresarios alemanes*, examines German investments in Mexico in great depth. For a complete list of German companies in Mexico from 1933 to 1942, see ibid., 172–91.

44. Memo from Nelson Rockefeller on Latin America, June 15, 1940, RUA, Nelson Rockefeller, Washington, D.C., Files, RG 4, series O, subseries 9, box 9, folder 76.

45. John Bankhead, December 1939, USNA, RG 151, Records of the Bureau of Foreign and Domestic Commerce, Records relating to Commercial Attachés, Reports, Mexico City, Assistant Trade Commissioner, General Records, box 1144.

46. Ibid.

47. Ibid.

48. Ibid.

49. Wallace Harrison to E. Dadley Jr., March 14, 1942, USNA, RG 229, OIAA, General Records, Commercial and Financial, box 194.

50. María Emilia Paz, *Strategy, Security, and Spies*, 26–30, 34.

51. Ibid.

52. Lorenzo Meyer, *México y los Estados Unidos*, 374–76, 389, 435, 470–72, suggests that Daniels's "advanced form of capitalism," Roosevelt's New Deal, and the threat created by Nazi Germany gave Cárdenas leverage and allowed him, unlike other presidents, to nationalize the oil companies. Meyer describes Daniels and Roosevelt as members of a progressive cadre of reformers who in principle did not object to Cárdenas by the late 1930s.

53. Memo from Nelson Rockefeller on Latin America, June 15, 1940, RUA, Nelson Rockefeller, Washington, D.C., Files, RG 4, series O, subseries 9, box 9, folder 76.

54. President Roosevelt to Members of the Cabinet, September 27, 1940, RUA, Nelson Rockefeller, Washington, D.C., Files, RG 4, series O, subseries 9, box 9, folder 76.

55. María Emilia Paz, *Strategy, Security, and Spies*, 128–32.

56. Niblo, *Mexico in the 1940s*, 117–18; Von Mentz, Radkau, Spencer, and Pérez Montfort, *Los empresarios alemanes*, 192–202.

57. Von Mentz, Radkau, Spencer, and Pérez Montfort, *Los empresarios alemanes*, 224–25.

58. Documentos de la Historia de la Casa Bayer, AGN, Archivo de la Casa Bayer, vol. 1, documentos 1–7, legajo 1, expediente 1–253.

59. Ibid.

60. María Emilia Paz, *Strategy, Security, and Spies*, 163.

61. American embassy in Mexico to Guy Ray, July 14, 1942, USNA, RG 229, OIAA, General Records, Information, Radio, box 345.

62. Documentos de la Historia de la Casa Bayer, AGN, Archivo de la Casa Bayer, vol. 1, documento 7, legajo 1, expediente 1–253.

63. Ibid., documentos 8–9, legajo 1, expediente 1–253.

64. Ibid.

65. Krauze, *La presidencia imperial*, 47–48; Agustín, *Tragicomedia mexicana*, 36.

66. Marcuse, *One-Dimensional Man*; Horkheimer and Adorno, *Dialectic of Enlightenment*; Adorno, *Minima Moralia*.

67. Ballagh & Thrall Export Sales to Harold Elterich, November 5, 1942, USNA, RG 229, OIAA, Records of the Department of Economic Development, Advertising Division, entry 21, box 603.

68. Horkheimer and Adorno, *Dialectic of Enlightenment*, 125.

69. "Mexican Newspapers," April 4, 1941, USNA, RG 229, OIAA, General Records, Commercial and Financial, box 194.

70. Ibid.

71. Ibid.

72. Ibid.

73. J. H. Carson to Hadley, June 4, 1941, USNA, RG 229, OIAA, General Records, Commercial and Financial, Regional Reports and Surveys, box 138.

74. Ibid.

75. "Newspaper Audience," J. H. Carson, May 4, 1941, USNA, RG 229, OIAA, General Records, Commercial and Financial, Regional Reports and Surveys, box 138.

76. Adler Lomnitz and Pérez-Lizaur, *Mexican Elite Family*.

77. "Newspaper Audience," report on *El Universal*, June 1941, USNA, RG 229, OIAA, General Records, Commercial and Financial, Regional Reports and Surveys, box 138.

78. Ibid.

79. "Newspaper Audience," J. H. Carson, May 4, 1941, USNA, RG 229, OIAA, General Records, Commercial and Financial, Regional Reports and Surveys, box 138.

80. "Newspaper Audience," report on *El Universal*, June 1941, USNA, RG 229, OIAA, General Records, Commercial and Financial, Regional Reports and Surveys, box 138.

81. "Newspaper Audience," J. H. Carson, May 4, 1941, USNA, RG 229, OIAA, Gen-

eral Records, Commercial and Financial, Regional Reports and Surveys, box 138.

82. "Newspaper Audience," report on *El Universal*, June 1941, USNA, RG 229, OIAA, General Records, Commercial and Financial, Regional Reports and Surveys, box 138.

83. "Report on Estimated Monthly Advertising Revenue of Mexican Newspapers," May–August 1941, USNA, RG 229, OIAA, General Records, Commercial and Financial, Regional Reports and Surveys, box 138.

84. Memo from Harley Cantril to Shelly Tracy, May 29, 1941, USNA, RG 229, OIAA, General Records, Commercial and Financial, Regional Reports and Surveys, box 130.

85. Ibid.

86. Report on surveys produced in Mexico from Herbert Cerwin to Nelson Rockefeller, March 10, 1943, 3, USNA, RG 229, OIAA, General Records, Information, Radio, box 344.

87. Ibid., 1.

88. Survey conducted by Sydney Ross Co., S.A., Mexico, D.F., June 27–August 13, 1942, USNA, RG 229, OIAA, General Records, Information, Radio, box 346.

89. Ibid.

90. "Commercial Survey Done in American and British Plants Employing Mexican Employees—Survey Done in a General Motors Plant in Mexico City," [January 1943], USNA, RG 229, OIAA, General Records, Information, Radio, box 346.

91. Transcriptions, [late 1942], 2, USNA, RG 229, OIAA, General Records, Information, Radio, box 344.

92. Ibid.

93. Henry Webel of GM Basford Company, "Advertising," lecture to the Industrial Advertising Association class, March 26, 1942, Export Advertising Association, USNA, RG 229, OIAA, General Records, Information, Radio, Script Material, Advertising and Publicity, box 286.

94. Transcriptions, [late 1942], 2, USNA, RG 229, OIAA, General Records, Information, Radio, box 344.

95. Ibid.

96. Herbert Cerwin to Joe Parker, July 20, 1944, USNA, RG 229, OIAA, General Records, Information, Radio, box 346.

97. Ibid.

98. Ibid.

99. Herbert Cerwin to Nelson Rockefeller, February 26, 1943, 3, USNA, RG 229, OIAA, General Records, Information, Radio, box 345.

100. Ibid.

101. "Memorandum sobre el viaje a Washington de don C.S.," n.d., AHAM, Carpetas Luis María Martínez, Gobierno Civil, Memorandums.

102. Ibid.

103. "El Inspector Federal de Educación al Sr. Arzobispo de Guadalajara," Janu-

ary 11, 1941, AHAM, Carpetas Luis María Martínez, Gobierno Civil, Memorandums.

104. "Memorandum Confidencial del Gobierno Civil," n.d., AHAM, Carpetas Luis María Martínez, Gobierno Civil, Memorandums.

105. Ibid.

106. "Memorandum Confidencial," December 22, 1943, AHAM, Carpetas Luis María Martínez, Gobierno Civil, Memorandums.

107. "Club Fraternal de Radio, Inc., al Arzobispado de México Luis María Martínez," July 19, 1944, AHAM, Carpetas Luis María Martínez, Gobierno Civil, Memorandums.

108. *Tide Magazine* report on OIAA advertising surveys, January 15, 1943, 20, USNA, RG 229, OIAA, General Records, Information, Radio, Script Material, Advertising and Publicity, Advertisers' Cooperation, box 287.

109. Memo to the Department of Commerce, June 4, 1942, 2, USNA, RG 229, OIAA, General Records, Commercial and Financial Development, Advertising, box 106.

110. Nelson Rockefeller to John Doe, president of Blank Manufacturing Company, June 4, 1942, 2, USNA, RG 229, OIAA, General Records, Commercial and Financial Development, Advertising, box 106.

111. Ibid.

112. Memo from Harold Elterich to Don Francisco, May 8, 1942, USNA, RG 229, OIAA, General Records, Commercial and Financial Development, Advertising, box 106.

113. R. T. Miller to J. H. Carson, September 23, 1941, USNA, RG 229, OIAA, General Records, Commercial and Financial, Reports and Surveys, box 138.

114. Harold Elterich to Don Francisco, May 8, 1942, USNA, RG 229, OIAA, General Records, Commercial and Financial Development, Advertising, box 106.

115. Gilbert Price to Walter Blumenthal, August 20, 1942, USNA, RG 229, OIAA, General Records, Information, Radio, Script Material, Advertising and Publicity, Advertisers' Cooperation, box 287.

116. Gilbert Price Jr. to Walter Blumenthal, August 20, 1942, 3, USNA, RG 229, OIAA, General Records, Information, Radio, Script Material, Advertising and Publicity, Advertisers' Cooperation, box 287.

117. Harold Elterich to J. C. Rovensky, August 17, 1942, USNA, RG 229, OIAA, General Records, Information, Radio, Script Material, Advertising and Publicity, box 287.

118. John Jensen to S. Weaver, April 30, 1942, USNA, RG 229, OIAA, General Records, Information, Radio, Script Material, Advertising and Publicity, box 287.

119. *Tide Magazine* report on OIAA advertising surveys, January 15, 1943, 19, USNA, RG 229, OIAA, General Records, Information, Radio, Script Material, Advertising and Publicity, box 287.

120. Ibid.

121. Don Francisco to John Wheaton, October 2, 1942, USNA, RG 229, OIAA, Gen-

eral Records, Information, Radio, Script Material, Advertising and Publicity, box 287.

122. Ibid.

123. Statement from J. W. Thompson to Harold Elterich, "American Advertising Will Not Decrease," [mid-1942], USNA, RG 229, OIAA, General Records, Information, Radio, Script Material, Advertising and Publicity, box 287.

124. Nelson Rockefeller to John Doe, president of Blank Manufacturing Company, June 4, 1942, USNA, RG 229, OIAA, General Records, Commercial and Financial Development, Advertising, box 106.

125. "Advertising and Publicity," n.d., USNA, RG 229, OIAA, General Records, Information, Radio, Script Material, Advertising and Publicity, box 287.

126. G. H. Smith Jr. to Carl B. Robbins, president of Axton-Fisher Tobacco Company, September 9, 1943, USNA, RG 229, OIAA, General Records, Commercial and Financial Development, Advertising, box 106.

127. Memo from Harold Elterich to Don Francisco, May 8, 1942, 2, USNA, RG 229, OIAA, General Records, Commercial and Financial Development, Advertising, box 106.

128. J. C. Rovensky to C. Chamber, president of the Chamber of Commerce, June 10, 1943, USNA, RG 229, OIAA, General Records, Information, Radio, box 334.

129. C. Parker Persons, address before the Florida State Chamber of Commerce, December 1, 1942, 1, USNA, RG 229, OIAA, Records of the Department of Economic Development, Advertising Division, entry 21, box 603.

130. Ibid., 2.

131. USNA, RG 229, OIAA, General Records, Commercial and Financial, Economic Development, Advertising, Advertising Rates, box 105.

132. Memo from H. A. Hayward to J. C. Rovensky, October 2, 1942, USNA, RG 229, OIAA, General Records, Commercial and Financial, Economic Development, Advertising, Advertising Rates, box 105.

133. Harold Elterich to Lawrence Levy, September 1, 1942, USNA, RG 229, OIAA, General Records, Commercial and Financial, Economic Development, Advertising, Advertising Rates, box 105.

134. Lord and Thomas to Harold Elterich, September 9, 1942, USNA, RG 229, OIAA, Records of the Department of Economic Development, Advertising Division, entry 21, box 603.

135. Ibid.

136. According to Chandler, *Visible Hand*, 412–13, the specialized role of middle management changed the rules of competition in corporate capitalism in America by the 1920s. Managers coordinated corporate resources at different stages of the production and distribution of merchandise based on research that allowed them to increase efficiency, thus becoming more competitive in the market by providing higher quality at lower prices.

137. USNA, RG 229, OIAA, General Records, Information, Radio, Script Material, Advertising and Publicity, Advertisers' Cooperation, box 287.

138. Report from M. Atkins to Advertising Division, July 18, 1941, 14, USNA, RG 229, OIAA, General Records, Commercial and Financial, Economic Development, Advertising, box 105.

139. "Confidential Memo regarding Information of American Advertisers in Latin America," August 12, 1942, USNA, RG 229, OIAA, General Records, Information, Radio, Script Material, Advertising and Publicity, box 286.

140. Ibid.

141. Ibid., 19.

142. USNA, RG 229, OIAA, General Records, Information, Radio, Script Material, Advertising and Publicity, Advertisers' Cooperation, 3, box 287.

143. Ibid., 2.

144. According to Gómez-Quiñones, *Roots of Chicano Politics*, 390–99, Rockefeller's programs also targeted Mexican communities in the United States and tried to raise some awareness in America.

145. Henry R. Webel, "Republic Steel Corporation's Plan for Building Good-Will in Latin America: Details and Reasons behind Its Pioneering Story of American Industry by Short-Wave Radio Broadcasts," *Export Trade and Shipper*, September 23, 1940, n.p., USNA, RG 229, OIAA, General Records, Information, Radio, Script Material, Advertising and Publicity, box 286.

146. Ibid.

147. Marchand, *Creating the Corporate Soul*, 4–10, 45, 124–25.

148. Henry R. Webel, "Republic Steel Corporation's Plan for Building Good-Will in Latin America: Details and Reasons behind Its Pioneering Story of American Industry by Short-Wave Radio Broadcasts," *Export Trade and Shipper*, September 23, 1940, n.p., USNA, RG 229, OIAA, General Records, Information, Radio, Script Material, Advertising and Publicity, box 286.

149. *Excélsior*, December 5, 12, 1943, n.p.

150. Ibid., December 12, 1943, n.p.

151. Advertising in *Guía de Importadores de Product Borg Warner*, March 1942, n.p., USNA, RG 229, OIAA, General Records, Commercial and Financial Development, Advertising, box 106.

152. Dixie-Vortex Company, June 1941, USNA, RG 229, OIAA, General Records, Commercial and Financial Development, Advertising, box 106.

153. John Jensen to S. Weaver, April 30, 1942, USNA, RG 229, OIAA, General Records, Information, Radio, Script Material, Advertising and Publicity, Advertisers' Cooperation, box 287.

154. John Jensen to J. J. Clarey Jr., April 23, 1942, USNA, RG 229, OIAA, General Records, Information, Radio, Script Material, Advertising and Publicity, Advertisers' Cooperation, box 287.

155. "Third Survey of Mexico, D.F., Conducted by the Radio Division of the Coordinator Committee for Mexico," December 27, 1943–January 30, 1944, 2, USNA, RG 229, OIAA, General Records, Information, Radio, box 347.

156. Radio script of Coca-Cola–sponsored programs, August 12, 1943, USNA, RG 229, OIAA, General Records, Information, Radio, box 345.

157. Crema de Miel y Almendras Hinds, *La Familia*, 195 (February 15, 1943): 19.

158. Esmalte para Uñas Cutex, *La Familia*, 198 (March 31, 1943): 23.

159. Walter Blumenthal, coordinator of OIAA, to Department of Commerce, October 6, 1942, USNA, RG 229, OIAA, General Records, Information, box 235.

160. Ibid.

161. Ibid.

162. Ibid.

163. Ibid.

164. McCann-Erickson Corporation to Harold Elterich, September 21, 1942, USNA, RG 229, OIAA, General Records, Commercial and Financial Development, Advertising, box 106.

165. Ibid.

166. Russell Pierce to Walter Blumenthal, August 14, 1942, 2, USNA, RG 229, OIAA, General Records, Information, Radio, Script Material, Advertising and Publicity, box 287.

167. Ibid.

168. Wrigley Company to J. Stanton Robins and Russell Pierce, August 20, 1943, USNA, RG 229, OIAA, General Records, Information, Radio, Script Material, Advertising Publicity, box 286.

169. Ibid.

170. Russell Pierce to Nelson Rockefeller, Don Francisco, and Wallace Harrison, n.d., 3, USNA, RG 229, OIAA, General Records, Information, Radio, Script Material, Advertising Publicity, box 286.

171. Mexican embassy to secretary of state, July 30, 1942, USNA, RG 229, OIAA, General Records, Information, Radio, box 343.

172. Ibid.

173. Walter Longan to Don Francisco, July 16, 1943, USNA, RG 229, OIAA, General Records, Information, Radio, box 343.

174. Herbert Cerwin to Nelson Rockefeller, March 2, 1944, USNA, RG 229, OIAA, General Records, Information, Radio, box 346.

175. Walter Longan to Nelson Rockefeller, November 23, 1943, USNA, RG 229, OIAA, General Records, Information, Radio, box 343.

176. Seth Fein, "Everyday Forms of Transnational Collaboration: U.S. Film Propaganda in Cold War Mexico," in Joseph, LeGrand, and Salvatore, *Close Encounters of Empire*, 400–450.

Chapter Three

1. *De Publicidad: Órgano Oficial de la AMAP* 11 (January–February 1987): 20.

2. Garza-Falcón, *Gente Decente*, 88–90.

3. Pogolotti, *La clase media*, 11–13.

4. Tenorio-Trujillo, *Mexico at the World's Fairs*, 48, 128–33; Pogolotti, *La clase media*, 26–27.

5. Pogolotti, *La clase media*, 98–102.
6. Carlos Marichal, "Obstacles to the Development of Capital Markets in Nineteenth-Century Mexico," in Haber, *How Latin America Fell Behind*, 118–45.
7. Ibid., 133–36.
8. Camp, *Entrepreneurs and Politics*, 66–75.
9. Derossi, *El empresario mexicano*, 139–43, 219.
10. Camp, *Entrepreneurs and Politics*, 66–75.
11. Derossi, *El empresario mexicano*, 219, 225–38.
12. "Principios de la publicidad," *Publicidad, Tarifas Oficiales: Revista para Ejecutivos de Negocios* 7 (October 1949): 14.
13. Bunker, "Consumers of Good Taste," 236–37.
14. Javier Hernández, "La Asociación Nacional de Publicidad, factor de optimismo y de progreso," *Publicidad, Tarifas Oficiales: Revista para Ejecutivos de Negocios* 1 (April 1949): 4–8.
15. "Principios de la publicidad," *Publicidad, Tarifas Oficiales: Revista para Ejecutivos de Negocios* 7 (October 1949): 14.
16. See Desideiro, *El anuncio en México*, 5.
17. Bunker, "Consumers of Good Taste," 231.
18. Johns, *City of Mexico*, 11, 37–38.
19. For a full account of advertisers' assessment of Mexico's commercial activity in the 1920s, see Desideiro, *El anuncio en México*.
20. Arreola and Scheffler, *México*, 40, 46, 47.
21. Johns, *City of Mexico*, 37–38.
22. Desideiro, *El anuncio en México*, 28–33.
23. Ibid.
24. Ibid.
25. Ibid., 5–17.
26. *Publicidad: Boletín Oficial de la Asociación Nacional de Publicistas* 71 (September 1944): n.p.
27. Demoscopia, S.A., y Medios Publicitarios Mexicanos, S.A. de C.V., *Publicidad mexicana*, 190–91.
28. "La producción nacional y la falta de publicidad," *Excélsior*, December 12, 1934, 9, AEBLT, "Publicidad: Propaganda, aranceles, relaciones públicas, comunicación de masas, México, 1925–1945," C07040.
29. "La regulación de la publicidad, se mueve la asamblea publicitaria," *Novedades*, September 23, 1944, 15, AEBLT, "Publicidad: Propaganda, aranceles, relaciones públicas, comunicación de masas, México, 1925–1945," C07040.
30. "Editorial," *Publicidad, Tarifas Oficiales: Revista para Ejecutivos de Negocios* 8 (November 1949): 2.
31. Ibid.
32. Rubenstein, *Bad Language, Naked Ladies*, 93–96.
33. "SPOTS," *Publicidad, Tarifas Oficiales: Revista para Ejecutivos de Negocios* 7 (October 1949): 22.

34. Ibid.
35. "Necesidad de reglamentar la profesión," *Publicidad: Boletín Oficial de la Asociación Nacional de Publicistas* 9 (November 1944): 1.
36. "El publicista sólo se hace en la práctica, así opina Humberto Sheridan," *Boletín de la Asociación Mexicana de Agencias de Publicidad* 6 (May 1958): n.p.
37. "Necesidad de reglamentar la profesión," *Publicidad: Boletín Oficial de la Asociación Nacional de Publicistas* 9 (November 1944): n.p.
38. Francisco Javier Hernández, "La Asociación Nacional de la Publicidad, factor de optimismo y progreso," *Publicidad, Tarifas Oficiales: Revista para Ejecutivos de Negocios* 1 (April 1949): 4.
39. "Necesidad de reglamentar la profesión," *Publicidad: Boletín Oficial de la Asociación Nacional de Publicistas* 9 (November 1944): 1.
40. Ibid., 4.
41. Demoscopia, S.A., y Medios Publicitarios Mexicanos, S.A. de C.V., *Publicidad mexicana*, 187.
42. "Código y normas generales de la práctica de la publicidad," *Publicidad, Tarifas Oficiales: Revista para Ejecutivos de Negocios* 1 (April 1949): 3.
43. "SPOTS," *Publicidad, Tarifas Oficiales: Revista para Ejecutivos de Negocios* 7 (October 1949): 23.
44. "Bases constitutivas de la Federación Pan-Americana de la Publicidad," *Publicidad, Tarifas Oficiales: Revista para Ejecutivos de Negocios* 3 (July 1949): 11.
45. Ibid., 27.
46. "Editorial," *Publicidad, Tarifas Oficiales: Revista para Ejecutivos de Negocios* 3 (July 1949): 2.
47. Rubén Acuña, "Publicidad en la provincia," *Publicidad, Tarifas Oficiales: Revista para Ejecutivos de Negocios* 7 (October 1949): 43.
48. Ibid.
49. "Carta al Director General de Industria y Comercio," September 24, 1943, AGN, Ávila Camacho, Economía Nacional, 521.1, Departamento de Artes y Consumo Necesario.
50. Ibid.
51. Publicistas Mexicanos ad, *Directorio Telefónico*, Classified Section, 1945–46, 36, Hemeroteca Nacional, Universidad Nacional Autónoma de México, Mexico City.
52. Ibid.
53. Interestingly enough, some upper-middle-class women adopted this approach as they organized in the 1940s to promote the importance of educating women so they could produce well-educated sons.
54. Cano Farías, "Charlas de publicidad," *Publicidad, Tarifas Oficiales: Revista para Ejecutivos de Negocios* 8 (November 1949): 8.
55. Interview with Jorge Berlie, Mexico City, August 7, 1999. Berlie worked for El Palacio de Hierro from the early 1950s to 1999.
56. Gómez-Gavarito Freer, "Impact of Revolution," 63–67, eloquently describes

Palacio de Hierro operations and the role of *viajeros*, although it does not specifically use that term. Jorge Berlie, Margarita Rostan, María Teresa Vargas,
and other Palacio de Hierro executives I interviewed did use the term.

57. Interview with Margarita Rostan, Mexico City, August 5, 1999.
58. Daniel López Palacio, "Habla el cliente: Manuel Muñiz," *AMAP: Vocero de la
    Publicidad Organizada* 1 (January 1957): 14.
59. "En la publicidad colectiva descansa el brillante futuro de la industria dul-
    cera," *Dulcería: Industrias Alimenticias, Revista Técnico Profesional Dedicada a
    la Industria de Productos Alimenticios en General* 55 (February 1945): 24.
60. *Dulcería: Órgano Oficial de la Asociación de Fabricantes de Chocolates, Dulces y
    Similares de la República de México* 40 (November 1943): 10.
61. "En la publicidad colectiva descansa el brillante futuro de la industria dul-
    cera," *Dulcería: Industrias Alimenticias, Revista Técnico Profesional Dedicada a
    la Industria de Productos Alimenticios en General* 55 (February 1945): 24.
62. "Investigación del mercado," *Publicidad, Tarifas Oficiales: Revista para Ejecu-
    tivos de Negocios* 2 (May 1949): 8.
63. Cervecería Cuauhtémoc, S.A., *Boletín Mensual de la Cerveza Carta Blanca* 4
    (September 1935): n.p.
64. Ibid.
65. "Investigación del mercado," *Publicidad, Tarifas Oficiales: Revista para Ejecu-
    tivos de Negocios* 2 (May 1949): 8–9.
66. Daniel López Palacio, "Habla el cliente: Manuel Muñiz," *AMAP: Vocero de la
    Publicidad Organizada* 1 (January 1957): 9–14.
67. "Si en China se habla Chino, tiene que aprender Chino," *Publicidad, Tarifas
    Oficiales: Revista para Ejecutivos de Negocios* 8 (November 1949): 6.
68. "Principios de la publicidad," and Manuel Acuña, "No es lo mismo publicidad
    que propaganda," *Publicidad, Tarifas Oficiales: Revista para Ejecutivos de Nego-
    cios* 8 (November 1949): 16, 1 (April 1949): n.p.
69. Cano Farías, "Charlas de publicidad," *Publicidad, Tarifas Oficiales: Revista para
    Ejecutivos de Negocios* 8 (November 1949): 8.
70. They made reference to Elma Lewis's 1898 work, *Psychological Functions of
    Advertising*, and H. D. Kitson's 1921 book, *The Mind of the Buyer*.
71. "Psychological Functions of Advertising," *Publicidad, Tarifas Oficiales: Revista
    para Ejecutivos de Negocios* 8 (November 1949): 20–21. This article included
    excerpts from Kitson's *Mind of the Buyer*.
72. Manuel Acuña, "No es lo mismo publicidad que propaganda," *Publicidad, Tari-
    fas Oficiales: Revista para Ejecutivos de Negocios* 1 (April 1949): n.p.
73. Cano Farías, "Charlas de publicidad," *Publicidad, Tarifas Oficiales: Revista para
    Ejecutivos de Negocios* 8 (November 1949): 40.
74. "Investigación del mercado," *Publicidad, Tarifas Oficiales: Revista para Ejecu-
    tivos de Negocios* 2 (May 1949): 8.
75. Ibid., 9.
76. Ibid., 10–12.

77. "Anuncios de ayer y de hoy," *Publicidad, Tarifas Oficiales: Revista para Ejecutivos de Negocios* 6 (September 1949): 11.

78. "Una nueva inversión de 7 millones en la editora de periódicos," *Publicidad y Ventas: Revista Técnica de Divulgación Publicitaria* 2 (June 1949): 16.

79. "La radio como medio de publicidad," *Publicidad y Ventas: Revista Técnica de Divulgación Publicitaria* 1 (May 1949): 9.

80. "Obteniendo resultados con publicidad radiofónica," *Publicidad y Ventas: Revista Técnica de Divulgación Publicitaria* 3 (July 1949): 12.

81. Ibid., 13.

82. Ibid.

83. Rubén Acuña, "Hablando de radio," *Publicidad, Tarifas Oficiales: Revista para Ejecutivos de Negocios* 4–5 (July–August 1949): 6.

84. Ibid.

85. Ibid.

86. The dissemination of Mexican music through Picot *cancioneros* offers a glimpse of the use of music for commercial purposes. It raises issues instrumental in understanding nation building and the formation of national identity considering that *ranchera* music became a symbol of Mexican identity along with muralist art, indigenous sites, *charreadas*, and other folk traditions. See Sands, *Charrería Mexicana*, and Delpar, *Enormous Vogue of Things Mexican*.

87. Krauze, *La presidencia imperial*, 71.

88. Interview with Ubaldo Riojas, San Francisco, California, March 2001. Like millions of Mexicans during the 1940s, Riojas moved from a northern provincial area to Mexico City, where he began studying medicine in 1945.

89. Bunker, "Consumers of Good Taste," 228.

90. "Anuncios espectaculares," *Publicidad, Tarifas Oficiales: Revista para Ejecutivos de Negocios* 7 (October 1949): 7.

91. Ibid., 6.

92. Ibid.

93. Ibid.

94. Novo, *Nueva grandeza mexicana*, 84, 128.

95. "La publicidad en México para la mente del mexicano," *Publicidad, Tarifas Oficiales: Revista para Ejecutivos de Negocios* 7 (October 1949): 26.

96. Ibid.

97. Octavio Paz, *Labyrinth of Solitude*, and Fuentes, *Death of Artemio Cruz*, eloquently capture the Mexican experience as one of individual struggle in which death, suffering, and pride are intrinsically linked and expressed through humor and fatalism.

98. "Por el mundo de la publicidad," *Publicidad, Tarifas Oficiales: Revista para Ejecutivos de Negocios* 1 (April 1949): 20.

99. Ibid.

100. Ibid.

101. Ferrer Rodríguez, *El diario de un publicista*, 131.

102. Ibid.
103. Ibid., 75.
104. Ibid., 208.
105. "La publicidad a través de la vida," Conferencia pronunciada por el Señor Francisco Sayrols ante el Instituto Mercantil de la Confederación de Cámaras de Comercio, México, D.F., *Miscelánea mexicana*, 594, Hemeroteca Nacional, Universidad Nacional Autónoma de México, Mexico City.
106. *De Publicidad: Órgano Oficial de la AMAP* 11 (January–February 1987): 20.

Chapter Four

1. UNAM, "Tiempos de Guerra," *18 lustros la vida en México en este siglo*, 1940–44, University of California at Los Angeles Film Archives.
2. Wells and Joseph, *Summer of Discontent*, 122–23.
3. Knight, *Mexican Revolution*, 1:127–28.
4. See Wells and Joseph, *Summer of Discontent*, 132.
5. Ibid., 124–25.
6. Johns, *City of Mexico*, 11, 37–38.
7. Strode, *Now in Mexico*, 68–69.
8. Joseph and Nugent, *Everyday Forms of State Formation*; Vaughan, *Cultural Politics of Revolution*.
9. See Sands, *Charrería Mexicana*.
10. Steven Topik, "Economic Domination by the Capital: Mexico City and Rio de Janeiro, 1888–1910," in UNAM, *La ciudad y el campo*, 185–97.
11. Mosk, *Industrial Revolution in Mexico*, 133–38.
12. *La Familia* 355 (March 15, 1950): 7.
13. Ibid. 357 (April 15, 1950): 47.
14. Ibid. 359 (May 15, 1950): 5.
15. Wilkie, *Mexican Revolution*; Cline, *Mexico*; Hansen, *Politics of Mexican Development*; Mosk, *Industrial Revolution in Mexico*.
16. Reyes Heroles, *El liberalismo mexicano: La integración de las ideas*, 470–83.
17. Reyes Heroles, *El liberalismo mexicano: La sociedad fluctuante*, vii–viii.
18. Reyes Heroles, *La historia y la acción*, 57, 140; Córdova, *La ideología de la Revolución Mexicana*, 87–88; Hale, *Transformation of Liberalism*, 121–23; Molina Enríquez, *Los grandes problemas nacionales*, 20–21.
19. Brading, *First America*, 310, 361–73, and *Los orígenes del nacionalismo*, 73–82.
20. Tenorio-Trujillo, *Mexico at the World's Fairs*, 53, 65–68, 71.
21. *El Universal*, December 3, 1943, sect. 1, 7.
22. *La Familia* 345 (March 15, 1950): 3.
23. *Excélsior*, December 5, 12, 1943, n.p.
24. Ibid., December 12, 1943, n.p.
25. *El Universal*, December 4, 1944, sect. 2, 6.
26. Ibid., December 18, 1949, n.p.

27. Ibid., December 1, 1946, sect. 1, 7.
28. Ibid., December 1, 1945, n.p.
29. *Excélsior*, December 2, 1945, n.p.
30. Rosenberg, *Spreading the American Dream*, 7.
31. Ibid., 12.
32. According to Eckes, *Opening America's Market*, 55–56, 144–48, the State Department under the leadership of Cordell Hull equated free trade with economic stability and peace by the 1930s and 1940s. It considered trade a diplomatic tool. Similarly, Zeiler, *Free Trade, Free World*, 2, 6–12, 47, 108–9, suggests that Hull, Franklin Roosevelt, the State Department, and President Truman all perceived free trade as an important diplomatic and ideological tool against Nazis and communists throughout the 1930s and 1940s.
33. O'Brien, *Revolutionary Mission*, 274–75.
34. Pike, *The United States and Latin America*, 167–68.
35. Molina Enríquez, *Los grandes problemas nacionales*, 293, 406–7.
36. Knight, "Racism, Revolution, and Indigenismo."
37. Vasconcelos, *Cosmic Race*.
38. Stepan, *Hour of Eugenics*, 55, 105–6, 151.
39. Ibid., 146–50.
40. Brading, *First America*, 361.
41. Brading, *Mexican Phoenix*, 8–9, 312–14.
42. Krauze, *La presidencia imperial*, 142.
43. Cerwin, *These Are the Mexicans*, 284.
44. Ibid., 284–85.
45. *El Universal*, January 20, 1947, sect. 1, 12.
46. Ibid., December 2, 1946, sect. 1, 16.
47. Ibid., December 18, 1949, sect. 3, 3.
48. *Excélsior*, December 23, 1949, n.p.
49. Ibid.
50. Mora, *Mexican Cinema*.
51. *El Universal*, April 18, 1945, n.p.
52. "Cuidando su belleza," ibid., December 9, 1940, sect. 3, 12.
53. Ibid., December 2, 1945, sect. 1, 3; December 21, 1949, sect. 1, 40.
54. Ibid., December 9, 1940, sect. 3, 12.
55. "Belleza femenina," ibid., December 2, 1945, sect. 3, 3.
56. Ibid., December 6, 1943, sect. 1, 12.
57. Ibid., December 2, 1946, sect. 3, 4.
58. Interview with Margarita Rostan, Mexico City, July 6, 1999.
59. *Revista de Revistas* 1638 (October 19, 1944): n.p.
60. *La Familia* 198 (March 31, 1943): 12; 312 (May 31, 1948): 7; 358 (April 30, 1950): 19.
61. *Revista de Revistas* (August 1934): 31; *La Familia* 70 (October 30, 1937): 23, 25; 105 (May 15, 1939): 39, 61; 134 (July 31, 1940): 34, 45, 55; *El Universal*,

December 4, 1945, sect. 1, 18; *La Familia* 277 (September 15, 1946): 1, 45; 312 (May 31, 1948): 53; 364 (July 30, 1950): 103.

62. "Report on Ponds Global Advertising," 7, HCAMR, JWTCA, E. G. Wilson Papers, International Series, Offices of Italy–Mexico, box 13.

63. Ibid.

64. *Revista de Revistas* 1149 (May 22, 1932): n.p.

65. *La Familia* 198 (March 31, 1943): 12.

66. Ibid. 312 (May 31, 1948): n.p.

67. "Report on Ponds Global Advertising," 9, HCAMR, JWTCA, E. G. Wilson Papers, International Series, Offices of Italy–Mexico, box 13.

68. Ibid.

69. *El Universal*, December 3, 1930, sect. 2, 8; *Revista de Revistas* 1202 (May 28, 1933): n.p.

70. *Revista de Revistas* 1359 (May 31, 1936): n.p.; 1395 (February 14, 1937): n.p.; 1414 (June 27, 1937): n.p.

71. *La Familia* 198 (March 31, 1943): 25; 244 (March 15, 1945): 37; 312 (May 31, 1945): 51.

72. "Cuénteme su problema," ibid. 242 (February 15, 1945): 12.

73. Franco, *Plotting Women*, 81–82, 131.

74. Ibid., 97.

75. Rubenstein, *Bad Language, Naked Ladies*, 42.

76. Hershfield, *Mexican Cinema, Mexican Women*, 3, 8, 34, 134.

77. Ibid., 3; Rubenstein, *Bad Language, Naked Ladies*, 58, 84. According to Rubenstein, narratives addressing an opposition between the country and the city were often resolved in favor of the country but left a sense of ambiguity by not classifying such a resolution as being good or bad.

78. Schaefer, *Textured Lives*, 3–36. Schaefer identifies Frida Kahlo's artistic expression as an antiliberal discourse rather than suggesting that the ambiguity was a spin-off from the liberal discourse.

79. *Revista de Revistas* 1312 (July 7, 1935): n.p.

80. "Los frutos productos de belleza," *La Familia* 70 (October 30, 1937): 44–45.

81. Ibid. 196 (March 31, 1943): 20–21.

82. Ibid. 150 (March 31, 1941): 68 and 303 (January 15, 1948): 58 offer examples of this type of hair-removal product advertising in the 1940s.

83. "Páginas de belleza," ibid. 276 (August 30, 1946): 20–21.

84. Ibid.

85. Ibid. 196 (February 28, 1943): 20–21; 244 (March 15, 1945): 20–21; 277 (September 15, 1946): 20–21; 312 (May 31, 1948): 20–21.

86. "Belleza," ibid. 105 (May 15, 1939): 52–53.

87. "Páginas de belleza," ibid. 164 (October 31, 1941): 20–21.

88. Ibid.

89. Ibid. 327 (January 5, 1949): 25.

90. Ibid., 32.

91. Palmolive ads in *El Universal*, December 3, 1930, sect. 2, 8; *Revista de Revistas* 1202 (May 28, 1933): n.p.; 1312 (July 7, 1935): n.p.; 1359 (May 31, 1936): n.p.; 1414 (June 27, 1937): n.p.; *La Familia* 154 (May 31, 1941): 65; 198 (March 31, 1943): 25; 244 (March 15, 1945): 37; 327 (January 5, 1949): 25.

92. *Revista de Revistas* 1149 (May 22, 1932): n.p.; *Negro y Blanco* 2 (August 1934): 31; *La Familia* 89 (September 30, 1938): 25, 29; 70 (October 30, 1937): 25; 143 (December 15, 1940): 55.

93. *La Familia* 70 (October 30, 1937): 25.

94. Ibid. 143 (December 15, 1940): 29.

95. *Negro y Blanco* 2 (August 1934): 31; *La Familia* 70 (October 30, 1937): 23, 25; 89 (September 16, 1938): 29; 154 (May 31, 1941): 49; 239 (August 15, 1944): 19; 260 (December 30, 1945): 13; *Negro y Blanco* 10 (April 7, 1948): 19.

96. *El Universal*, December 4, 1945, sect. 1, 18.

97. Ibid., December 1, 1947, sect. 2, 3.

98. Ibid., December 2, 1948, sect. 1, 16.

99. *La Familia* 118 (November 30, 1939): 57; 154 (May 31, 1941): 49; *Negro y Blanco* 12 (July 7, 1942): 14; *La Familia* 230 (August 15, 1944): 19; *El Universal*, December 1, 1946, supplemental sect., 3; *La Familia* 277 (September 15, 1946): 1; *Negro y Blanco* 10 (April 7, 1948): 17.

100. Valdés, *Shattered Mirror*, 14–19, 29; Lindauer, *Devouring Frida*, 39–41. Both Valdés and Lindauer suggest that gender boundaries were very rigid and that women who operated outside acceptable norms suffered drastic consequences.

101. Rubenstein, *Bad Language, Naked Ladies*, 47–48.

102. *Excélsior*, December 31, 1939, n.p.

103. *El Universal*, April 18, 1945, n.p.

104. Ibid., December 4, 1945, sect. 1, 7.

105. Ibid., 18.

106. Ibid., December 5, 1945, sect. 1, 8.

107. Ibid.

108. Ibid., December 1, 1948, sect. 1, 13.

109. Ibid., December 2, 1948, sect. 1, 6.

110. Ibid., December 1, 1947, sect. 2, 3.

111. Ibid., December 2, 1948, sect. 2, 11.

112. Ibid., December 7, 1947, sect. 1, 16.

113. Ibid., December 7, 1946, sect. 1, 16.

114. Ibid., December 4, 1940, sect. 3, 3.

115. Ibid., December 1, 1944, sect. 1, 1.

116. Ibid., December 2, 1945, sect. 1, 7.

117. Ibid., 6.

118. Ibid., sect. 3, 4.

Chapter Five

1. "Report about JWT Operations in Mexico," February 1964, 19, HCAMR, JWTCA, E. G. Wilson Papers, International Series, Offices of Italy–Mexico, box 13.
2. Ibid.
3. Ibid.
4. James Playsted Wood, *Story of Advertising*, 230–31.
5. Walker, *Advertising Progress*, 168–70.
6. Pope, *Making of Modern Advertising*, 119–21.
7. James Playsted Wood, *Story of Advertising*, 456–57.
8. Pope, *Making of Modern Advertising*, 142.
9. James Playsted Wood, *Story of Advertising*, 458.
10. Pope, *Making of Modern Advertising*, 142.
11. James Playsted Wood, *Story of Advertising*, 159–61.
12. Borden, *Economic Effects of Advertising*, 89–92.
13. "Analysis of an Expanding Venture with Policy Recommendations: Confidential Report on International Operations by Carol Wilson," December 15, 1954, iii, HCAMR, JWTCA, E. G. Wilson Papers, International Series, box 20.
14. Luther O. Lemon (assistant treasurer of Mexico City branch) to Bashman, Ringe, and Correa Law Firm, October 7, 1943, HCAMR, JWTCA, Treasurer's Office, International Offices, London–Mexico City, box 10.
15. Pope, *Making of Modern Advertising*, 176.
16. "Analysis of an Expanding Venture with Policy Recommendations: Confidential Report on International Operations by Carol Wilson," December 15, 1954, 8–9, 13–20, HCAMR, JWTCA, E. G. Wilson Papers, International Series, box 20.
17. "Company File Report," n.d., 12, HCAMR, JWTCA, Ralph Bernstein, Company History Files, box 5.
18. J. Kuneau to Samuel Meek, January 29, 1944, HCAMR, JWTCA, Treasurer's Office, International Offices, London–Mexico City, box 10.
19. "Company File Report," February 1964, n.p., HCAMR, JWTCA, Ralph Bernstein, Company History Files, box 5.
20. "Report on Thompson de México, SA," February 1964, 25–27, HCAMR, JWTCA, Ralph Bernstein, Company History Files, box 5.
21. Ibid. Thompson's report did not include the actual wording of the client's complaint, but it stated that according to the client the commercial had a sexual connotation.
22. Anonymous report addressed to Luther O. Lemon, March 14, 1944, HCAMR, JWTCA, Treasurer's Office, International Offices, London–Mexico City, box 10.
23. Ibid.
24. "Report on Thompson de México, SA," February 1964, 16, HCAMR, JWTCA, Ralph Bernstein, Company History Files, box 5.

25. Adler Lomnitz and Pérez-Lizaur, *Mexican Elite Family*.

26. Ibid. and Derossi, *El empresario mexicano*, offer a great analysis of how family business networks operated in Mexico.

27. "Report on Thompson de México, SA," February 1964, 16, HCAMR, JWTCA, Ralph Bernstein, Company History Files, box 5.

28. Ibid., 5.

29. Ibid., 16.

30. Ibid. Camp, *Entrepreneurs and Politics*, supports this view.

31. "Personnel Report," Thompson de Mexico, April 25, 1945, n.p., HCAMR, JWTCA, Treasurer's Office, International Offices, London–Mexico City, box 10.

32. Donald Thorburn to Donald Foote, December 13, 1946, HCAMR, JWTCA, Treasurer's Office, International Offices, London–Mexico City, box 10.

33. Ibid.

34. Ibid.

35. Ibid.

36. "Analysis of an Expanding Venture with Policy Recommendations: Confidential Report on International Operations by Carol Wilson," December 15, 1954, vi, E. G. Wilson Papers, International Series, box 20.

37. "Report on Thompson de México, SA," February 1964, 21, HCAMR, JWTCA, Ralph Bernstein, Company History Files, box 5.

38. Ibid.

39. Johns, *City of Mexico*, 49–59.

40. Ibid., 53, 55.

41. "Report on Thompson de México, SA," February 1964, 20, HCAMR, JWTCA, Ralph Bernstein, Company History Files, box 5.

42. Ibid.

43. *Thompson de México, S.A.*, October 1952, n.p., HCAMR, JWTCA, Treasurer's Office, International Offices, London–Mexico City, box 10.

44. Ibid.

45. Ibid.

46. Ibid.

47. "The Force Nobody Knows—American Industry," address by Don Francisco, president of Lord and Thomas, to the Congress of American Industry, sponsored by the National Association of Manufacturers, New York, December 7, 1938, HCAMR, JWTCA, Writings and Speeches Collection, Miscellaneous, Hanson, box 4.

48. Address by Don Francisco, vice president of J. Walter Thompson, at a dinner given by the Association of Advertising Men in honor of visiting delegates of Alpha Delta Sigma, New York Advertising Club, June 16, 1950, 8–10, 14–16, HCAMR, JWTCA, Speeches, Don Francisco, box 5.

49. The attitude, approach, and performance of Thompson representatives resembled the experience of U.S. financial advisers or, to use Rosenberg's phrase,

"financial missionaries," sent to Latin America prior to the 1930s. Like these advisers, Thompson advertising agents were highly ignorant of Mexican culture and expected Mexicans to adjust to their advertising strategies, which the agents considered superior to Mexican advertising. See Rosenberg, *Financial Missionaries*, 225–26.

50. Borden, *Economic Effects of Advertising*, 87–88.
51. James Playsted Wood, *Story of Advertising*, 461.
52. Borden, *Economic Effects of Advertising*, 87–88.
53. "Report on Thompson de México, SA," February 1964, 39, HCAMR, JWTCA, Ralph Bernstein, Company History Files, box 5.
54. Ibid., 45.
55. Ibid. See also J. W. Thompson, *The Mexican Market* (1959, 1963), HCAMR, JWTCA, Company Publications, International Offices, Consumer Index of Markets, India, Italy, Mexico–The Mexican Market, box 29.
56. "Mexico: Market for Dentifrice," June 1947, n.p., HCAMR, JWTCA, Microfilm Collection.
57. Ibid., 2.
58. Ibid., 14.
59. Ibid., 15.
60. Ibid., 14.
61. Ibid., 7.
62. Becker, *Setting the Virgin on Fire*, 89.
63. "Mexico: Market for Dentifrice," June 1947, 26, HCAMR, JWTCA, Microfilm Collection.
64. Ibid., 27.
65. Ibid., 22.
66. Ibid., 11.
67. Ibid., 12.
68. Ibid., 14.
69. "News of Vision Incorporated: An Advertising Case Study from JWT de Mexico," n.d., n.p., HCAMR, JWTCA, E. G. Wilson Papers, International Series, Italy–Mexico, box 13.
70. Ibid.
71. "Report on Thompson de México, SA," February 1964, 47, HCAMR, JWTCA, Ralph Bernstein, Company History Files, box 5.
72. Ibid.
73. *JWT Weekly News* 28 (December 9, 1946): n.p., HCAMR, JWTCA, Newsletter Collection, Main Series, Main Research, 1946–51, box 5.
74. Brandenburg, *Making of Modern Mexico*, 291.
75. Ibid.
76. *JWT Weekly News* 28 (December 9, 1946): n.p., HCAMR, JWTCA, Newsletter Collection, Main Series, Main Research, 1946–51, box 5.

77. "Regulation Forbids Gold Imports," memo submitted by Shirley Woodell, August 14, 1947, n.p., HCAMR, JWTCA, Shirley Woodell Papers, Office Files and Correspondence, box 1.

78. Ibid.; Don Thorburn to Shirley Woodell, July 11, 1947, HCAMR, JWTCA, Shirley Woodell Papers, Office Files and Correspondence, box 2.

Chapter Six

1. *Sears News Graphic: The All Employees Picture Newspaper* 2 (March 27, 1947): n.p., SRA.

2. According to Cerwin, the head of the Coordinator's Office for the OIAA in Mexico, 95 percent of the Mexican population was Catholic by 1945 (*These Are the Mexicans*, 286).

3. According to Jean Meyer, *Cristero Rebellion*, the essence of the church-state struggle revolved around the issue of state legitimacy. The church's theological rationale for governance implicitly challenged state authority by placing God's law at a higher level than civil law. Enforcing the anticlerical measures in the midst of social and political upheaval made sense during the 1920s and 1930s. Meyer accurately interpreted church-state tensions along ideological lines during the Cristero Revolt. Religious authorities like Archbishop Luis María Martínez placed Christian authority above civil law during the 1920s. See Martínez, "El corazón de Cristo." However, the legitimacy and stability the Mexican state had acquired by the 1940s made the church and public religious performances less threatening to the state.

4. According to Krauze, *La presidencia imperial*, 106, the political consensus reached by the revolutionary government in the 1940s was based on the belief that every individual and group could climb up the social or economic ladder. This belief "stressed that social and economic conditions in the country had finally made it possible for Mexicans to improve the social status within the political system and not independently outside the government."

5. Agustín, *Tragicomedia mexicana*, 12; Krauze, *La presidencia imperial*, 142.

6. LaFaye, *Quetzalcóatl and Guadalupe*, and Brading, *First America*, suggest that the Virgin of Guadalupe served as a symbol for the growth of an elite Creole identity during the seventeenth century. Jean Meyer, in *Cristero Rebellion*, claims that the Virgin of Guadalupe had become a popular nationalist and revolutionary ideological figure by the 1920s for whom peasants were willing to fight.

7. Martínez, "El corazón de Cristo," 132.

8. Cerwin, *These Are the Mexicans*, 296.

9. Jacoby, *Modern Manors*, 95–142.

10. *Sears News Graphic: The All Employees Picture Newspaper* 2 (March 27, 1947): n.p., SRA.

11. Ibid.

12. "Foreign Procedures," n.d., 3, SRA, 100.15 IOF, box 1.

13. "Mexico City 'A' Store Opens!," *Sears News Graphic: The All Employee Picture Newspaper* 2 (March 17, 1947): n.p., SRA.

14. Grand opening celebrations changed during the 1950s when Sears's management began opening new stores with the traditional "cutting of ribbons" practiced in the United States, but they still included processions led by religious authorities (interview with Jorge Bonilla, Mexico City, July 30, 1999).

15. Jacoby, *Modern Manors*, 96–106.

16. Sears Publication Department, *Merchant to the Millions*, 10.

17. Ibid., 11.

18. "Sears in Mexico—History," n.d., n.p., SRA, 100.15 IOF, box 48.

19. "Latinoamérica: Oportunidades y Responsabilidades," John F. Gallagher, vice president of the Latin American Sears Division, speech to the International Trade Club of Chicago, n.d., 5, SRA, 100.15 IOF, box 49.

20. Jacoby, *Modern Manors*, 123–25.

21. Interview with Jorge Bonilla, Mexico City, August 2, 1999.

22. Ibid.

23. Ibid., July 30, 1999; interview with Ernesto Zatarain, Mexico City, July 2, 1999.

24. Interview with Jorge Bonilla, Mexico City, August 2, 1999.

25. "South of the Border: Sears Stirring Up Merchandising Revolution as Top Single Retailer in Latin America with 12 Big Stores," *Wall Street Journal*, June 8, 1951, n.p., "Mexico—History Files," SRA, 100.15 IOF, box 48.

26. Article by Phil Querido, in "General Wood Lands Results of Sears—Mexico Operations," n.d., SRA, 100.15 IOF, box 48.

27. General Wood, "Story to Date, Prospects for Latin American Expansion, as Told by General Wood," *Sears News Graphic: The All Employee Picture Newspaper* 9 (November 26, 1948): 3, SRA.

28. Ibid.

29. Marchand, *Creating the Corporate Soul*, 14.

30. Jacoby, *Modern Manors*, 97–98.

31. Chandler, *Visible Hand*, 224–27, 236.

32. Ibid., 7–8, 11, 224.

33. Marchand, *Creating the Corporate Soul*, 4.

34. Rosenberg, *Financial Missionaries*, 32–33, 62–65.

35. Marchand, *Creating the Corporate Soul*, 4.

36. Jacoby, *Modern Manors*, 3.

37. Marchand, *Creating the Corporate Soul*, 5–9.

38. Ibid., 44–45, 100–101.

39. Ibid., 197–201, 245.

40. Jacoby, *Modern Manors*, 5, 46.

41. O'Brien, *Revolutionary Mission*, 31–32, 258–59, 275–84.

42. See Leach, *Land of Desire*; Frederick Jackson Turner, "The Significance of the

Frontier in American History," in *The Frontier in American History*; Potter, *People of Plenty*; and Heinze, *Adapting to Abundance*.

43. Other studies of the U.S. Cold War illustrate the ways in which anticommunism served as a mechanism to instill, within the context of consumer culture, family values. See May, *Homeward Bound*; Gilbert, *Cycle of Outrage*; and Inglis, *Cruel Peace*. The film *Atomic Cafe* includes original footage of authority figures in the U.S. government attempting to persuade the public to defend capitalism against communism by stating that the individual choice and abundance Americans enjoy could turn into misery and scarcity under communism. U.S. government officials during World War II used the contrast between abundance, consumption, and democracy in the United States and life in Nazi Germany in their anti-Nazi campaign. María Emilia Paz, *Strategy, Security, and Spies*, and Seth Fein, "Everyday Forms of Transnational Collaboration: U.S. Film Propaganda in Cold War Mexico," in Joseph, LeGrand, and Salvatore, *Close Encounters of Empire*, 400–450, suggest that a similar strategy continued as part of the anticommunist propaganda carried out by the U.S. State Department in Mexico during the late 1940s and early 1950s.

44. Fein, "Everyday Forms of Transnational Collaboration," 412, 417, 421–22.

45. John F. Gallagher, speech to the War National College, September 3, 1970, 10, SRA, 100.15 IOF, box 3.

46. Ibid.

47. Nelson Rockefeller, chairman of the International Development Advisory Board, address before the Conference of National Organization, Atlantic City, New Jersey, July 9, 1951, 2–3, 8, RUA, Nelson Rockefeller, Washington, D.C., Files, RG 4, series O, subseries 9, box 9, folder 312.

48. Ibid., 8–15.

49. Nelson Rockefeller, "Industrialization of Latin America to Open New Markets for U.S. Goods," *Sales Management*, November 1, 1944, 80, RUA, RG 4, series O, subseries 9, box 9, folder 75.

50. Ibid.

51. Ibid., 84.

52. "Foreign Operation" documents, 1946, SRA, 100.15 IOF, box 52.

53. Ibid., 14.

54. "Sears: La Institución que Conquistó a México en 3 Días," *Publicidad y Ventas: Revista Técnica de Divulgación Publicitaria* 2 (June 1949): 12.

55. Jerry Jeran to T. V. Houser, December 1946, SRA, 100.15 IOF, box 52.

56. Ibid.

57. G. D. Downey to Mr. Shykind, January 18, 1946, SRA, 100.15 IOF, box 52.

58. "Sears Roebuck's Mexican Revolution," *Harper's Magazine*, April 1964, n.p., Sears News Service, SRA, 100.15 IOF, box 1.

59. Cerwin, *These Are the Mexicans*, 88.

60. According to speakers at the Ateneo Nacional de Ciencias y Artes de México like José Domingo Lavín, the degree to which a modern nation could satisfy

the basic necessities of "civilized life" depended on its ability to extract and manufacture its natural resources. See José Domingo Lavín, "La industrialización de México: Relaciones obrero—patronales," conference hosted by the Ateneo Nacional de Ciencias y Artes de México, April 13, 1945, 5–35.

61. Daniel Seligman, "The Maddening Promising Mexican Market," *Fortune Magazine,* January 1956, 108, SRA, 100.15 IOF, box 52.

62. Cosío Villegas criticized this approach by suggesting that no economic theory or technique for industrialization modeled on the United States or Europe would be effective in Mexico because such theories were designed to benefit only industrialized countries. See Daniel Cosío Villegas, "La riqueza legendaria de México," in *Ensayos y notas,* 71.

63. Peter Smith, "Mexico since 1946"; Camp, *Entrepreneurs and Politics.*

64. According to Cline, *Mexico,* 249, foreign investment in the Mexican mining industry declined from 48 percent in 1940 to 17.5 percent in 1958. In contrast, foreign control over Mexico's manufacturing, commerce, and electrical and gas industries increased from 17 percent in 1940 to 40 percent in 1957. Sixty-five percent of private American investment in Mexico was targeted at manufacturing, commerce, and the electrical and gas industries.

65. Robert Wood to N. A. Barron and the Mexican minister of commerce, April 14, 1949, SRA, 100.15 IOF, box 48.

66. A. M. Fresneda to T. V. Houser, n.d., SRA, 100.15 IOF, box 53.

67. "El nuevo reglamento de anuncios," *El Universal,* October 23, 1938, 9, AEBLT, "Publicidad: Propaganda, aranceles, relaciones públicas, comunicación de masas, México, 1925–1945," C07040; Charles Mann, "Sears: A Cross-Cultural Analysis," *Social Science* 3 (June 1965): 154, SRA, 100.15 IOF, box 51; Secretaría de Gobernación, *Leyes de patentes y de marcas.*

68. Charles Mann, "Sears: A Cross-Cultural Analysis," *Social Science* 3 (June 1965): 155, SRA, 100.15 IOF, box 50.

69. Paul Rauvil to General Wood, February 12, 1952, 6, SRA, 100.15 IOF, box 51.

70. Ibid., 8.

71. The most radical aspects of the 1917 constitution outlined in Articles 27 and 123 established the legal foundation for nationalizing foreign companies, creating a minimum wage, an eight-hour workday, paid vacations, and equal salaries for comparable work performed by men and women. See Gilly, *El Cardenismo,* 179–87; González y González, *Los días del Presidente Cárdenas,* 152–57; and de la Cueva, *Derecho mexicano del trabajo,* 524–69.

72. Interview with Jorge Bonilla, Mexico City, August 30, 1999.

73. Interview with Ernesto Zatarain, Mexico City, July 1, 1999. Zatarain received a Sears scholarship in 1956 to finish his degree in accounting at the Universidad Autónoma de Guadalajara before he joined the company's corporate operations in the early 1960s. According to him, some Sears employees retired with over a million pesos as a result of Sears' profit-sharing program.

74. Interview with Jorge Bonilla, Mexico City, August 12, 1999.

75. Ibid.

76. Scholars like Hamilton, in *Limits of State Autonomy*, 138–41, classify Lázaro Cárdenas's paternalist and revolutionary reforms and policies as horizontally based in defense of peasants and workers. Although Hamilton's approach eloquently discusses the relationship between workers, peasants, and Cárdenas in the context of Mexico's revolutionary state, her analysis focuses primarily on defining the Cárdenas administration as a socialist rather than a populist government. She places her work within the context of studies of populism such as Drake, *Socialism and Populism in Chile*, and LaClau, *Politics and Ideology in Marxist Theory*. According to Drake, populism in Chile was an ideological tool with a hierarchical structure that depoliticized radical socialists and revolutionary goals in Chile. According to LaClau, populism is a coercive hegemonic and ideological mechanism that leads to the articulation of elite values and worldviews that define hegemony as an "ideological class." Hamilton's interpretation of Cárdenas as a paternal figure who defended the lower sectors of society led her to classify his administration as "socialist" rather than "populist." Sears saw Cárdenas as a socialist and nationalist "paternal" caretaker of the Mexican people who patriotically defended Mexican sovereignty.

77. Ochoa, *Feeding Mexico*, 99–104.

78. Nelson Rockefeller, chairman of the International Development Advisory Board, address before the Conference of National Organization, Atlantic City, New Jersey, July 9, 1951, 8–15, RUA, Nelson Rockefeller, Washington, D.C., Files, RG 4, series O, subseries 9, box 9, folder 312.

79. Wilkie, *Mexican Revolution*, 203.

80. Krauze, *La presidencia imperial*, 68.

81. Ibid.

82. Ibid., 103.

83. Richardson Wood, *Sears Roebuck de México*, 14. Sources indicate that the survey was conducted prior to 1949.

84. Hernal Gastrel Seely, "Mexico Booming: Sears Takes Advantage of New Revolution," *Daily News*, June 6, 1951, n.p., SRA, 100.15 IOF, box 48.

85. Chandler, *Visible Hand*, 286–89, 372.

86. Hernal Gastrel Seely, "Mexico Booming: Sears Takes Advantage of New Revolution," *Daily News*, June 6, 1951, n.p., SRA, 100.15 IOF, box 48.

87. Ibid., 1.

88. Ibid., 2.

89. Imperialism in this case is strictly defined at a cultural level and specifically refers to a company's persistence in expanding its American ideas and ways of operating without considering local conditions or social economic status in other countries, as discussed by scholars like Pike, *The U.S. and Latin America*, who follow a Frankfurt school approach to mass culture. Pike eloquently defines American imperialism as a historical construction identified with "civilization," which implies that disseminating American values and practices

throughout Latin America would progressively help improve the "primitivism" of the region. The problem with Pike's approach is that it offers no agency to Latin Americans. Scholars such as Joseph, LeGrand, and Salvatore, in *Close Encounters of Empire*, are reinterpreting the traditional Frankfurt school view of U.S.–Latin American relations as described by Pike by granting agency to Latin Americans as they interact with or encounter different facets of American culture, agencies, industries, etc.

90. This approach does not credit American investments and modern industrial capitalism for thoroughly transforming Latin American economies and societies by stimulating economic and industrial growth. See Cline, *Mexico*; Hansen, *Mexican Economic Development*; and Tony Smith, *America's Mission*. Crediting American political and business leaders for Latin America's development, as shown in Joseph, LeGrand, and Salvatore, *Close Encounters of Empire*, and O'Brien, *Revolutionary Mission*, ignores the ways in which Latin Americans shaped, often collectively with U.S. authorities, their own history. On the other hand, this approach invites scholars to further examine historical interpretations that suggest that American investments and expansion into Latin America during the 1940s undermined revolutionary ideals, brought exploitation, and "wiped out" Latin American culture. See Carlos Monsiváis, "La cultura mexicana en el siglo XX," in Wilkie, Meyer, and Wilkie, *Contemporary Mexico*, 624–70; Agustín, *Tragicomedia mexicana*; Hamilton, *Limits of State Autonomy*; Aguilar Camín and Meyer, *In the Shadow of the Mexican Revolution*; and Daniel Cosío Villegas, "La crisis de México," in *Ensayos y notas*.

91. Mexican intellectuals in the 1940s presented a rather optimistic view of Mexico's middle class and its place in national identity. See, for example, Samuel Ramos, *Profile of Man*. Others criticized the increasing commercialization of life in Mexico during the 1940s. See, for example, the fictional account in Pacheco, *Las batallas en el desierto*. Both Ramos and Pacheco discuss Mexico's middle class and the commercialization of life in Mexico as a cultural rather than a socioeconomic phenomenon. My view of Sears as an agent that defined middle-class status through consumption focuses on the cultural construction of the middle class. I have been influenced by studies such as Abelson, *When Ladies Go a-Thieving*. According to Abelson, department stores transformed American society by creating a culture of consumption and played a "crucial role in determining the essentials of middle-class life and aspirations" (4–5). She presents them as "cultural authorities selling a 'middle class life style' and creating images that women used for authenticating their own social status and ambitions" (51, 46).

92. "Sears 25 años en México, 1947–1972," February 1972, 19, SRA, 100.15 IOF, box 48.

93. F. M. Judson to C. T. Seitz, October 16, 1951, SRA, 100.15 IOF, box 52. See also Wilkie, *Mexican Revolution*, 203.

94. Interview with Jorge Bonilla, Mexico City, August 2, 1999.

95. Robert Wood, "Sears Roebuck Will Continue Expansion in Latin America," *New York Journal of Commerce*, April 14, 1949, Sears News Releases, SRA; *Sears News Graphic: The All Employee Picture Newspaper*, February 1951–January 1953, n.p., SRA.

96. Derossi, *El empresario mexicano*, 91–92, 109–10.

97. Ibid.

98. George Lynch to A. E. Hegewisch, October 28, 1949, SRA, 100.15 IOF, box 49.

99. Ibid.

100. Theodore Houser, chairman of the Board of Sears Roebuck and Company, address at Columbia University, May 14, 1957, 8, SRA, Speeches: Latin America.

101. T. F. Filline to Theodore Houser, December 20, 1949, 7, SRA, 100.15 IOF, box 51.

102. David L. Cohn, "Private Point Four: South of the Border," *Nation's Business*, May 1954, n.p., SRA, 100.15 IOF, box 29.

103. Jacoby, *Modern Manors*, 100.

104. The information that Margarita Rostan provided indicates that El Palacio de Hierro continued this service until the early 1950s. Interview with Margarita Rostan, Mexico City, July 5, 1999.

105. Robert Vanderpoel, "Sears Strengthening International Good Will," *Chicago Sun Times*, June 13, 1951, n.p., SRA, 100.15 IOF, box 48.

106. J. M. Baskin, *Women's Quarterly*, June 27, 1951, n.p., SRA, 100.15 IOF, box 48.

107. J. M. Baskin, "Sears in Mexico to Sell Fall Suits of 13 Ounce Rayon," *New York Daily News Record*, June 8, 1951, n.p., SRA, 100.15 IOF, box 48.

108. Ibid.

109. Ibid.

110. Richardson Wood, *Sears Roebuck de México*, 17.

111. Interview with Jorge Bonilla, Mexico City, July 30, 1999.

112. Sears Publication Department, *Merchant to the Millions*, 12.

113. Ibid., 13.

114. Bunker, "Consumers of Good Taste."

115. "El aparador mexicano," *Publicidad, Tarifas Oficiales: Revista para Ejecutivos de Negocios* 8 (November 1949): 13.

116. Ibid.

117. "Sears Roebuck's Mexican Revolution," *Harper's Magazine*, April 1964, n.p., Sears News Service, SRA, 100.15 IOF, box 1.

118. Ibid.

119. Richardson Wood, *Sears Roebuck de México*, 4.

120. Ibid.

121. General Wood, "Sears presenta con orgullo: Su nueva tienda en puebla," n.d., n.p., SRA, 100.15 IOF, box 52.

122. E. W. Fitz to George Lynch, December 3, 1949, SRA, 100.15 IOF, box 51.

123. Phillip Querido, "Sears, Mexico City, Makes Its Mark through Catalogs and Trading Up," *Women's Wear*, n.p., Sears News Service, SRA, 100.15 IOF, box 51.

124. Ibid.

125. T. F. Filline to T. V. Houser, December 20, 1949, SRA, 100.15 IOF, box 51.

126. "Sears in Mexico—History," n.d., n.p., SRA, 100.15 IOF, box 48.

127. For sample catalogs, see *El Palacio de Hierro, Catálogo*, no. 110 (Mexico City, [1910–14]), and *El Palacio de Hierro, Catálogo de Lutos*, no. 112 (Mexico City, [1912–13]).

128. For examples, see the "Entre Nosotras" column in *Negro y Blanco* 12 (June 7, 1942): 55–57; 10 (April 7, 1948): 50–52; and 5 (November 7, 1945): 50–53.

129. "¡Entérate compañero de Sears! Carta que los empleados de Sears dirigen al Secretario de Gobernación," May 1949, n.p., SRA, 100.15 IOF, box 48.

130. Ibid.

131. Ibid.

132. Ibid.

133. Ibid.

134. Ringe, Bashman, and Correa to General Wood, June 1949, SRA, 100.15 IOF, box 48.

135. Ibid.

136. Ibid.

137. Robert La Follette to General Wood, July 15, 1949, 3, SRA, 100.15 IOF, box 48.

138. Ibid.

139. Ibid., 4.

140. "Sears in Mexico—History," n.d., n.p., SRA, 100.15 IOF, box 48.

141. Ibid.

142. Interview with Jorge Bonilla, Mexico City, August 3, 1999.

143. Interview with Ernesto Zatarain, Mexico City, July 12, 1999.

144. Ibid., July 1, 1999.

145. Sears Roebuck Company, *Manual para jefes de división*.

146. Interview with Jorge Bonilla, Mexico City, July 7, 9, 1999.

147. Ibid., July 12, 1999.

148. Interview with Ernesto Zatarain, Mexico City, July 1, 1999.

149. Interview with Jorge Bonilla, Mexico City, July 12, 1999.

150. Ibid.; interview with Ernesto Zatarain, Mexico City, July 1, 1999.

151. Interviews with Jorge Bonilla, Mexico City, July 12, 1999, and Ernesto Zatarain, Mexico City, July 1, 1999.

152. Interview with Jorge Bonilla, Mexico City, July 30, 1999.

153. Ibid., July 5, 1999; interview with Ernesto Zatarain, Mexico City, July 1, 1999.

154. George Lynch to General Wood, August 5, 1951, 4, SRA, 100.15 IOF, box 48.

155. Ibid.

156. Ibid.

157. Ibid.

158. Ibid., 2.

159. Ibid., 3.

160. Ibid.

161. Ibid.

162. Ibid., 4.

163. "South of the Border: Sears Stirring Up Merchandising Revolution as Top Single Retailer in Latin America with 12 Big Stores," *Wall Street Journal*, June 8, 1951, n.p., Sears News Service, SRA, 100.15 IOF, box 48.

164. Ibid.

165. *New York Daily News Record*, June 13, 1951, n.p., Sears News Service, SRA, 100.15 IOF, box 48.

166. "South of the Border: Sears Stirring Up Merchandising Revolution as Top Single Retailer in Latin America with 12 Big Stores," *Wall Street Journal*, June 8, 1951, n.p., Sears News Service, SRA, 100.15 IOF, box 48.

167. Ibid.

168. *New York Daily News Record*, June 13, 1951, n.p., Sears News Service, SRA, 100.15 IOF, box 48.

169. Mexican male honor and pride have often been defined as "machismo," a destructive force that includes male dominance, violence, heavy drinking, and the expectation that wives and daughters perform household duties. See LeVine, *Dolor y Alegría*.

170. Gutman, *Meanings of Macho*.

171. This claim, as I interpret it, does not mean power relations across gender have changed to the point that male-female equality exists within the domestic sphere. See ibid., which does an excellent job of deconstructing previous interpretations of male pride and machismo in Mexico.

172. Interview with Jorge Bonilla, Mexico City, July 12, 1999.

173. Ibid.

174. Phillip Querido, "Sears, Mexico City, Makes Its Mark through Catalogs and Trading Up," 1948, n.p., Mail Order Catalogs, Profit Sharing, Sources, Stocks, SRA, 100.15 IOF, box 51.

175. Oral interview with Ubaldo Riojas, San Francisco, California, March 2001.

176. Audience comments, Julio Moreno, "Sears, Roebuck de México y el patrimonio cultural mexicano durante la década de los cuarenta," paper presented at the Primer Congreso de Historia Económica de México de la Asociación Mexicana de Historia Económica, UNAM, Mexico City, October 23–25, 2001.

177. Interview with Jorge Bonilla, Mexico City, July 30, 1999.

178. Agustín, *Tragicomedia mexicana*, 106–7.

Chapter Seven

1. "Cartas que se extraviaron," *La Familia* 364 (July 30, 1950): 10. *La Familia* often published lost letters in the hope that readers would recognize the letters when they read them in the magazine. There are no records of how many readers (if any) actually recognized lost letters published in the magazine.

2. "Cartas premiadas," ibid. 363 (July 15, 1950): 10. *La Familia* also requested letters from readers to be published in its "Cartas premiadas" section.

3. Lears, *No Place of Grace*, vi–xvii, 4–6, 46–47, 54–58, 300–301.

4. "Editorial, La calma espiritual," *La Familia* 260 (December 15, 1945): 53.

5. "Editorial, ¿Qué es el tiempo?," ibid. 323 (November 15, 1948): 4.

6. Ibid.

7. "Editorial, Cruzada en pro de la cortería," ibid. 266 (March 30, 1946): 6.

8. "Editorial, Desertores de la vida," ibid. 153 (May 15, 1941): 8.

9. Lewis, *Five Families*, 2, 10–11.

10. Lewis, *Children of Sánchez*, xxiv–xxvii.

11. Levine, *Highbrow Lowbrow*, 129–46, 160–68, suggests that the cultural hierarchy was defined in the United States during the second half of the nineteenth century as society gave culture meaning and made distinctions between highbrow and lowbrow culture.

12. Rubin, *Making of a Middle Brow Culture*.

13. Pogolotti, *La clase media en México*, 191–215, offers a good overview of themes in nineteenth-century Mexican literature that addressed middle-class efforts to preserve high moral standards.

14. Vázquez Amaral, *México*, 137–38.

15. Gutierrez, *La humanidad arrodillada*, 10–11; Sepúlveda, *Santa María de Guadalupe*, 137–39.

16. Leal, *La educación para la post-guerra*, 56.

17. "¿Qué teme usted?," *La Familia* 277 (June 15, 1944): 18.

18. "Editorial, La calma espiritual," *La Familia* 260 (December 15, 1945): 53.

19. "Cuénteme su problema," ibid. 364 (July 30, 1950): 32.

20. "Cartas que se extraviaron," ibid. 242 (February 15, 1945): 11.

21. "Carta premiada," ibid., 10.

22. "Carta premiada," ibid. 225 (May 15, 1944): 10.

23. "Editorial," ibid. 164 (October 31, 1941): 8.

24. "Cartas que se extraviaron," ibid. 150 (March 31, 1941): 11.

25. Emilio G. Escalante to Luis María Martínez, October 19, 1940, AHAM, Oficiales, Particular, Carpeta 68.

26. Ibid.

27. Ibid.

28. Interview with Margarita Rostan, Mexico City, July 7, 1999.

29. Ibid.

30. Abelson, *When Ladies Go a-Thieving*, 4–12, 174, 179–81.

31. "Editorial, Balance," *La Familia* 141 (January 31, 1941): 7.

32. "Carta premiada," ibid. 195 (February 15, 1943): 8.

33. Ibid. 266 (March 30, 1946): 8.

34. Ibid.

35. "Cuáles son los deberes que contraen las mujeres con el matrimonio," ibid. 277 (June 15, 1944): 72.

36. "Cuénteme su problema," ibid. 196 (February 28, 1943): 12.

37. Ibid. 360 (May 30, 1950): 70.

38. Ibid. 225 (May 15, 1944): 10.

39. Ibid. 277 (June 15, 1944): 14.

40. Ibid.

41. Ibid. 359 (May 15, 1950): 28.

42. "Carta premiada," addressed to Irene, ibid. 360 (May 30, 1950): 8.

43. "Cuénteme su problema," ibid. 357 (April 15, 1950): 12.

44. Ibid.

45. Seed, *To Love, Honor, and Obey*.

46. "Cuénteme su problema," *La Familia* 261 (January 15, 1946): 15.

47. Ibid. 233 (September 15, 1944): 12.

48. José Valencia Alvares to Luis M. Martínez, May 31, 1942, AHAM, Oficiales, Particular, Carpeta 68.

49. Guadalupe Hernández to Luis M. Martínez, September 24, 1946, AHAM, Oficiales, Particular, Carpeta 68.

50. Ibid.

51. "Causas matrimoniales, ex capite ligaminis mulieris-tercera instancia-sentencia," March 10, 1941, 3–6, AHAM, Monseñor Luis María Martínez, Clasificado, 1940–49.

52. Ibid.

53. Luz de la Mora de Orbe to José A. Romero, 1951, AHUIA, AHAC, Campaña de Moralización del Ambiente.

54. Carta Pastoral Colectiva del Episcopado Nacional sobre la Moralización de las Costumbres, 1936, AHUIA, AHAC, Campaña de Moralización del Ambiente.

55. "Conclusiones de la Cuarta Asamblea Nacional del tema de propagandistas," June 1938, AHUIA, AHAC, Propaganda y Estadística, 1938–44.

56. Junta Central de Acción Católica, Estatuto y Reglamento de la Comisión Central de Propaganda y Censo, December 1938, AHUIA, AHAC, Propaganda y Estadística, 1938–44.

57. Escuela Diocesana para Dirigentes de A.C., "Cuestionario de Formación de Propagandistas," 1941, AHUIA, AHAC, Correspondencia, 1940–41.

58. Jesús F. Rosas, "Como dar cumplimiento a las conclusiones aprobadas por la Cuarta Asamblea Nacional relativa al tema de propagandistas," December 3, 1938, AHUIA, AHAC, Correspondencia, 1940–41.

59. Carta Pastoral Colectiva del Episcopado Nacional sobre la Moralización de las Costumbres, 1936, AHUIA, AHAC, Campaña de Moralización del Ambiente.

60. UFCM to P. Barragán, September 7, 1951, AHUIA, AHAC, Campaña de Moralización del Ambiente.

61. José González Torres, president's report on the Comisión Central de Propaganda y Estadística, October 18, 1943, AHUIA, AHAC, Propaganda y Estadística.

62. Juan Correa Delgado, circular from the president of the Comisión Central de Propaganda y Estadística, November 11, 1944, 1, AHUIA, AHAC, Circulares, 1944–46, Propaganda y Estadística.

63. Carlos Acosta and José González Torres, circular from the president of the

Junta Central de Acción Católica, November 24, 1950, 4, AHUIA, AHAC, Comisión Central de Propaganda, 1948–52.

64. Rubenstein, *Bad Language, Naked Ladies*, 6–7.

65. Alicia Lozano, report from the president of UFCM, November 9, 1951, AHUIA, AHAC, Campaña de Moralización del Ambiente, 1951–56.

66. Instructivo de Radio, August 1951, AHUIA, AHAC, Campaña de Moralización del Ambiente, 1951–52.

67. Alicia Lozano, report from the vice president of UFCM, November 9, 1951, AHUIA, AHAC, Campaña de Moralización del Ambiente, 1951–56.

68. Carlos F. Acosta, recommendations to the Junta Central de Acción Católica, October 15, 1951, AHUIA, AHAC, Campaña de Moralización del Ambiente, 1951–56.

69. Martín del Campo, circular from the president of ACM, November 26, 1951, 39, AHUIA, AHAC, Campaña de Moralización del Ambiente.

70. Comité Central de Acción Católica de los Jóvenes Mexicanos, "Tercera parte de la campaña de moralización," early 1952, AHUIA, AHAC, Campaña de Moralización del Ambiente, 1951–56. See also "Reunión de Presidentes Diocesanos de la Comisión Central de Propaganda," May 1951, AHUIA, AHAC, Campaña de Moralización del Ambiente, 1951–56.

71. Ibid.

72. Juan Sánchez Navarro, corporate executive at Cervecería Modelo, S.A., to Ignacio Martín del Campo, May 29, 1952, AHUIA, AHAC, Campaña de Moralización del Ambiente, 1952–58.

73. Report from UFCM to Father Barragán, September 7, 1951, AHUIA, AHAC, Campaña de Moralización del Ambiente, 1951–56.

74. José Antonio Romero, S.J., to Luis Logorreta, July 6, 1954, AHUIA, AHAC, Campaña de Moralización del Ambiente, 1952–58.

75. Honor Pact signed by the Cámara Nacional de la Radiodifusión, the Asociación Nacional de la Publicidad, the Asociación Mexicana de Agencias de Publicidad, and the Sociedad de Autores y Compositores de México, 1951, AHUIA, AHAC, Campaña de Moralización del Ambiente, 1951–56.

76. Ibid.

77. *La hora guadalupana*, radio script, December 30, 1943, AHAM, Documentos de Luis María Martínez, Clasificación de 1943.

78. See ibid., December 23, 27, 1943.

79. Ramón Paniagua Jiménez, "El dinero," lesson 12, radio script, n.d., AHUIA, AHAC, Campaña de Moralización del Ambiente, 1951–56.

80. Ramón Paniagua Jiménez, "Capacidad de consumo," lesson 13, radio script, n.d., AHUIA, AHAC, Campaña de Moralización del Ambiente, 1951–56.

81. Ramón Paniagua Jiménez, "El ahorro, primera y segunda parte," lesson 18, radio script, n.d., AHUIA, AHAC, Campaña de Moralización del Ambiente, 1951–56.

82. "Editorial," *La Familia* 323 (November 15, 1948): 4.

83. Ibid. 360 (May 30, 1950): 4.
84. See ibid. 363 (July 15, 1950): 109 for an example of a Tampax ad.
85. See ibid. 282 (September 15, 1944): 9 for an example of a Formfit ad.

Conclusion

1. "Lost in the Translation: Milk Board Does without Its Famous Slogan When It Woos a Latino Audience," *San Francisco Chronicle*, August 25, 2001, business section, 1, 3.
2. Ibid.

Bibliography

Archives and Research Centers

Advertising Research Foundation, New York
Archivo General de la Nación, Mexico City
   Colección de la Casa Bayer
   Dirección General de Información
   Galería Presidencial
   Propiedad Artística y Literaria
   Registro de Patentes
Archivo Histórico del Arzobispado de México, Mexico City
Archivos Económicos de la Biblioteca Lerdo de Tejada, Mexico City
Archivos Históricos de Banamex, Mexico City
Asociación de Radiodifusores del Valle de México, Mexico City
Asociación Mexicana de Agencias de Publicidad, Mexico City
Asociación Nacional de Publicidad, Mexico City
Bancroft Library, University of California, Berkeley
Biblioteca del Instituto Mora, Mexico City
Biblioteca Francisco Xavier Clavigero, Acervos Históricos, Universidad Iberoamericana, Mexico City
   Archivo Histórico de Acción Católica
Biblioteca Fundación Miguel Alemán, Mexico City
Center for Advertising and Marketing Research, New York
Hartman Center for Sales, Advertising, and Marketing Research, Duke University, Durham, North Carolina
   J. Walter Thompson Company Archives
Hemeroteca Nacional, Universidad Nacional Autónoma de México, Mexico City
Jorge Berlie's Private Archival Collections, El Palacio de Hierro, Mexico City
Library of Congress, Washington, D.C.
Margarita Rostan's Private Archival Collections, El Palacio de Hierro, Mexico City
Nettie Lee Benson Library, University of Texas, Austin
Rockefeller University Archives, New York
   Nelson Rockefeller Records
Sears Roebuck and Company Archives, Chicago
   International Office Files
   Records for Mexican and Latin American Operations
U.S. National Archives, College Park, Maryland
   Record Group 229, Office of Inter-American Affairs
University of California at Los Angeles Film Archives, Los Angeles

Newspapers and Magazines

Abside: Revista de Cultura Mexicana, Mexico City, 1946
AMAP: Vocero de la Publicidad Organizada, 1950s
Boletín de la Asociación Mexicana de Agencias de Publicidad, 1950s
Boletín Mensual de la Cerveza Carta Blanca, 1935
Excélsior, Mexico City, 1920s–30s
La Familia: Revista de Labores para el Hogar, 1930–50
El Heraldo, Mexico City, 1930s–40s
Hoy! La Revista Supergráfica, 1940s
El Nacional, Mexico City, 1930s–40s
Negro y Blanco y Labores: Revista Mensual de la Mujer, 1930s–40s
El Popular, Mexico City, 1930s–40s
Publicidad: Boletín Oficial de la Asociación Nacional de Publicistas, 1940s
Publicidad, Tarifas Oficiales: Revista para Ejecutivos de Negocios, 1940s
Publicidad y Ventas: Revista Técnica de Divulgación Publicitaria, 1949–50
Revista de Revistas, el Semanario Nacional, 1930s–40s
El Universal, Mexico City, 1920s–40s

Interviews

Jorge Berlie, business executive, El Palacio de Hierro, Mexico City, July–August 1999.
Jorge Bonilla, director of Latin American Translating Unit, Sears de México, Mexico City, July–August 1999.
María Licona, sales representative at La Esmeralda Jewelry (1950s) and El Palacio de Hierro (1960s–90s), Mexico City, August 1999.
Raul Prado, director of credit, El Palacio de Hierro, Mexico City, July 1999.
Ubaldo Riojas, medical student in Mexico City during the 1940s, San Francisco, California, March 2001.
Margarita Rostan, director of fashion department (1929–40s), public relations executive (1950s–70s), Artesanías (1980s–90s), El Palacio de Hierro, Mexico City, July–August 1999.
María Teresa Vargas, advertising director, El Palacio de Hierro, Mexico City, July 1999.
Ernesto Zatarain, corporate executive, Sears de México, Mexico City, July–August 1999.

Books, Articles, and Dissertations

Abelson, Elaine. *When Ladies Go a-Thieving: Middle-Class Shoplifters in the Victorian Department Store*. New York: Oxford University Press, 1989.
Acosta, Homero. *La canción olvidada: Poemas*. Mexico City, 1948.

Adler Lomnitz, Larissa, and Marisol Pérez-Lizaur. *A Mexican Elite Family, 1820–1980: Kinship, Class, and Culture*. Princeton: Princeton University Press, 1987.

Adorno, Theodor. *Minima Moralia*. London: Verso, 1978.

Aguayo Quezada, Sergio. *El panteón de los mitos: Estados Unidos y el nacionalismo mexicano*. Mexico City: Editorial Grijalbo, 1998.

Aguilar, Alonso M., and Fernando Carmona. *México: Riqueza y miseria*. Mexico City: Editorial Nuestro Tiempo, 1988.

Aguilar Camín, Héctor, and Lorenzo Meyer. *In the Shadow of the Mexican Revolution: Contemporary Mexican History, 1910–1989*. Translated by Luis A. Fierro. Austin: University of Texas Press, 1993.

Aguilar Camín, Héctor, Lourdes Arizpe, José Blanco, Guillermo Bonfil, Rolando Cordera Aguirre, and Alvaro Matute. *Pensamiento historiográfico mexicano del siglo XX: La desintegración del positivismo, 1911–1935*. Mexico City: Fondo de Cultura Económica, 1999.

Agustín, José. *Tragicomedia mexicana: La vida en México de 1940 a 1970*. Vol. 1. Mexico City: Editorial Planeta Mexicana, 1990.

Alemán Valdés, Miguel. *Un México mejor: Pensamientos, discursos e información, 1936–1952*. Mexico City: Editorial Diana, 1988.

———. *Remembranzas y testimonios*. Mexico City: Editorial Grijalbo, 1986.

Alvarado, Salvador. *La reconstrucción de México*. Vols. 1–3. Mexico City: Instituto Nacional de Estudios Históricos de la Revolución Mexicana, 1985.

Alvarez, Oscar C. *La cuestión social en México: El trabajo, manual para círculos de estudio*. Mexico City: Publicaciones Mundiales, 1950.

Amaral, José V. *México: Datos para su biografía*. Mexico City, 1945.

American Council on Public Affairs. *The Economic Defense of the Western Hemisphere: A Study in Conflicts*. Symposium of the Latin American Economic Institute. Washington, D.C.: American Council on Public Affairs, 1941.

Anderson, Benedict. *Imagined Communities: Reflections on the Origin and Spread of Nationalism*. London: Verso, 1992.

Andrade, Manuel. *Cooperativas y asociaciones: Código de comercio reformado*. Mexico City: Información Aduanera de México, 1953.

Araujo, Roberto G. *Palabras de libertad y democracia*. Mexico City: Ediciones de America, 1944.

Arbena, Joseph. "Sport and the Study of Latin American Society: An Overview." In *Sport and Society in Latin America: Diffusion, Dependency, and the Rise of Mass Culture*, 1–14. New York: Greenwood Press, 1988.

Arreola, José, and Lilian Scheffler. *México, ¿Quieres tomarte una foto conmigo?: Cien años de consumo*. Mexico City: Editorial Gustabo Casasola, 1996.

Arriaga, Patricia. *Publicidad, económica y comunicación masiva: México–Estados Unidos*. Mexico City: Editorial Nueva Imagen, 1980.

Baklanoff, Jay Driskell. "From the Mass-Media to the Bars: An Ethnomusicological Perspective on Contemporary Musical Activities in Mérida, Yucatán." *Studies in Latin American Popular Culture* 5 (1986): 127–33.

Balderrama, Francisco, and Raymond Rodríguez. *A Decade of Betrayal: Mexican Repatriation in the 1930s*. Albuquerque: University of New Mexico Press, 1995.

Banamex. *Examen de la situación económica de México en el contexto mundial*. Mexico City: Fondo Cultural Banamex, 1978.

Banco de México. *Comentarios al estudio sobre México de Higgins Industries, Inc.* Mexico City: Banco de México, 1954.

Baudrillard, Jean. *The Mirror of Production*. St. Louis: Telos Press, 1975.

———. *Selected Writings*. Edited by Mark Poster. Stanford: Stanford University Press, 1988.

Becker, Marjorie. *Setting the Virgin on Fire: Lázaro Cárdenas, Michoacán Peasants, and the Redemption of the Mexican Revolution*. Berkeley: University of California Press, 1995.

Beezley, William H. *Judas at the Jockey Club and Other Episodes of Porfirian Mexico*. Lincoln: University of Nebraska Press, 1987.

———. "Sports." *Studies in Latin American Popular Culture* 4 (1985): 213–17.

Bejar, Raúl, and Héctor Rosales. *La identidad nacional mexicana como problema político y cultural*. Mexico City: Siglo Veintiuno Editores, 1999.

Benjamin, Thomas. *La Revolución: Mexico's Great Revolution as Memory, Myth, and History*. Austin: University of Texas Press, 2002.

Benjamin, Thomas, and Mark Wasserman. *Provinces of the Revolution: Essays on Regional Mexican History, 1920–1929*. Albuquerque: University of New Mexico Press, 1990.

Bensusan, Guy. "Mexican Popular Music." *Studies in Latin American Popular Culture* 2 (1983): 213–17.

Bermudez, María Teresa. "La decencia en oferta: Anuncios periodísticos y escuelas particulares, 1857–1867." *Historia Mexicana* 33 (1984): 214–53.

Bernal Sahagún, Victor Manuel. *Anatomía de la publicidad en México: Temas de la actualidad*. 9th ed. Mexico City: Editorial Nuestro Tiempo, 1993.

Besse, Susan K. *Restructuring Patriarchy: The Modernization of Gender Inequality in Brazil, 1914–1940*. Chapel Hill: University of North Carolina Press, 1996.

Beteta, Ramón. *Pensamiento y dinámica de la Revolución Mexicana: Antología de documentos políticosociales*. Mexico City: Editorial México Nuevo, 1950.

———. *Programa económico y social de México*. Mexico City, 1935.

Bethel, Leslie. *Latin America: Economy and Society since 1930*. Cambridge: Cambridge University Press, 1998.

———. *Mexico since Independence*. New York: Cambridge University Press, 1991.

Blacarte, Roberto, ed. *Cultura e identidad nacional*. Mexico City: Fondo de Cultura Económica, 1994.

———. *El pensamiento social de los católicos mexicanos*. Mexico City: Fondo de Cultura Económica, 1996.

Bonfíl Batalla, Guillermo. *México profundo: Una civilización negada*. Mexico City: Editorial Grijalbo, 1989.

Bonilla, José María. *Los derechos políticos*. Mexico City: Herrero Hermanos Sucesores, 1923.

Borden, Neil H. *The Economic Effects of Advertising*. Chicago: Richard D. Irwing, 1942.

Borden, Neil H., Malcolm Taylor, and Howard Hovde. *National Advertising in Newspapers*. Cambridge: Harvard University Press, 1946.

Brading, David. *The First America: The Spanish Monarchy, Creole Patriots, and the Liberal State, 1492–1864*. Cambridge: Cambridge University Press, 1991.

———. *Mexican Phoenix, Our Lady of Guadalupe: Image and Tradition across Five Centuries*. Cambridge: Cambridge University Press, 2001.

———. *Los orígines del nacionalismo mexicano*. Mexico City: Ediciones Era, 1998.

Brandenburg, Frank. *The Making of Modern Mexico*. Englewood: Prentice-Hall, 1965.

Britton, John A. *Revolution and Ideology: Images of the Mexican Revolution in the United States*. Lexington: University of Kentucky Press, 1995.

Bronner, Simon, ed. *Consuming Visions: Accumulation and Display of Goods in America, 1880–1920*. New York: Henry Francis du Pont Winterthur Museum, 1989.

Brown, Bruce. *Images of Family Life in Magazine Advertising, 1920–1978*. New York: Praeger, 1981.

Browner, Carole, and Jane H. Hill. "Gender Ambiguity and Class Stereotyping in the Mexican Fotonovela." *Studies in Latin American Popular Culture* 1 (1982): 43–61.

Bunker, Steve. "Consumers of Good Taste: Marketing Modernity in Northern Mexico, 1890–1900." *Estudios Mexicanos/Mexican Studies* 13, no. 2 (1997): 226–37.

Bushman, Richard. *The Refinement of America: Persons, Houses, Cities*. New York: Vintage Books, 1993.

Cacho, José P., and Celia Balcarcel. *Correspondencia mercantil y oficial*. Mexico City: Ediciones ECA, 1948.

Calderón, José María. *Génesis del presidencialismo en México*. Mexico City: Ediciones El Caballito, 1972.

Calva, José Luis. *Los campesinos y su devenir en las economías del mercado*. Mexico City: Siglo Veintiuno Editores, 1988.

Cámara de Diputados al H. Congreso de la Unión (XXXVIII Legislatura). *Un continente, un pueblo, un hombre*. Mexico City, 1941.

Cámara Nacional de la Industria de Transformación. *Selección, registro y uso de marcas: Instructivo*. Mexico City: Cámara Nacional de la Industria de Transformación, 1948.

Camp, Roderic. *Entrepreneurs and Politics in Twentieth Century Mexico*. New York: Oxford University Press, 1988.

Cardoso, Fernando Henrique. *Dependency and Development in Latin America*. Translated by Marjory Mattingly Urquidi. Berkeley: University of California Press, 1979.

Carmona, Fernando, Guillermo Montaño, Jorge Carrión, and Alonso Aguilar. *El milagro mexicano*. Mexico City: Editorial Nuestro Tiempo, 1999.

Carniado, Enrique. *La capacitación técnica del obrero en México: Conferencia sustentada en el Palacio de Bellas Artes*. Mexico City: CTM, Federación de Trabajadores del Distrito Federal, 1951.

Carpizo, Jorge. *El presidencialismo mexicano*. Mexico City: Siglo Veintiuno Editores, 1978.

Carranza, Javier. *Métodos naturales de la enseñanza*. Mexico City, 1940.

Carrillo Zalce, Ignacio, Agustín de la Llera, and Mariano Alcócer. *Documentación y prácticas comerciales*. Mexico City: Editorial Banca y Comercio, 1947.

Carson, W. E. *México: The Wonderland of the South*. New York: Macmillan, 1909.

Casanova, Pablo G. *La democracia en México*. Mexico City: Ediciones Era, 1965.

Caso, Antonio. *El problema de México y la ideología nacional*. Mexico City: Biblioteca Universo, 1924.

Castañeda Ramos, Gonzálo. *La empresa mexicana y su gobierno corporativo: Antecedentes y desafíos para el siglo XXI*. Puebla: Universidad de las Américas and Alter Ego Editores, 1998.

Castorena, Jesús. *Problemas del trabajo en la post-guerra*. Mexico City: S/E, 1944.

Cepeda Villareal, Rodolfo. *Apuntes de derecho del trabajo, segundo curso*. Mexico City, 1947.

Cervantes Ahumada, Raúl. *La sociedad de responsabilidad limitada en el derecho mercantil mexicano: Breve monografía, que incluye un estudio sobre empresas individuales de responsabilidad limitada*. Mexico City: Imprenta Universitaria, 1943.

Cerwin, Herbert. *These Are the Mexicans*. New York: Reynal & Hitchcock, 1947.

Chandler, Alfred D. *The Visible Hand: The Managerial Revolution in American Business*. Cambridge: Harvard University Press, 1977.

Christiansen, Olaf. *El conflicto entre la gran bretaña y México por la expropriación petrolera: Documentos confidenciales del Foreign Office*. Mexico City: Editorial ASBE, 1997.

Cline, Howard. *Mexico: Revolution to Evolution, 1940–1960*. Westport: Greenwood Press, 1962.

Coatsworth, John. *Growth against Development: Economic Impact of Railroads in Porfirian Mexico*. De Kalb: Northern Illinois University Press, 1981.

Cocena, José Luis. *México en la orbita imperial: Las empresas transnacionales*. Mexico City: Ediciones El Caballito, 1999.

Cohen, Lizabeth. "The Class Experience of Mass Consumption: Workers as Consumers in Inter-War America." In *The Power of Culture: Critical Essays in American History*, edited by Richard Wightman Fox and T. J. Jackson Lears, 135–60. Chicago: University of Chicago Press, 1993.

———. *Making a New Deal: Industrial Workers in Chicago, 1919–1939*. Cambridge: Cambridge University Press, 1990.

El Colegio de México. *Historia general de México*. Vol. 2. Mexico City: El Colegio de México, 1998.

Comité Nacional Alemanista. *El problema nacional de la industria azucarera: Conferencia de mesa redonda*. Cuernavaca: Comité Nacional Alemanista, 1945.

———. *El problema nacional de la industria textil: Conferencia de mesa redonda*. Puebla: Comité Nacional Alemanista, 1946.

Córdova, Arnaldo. *La formación del poder político en México*. Mexico City: Ediciones Era, Colección Problemas de México, 1998.

———. *La ideología de la Revolución Mexicana: La formación del nuevo régime*. Mexico City: Ediciones Era, Colección Problemas de México, 1997.

Córdova, Arnaldo, Fátima Fernández, Julio Frenk, Adolfo Gilly, Miguel A. González Block, Luis González, Hugo Hiriart, Lorenzo Meyer, Ruy Pérez Tamayo, Carlos Tello, Arturo Warman, and José Warman. *México mañana*. Mexico City: Océano Nexos, 1988.

Coronil, Fernando. *The Magical State: Nature, Money, and Modernity in Venezuela*. Chicago: University of Chicago Press, 1997.

Cosío Villegas, Daniel. *Ensayos y notas*. Vol. 1. Mexico City: Editorial Hermes, 1966.

———. *Llamadas*. Mexico City: El Colegio de México, 1980.

———. *Memorias*. Mexico City: Editorial Joaquín Mortiz, 1976.

Cossio, José L. *Del México viejo*. Mexico City, 1934.

———. "Prólogo." In *En gran despojo nacional o de manos muertas a manos vivas: Datos sobre las propiedades urbanas de la intrucción iúblicas y de la beneficiencia privada*. Mexico City: Polis, 1945.

Cremoux, Raúl, and Alfonso Millán. *La publicidad os hará libres*. Mexico City: Fondo de Cultura Económica, 1970.

Cronon, David E. *Josephus Daniels in Mexico*. Madison: University of Wisconsin Press, 1960.

Cross, Gary. *An All-Consuming Century: Why Commercialism Won in Modern America*. New York: Columbia University Press, 2000.

Curiel Benfield, José Luis. *El dinero: Fenómeno económico-jurídico*. Mexico City: Universidad Nacional Autónoma de México, 1943.

Daviddoff, Leonore, and Catherine Hall. *Family Fortunes: Men and Women of the English Middle Class, 1780–1850*. Chicago: University of Chicago Press, 1987.

De la Cueva, Mario. *Derecho mexicano del trabajo*. 2d ed. Mexico City: Libreria de Porrúa Hnos. y Cia., 1943.

De la Hidalga, Luis. *El equilibrio del poder en México*. Mexico City: Universidad Nacional Autónoma de México, 1986.

De la Maza, Francisco. *El guadalupanismo mexicano*. Mexico City: Fondo de Cultura Económica, 1981.

Delpar, Helen. *The Enormous Vogue of Things Mexican: Cultural Relationships between the U.S. and Mexico, 1920–1935*. Tuscaloosa: University of Alabama Press, 1992.

De Mendizabal, Miguel Othón, José María Luis Mora, Mariano Otero, Andrés Molina Enriquez, Nathan L. Whetten, Angel Palerm Vich, Rodolfo Stavenhagen, and Pablo González Casanova. *Las clases sociales en México*. Mexico City: Editorial Nuestro Tiempo, 1972.

Deming, Edwards. *El control estadístico de calidad*. Mexico City: Secretaria de Economía, 1954.

Demoscopia, S.A., y Medios Publicitarios Mexicanos, S.A. de C.V., *Publicidad mexicana*. Mexico City: Valencia, 1971.

Departamento del Distrito Federal. *Resumen de actividades, 1950*. Mexico City: S/E, 1950.

Derossi, Flavia. *El empresario mexicano*. Mexico City: Instituto de Investigaciones Sociales, Universidad Nacional Autónoma de México, 1977.

Desideiro, Marcos. *El anuncio en México*. Mexico City: Imprenta Nacional, 1922.

Díaz y de Ovando, Clementina. *Odontología y publicidad en la prensa mexicana del siglo XIX*. Mexico City: Universidad Nacional Autónoma de México, Instituto de Investigaciones Históricas, 1990.

Drake, Paul. *Socialism and Populism in Chile, 1932–1952*. Urbana: University of Illinois Press, 1978.

Duarte, Jacinto A. *Brevísima historia y técnica del aviso en la revista*. Montevideo, 1946.

Dunbaugh, Frank Montgomery. *Marketing in Latin America*. New York: Printers' Ink, 1960.

Durán Ochoa, Julio. *Población*. Mexico City: Fondo de Cultura Económica, 1955.

Eckes, Alfred, Jr. *Opening America's Market: U.S. Foreign Policy since 1776*. Chapel Hill: University of North Carolina Press, 1995.

Ediciones Jackson. *Práctica comercial norteamericana: Bancos, capital, finanzas y organización*. Vol. 1. Buenos Aires: Editorial Jackson, n.d.

———. *Práctica comercial norteamericana: Créditos, procedimientos corporativos e inversions*. Vol. 9. Buenos Aires: Editorial Jackson, n.d.

———. *Práctica comercial norteamericana: Exportación, tránsito y sistema de oficinas*. Vol. 5. Buenos Aires: Editorial Jackson, n.d.

———. *Práctica comercial norteamericana: Personal de la fábrica, compra de equipos*. Vol. 10. Buenos Aires: Editorial Jackson, n.d.

Editorial Superación. *México: Realización y esperanza*. Mexico City: Editorial Superación, 1952.

Encinas, Luis. *Proceso y problemas de México*. Mexico City: Editorial Stylo, 1954.

Enriquez Filio, Antonio. *Problemas sociales mexicanos*. Mexico City: Talleres Gráficos de la Nación, 1929.

Ewen, Stuart. *Captains of Consciousness: Advertising and the Social Roots of Consumer Culture*. New York: McGraw-Hill, 1976.

Ferrero, Rómulo A. *Comercio y pagos internacionales*. Mexico City: Centro de Estudios Monetarios Internacionales, 1963.

Ferrer Rodríguez, Eulalio. *El diario de un publicista*. Mexico City: Editorial Diana, 1993.

———. *El lenguaje de la publicidad en México*. Mexico City: Ediciones EUFESA, 1966.

Florescano, Enrique. *El nuevo pasado mexicano*. Mexico City: Cal y Arena, 1991.

Florescano, Enrique, and Ricardo Pérez Montfort, eds. *Historiadores de México en el siglo XX*. Mexico City: Fondo de Cultura Económica, 1995.

Flores Zavala, Ernesto. *Elementos de finanzas públicas mexicanas, los impuestos*. Vol. 1. Mexico City: Camarena y Ramírez, 1946.

Fouque, Agustín. *El tratado de comercio México-Americano, guión para una revisión equitativa: Colección de temas económicos y políticos contemporáneos de México*. Mexico City: EDIAPSA, 1949.

Fowler-Salamini, Heather, and Mary Kay Vaughan. *Women of the Mexican Countryside, 1850–1990*. Tucson: University of Arizona Press, 1994.

Fox, Richard Wightman, and T. J. Jackson Lears, eds. *The Culture of Consumption: Critical Essays in American History, 1880–1980*. New York: Pantheon Books, 1983.

Franco, Jean. *Plotting Women: Gender and Representation in Mexico*. New York: Columbia University Press, 1988.

Freithaler, William O. *Comercio exterior y desarrollo económico de México*. Mexico City: Editorial Diana, 1968.

Fuentes, Carlos. *The Death of Artemio Cruz*. New York: Farrar, Straus and Giroux, 1991.

Fundación Miguel Alemán. *Remembranzas y testimonios*. Mexico City: Editorial Grijalbo, 1987.

Furtado, Celso. *Economic Development of Latin America: Historical Background and Contemporary Problems*. Translated by Suzette Macedo. Cambridge: Cambridge University Press, 1976.

García Canclini, Nestor. *Transforming Modernity: Popular Culture in Mexico*. Translated by Lidia Lozano. Austin: University of Texas Press, 1993.

García Rivas, Heriberto. *Dádivas de México al mundo*. Mexico City, 1965.

García Rivera, Emilio. *Historia documental del cine mexicano, 1938–1942*. Vol. 2. Guadalajara: Universidad de Guadalajara, 1992.

Garrido, Luis, ed. *Conferencias de orientación vocacional*. Mexico City: Universidad Nacional Autónoma de México, 1950.

Garza-Falcón, Leticia M. *Gente Decente: A Borderlands Response to the Rhetoric of Dominance*. Austin: University of Texas Press, 1988.

Gaytán, Ricardo T. *Teoría del comercio internacional*. Mexico City: Siglo Veintiuno Editores, 1972.

Gellman, Irwin F. *Good Neighbor Diplomacy: U.S. Policies in Latin America, 1933–1945*. Baltimore: Johns Hopkins University Press, 1979.

Gilbert, James. *A Cycle of Outrage: America's Reaction to Juvenile Delinquents in the 1950s*. New York: Oxford University Press, 1986.

Gilly, Adolfo. *El Cardenismo: Una utopía mexicana*. Mexico City: Aguilar, León y Cal Editores, 1994.

Gobierno del D.F. Sexenio 1940–46. *C. presidente constitucional de la república general de la división, Ávila Camacho*. Mexico City: Gobierno del D.F., 1946.

Gobierno Federal de México. *Industrialización de México: El tratado comercial con los Estados Unidos, opiniones de la cámara nacional de la industria de transformación*. Mexico City, 1947.

———. *Manual para uso de los fundadores y administradores de las cooperativas en México*. Mexico City: Talleres Gráficos de la Nación, 1925.

Gómez-Gavarito Freer, Aurora. "The Impact of Revolution: Business and Labor in the Mexican Textile Industry, Orizaba, Veracruz, 1900–1930." Ph.D. diss., Harvard University, 1999.

Gómez Moraga, Mauricio. *La ciudad y la gente*. Vols. 1 and 2. Mexico City: Editorial Jus, 1979.

Gómez-Quiñones, Juan. *Roots of Chicano Politics, 1600–1940*. Albuquerque: University of New Mexico Press, 1988.

González Casanova, Pablo. *La democracia en México*. Mexico City: Ediciones Era, 1965.

González y González, Luis. *Obras completas: Invitación a la microhistoria*. Vol. 9. Mexico City: Clío, 1997.

———. *Obras completas: Modales de la cultura nacional*. Mexico City: Clío, 1998.

———. *Los días del Presidente Cárdenas*. Mexico City: Colegio de México, 1981.

———. *San José de Gracia: Mexican Village in Transition*. Translated by John Upton. Austin: University of Texas Press, 1972.

Gradante, William. "Mexican Popular Music at Midcentury: The Role of José Alfredo Jimenez and the Canción Ranchera." *Studies in Latin American Popular Culture* 1 (1983): 99–113.

Graham, Richard. *The Idea of Race in Latin America, 1870–1940*. Austin: University of Texas Press, 1990.

Gramsci, Antonio. *Sections from the Prison Notebooks*. New York: International Publishers, 1971.

Granados Roldán, Otto, Rogelio Montemayor, Sergio Reyes Osorio, Ma. de Los Angeles Moreno, René Villarreal, Francisco Suárez Dávila, and Emilio Lozoya. *México: 75 años de revolución, desarrollo económico*. Vol. 1. Mexico City: Fondo de Cultura Económica, 1988.

Greenberg, David, and Marían Greenberg. *The Shopping Guide to Mexico*. New York: Trade Winds Press, 1955.

Gutierrez, Marín. *La humanidad arrodillada: Panorama de la fe religiosa universal*. Mexico City: Casa Unida de Publicaciones, 1955.

Gutiérrez, Mateo Solana. *Las devaluaciones en México: Cuál será la política de Adolfo López Mateos*. Mexico City: Libro Mex Editores, 1958.

Gutman, Matthew. *The Meanings of Macho: Being a Man in Mexico City*. Berkeley: University of California Press, 1996.

Haber, Stephen. *How Latin America Fell Behind: Essays in the Economic Histories of Brazil and Mexico, 1800–1914*. Stanford: Stanford University Press, 1997.

———. *Industry and Underdevelopment: The Industrialization of Mexico, 1890–1940*. Stanford: Stanford University Press, 1989.

Habermas, Jürgen. *Moral Consciousness and Communicative Action*. Translated by Christian Lenhardt and Shierry Weber Nicholsen. Cambridge: MIT Press, 1991.

———. *The Theory of Communicative Action*. Vol. 2, *Lifeworld and System: A Critique of Functionalist Reason*. Translated by Thomas McCarthy. Boston: Beacon Press, 1981.

Haineault, Doris-Louise, and Jean-Yves Roy. *Unconscious for Sale: Advertising, Psychoanalysis, and the Public*. Translated by Kimball Lockhart with Barbara Kerslake. Minneapolis: University of Minnesota Press, 1993.

Hale, Charles. *The Transformation of Liberalism in Late Nineteenth Century Mexico*. Princeton: Princeton University Press, 1989.

Hamilton, Nora. *The Limits of State Autonomy: Post Revolutionary Mexico*. Princeton: Princeton University Press, 1982.

Hansen, Roger. *Mexican Economic Development: The Roots of Rapid Growth*. Studies Development in Progress, no. 2. Washington, D.C.: National Planning Association, 1971.

———. *The Politics of Mexican Development*. Baltimore: Johns Hopkins University Press, 1971.

Hart, John Mason. *Revolutionary Mexico: The Coming and Process of the Mexican Revolution*. Berkeley: University of California Press, 1987.

Hayes, Joy Elizabeth. "Historical Perspectives on Mass Media, Popular Culture, and Nationalism in Mexico." *Studies in Latin American Popular Culture* 15 (1996): 319–23.

Heinze, Andrew. *Adapting to Abundance: Jewish Immigrants, Mass Consumption, and the Search for American Identity*. New York: Columbia University Press, 1990.

Hernández Chávez, Alicia, and Manuel Miño Grijalba, eds. *Cincuenta años de historia en México*. Vol. 2. Mexico City: El Colegio de México, 1993.

Hernández Rodríguez, Rogelio. *Amistades, compromisos y lealtades: Líderes y grupos políticos en el estado de México, 1942–1993*. Mexico City: El Colegio de México, 1998.

Hershfield, Joanne. *Mexican Cinema, Mexican Women, 1940–1950*. Tucson: University of Arizona Press, 1996.

Hewitt de Alcántara, Cynthia. *La modernización de la agricultura mexicana, 1940–1970*. Mexico City: Siglo Veintiuno Editores, 1999.

Hinds, Harold E., Jr. "Recent Studies of Mexican Sport and Ritual: Elite Intentions and Popular Renderings." *Studies in Latin American Popular Culture* 15 (1996): 301–10.

Homs, Ricardo. *Creadores de imagen mexicana*. Mexico City: Planeta, 1992.

Horkheimer, Max, and Theodor Adorno. *Dialectic of Enlightenment*. Translated by John Cumming. New York: Continuum, 1991.

Hornedo, Eduardo. *Política económica mexicana: Abatimiento del costo de la vida*. Mexico City: Editorial B. Costa-Amic, 1958.

Impresora Editora Revolucionaria. *Reseña gráfica presidencial correspondiente al primer año de labores del C. Gral. de división, Manuel Ávila Camacho*. Mexico City: Empresa Editora Revolucionaria, 1946.

Inglis, Fred. *The Cruel Peace: Everyday Life and the Cold War*. New York: Basic Books, 1991.

Iturbide, Eduardo. *Mi paso por la vida*. Mexico City: Editorial CVLTVRA, 1941.

Iturriaga, José. *La estructura social y cultural de México*. Mexico City: Fondo de Cultura Economica, 1951.

Jacoby, Sanford M. *Modern Manors: Welfare Capitalism since the New Deal*. Princeton: Princeton University Press, 1997.

Jaimes, Graciela M. *Elementos de historia del derecho mexicano*. Mexico City: Universidad Autónoma del Estado de México, 2000.

Jameson, Fredric. *Postmodernism, or, The Cultural Logic of Late Capitalism*. Durham: Duke University Press, 1991.

Johns, Michael. *The City of Mexico in the Age of Díaz*. Austin: University of Texas Press, 1997.

Joseph, Gilbert, and Daniel Nugent, eds. *Everyday Forms of State Formation: Revolution and Negotiation of Rule in Modern Mexico*. Durham: Duke University Press, 1994.

Joseph, Gilbert, Catherine C. LeGrand, and Ricardo D. Salvatore, eds. *Close Encounters of Empire: Writing the Cultural History of U.S.–Latin American Relations*. Durham: Duke University Press, 1998.

Kammen, Michael G. *American Culture, American Tastes: Social Change and the Twentieth Century*. New York: Knopf, 1999.

Kandal, Jonathan. *La Capital: The Biography of Mexico City*. New York: Random House, 1988.

Kaplan, Amy, and Donald E. Pease, eds. *Cultures of United States Imperialism*. Durham: Duke University Press, 1993.

Katz, Friedrich. *The Secret War in Mexico: Europe, the U.S., and the Mexican Revolution*. Chicago: University of Chicago Press, 1981.

Kilpatrick, Carroll, ed. *Roosevelt and Daniels: A Friendship in Politics*. Chapel Hill: University of North Carolina Press, 1952.

Klein, Lawrence R. *La revolución keynesiana*. Madrid: Editorial Revista de Derecho Privado, 1952.

Knight, Alan. *The Mexican Revolution: Counter-Revolution and Reconstruction*. Vols. 1 and 2. Lincoln: University of Nebraska Press, 1986.

———. "Racism, Revolution, and Indigenismo: Mexico, 1910–1940." In *The Idea of*

Race in Latin America, 1870–1940, edited by Richard Graham, 71–113. Austin: University of Texas Press, 1990.

———. "Revolutionary Project, Recalcitrant People: Mexico, 1910–40." In *The Revolutionary Process in Mexico: Essays on Political and Social Change, 1880–1940*, edited by Jaime E. Rodríguez, 227–64. Wilmington: Scholarly Resources, 1990.

Krauze, Enrique. *Caudillos culturales de la Revolución Mexicana*. Mexico City: Siglo Veintiuno Editores, 1985.

———. *Daniel Cosío Villegas: Una biografía intelectual*. Mexico City: Joaquín Mortiz, 1980.

———. *Mexico, Biography of Power: A History of Modern Mexico, 1810–1996*. New York: Harper Collins, 1997.

———. *La presidencia imperial: Ascenso y caída del sistema político mexicano, 1940–1996*. Mexico City: Tus Quets Editores, 1997.

Kuisel, Richard. *Seducing the French: The Dilemma of Americanization*. Berkeley: University of California Press, 1993.

LaClau, Ernesto. *Politics and Ideology in Marxist Theory: Capitalism, Fascism, and Populism*. London: NLB, 1977.

LaFaye, Jacques. *Quetzalcóatl and Guadalupe: The Formation of Mexican National Consciousness, 1531–1831*. Chicago: University of Chicago Press, 1974.

Lavín, José Domingo. *En la brecha mexicana: Temas económicos para México y Latinoamérica*. Mexico City: EDIAPSA, 1948.

———. *La industrialización de México, relaciones obrero patronales, presentación en el teatro de bellas artes presidida por el Sr. Ingeniero Don Gustavo P. Serrano, secretario de economía nacional*. Mexico City: Ateneo Nacional de Ciencias y Artes de México, 1947.

———. *Inversiones extranjeras: Análisis, experiencias y orientaciones para la conducta mexicana*. Mexico City: EDIAPSA, 1954.

Lawrence, D. H. *Mañanas en México*. Translated by Octavio Barreda. Mexico City: Letras de México, 1942.

Leach, William. *Land of Desire: Merchants, Power, and the Rise of a New American Culture*. New York: Vintage Books, 1993.

Leal, Miguel. *La educación para la post-guerra*. Vol. 2. Mexico City: Ediciones Educación, 1944.

Lears, T. J. Jackson. *Fables of Abundance: A Cultural History of Advertising in America*. New York: Basic Books, 1994.

———. *No Place of Grace: Antimodernism and the Transformation of American Culture, 1880–1920*. Chicago: University of Chicago Press, 1981.

Lerner, Victoria. *Historia de la Revolución Mexicana: La educación socialista, 1934–1940*. Mexico City: El Colegio de México, 1998.

Levine, Lawrence W. *Highbrow Lowbrow: The Emergence of Cultural Hierarchy in America*. Cambridge: Harvard University Press, 1988.

LeVine, Sarah. *Dolor y Alegría: Women and Social Change in Urban Mexico*. Madison: University of Wisconsin Press, 1993.

Lewis, Oscar. *The Children of Sánchez: Autobiography of a Mexican Family*. London: Penguin Books, 1961.

———. *Five Families: Mexican Case Studies in the Culture of Poverty*. New York: Basic Books, 1959.

Leyva Ordorica, José. "La publicidad y sus efectos en el desarrollo económico de México." B.A. thesis, Universidad Nacional Autónoma de México, 1965.

Lindauer, Margaret. *Devouring Frida: The Art History and Popular Celebrity of Frida Kahlo*. Middletown, Conn.: Wesleyan University Press, 1999.

Lobato López, Ernesto. *El crédito en México: Esbozo histórico hasta 1925*. Mexico City: Fondo de Cultura Económica, 1945.

López Mateos, Adolfo. *Ser mexicano es ser libre*. Mexico City: Editorial La Justicia, 1959.

López Romero, Adolfo. *Plan México sugerencias para una política económica del próximo gobierno*. Mexico City: Libro Mex, 1958.

López Rosado, Diego G. *Historia y pensamiento económico de México*. Mexico City: Universidad Nacional Autónoma de México, 1972.

———. *Los servicios públicos de la ciudad de México*. Mexico City: Editorial Porrúa, 1976.

López Rosado, Felipe. *Vida cívica y juventud*. Mexico City: Editorial Porrúa, 1964.

Lorenzano, Luis. *La publicidad en México*. Mexico City: Quinto Sol, 1986.

Ludlow, Leonor, and Jorge Silva Riquer. *Los negocios y las ganancias de la colonia al México moderno*. Mexico City: Instituto de Investigaciones Dr. José María Luis Mora, 1999.

Maciel, David R. "The Cinema of Mexico." *Studies in Latin American Popular Culture* 9 (1990): 343–52.

Mallon, Florencia E. *Peasant and Nation: The Making of Postcolonial Mexico and Peru*. Berkeley: University of California Press, 1995.

Manero, Antonio. *Organización y financiamiento de empresas*. Mexico City: Ediciones Minerva, 1944.

———. *Promoción, organización y financiamiento de empresas*. Mexico City: Editorial Porrúa, 1958.

Manero, Federico G. *Origen y evolución de la contabilidad*. Mexico City: Secretaría de Educación Pública, 1968.

Mannheim, Karl. *Ideology and Utopia: An Introduction to the Sociology of Knowledge*. Translated by Lois Wirth and Edward Shils. New York: Harvest/Harcourt Brace Jovanovich, 1936.

Marchand, Roland. *Advertising the American Dream: Making Way for Modernity, 1920–1940*. Berkeley: University of California Press, 1985.

———. *Creating the Corporate Soul: The Rise of Public Relations and Corporate Imagery in American Big Business*. Berkeley: University of California Press, 1998.

Marcuse, Herbert. *One-Dimensional Man*. Boston: Beacon Press, 1964.

Marichal, Carlos. *A Century of Debt Crises in Latin America*. Princeton: Princeton University Press, 1989.

Márquez Padilla, Tarsicio. "Consideraciones sobre la interpretación mexicana de la política del Buen Vecino." B.A. thesis, Universidad Nacional Autónoma de México, 1944.

Marroquí, José María. *La ciudad de México: El origen de los nombres de sus calles y plazas, de varios establecimientos públicos y privados, y no pocas noticias curiosas y entretenidas*. Mexico City: Aguilar Vera y Compañía, 1903.

Martínez, D. Guillermo. *Intentos de control de precios en México*. Mexico City: Secretaría de Educación Pública, 1950.

Martínez, Luis María. "El corazón de Cristo y el corazón de la patria: Sermón predicado en la solemne consagración de México al santísimo corazón de Jésus." In Congreso Eucarístico Nacional, *Jésus*, 10th ed., 125–34. Mexico City: Editorial La Cruz, 1992.

Martínez, Luis María. *Divina obsesión*. Mexico City: Editorial La Cruz, 1991.

Marvin, Carolyn. *When Old Technologies Were New: Thinking about Electric Communication in the Late Nineteenth Century*. New York: Oxford University Press, 1988.

Maurois, André. *Un arte de vivir*. Mexico City: Editorial Hispanoamericana, 1947.

May, Elaine Tyler. *Homeward Bound: American Families in the Cold War Era*. New York: Basic Books, 1988.

McConnell, Burt. *Mexico at the Bar of Public Opinion: A Survey of Editorial Opinion in Newspapers of the Western Hemisphere*. New York: Mail and Express Publishing Company, 1939.

McLuhlan, Marshall. *Understanding Media: The Extensions of Man*. New York: McGraw-Hill, 1965.

Medina, José Francisco. "The Impact of Modernization on Developing Nation Consumption Patterns: The Case of Mexico." Ph.D. diss., University of California, San Diego, 1989.

Medina Peña, Luis. *Hacia el nuevo estado: México, 1920–1994*. Mexico City: Fondo de Cultura Económica, 1994.

Mesa, Antonio. *La propaganda y sus secretos*. Buenos Aires: Monogram, 1959.

Meyer, Jean. *The Cristero Rebellion: The Mexican People between Church and State, 1926–1929*. Translated by Richard Southern. Cambridge: Cambridge University Press, 1976.

Meyer, Lorenzo. *México y los Estados Unidos en el conflicto petrolero, 1917–1942*. Mexico City: El Colegio de México, 1981.

Middlebrook, Kevin. *The Paradox of Revolution*. Baltimore: Johns Hopkins University Press, 1995.

Mijares Palencia, José. *El gobierno mexicano: Su organización y funcionamiento*. Mexico City: Sociedad Mexicana de Publicaciones, 1936.

Milan, Verna Carleton. *Mexico Reborn*. Boston: Houghton Mifflin, 1939.

Miller, Nicola. *In the Shadow of the State: Intellectuals and the Quest for National Identity in Twentieth-Century Spanish America*. London: Verso, 1999.

Mistron, Deborah. "A Hybrid Subgenre: The Revolutionary Melodrama in the Mexican Cinema." *Studies in Latin American Popular Culture* 3 (1984): 47–56.

Moats, Leone, and Alice-Leone Moats. *Off to Mexico*. New York: Charles Scribner's Sons, 1940.

Molina Enríquez, Andrés. *Los grandes problemas nacionales, 1909, y otros textos, 1911–1919, colección problemas de México*. Mexico City: Ediciones Era, 1978.

Monnet, Jerome. *Usos e imagenes del centro histórico de la ciudad de México*. Mexico City: Departamento del Distrito Federal, 1995.

Monsiváis, Carlos. *Mexican Postcards*. London: Verso, 1997.

Monsiváis, Carlos, and Carlos Bonfíl. *A través del espejo: El cine mexicano y su público*. Mexico City: Instituto Mexicano de Cinematografía, 1994.

Mora, Carl. *Mexican Cinema: Reflections of a Society, 1896–1980*. Berkeley: University of California Press, 1982.

Mosk, Sanford A. *Industrial Revolution in Mexico*. Berkeley: University of California Press, 1950.

Murillo, Guilebaldo. *De lo íntimo del corazón*. Mexico City: Imprenta Adiana-Rossel y Sordo Noriega, 1948.

Nacional Financiera. *Estructura económica y social de México: El mercado de trabajo, relaciones obrero-patronales*. Mexico City: Fondo de Cultura Económica, 1955.

———. *Nacional Financiera, 1934–1984: Medio siglo de banca de desarrollo, testimonios de sus directores generales*. Mexico City: Nacional Financiera, 1985.

Newman, Kathleen. "Recent Books on Mexican Cinema." *Studies in Latin American Popular Culture* 13 (1994): 212–16.

Niblo, Stephen. *Mexico in the 1940s: Modernity, Politics, and Corruption*. Wilmington: Scholarly Resources, 1999.

———. *War, Diplomacy, and Development: The U.S. and Mexico, 1938–1954*. Wilmington: Scholarly Resources, 1995.

Nietzsche, Friedrich. *The Birth of Tragedy and the Genealogy of Morals*. Translated by Francis Golffing. New York: Anchor Books, 1956.

———. *The Will to Power*. Translated by Walter Kaufmann and R. J. Hollingdale. New York: Vintage Books, 1967.

Norris, James D. *Advertising and the Transformation of American Society, 1865–1920*. New York: Greenwood Press, 1990.

Novo, Salvador. *Apuntes para una historia de la publicidad en la ciudad de México*. Mexico City: Organización Editorial Novaro, 1968.

———. *Las locas, el sexo y los burdeles*. Mexico City: Editorial Diana, 1979.

———. *Nueva grandeza mexicana*. Buenos Aires: Espalsa-Calpe, 1947.

———. *Seis siglos de la ciudad de México*. Mexico City: Fondo de Cultura Económica, 1974.

———. *La vida en México en el periodo presidencial de Lázaro Cárdenas, compilación y nota preliminar de José Emilio Pacheco*. Mexico City: INAH, 1994.

———. *La vida en México en el periodo presidencial de Manuel Ávila Camacho, compilación y nota preliminar de José Emilio Pacheco*. Mexico City: INAH, 1994.

———. *La vida en México en el periodo presidencial de Miguel Alemán, compilación y nota preliminar de José Emilio Pacheco*. Mexico City: INAH, 1994.

O'Barr, William. *Culture and the Ad: Exploring Otherness in the World of Advertising*. Boulder: Westview Press, 1994.

O'Brien, Thomas F. *The Century of U.S. Capitalism in Latin America*. Albuquerque: New Mexico University Press, 1999.

———. *The Revolutionary Mission: American Enterprise in Latin America, 1900–1945*. Cambridge Latin American Studies. Cambridge: Cambridge University Press, 1996.

Ochoa, Enrique. *Feeding Mexico*. Wilmington: Scholarly Resources, 2000.

O'Malley, Ilene V. *The Myth of the Revolution: Hero Cults and the Institutionalization of the Mexican State, 1920–1940*. New York: Greenwood Press, 1986.

Ortíz Mena, Antonio. *Las finanzas publicas en el desarrollo socioeconomico de México*. Mexico City: LIBROS SELA, 1969.

Pacheco, José Emilio. *Las batallas en el desierto*. Mexico City: Ediciones Era, 1981.

Padilla, Ezequiel. *Seguridad económica y régimen democrático en la post-guerra*. Mexico City: Serie Problemas Nacionales e Internacionales, Talleres Gráficos de la Nación, 1943.

Palencia, José Minjares. *El gobierno mexicano: Su organización y funcionamiento*. Mexico City: Sociedad Mexicana de Publicaciones, 1936.

Parra, Manuel G. *La industrialización de México*. Mexico City: Imprenta Universitaria, 1954.

Partido Nacional Revolucionario. *Plan sexenal de partido nacional revolucionario*. Mexico City: PNR, 1937.

Partido Revolucionario Institucional. *Reunión nacional para el estudio del desarrollo industrial de México: Nuevos desarrollos industriales*. Mexico City: PRI, 1970.

Partner, Simon. *Assembled in Japan: Electrical Goods and the Making of the Japanese Consumer*. Berkeley: University of California Press, 1999.

Paz, María Emilia. *Strategy, Security, and Spies: Mexico and the U.S. as Allies in World War II*. University Park: Pennsylvania State University Press, 1997.

Paz, Octavio. *The Labyrinth of Solitude*. New York: Grove Press, 1961.

Paz, Octavio, and Luis Mario Schneider. *El peregrino en su patria: Historia y política de México*. Vol. 1. Mexico City: Fondo de Cultura Económica, 1956.

Peiss, Kathy. *Cheap Amusements: Working Women and Leisure in Turn-of-the-Century New York*. Philadelphia: Temple University Press, 1986.

Pérez Jimenez, Gustavo. *Vigencia del pensamiento político, económico y social de la Revolución Mexicana en la vida institucional de la nación*. Oaxaca: Instituto de Investigaciones Sociales y Económicas de la Escuela de Jurisprudencia, 1951.

Perzabal, Carlos. *Acumulación de capital e industrialización compleja en México*. Mexico City: Siglo Veintiuno Editores, 1988.

Petricioli, Gustavo, and Leopoldo Solís. *México: 75 años de revolución—desarrollo económico*. Vol. 2. Mexico City: Fondo de Cultura Económica, 1988.

Pike, Fredrick B. *The United States and Latin America: Myths and Stereotypes of Civilization and Nature*. Austin: University of Texas Press, 1992.

Podalsky, Laura. "Consuming Passions: Popular Urban Culture in Mexico." *Studies in Latin American Popular Culture* 15 (1996): 325–31.

Pogolotti, Marcelo. *La clase media en México: Prólogo y selección de antologías temáticas*. Mexico City: Editorial Diógenes, 1972.

Pope, Daniel. *The Making of Modern Advertising*. New York: Basic Books, 1983.

Poster, Mark. *Critical Theory and Poststructuralism: In Search of a Context*. Ithaca: Cornell University Press, 1989.

———. *The Mode of Information: Poststructuralism and Social Context*. Chicago: University of Chicago Press, 1990.

Potter, David. *People of Plenty: Economic Abundance and the American Character*. Chicago: University of Chicago Press, 1966.

Powelson, John P. *Contabilidad económica*. Mexico City: Fondo de Cultura Económica, 1958.

Pratt, May Louise. *Imperial Eyes: Travel Writing and Transculturation*. New York: Routledge, 1992.

Preciado, Abram A. *How to Sell to Latin America*. New York: Funk & Wagnalls, 1949.

Presas, Roberto. *¿Qué es la publicidad?* Buenos Aires: Editorial Columba, Colección Esquemas, 1967.

Presidencia de la República. *50 años de la Revolución Mexicana en cifras*. Mexico City: Nacional Financiera, 1963.

Procuraduría General de Justicia del D.F. *Territorios federales, memoria, 1946–1951*. Mexico City: S/E, 1952.

Pruneda, Salvador. *La caricatura como arma política*. Mexico City: Biblioteca del Instituto Nacional de Estudios Históricos de la Revolución Mexicana, 1958.

Publicaciones Rolland. *Confederación de cámaras industriales de los Estados Unidos Mexicanos, primer directorio industrial nacional, 1947–1948*. Mexico City, 1948.

Purnell, Jennie. *Popular Movements and State Formation in Revolutionary Mexico: The Agraristas and Cristeros of Michoacán*. Durham: Duke University Press, 1999.

Ramírez, Ignacio. *Obras: Economía política*. Vol. 2. Mexico City: Editora Nacional, 1952.

Ramírez Saiz, Juan Manuel, Enrique Jiménez Espiriú, Francisco Covarrubias, María Emilia Farías, José Cueli, and Jorge Bustamante. *México: 75 años de revolución, desarrollo social*. Vol. 2. Mexico City: Fondo de Cultura Económica, 1988.

Ramos, Samuel. *Obras completas: Hacia un nuevo humanismo veinte años de educación en México, historia de la filosofía en México*. Mexico City: Universidad Nacional Autónoma de México, 1976.

———. *The Profile of Man and Culture in Mexico*. New York: McGraw-Hill, 1962.

Ramos Garza, Oscar. *Los extanjeros y la propiedad territorial en México: Fideicomisos de zona prohibida, origen, legislación y prácticas*. Mexico City: Dofiscal Editores, 1989.

———. *México ante la inversión extranjera: Legislación, política y prácticas*. Mexico City: La Impresora Azteca, 1971.

Ramos Pedrueza, Rafael. *La lucha de clases a través de la historia de México: Revolución democráticoburguesa*. Mexico City: Talleres Gráficos de la Nacion, 1941.

Range, Willard. *Franklin D. Roosevelt's World Order*. Athens: University of Georgia Press, 1959.

Rangel Cuoto, Hugo. *Cooperativas de consumo oganizadas sindicalmente en México*. Mexico City: Ediciones Minerva, 1944.

Rautenstrauch, Walter, and Raymond Villers. *Economía de las empresas industriales*. Mexico City: Fondo de Cultura Económica, 1949.

Reyes Espaza, Ramiro, Enrique Olivares, Emilio Leyva, and Ignacio Hernández G. *La burguesía mexicana: Cuatro ensayos*. Mexico City: Editorial Nuestro Tiempo, 1973.

Reyes Heroles, Jesús. "Función social de las obras públicas." In *México: Realización y esperanza*, 675–80. Mexico City: Editorial Superación, 1952.

———. *La historia y la acción: La revolución y el desarrollo político de México*. Mexico City: Ediciones Oasis, 1972.

———. *El liberalismo mexicano: La integración de las ideas*. Vol. 3. Mexico City: Fondo de Cultura Económica, 1988.

———. *El liberalismo mexicano: La sociedad fluctante*. Vol. 2. Mexico City: Fondo de Cultura Económica, 1988.

Reynolds, Clark W. *The Mexican Economy: Twentieth-Century Structure and Growth*. New Haven: Yale University Press, 1970.

Richards, Thomas. *The Commodity Culture of Victorian England: Advertising and Spectacle, 1851–1914*. Stanford: Stanford University Press, 1990.

Riding, Alan. *Distant Neighbors: A Portrait of the Mexicans*. New York: Vintage Books, 1989.

Rock, David, ed. *Latin America in the 1940s: War and Postwar Transitions*. Berkeley: University of California Press, 1994.

Rodríguez, Eulalio. *El lenguaje de la publicidad en México*. Mexico City: Editores Eufesa, 1946.

Rodríguez, Jaime E., ed. *The Revolutionary Process in Mexico: Essays on Political and Social Change, 1880–1940*. Wilmington: Scholarly Resources, 1990.

Rodríguez, Joaquín. *Curso de derecho mercantil*. Vol. 2. Mexico City: Editorial Porrúa, 1957.

———. *Tratado de sociadades mercantiles*. Vols. 1 and 2. Mexico City: Editorial Porrúa, 1947.

Rojas Coria, Rosendo. *Tratado de cooperativismo mexicano*. Mexico City: Fondo de Cultura Económica, 1952.

Rojas de la Torre, Francisco, and Vicente Castro. *Banco mexicano de comercio e industria, S.A., en liquidación VS testamentaria de don Carlos Herrera*. Mexico City: Antigua Imprenta de Murguía, 1926.

Romero Flores, Jesús. *Anales históricos de la Revolución Mexicana: Del porfirismo a la revolución constitucionalista*. Vol. 1. Mexico City: Libro Mex Editores, 1959.

———. *Anales históricos de la Revolución Mexicana: La constitución de 1917 y los primeros gobiernos revolucionarios*. Vol. 2. Mexico City: Libro Mex Editores, 1960.

Rosenberg, Emily S. *Financial Missionaries to the World: The Politics and Culture of Dollar Diplomacy, 1900–1930*. Cambridge: Harvard University Press, 1999.

———. *Spreading the American Dream: American Economic and Cultural Expansion, 1890–1945*. New York: Hill and Wang, 1982.

Rubenstein, Anne. *Bad Language, Naked Ladies, and Other Threats to the Nation: A Political History of Comic Books in Mexico*. Durham: Duke University Press, 1998.

Rubin, Joan Shelley. *The Making of a Middle Brow Culture*. Chapel Hill: University of North Carolina Press, 1992.

Ruiz, Vicki L. *From out of the Shadows: Mexican Women in Twentieth Century America*. New York: Oxford University Press.

Ruiz Cortines, Adolfo. *Discursos de Ruiz Cortines pronunciados del 14 de octubre de 1951 al 22 de junio de 1952, durante su campaña política como candidato a la presidencia de la república*. Mexico City, 1952.

Salas, Elizabeth. *Soldaderas in the Mexican Military: Myth and History*. Austin: University of Texas Press, 1990.

Sálazar, Rosendo. *Los primeros de mayo en México: Contribución a la historia de la revolución*. Mexico City: B. Costa-AMIC, 1965.

Sánchez, George J. *Becoming Mexican American: Ethnicity, Culture, and Identity in Chicano Los Angeles, 1900–1945*. New York: Oxford University Press, 1993.

Sandoval, Alfonso, Alejandro Rodríguez, Arturo Romo, Jorge Sayeg Helú, Raúl Salinas de Gortari, Raúl Lemus García, Arturo Warman, and Miguel Limón. *México: 75 años de revolución, desarrollo social*. Vol. 1. Mexico City: Fondo de Cultura Económica, 1988.

Sands, Kathleen Mullen. "Charreada: Performance and Interpretation of an Equestrian Folk Tradition in Mexico and the U.S." *Studies in Latin American Popular Culture* 13 (1994): 77–97.

———. *Charrería Mexicana: An Equestrian Folk Tradition*. Tucson: University of Arizona Press, 1993.

Schaefer, Claudia. *Textured Lives: Women, Art, and Representation in Modern Mexico*. Tucson: University of Arizona Press, 1992.

Schuler, Friedrich E. *Mexico between Hitler and Roosevelt: Mexican Foreign Relations in the Age of Lázaro Cárdenas, 1934–1940*. Albuquerque: University of New Mexico Press, 1998.

Sears Publication Department. *Merchant to the Millions: A Brief History of the Origins and Development of Sears*. Chicago, 1950s.

Sears Roebuck and Company. *Manual para jefes de división Sears and Company: Adiestramiento*. Translated by Jorge Bonilla. Mexico City: Latin American Translating Unit, 1967.

Secretaría de Comunicaciones y Obras Públicas. *Memoria presentada por el C. secretario del ramo, general de división, Máximo Ávila Camacho*. Mexico City: Secretaría de Comunicaciones y Obras Públicas, 1943–44.

———. *Memoria presentada por el C. secretario del ramo, Ing. Pedro Martínez Tornel*. Mexico City: Secretaría de Comunicaciones y Obras Públicas, 1945–46.

Secretaría de Economía, Dirección General de Estadística. *Published Workshops of Dr. Edwards Deming: El control estadístico de calidad, María Lomeli y Nieto de Pascual*. Translated by Departamento de Muestreo. Mexico City, 1954.

———. *Segundo censo comercial de los Estados Unidos Mexicanos, 1945, resumen general*. Mexico City, 1950.

Secretaría de Educación Pública. *Vasconcelos, prólogo de Génaro Fernández MacGregor*. Mexico City: Ediciones de la Secretaría de Educación Pública, 1942.

Secretaría de Estado. *Ley sobre relaciones familiares, editada por el C. Venustiano Carranza, primer jefe del ejército constitucionalista encargado del poder ejecutivo de la nación*. Mexico City: Imprenta del Gobierno, 1917.

Secretaría de Gobernación. *Leyes de patentes y de marcas, avisos y nombres comerciales: Reglamentos de las mismas y disposiciones relativas*. Mexico City: Talleres Gráficos de la Nación, 1941.

———. *Los problemas de la guerra y la preparación de la paz: Una America libre, fuerte y culta, inestimable promesa para el mundo*. Mexico City: Secretaría de Gobernación, 1945.

Secretaría de Hacienda y Crédito Público. *La secretaría de hacienda y las convenciones bancarias, 1934–1981*. Mexico City: Secretaría de Hacienda y Crédito Público, 1981.

Secretaría de la Economía Nacional. *Anteproyecto del libro primero del código de comercio*. Mexico City: Talleres Gráficos de la Nación, 1943.

———. *Leyes de patentes y de marcas, avisos y nombres comerciales: Reglamentos de las mismas disposiciones relativas*. Mexico City: Talleres Gráficos de la Nación, 1936.

Secretaría de la Economía Nacional, Dirección General de Estadística. *Padrón de establecimientos comerciales, 1939*. Mexico City, 1941.

Secretaría de Relaciones Exteriores. *México en la IX conferencia internacional Americana*. Mexico City: Talleres Gráficos de la Nación, 1948.

Secretaría Industrial de Comercio. *Censo industrial: Resumen general, 1956*. Vols. 1 and 2. Mexico City: Secretaría Industrial de Comercio, 1959.

Seed, Patricia. *To Love, Honor, and Obey in Colonial Mexico: Conflicts over Marriage, 1574–1821*. Stanford: Stanford University Press, 1988.

Senado de la República. *Tratados ratificados y convenios ejecutivos celebrados por México*. Vol. 12. Mexico City: Talleres Gráficos de la Nación, 1972.

Sepúlveda, Monseñor, ed. *Santa María de Guadalupe Madre reina protectora: Algunos sermones guadalupanos de Monseñor Sepúlveda*. Mexico City: Imprenta Guanajuato, 1945.

Sierra, Justo. *The Political Evolution of the Mexican People*. Austin: University of Texas Press, 1969.

Silva Herzog, Jesús. *Nueve estudios mexicanos*. Mexico City: Imprenta Universitaria, 1953.

Simpson, Lesley Byrd. *Many Mexicos*. Berkeley: University of California Press, 1966.

Sindicato Nacional de Trabajadores de Hacienda. *Las repercusiones de la guerra en el comercio exterior de México, Conferencia del Sr. Lic. Ramón Beteta*. Mexico City: CTM, 1942.

Siqueiros Prieto, José Luis. *Las reclamaciones internacionales por intereses extranjeros en sociedades mexicanas*. Mexico City: Facultad de Derecho y Ciencias Sociales, Universidad Nacional Autónoma de México, 1947.

Sklar, Martin. *The Corporate Reconstruction of American Capitalism, 1890–1916*. Cambridge: Cambridge University Press, 1988.

Smith, Peter. *Labyrinths of Power: Political Recruitment in Twentieth Century Mexico*. Princeton: Princeton University Press, 1979.

———. "Mexico since 1946: Dynamics of an Authoritarian Regime." In Leslie Bethel, *Mexico since Independence*, 321–96. New York: Cambridge University Press, 1991.

Smith, Tony. *America's Mission: The United States and the Worldwide Struggle for Democracy in the Twentieth Century*. Princeton: Princeton University Press, 1994.

Sociedad Mexicana de Geografía y Estadística. *Los centros históricos en nuestro tiempo*. Mexico City: CONACULTA, 1999.

———. *Estudios de geografía, ciclo de conferencias sustentadas en el ejercicio social, 1942–1943*. Mexico City: Secretaría de Agricultura y Fomento, 1943.

Sotomayor, Arturo. *Expansión de México*. Mexico City: Fondo de Cultura Económica, 1975.

Spenser, Daniela. *The Impossible Triangle: Mexico, Soviet Russia, and the U.S. in the 1920s*. Durham: Duke University Press, 1999.

Stanley, Alexander O. *Approach to Latin American Markets*. New York: Dun & Bradstreet, 1941.

Stepan, Nancy L. *The Hour of Eugenics: Race, Gender, and Nation in Latin America*. Ithaca: Cornell University Press, 1991.

Strigberg, David. "Mexican Popular Musical Culture and the Tradition of Musica

Tropical in the City of Veracruz." *Studies in Latin American Popular Culture* 1 (1982): 151–63.

Strode, Hudson. *Now in Mexico*. New York: Harcourt, Brace, 1946.

Suárez, José I. "Advertising in Latin America." *Studies in Latin American Popular Culture* 14 (1995): 245–50.

Suárez, Mario. *Hacia una nueva conquista social la vivienda popular*. Mexico City: ICD, 1945.

Tannenbaum, Frank. *Mexico: The Struggle for Peace and Bread*. New York: Knopf, 1950.

Tenorio-Trujillo, Mauricio. *Mexico at the World's Fairs: Crafting a Modern Nation*. Berkeley: University of California Press, 1996.

Thompson, E. P. *The Making of the English Working Class*. New York: Vintage Books, 1963.

Thompson Company. *The Latin American Markets*. New York: McGraw-Hill, 1956.

Tischendorf, Alfred. *Great Britain and Mexico in the Era of Porfirio Díaz*. Durham: Duke University Press, 1961.

Topik, Steven. "Economic Denomination by the Capital: Mexico City and Rio de Janeiro, 1888–1910." In *La ciudad y el campo en la historia de México: Memoria de la VII reunión de historiadores mexicanos y norteamericanos*, 185–97. Mexico City: Universidad Nacional Autónoma de México, 1985.

Topik, Steven, and Allen Wells, eds. *The Second Conquest of Latin America: Coffee, Henequen, and Oil during the Export Boom, 1850–1930*. Austin: University of Texas Press, 1998.

Torres, María Eloida. *La ciudad de México: Sus orígenes y desarrollo*. Mexico City: Editorial Porrúa, 1977.

Torres-Bodet, Jaime. *Memorias equinoccio*. Mexico City: Editorial Porrúa, 1974.

Torres Gaitán, Ricardo. *Curso de teoría del comercio internacional*. Mexico City: Editorial Cátedra, 1954.

Torres Septién, Valentina. *La educación privada en México, 1903–1976*. Mexico City: El Colegio de México, 1988.

Toscano Moreno, Alejandra, ed. *Ciudad de México: Ensayo de construcción de una historia*. Mexico City: INAH, 1978.

Tovar de Arechederra, Isabel. *Metrópoli cultural*. Mexico City: Cuidad de México, 1994.

Townsend, William Cameron. *Lázaro Cárdenas: Mexican Democrat*. Ann Arbor: George Wahr Publishing, 1952.

Treviño, J. G. *Monseñor Martínez*. Mexico City: Editorial La Cruz, 1986.

Tunon, Julia. "Between the Nation and Utopia: The Image of Mexico in the Films of Emilio 'Indio' Fernández." *Studies in Latin American Popular Culture* 12 (1993): 159–72.

———. "Mexico and the Mexican on the Screen: The Construction of an Image." *Studies in Latin American Popular Culture* 10 (1991): 329–37.

Turner, Frederick Jackson. *The Frontier in American History*. New York, 1920.

Tzvi, Medin. *El sexenio Alemanista: Ideología y praxis política de Miguel Alemán*. Mexico City: Ediciones Era, 1990.

Universidad Nacional Autónoma de México. *La ciudad y el campo en la historia de México: Memoria de la VII reunión de historiadores mexicanos y norteamericanos*. Mexico City: Universidad Nacional Autónoma de México, 1985.

Valdés, María Elena. *The Shattered Mirror: Representations of Women in Mexican Literature*. Austin: University of Texas Press, 1998.

Valdés Ugalde, Francisco. *Autonomía y legitimidad: Los empresarios, la política y el estado en México*. Mexico City: Siglo Veintiuno Editores, 1997.

Valles, Jorge. *Un médico en una guerra*. Mexico City: Costa-Propaganda Impresa, 1942.

Vasconcelos, José. *The Cosmic Race, La Raza Cósmica*. Baltimore: Johns Hopkins University Press, 1997.

Vaughan, Mary Kay. *Cultural Politics of Revolution: Teachers, Peasants, and Schools in Mexico, 1930–1940*. Tucson: University of Arizona Press, 1997.

Vázquez, Josefina, and Lorenzo Meyer. *México frente a Estados Unidos*. Mexico City: Fondo de Cultura Económica, 1999.

Vázquez Amaral, José. *México: Datos para su biografía*. Mexico City: Costa-Amic Editor, 1945.

Velasco, Gustavo R. *El camino de la abundancia: Una política social y económica para México*. Mexico City: Editorial Humanidades, 1973.

Velázquez, Pedro H. *Miseria de México: Tierra desconocida*. Mexico City: Secretariado Social Mexicano, 1946.

Velíz, Claudio, ed. *Obstacles to Change in Latin America*. London: Oxford University Press, 1965.

Velling, Menno. *Industrialización, burguesía y clase obrera en México*. Mexico City: Siglo Veintiuno Editores, 1989.

Vernon, Raymond. *The Dilemma of Mexico's Development*. Cambridge: Harvard University Press, 1965.

Villarreal, René. *Industrialización, deuda y desequilibrio externo en México*. Mexico City: Fondo de Cultura Económica, 1988.

Vitali, Federico. *De mi labor publicitaria, 1918–1943*. Buenos Aires: Compañía General Fabril Financiera, 1944.

Von Humboldt, Alexander. *Political Essay on the Kingdom of New Spain*. Norman: University of Oklahoma Press, 1972.

Von Mentz, Brígida, Verena Radkau, Daniela Spencer, and Ricardo Pérez Montfort. *Los empresarios alemanes, el tercer reich y la oposición de derecha a Cárdenas*. Vol. 1. Colección Miguel Othón de Mendizabal, no. 11. Mexico City: Centro de Investigaciones y Estudios Superiores en Antropología Social, Ediciones de la Casa Chata, 1988.

Walker, Laird. *Advertising Progress: American Business and the Rise of Consumer Demand*. Baltimore: Johns Hopkins University Press, 1998.

Watson, James. *Golden Arches East*. Stanford: Stanford University Press, 1997.

Weber, Max. *From Max Weber: Essays in Sociology*. Edited by H. H. Gerth and C. Wright Mills. New York: Oxford University Press, 1946.

Weintraub, Sidney. *A Marriage of Convenience: Relations between Mexico and the United States, a Twentieth Century Fund Report*. New York: Oxford University Press, 1990.

Wells, Allen, and Gilbert M. Joseph. *Summer of Discontent, Seasons of Upheaval*. Stanford: Stanford University Press, 1996.

White, Richard. *The Middle Ground: Indians, Empires, and Republics in the Great Lakes Region, 1650–1815*. Cambridge: Cambridge University Press, 1991.

Wilkie, James. *The Mexican Revolution: Federal Expenditures and Social Changes since 1910*. Berkeley: University of California Press, 1967.

Wilkie, James W., and Edna Monson de Wilkie. *México visto en el siglo XX*. Mexico City: Instituto Mexicano de Investigaciones Económicas, 1969.

Wilkie, James, Michael Meyer, and Edna Monzon de Wilkie, eds. *Contemporary Mexico: Papers of the IV International Congress of Mexican History*. Berkeley: University of California Press, 1976.

Willard, Range. *Franklin D. Roosevelt's New World Order*. Athens: University of Georgia Press, 1959.

Williams, Rosalind H. *Dream Worlds: Mass Consumption in Late Nineteenth Century France*. Berkeley: University of California Press, 1982.

Williamson, Judith. *Decoding Advertisement: Ideology and Meaning in Advertising*. London: Marion Boyars, 1978.

Wise, George. *El México de Alemán*. Translated by Octavio Novaro. Mexico City: Editorial Atlante, 1952.

Womack, John. *Zapata and the Mexican Revolution*. New York: Vintage Books, 1968.

Wood, James Playsted. *The Story of Advertising*. New York: Ronald Press, 1958.

Wood, Richardson. *Sears Roebuck de México, S.A.* Washington, D.C.: National Planning Association, 1953.

Yamanouchi, Yasushi, J. Victor Koschmann, and Ryuichi Narita, eds. *Total War and Modernization*. Ithaca: Cornell University Press, 1998.

Zaragoza, Alex M. *The Monterrey Elite and the Mexican State, 1880–1940*. Austin: University of Texas Press, 1988.

Zeiler, Thomas W. *Free Trade, Free World: The Advent of GATT*. Chapel Hill: University of North Carolina Press, 1999.

Zimmerman, M. M. *Los supermercados*. Madrid: Ediciones Rialp, 1961.

Index